Planning Under Pressure

The Strategic Choice Approach

Titles of Related Interest

EDEN, JONES & SIMS
Messing About in Problems

FALUDI
A Decision-Centred View of Environmental Planning

FALUDI
Planning Theory

FRIEND & JESSOP
Local Government and Strategic Choice, 2nd Edition

HUSSEY
Introducing Corporate Planning, 3rd Edition

LITCHFIELD, KETTLE & WHITBREAD
Evaluation in the Planning Process

MCNAMEE
Tools and Techniques for Strategic Management

Related Pergamon Journals

LONG RANGE PLANNING*

OMEGA
The International Journal of Management Science*

*Free specimen copy available on request

Planning Under Pressure

The Strategic Choice Approach

by

JOHN FRIEND
IOP Consulting, Sheffield

and

ALLEN HICKLING
Allen Hickling & Associates, Warwickshire

PERGAMON PRESS

OXFORD · NEW YORK · BEIJING · FRANKFURT
SÃO PAULO · SYDNEY · TOKYO · TORONTO

U.K.	Pergamon Press plc, Headington Hill Hall, Oxford OX3 0BW, England
U.S.A.	Pergamon Press, Inc., Maxwell House, Fairview Park, Elmsford, New York 10523, U.S.A.
PEOPLE'S REPUBLIC OF CHINA	Pergamon Press, Room 4037, Qianmen Hotel, Beijing, People's Republic of China
FEDERAL REPUBLIC OF GERMANY	Pergamon Press GmbH, Hammerweg 6, D-6242 Kronberg, Federal Republic of Germany
BRAZIL	Pergamon Editora Ltda, Rua Eça de Queiros, 346, CEP 04011, Paraiso, São Paulo, Brazil
AUSTRALIA	Pergamon Press Australia Pty Ltd., P.O. Box 544, Potts Point, N.S.W. 2011, Australia
JAPAN	Pergamon Press, 5th Floor, Matsuoka Central Building, 1-7-1 Nishishinjuku, Shinjuku-ku, Tokyo 160, Japan
CANADA	Pergamon Press Canada Ltd., Suite No. 271, 253 College Street, Toronto, Ontario, Canada M5T 1R5

Copyright© 1987 J.K. Friend and A. Hickling

First edition 1987
Reprinted with revisions 1988

Library of Congress Cataloging-in-Publication Data
Friend, John.
Planning under Pressure.
(Urban and regional planning series; 37)
Bibliography: p.
Includes index.
1. Strategic planning. I. Hickling, Allen. II. Title. III. Series.
HD30.28.F75   1987   658.4'012   86-25219

British Library Cataloguing in Publication Data
Friend, J.K.
Planning under pressure: the strategic choice approach. — (Urban & regional planning series, ISSN 0305-5582; v. 37)
1. Social policy
I. Title II. Hickling, Allen III. Series 361.6' 1 HN18

ISBN 0-08-018766-8 (Hardcase)
ISBN 0-08-018765-X (Flexicover)

178966 4

Printed in Great Britain by A. Wheaton & Co. Ltd., Exeter

Contents

A fuller description of the contents of Chapters 1 to 10 appears in the Quick Access Guide

Foreword

WHEN Neil Jessop's and John Friend's seminal work *Local Government and Strategic Choice* appeared in 1969, I was teaching in the Department of Town and Country Planning at the University of Sydney. I was so impressed that I reviewed it for the then *Journal of the Australian Institute of Planners*, and it has had a marked influence on my work since.

I had the profit and pleasure of spending a sabbatical year with John Friend, Allen Hickling and their colleagues in 1973. This book appears many years afterwards, and it is enlightening to turn back to my impressions of the strategic choice approach at that time. These impressions followed not only from extensive discussions with the authors of this present book, but also from a programme of visits to most of the planners, managers and others who had then begun to use the approach. We generally agreed that the process of strategic choice would benefit from being presented as more cyclic rather than lineal and sequential; should be extended to address policy questions of major significance; and could be applied and used in fields of activity other than urban and regional development. This present book shows how much developmental work has taken place in these directions since the early 1970s.

It would be a pity if the comprehensiveness and thoroughness of this book led to the neglect of opportunities to use the strategic choice approach in partial or informal ways. This is particularly important in working situations where it is difficult to use the approach deliberately and deliberatively, because policies and problems have to be shaped and addressed through a diffuse process of negotiation with many different people and groups. One major example of this style of working was the joint Commonwealth-States study of soil conservation in Australia which I co-ordinated as a Commonwealth public servant in the mid-1970s.

This study had become static and rigidly programmatic. It was dominated by the current technology of soil conservation and by construction of capital works to arrest land degradation with little consideration of any national interests or priorities. The study had been in progress for two or three years, and in the circumstances of that time, it was not feasible for me to introduce strategic choice explicitly to all the various groups of inter-governmental officers who were involved in different ways. But the study was able to conclude with a principal recommendation, agreed to by all parties, about the need for mutual commitments to raise the level of soil conservation effort. This, of course, was supported by a series of statements about what that meant in terms of substance and priorities. These conclusions were then supported by a series of subsidiary recommendations which defined the principles of resource allocation needed to support an enhanced soil conservation effort; the organisational requirements of this expanded programme; and the dynamics of its continued development and modification. Inter-governmental relations were a particularly important part of this operation, and the recommendations were structured to express these.

In effect, the study was changed from one dominated by the heavily structured characteristics of traditional planning, towards an emphasis on the qualities of the strategic choice approach as expressed in this book. This soil conservation study accordingly represents an example of the approach being introduced informally but effectively to address the crucial aspects of process and organisation in policy-making and programme/project development and operation.

In an educational context, the strategic choice approach can be used in quite comprehensive and explicit ways. At the most ambitious level, I believe that it can be used as the major structuring element in the design of courses in town and country planning. More pragmatically, I have used it both as a means of illuminating different philosophies of planning, and as a vehicle for problem-solving in planning exercises. Either it can be taught carefully and comprehensively along the lines shown in this book; or students can be thrown into the deep end in dealing with a planning situation, after only a brief introduction to strategic choice. In a recent exercise of this latter kind, at the South Australian Institute of Technology, I defined the broad attributes of a planning situation, divided students into three groups and asked them to develop different solutions. Each group acted as a professional planning group advising the local council and taking the problem through a series of progressive decisions over three or four months. To encourage their imagination and to save time on the laborious collection of data and information, I asked them to write up the exercise as three different short stories, inventing information along the way which was supportive of, and consistent with, the progressive series of decisions of different kinds. The three answers showed the leading importance, respectively, of cash flow to the development agency; of an opportunity to accommodate a major metropolitan showground facing relocation; and of the resolution of land use conflicts with adjoining activities. Along the way the students learned a lot about the roles and relationships of decision-makers and decision-takers.

The way strategic choice is used in teaching depends on the educational environment. In the example cited above, the students were in the third year of an undergraduate course: but ideally the students should be introduced to the concepts of strategic choice in the first year, and the approach built up throughout the course.

Finally, I believe the stage of development of strategic choice in this book is not the final one. One of its greatest contributions has been to break down the rigidities attending planning, problem-solving and policy-making. I feel that too many people see implementation of plans and policies as simply the routine carrying out of decisions. Yet, I am convinced that aspects and instruments of implementation often need to be shaped, adapted, or accepted as given, right from the beginning of addressing a problem. Otherwise, we will continue to have too many ineffective policies and too many pigeonholed plans.

RAYMOND BUNKER

Authors' Preface

Historical Perspective

Twelve years have passed between the conception and completion of this book. For a book concerned with planning under pressure, that may seem a surprisingly long time. But the twelve years of gestation have seen much in the way of development both in the practice and the theory of the general approach to planning about which we write. Over this period, we have found ourselves collaborating with users in many kinds of organisations, public and private, throughout the world. So several thousands of managers, planners and policy-makers have now become exposed to the strategic choice approach; and there are hundreds of these who have played a part alongside us in its development. There have been many interim publications too; some of them reporting on particular research and application projects, others emanating from training programmes designed to introduce the essentials of the approach to prospective users in particular countries.

The origins of the approach — and of this book — are to be found in the work of IOR — the Institute for Operational Research. IOR was formed in 1963, as a unit of the Tavistock Institute of Human Relations in London, as the result of a joint initiative on the part of the Councils of the Tavistock Institute and the national Operational Research Society. Its dual aims were to extend the realm of application of operational research towards broader policy issues, and to build stronger links between OR and the social sciences. These are aims that have remained to the fore through many subsequent organisational changes, with the impetus now being maintained through an extensive network of individuals and groups in several parts of the world.

The first book on the strategic choice approach was published in 1969 (Friend and Jessop, 1969/77), followed tragically soon by the death of its co-author Neil Jessop, the first Director of IOR. The first experimental applications of the approach to practical planning problems were conducted in 1970, in collaboration with six teams of British local government officers; and the first training courses for managers were launched in 1971 at a Coventry hotel. Many other colleagues from the IOR Coventry and London offices had become involved in these early experiences. Then, in 1973 we were also joined in Coventry by Ray Bunker — the contributor of our foreword — who was revisiting the county of his birth on sabbatical leave from the University of Sydney in Australia. As a professional planner, he readily agreed to make it his task to visit as many as possible of the planners and other professionals who had taken part in our experiment in application three years earlier, in order to discover what influence, if any, the experience had had on the organisations and individuals taking part.

At that stage, it appeared that the impact on individuals had been generally more substantial than that on organisations. But the extent of that impact was both variable and elusive; and if dissemination was to proceed further, an obvious next aim was for us to produce a readable, accessible 'how to do it' guide to the approach. So, the understanding at the end of 1973 was that the three of us would work on this task together. Soon, however, the time came for Bunker to return to Australia — sailing by the long sea route, with prospects of plenty of writing time on the voyage. Then time scales became extended and, gradually, the idea of Bunker remaining a co-author became a less practical one — to be replaced by the idea of his providing some introductory remarks from his varied experiences as planning practitioner, consultant, teacher and researcher.

Meanwhile, another prospective co-author had emerged: Alan Sutton, an IOR colleague who became closely involved with the two of us in developing training programmes in Canada, and subsequently in a major government-financed project in Britain to apply strategic choice methods to the exploration of policy alternatives in County Council Structure Plans. But then Sutton too receded as a prospective co-author when, in 1977, he moved to a new base in Western Canada; so, the responsibilities of authorship reverted to the two of us.

Shifting Pressures

Work on this book continued during the later seventies — but in a sporadic way as we were both working under high pressure on IOR consulting and research projects for clients in Britain and overseas. For one of us, Hickling, the thrust continued to be on practical applications of the strategic choice approach; but for the other, Friend, it shifted towards research on the organisational and inter-organisational dimensions of complex planning processes, bringing a contrasting perspective to our training activities and our continuing work on the manuscript of this book.

The late seventies were, for both of us, a difficult time in terms of continuity of our project work. In 1980, Hickling set up as an independent consultant; Friend continued to work part-time at the Institute while also taking up an Honorary Senior Visiting Fellowship at the Management Centre of the University of Bradford. Around this time we were both becoming immersed in quite different ventures as well. Hickling, having recently relinquished the management of the village stores and post office adjoining his home, launched a company called Endless Games, through which to enter the burgeoning market of fantasy role-playing games. Meanwhile, Friend, from a new home location in West Yorkshire, found himself working in partnership with his wife to set up a countryside interpretive centre, as an initiative in environmental education run on small business lines.

For both of us, the involvement in work on planning processes continued; and with it our efforts to bring the book to completion. The members of Pergamon's advisory committee for the Urban and Regional Planning Series — of which Friend was a long-standing member — offered a judicious blend of encouragement and exhortation, supported by the editorial staff. We met together whenever we could, usually at least once a month, to progress the writing work. These meetings took place in all kinds of locations — not only in offices but in hotels and restaurants, at motorway service stations, in airport lounges and railway buffets. We met often at our respective homes; indeed, we have photographs of our working one sunny day in an English country garden, with flip charts hung among the greenery climbing up the walls of the cottage behind. Meanwhile, our children grew up and started to go their separate ways; and our wives continued to tolerate our joint writing endeavours with surprising good humour, while developing their own careers in their respective fields of creative art.

The breakthrough finally came in the latter half of 1985. By this time, we had both disposed of most of our other entrepreneurial interests and Friend was again working full time from the Tavistock Centre in London. Hickling was now fully stretched in some challenging applications of the strategic choice approach for Dutch governmental agencies, while Friend was becoming drawn into running strategic choice workshops in new fields ranging from community health planning to information technology strategy within the firm. A high point came during the new year break in January 1986, when a conjunction of circumstances allowed a brief reunion, at Hickling's home, of key people who had been associated with the earlier stages of preparation of the book — including both Ray Bunker and Alan Sutton, who was now resident again in Europe. This was not only a convivial occasion, it also saw a significant step forward in the consolidation of our ideas about technology, organisation, process and product, as presented in Chapter 4. There were still to be six agonising months of meetings, long telephone calls and redraftings before we were finally able to commit our finished text to the publishers. It was far from easy, but the sense of relief was overwhelming.

Complementarities

Our different experiences and work patterns over the twelve years, along with different and complementary personal skills, have led us to recognise differences and complementarities in our respective contributions to the writing process. For much of the time, the main load of drafting and co-ordination has fallen on one of us, Friend, as and when pauses in the pressures to maintain a continuing flow of project work have allowed. Yet the endeavour has been a joint one, which neither of us could have brought to fruition without the other. For Hickling's immersion over this period in practical applications of the strategic choice approach provided an all-important base of experience against which to judge the realism of the advice we wish to offer and the most practical way of presenting it; and the interdependence of our contributions became more and more apparent during the final nine-month period of intensive collaboration in the writing process.

We found during this period that some significant differences had developed between us on matters of emphasis and terminology; and we had to work long and hard at these before reaching agreement on simple, practical ways in which they could be overcome. We recognised too that there were differences in our styles of presentation — written, verbal, graphical — but we agreed that these stylistic differences could be a source of strength rather than weakness, if only we could achieve a creative synthesis between them. Some clues to the complementarities between our perspectives can be found in our respective biographical notes. Among the many facets of his early work experience, Hickling admits to operating as a semi-professional magician; Friend, meanwhile, admits to having graduated in the abstract discipline of mathematics before embarking on his early career in industrial operational research. So, a background of magic comes together with a background in logic; a contrast which, at first sight, seems to sum up neatly enough the main differences in our backgrounds and their influence on our respective styles.

But the potential for creative collaboration would not have existed had we not been capable of meeting each other at least half way. For, in the late sixties, when Friend was struggling to adapt his ingrained belief in rationality, quantification and logical rigour to the untidy social and political realities of decision-making on Coventry City Council, Hickling was taking his postgraduate degrees at the University of Pennsylvania, to become both Master of Architecture and Master of City Planning. It was here that he became exposed to the influence of Ackoff and others in the field of operational research; and it was through the convergence of this experience with Friend's searing experiences of decision-making in Coventry — together with a shared inclination towards use of graphics in expressing ideas and their relationships — that the basis for a productive collaboration was forged.

The logic/magic tensions surfaced repeatedly when Friend's writing tended to become laboured, in the attempt to pin down more formally aspects of the strategic choice approach which had hitherto developed in quite an intuitive way. Sometimes, this led to proposed changes in terminology or technique which did not fit well with Hickling's evolving base of experience in the field; so we found we had to make many fine adjustments — a little more magic here, a little more logic there. In retrospect, the opportunity which the writing task has provided for us to consolidate, review and modify the concepts and methods of the strategic choice approach has been an important one for both of us. The hope now must be that the fruits of this labour will be of as much value to our readers, whether they be practitioners, students, teachers or researchers.

The demand for an authoritative, practical guide to the strategic choice approach has been expressed to us often enough since 1973 and, indeed, earlier. Our hope now is that this volume will succeed in meeting the demand and thereby help in sustaining the momentum of application, teaching and development of ideas. If the past is any guide, the practice of strategic choice is likely to continue to evolve in different ways in different places in response to different demands and pressures. So, we hope that this book can provide a significant milestone in maintaining the wide-ranging collaborative endeavour on which the advance of the strategic choice approach has been built over the last twelve years.

Acknowledgements

There have been enough references to other people already in this preface for us to have gone some way towards the important and congenial task of acknowledging the contributions by others in this work. The contribution of the late Neil Jessop was seminal and has been acknowledged more fully in the second edition of *Local Goverment and Strategic Choice* (Friend and Jessop,1969/1977). The far-reaching contributions of Raymond Bunker and Alan Sutton over the twelve-year writing period have already been mentioned in earlier sections. Another major contribution to be acknowledged is that of Andreas Faludi who, from his Chair in Planning at the University of Amsterdam, has persistently sought to encourage development of the comparatively neglected academic perspectives of the strategic choice approach, and the study of its relatedness to other bodies of planning theory.

Others who have contributed to the development of the approach over the years include many past and present members of IOR and Tavistock Institute staff — Eric Trist, Hugh Murray, Paul Spencer, John Stringer, John Luckman, Don Bryant, James Morgan, Michael Luck, Chris Yewlett, Ken Carter, Hadley Hunter, John Pollard, Brian Quarterman, Gloria Overton, Martin Elton, David Millen, Peter Spink, Michael Floyd and Michael Norris — the last of whom has contributed many incisive comments in recent years. Other significant collaborators and sources of ideas in Britain and elsewhere have included Russell Ackoff, Felix Wedgwood-Oppenheim, Jonathan Rosenhead, Peter Fishburn, John Power, Fritz Scharpf, Bill Ogden, Harry Lash, Robin Fried, Arnold de Jong, Luc Wilkin, Fernand Debreyne, Hans Mastop, Angela de Melo, Robert Glass, Nathaniel Lichfield, Morris Hill, Martin Payne, Doug Spencer, Don Miller, Obbo Hazewinkel, Bram Breure, Paul de Jongh, Fernando Galvão Maximino Loschiavo de Barros, Moacyr Parahyba, Ken Bowen, Peter Bennett, Colin Eden, Sue Jones, Stephen Cropper, Christine Huxham, Jim Bryant and Tsunekazu Toda. But even to list the academic, international and other affiliations of these and other individuals would take up too much space — let alone to describe the rich and varied nature of their contributions.

Contributors to the typing of successive chapter drafts have also been numerous over the twelve years since this book was conceived — but special acknowledgement must go to Betty Fox, for long the key resource person in IOR's Coventry office; to Ann Jamieson at the Tavistock Centre; and to Jayne Moore who, working from her home, was finally able to commit the text to disk in a way that we could scarcely have conceived in the dim and distant days of 1973.

A Quick Access Guide

The choice of how to read *Planning under Pressure* will depend on the nature of your interests; the time at your disposal; and the extent of your prior familiarity with the strategic choice approach.

The purpose of this Quick Access Guide is to help you in making your decisions about selective reading. It does so first by outlining the principals on which the book is designed; and then by making some suggestions to help establish priorities for further reading.

The Figures

One of the first things to be noticed on flicking through the pages is the number of diagrams. There are 89 full-page figures, all boldly numbered, and all on left-hand pages. Some are professionally drawn; some are drawn freehand. Others are photographs of the approach in use.

In the margins of the figures there are various keywords and symbols. These are designed to help the reader making rapid cross references within the text. Their meaning is explained in later sections of this Quick Access Guide.

The Structure

Three of the ten chapters present the main characteristics of the strategic choice approach at a general level:

Chapter 1 describes its *Foundations*, which are based on direct experience of the challenges facing decision-making in practice;

Chapter 4 draws out the general *Orientations* and shifts of attitude which are central to this approach;

Chapter 9 discusses the *Practicalities* of applying the approach in practice, based on wide experience over recent years.

Both Chapters 4 and 9 are expressed in terms of four complimentary aspects of the *Approach* — *Technology, Organisation, Process* and *Product*. Hence the acronym *A-TOPP* which appears in the bottom left-hand corner of the figures, with the relevant letter highlighted.

The intervening chapters are grouped in two sets:

Chapters 2 and 3, which introduce the basic *concepts* of the strategic choice approach;

Chapters 5, 6, 7 and 8, which describe the *skills* used in its application.

These six chapters are concerned primarily with technology and process. They cover four complementary modes of decision-making which are presented in Figure 8, and explained on page 19 — *shaping, designing, comparing* and *choosing*. In the bottom left-hand corner of each figure a small motif of four circles, based on the framework of Figure 8, is used to highlight the mode being described.

The concepts contained in these chapters are introduced in the text through the development of a story — the South Side story — in which they are applied to a semi-fictitious situation of planning under pressure.

The final chapter, **Chapter 10**, speculates about possible future *directions*.

The Introductory Chapters

The the first four chapters together give a general idea of what the strategic choice approach has to offer.

Chapter 1: Foundations explains the *philosophy* of planning as a process of strategic choice, and the roots in practice from which it has grown. One of the most important diagrams here is figure 3, which distinguishes three types of uncertainty in decision-making, that have to be managed in very different ways.

Chapter 2: Working into Problems introduces, at as simple a level as possible, a set of basic concepts and methods which have been found useful in guiding the work of the *shaping* and *designing* modes. Each is illustrated in a figure, with a more formal definition below. The core concepts are:

CONCEPTS FOR SHAPING	CONCEPTS FOR DESIGNING
Figure 10—the decision area	Figure 14—the decision option
Figure 11—the decision link	Figure 15—the option bar
Figure 12—the decision graph	Figure 16—the option graph
Figure 13—the problem focus	Figure 17—the decision scheme

Chapter 3: Working towards Decisions follows the same principle, and introduces a set of concepts and methods to guide the work of the *comparing* and *choosing* modes. The emphasis now switches to concerns

about the consequences and merits of different courses of action, and about the strategic management of uncertainty through time. The core concepts are:

CONCEPTS FOR COMPARING	CONCEPTS FOR CHOOSING
Figure 19—the comparison area	Figure 23—the uncertainty area
Figure 20—the relative assessment	Figure 24—the exploratory option
Figure 21—the advantage comparison	Figure 25—the action scheme
Figure 22—the working shortlist	Figure 26—the commitment package

A glance at Figure 26 is recommended here; it demonstrates the general format used to draw together the outputs of a process of strategic choice.

Chapter 4: Orientations offers an important bridge between the first three chapters and the five more practical chapters that follow. After drawing together the full set of basic concepts from Chapters 2 and 3, it elaborates the four complimentary aspects of the *Approach — Technology, Organisation, Process* and *Product.* Figure 29 summarises the shifts in orientation which the strategic choice approach calls for, taking each of the four aspects in turn. The next four figures interpret of these shifts in orientation in more practical terms.

The Later Chapters

Chapters 5, 6, 7 and **8** address the challenges readers are likely to meet and the skills they will need when setting out to apply the basic concepts of Chapters 2 and 3 to practical decision problems with which they are concerned.

They cover each of the four modes at a time. However, because experienced users of the approach tend to move flexibly and freely from one mode to another, these chapters highlight the subtle interrelationships between modes. It is for this reason that, in the corner motif in each figure, four circles have now been made to overlap.

Chapter 9: Practicalities starts by reviewing the expanding base of experience in applying the approach, and the principles of selectivity and adaptiveness that have emerged from this experience. Taking each of the four A-TOPP aspects in turn, various pieces of practical advice are offered, and summarised in the form of four *management checklists*:

> Figure 83 : Management Checklist : Technology
> Figure 83 : Management Checklist : Organisation
> Figure 86 : Management Checklist : Process
> Figure 88 : Management Checklist : Products

Chapter 10: Horizons is more speculative. It starts by reviewing the opportunities for new applications of the strategic choice approach in such fields as *publicity; corporate strategy;* and *inter-organizational working.* It then touches on some of the scope for further work in relating the approach to the insights of the social, political and psychological sciences, and to advances in *information technology* and more formal *management science* methods. Finally, it addresses the *educational challenge* to be faced if the decision-makers of the future are to be helped to take full advantage of ideas such as those presented in this book.

Reading Priorities

These guidelines are organised in terms of the results you may reasonably expect from different approaches to the book. They are to some extent cumulative, and we are presented in an order of increasing comprehensiveness

For **a first quick appreciation of the approach**, we recommend a fast read of Chapter 1; then a glance through the figures of the next three chapters — noting the definitions of those in Chapters 2 and 3 — ending with a closer look at the General Review on pages 105 to 108

For **a first basic grasp of the main concepts and principles**, we recommend a full read of the first four chapters. You can then reinforce your understanding by attempting the exercises which appear at the end of Chapters 2 and 3; and a useful extension can be gained from a quick skim of Chapter 9, focusing on figures 84, 87 and 89.

For **a thorough knowledge of how the approach is applied**, we recommend a complete familiarisation with the concepts introduced in Chapters 2 and 3; followed by a browse through Chapters 5, 6, 7, and 8, using Chapter 4 as the point of departure. Having developed a feel for what these four chapters have to say about the skills of putting the concepts and methods into practice, we suggest you read Chapter 9 — especially the section on selectivity and adaptiveness before returning to work through Chapters 5 to 8 in more depth.

For **ideas about directions of further development**, we recommend a thorough read of Chapter 10. This can be extended through a look at the Guide to Further Reading, which might provide the basis for fruitful discussions with others interested in the field.

For **a feel of using the approach in practice**, we recommend careful appraisal of the Illustrations from Practice in Chapters 5, 6, 7 and 8; and close study of the Management Checklists in Chapter 9. However — as with any other approach — one cannot expect to come to grips with the realities of practice through reading alone. Experience has to be gained either by trying out the approach on one's personal decisions or, preferably, by working with others on shared planning problems. And if this can be done with someone who has already acquired such experience, then so much the better.

1

Foundations

A Philosophy of Planning

There are many possible ways in which to approach the challenge of planning in an uncertain world.

The approach to be introduced in this chapter is one in which planning is viewed as a continuous process: a process of choosing strategically through time. This view of planning as a process of strategic choice is, however, not presented as a set of beliefs which the reader is expected to embrace uncritically at this stage. That would be too much to expect — especially of an introductory chapter, which is intended merely to open the door for the more specific concepts, methods and guidelines to be offered in those that follow. People involved in any kind of planning activity of course build up their own sets of beliefs about the practice of planning in the course of their working lives: beliefs which they will not wish to set aside lightly. Yet experience in applying the approach offered here has shown that its fundamentals can usually be accepted without much difficulty by those planners or managers whose working philosophy draws more on their own practice than on taught beliefs. This is because, in essence, the approach sets out to do no more than to articulate, as clearly as possible, the kinds of dilemma that experienced decision-makers repeatedly face in the course of their work, and the often intuitive judgements they make in choosing how to respond.

In practice, such judgements may sometimes be accompanied by a sense of discomfort or even guilt. For the decision-makers may feel they are departing from certain principles of rational behaviour which they have been taught to respect. Indeed, the view of planning as strategic choice is found to offer more of a challenge to such idealised principles of rationality than it does to the intuitive judgements and compromises that seem characteristic of planning practice. If this point can be accepted, the reader should be able to relax in following the ideas put forward in this chapter, and view them as offering perspectives that can help make sense of current practice — without necessarily demanding any revolutionary change in familiar ways of working.

1

The Craft of Choosing Strategically

It is important to emphasise that the view of strategic choice presented here is essentially about choosing in a strategic *way* rather than at a strategic *level*. For the idea of choosing at a strategic level implies a prior view of some *hierarchy* of levels of importance in decision-making; while the concept of strategic choice that will be developed here is more about the *connectedness* of one decision with another than about the level of importance to be attached to one decision relative to others.

It is not too surprising that these two senses of the word *strategic* have tended to fuse together in common usage. For it is often the more weighty and broader decisions which are most obviously seen to be linked to other decisions, if only because of the range of their implications and the long time horizons over which their effects are expected to be felt. This, in turn, can lead to a view that any process of strategic decision-making should aspire to be comprehensive in its vision and long-range in its time horizon, if it is to be worthy of its name.

But such a view of strategic choice can become a restrictive one in practice; for it is all too rarely that such idealistic aspirations can be achieved. The approach to strategic choice to be built up in this chapter is not only about making decisions at a supposedly strategic level. It goes beyond this in addressing the making of *any* decisions in the light of their links to other decisions, whether they be at a broader policy level or a more specific action level; whether they be more immediate or longer term in their time horizons; and no matter who may be responsible for them. This concept of strategic choice indicates no more than a readiness to look for patterns of connectedness between decisions in a manner that is selective and judgemental — it is *not* intended to convey the more idealistic notion that everything should be seen as inextricably connected to everything else.

So this view of planning as a process of strategic choice implies that planning can be seen as a much more *universal* activity than is sometimes recognised by those who see it as a specialist function associated with the preparation of particular sorts of plans. At the same time, it allows planning to be seen as a *craft*, full of subtlety and challenge; a craft through which people can develop their capacity to think and act creatively in coping with the complexities and uncertainties that beset them in practice.

Organisational Contexts of Strategic Choice

This relatively modest interpretation of the word *strategic* means that the view of planning as strategic choice is one that can be applied not only to decision-making in formal organisational settings, but to the choices and uncertainties which people face in their personal, family and community lives. For example, any of us might find ourselves involved in a process of strategic choice in addressing the problem of where and when to go on holiday next year, or how to sell an unwanted vehicle, or how to deal with a difficult request from a relative or friend. Of course, the craft of choosing strategically becomes more complicated where it involves elements of *collective* choice — of negotiation with others who view problems and possibilities in different ways. Indeed, most of the more demanding problems to which the strategic choice approach has been applied have involved challenges of collective decision-making, either in organisational or inter-organisational settings; and this can have the effect of blurring many of the familiar distinctions of task and discipline around which organisational structures are usually designed. For the skill of choosing strategically through time is one that can become just as essential to the manager or executive as to those in more formal planning roles. This point is illustrated schematically in Figure 1, through which is presented a view of planning under the practical pressures of organisational life. It is a view in which an organisation's arrangements for making plans, and those for making day-to-day decisions, tend to merge together into a less clearly bounded process through which progress is sustained. This is a process of choosing strategically in coping with difficult problems, amidst all the complex realities — or perceptions of reality — which contribute to organisational life.

The larger and more complex the organisation, the more it is to be expected that decision-making responsibilities will have become differentiated according to a multitude of operational, managerial or entrepreneurial roles. The more likely it is too that specialised plan-making functions will have been developed in an effort to maintain a co-ordinated, longer-term view isolated from everyday management pressures. However, no plan-making activity will remain valued within an organisation unless it can provide support for the more difficult and important of the decisions people face; and it is a common experience that carefully prepared plans can quickly lose their relevance under the pressures of day-to-day events. The combined pressures of urgency, competition for resources and turbulence in the world outside can soon lead to disenchantment and confusion in the arrangements for making plans; while the pressures of complexity, conflict and overload can lead to vacillation and inconsistency in the making of day-to-day decisions. To counter the resulting personal and organisational stresses, those responsible for organisational guidance sometimes look towards some overarching framework of *policies* or aims. But, in practice, such policy guidelines can often be difficult to agree — especially when working in inter-organisational settings — and their contributions towards sorting out the predicaments of day-to-day management can be disappointingly small.

The making of generalised policies is therefore given its place in Figure 1; but it is not given pride of place. Instead, the emphasis is on the more subtle

FIGURE
1

Planning Under Pressure: A View of the Realities

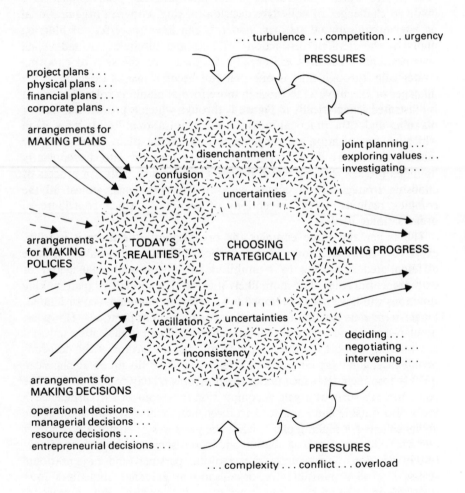

. . . turbulence . . . competition . . . urgency

PRESSURES

project plans . . .
physical plans . . .
financial plans . . .
corporate plans . . .

arrangements for
MAKING PLANS

joint planning . . .
exploring values . . .
investigating . . .

disenchantment

confusion

uncertainties

arrangements
for MAKING
POLICIES

TODAY'S
REALITIES

CHOOSING
STRATEGICALLY

MAKING PROGRESS

vacillation   uncertainties

inconsistency

deciding . . .
negotiating . . .
intervening . . .

arrangements for
MAKING DECISIONS

operational decisions . . .
managerial decisions . . .
resource decisions . . .
entrepreneurial decisions . . .

PRESSURES

. . . complexity . . . conflict . . . overload

process of making progress through time by choosing strategically; and on the creative management of multiple *uncertainties* as a crucial means towards this end. And progress through time can, itself, take many forms. Immediate progress can take the form of intervening, or negotiating with others, as well as taking decisions on matters where direct action is possible. Meanwhile, progress in building a base for later decisions can also take different forms — not only investigations but also clarification of values and cultivation of working relationships with other decision-makers.

So the term 'planning' will be used in this book to refer generally to this more loosely defined process of *choosing strategically*, in which the activities of making plans, decisions and policies can come together in quite subtle and dynamic ways. But with a wide variety of ways of making progress to be considered, the process can soon begin to appear as one not so much of planning but of scheming — to introduce a term which has a similar literal meaning but which carries very different undertones in its everyday usage. Whereas the notion of planning may invoke a sense of idealism and detachment, the notion of scheming tends to suggest working for sectional advantage in an often devious way. So there is a case to be made that people involved in planning must learn to become effective schemers; and furthermore that it is possible to exercise scheming skills in a responsible way. Those who are troubled about social responsibility in planning — and that includes both the authors of this book — may wonder whether there must always be a divide between responsible planners and irresponsible schemers — and if so, whether it must always be the latter who will win. As Chapter 10 will demonstrate, the concept of *responsible scheming* need not be considered a contradiction in terms. Indeed, it is towards the search for a theory and a practice of responsible scheming that the strategic choice view of planning can be said to be addressed.

It is, however, one thing for an individual to embrace a philosophy of planning as strategic choice; and quite another thing for a group of people working together to share such a philosophy as an unequivocal foundation for their work. Experience has shown that there are some settings where a sense of shared philosophy can indeed emerge — either where a set of close colleagues has learnt to work together as a coherent team, or where they discover that a common professional background allows them to proceed on shared assumptions as to how decisions should be made. Yet those whose work involves cutting across organisational boundaries must expect often to find themselves working alongside people with whom they do not share a philosophical base. So it is important to think of the philosophy presented in this chapter as a helpful frame of reference in making use of the more specific concepts and methods to be introduced in this book, rather than as a necessary foundation from which to build.

Indeed, it is a common enough experience, when working with strategic choice concepts, that people of quite diverse backgrounds can make solid progress towards decisions based on shared understandings, with little or no explicit agreement at a more philosophical level. Often it is only through the experience of working together on specific and immediate problems that they find they are beginning to break through some of the philosophical barriers which may have inhibited collaboration in the past.

Dilemmas of Practice

The view of strategic choice presented in this book gained its original impetus from the experience of a particular research project, which offered unusually extensive opportunities to observe the kinds of organisational processes indicated in Figure 1.

The setting of this research was the municipal council of a major English city — Coventry — which, between 1963 and 1967, agreed to act as host to a wide-ranging project on the processes of policy-making and planning in local government, viewed as a microcosm of government as a whole. This seminal research was supported by a grant from the Nuffield Foundation, and has been more fully reported elsewhere (Friend and Jessop, 1969/77). Over the four-year period, the research team was able to follow a wide range of difficult issues including the review of the city's first development plan; the redesign of its urban road network; the reorganisation of its school system; the renewal of its housing stock; the finance of public transport; and the scheduling of capital works. The researchers were able to hold many discussions with the various politicians, administrators, planners and professional experts involved, and to observe the processes of collective decision-making in which they came together — not only in the departmental offices and the formal meetings of Council and its committees, but also in the smoke-filled rooms of the opposing political groups.

Through these experiences, some impressions of the persistent *dilemmas* of decision-making in such complex circumstances gradually came to the fore. Among the clearest impressions were:

— that people held different and continually shifting views about the **shape** of the issues they faced and, not least, about how closely or widely the boundaries of their concern should be drawn;
— that there were persistent pressures for them to arrive at commitments to action in an **incremental** or piecemeal way, however committed they might be in theory to the idea of taking a broader, more comprehensive view of the issues before them;
— that there was a continuing dilemma of balancing **urgency** against **uncertainty** in decision-making through time;
— and that there were persistent difficulties in distinguishing the **technical** from the **political** aspects of the decision process, even

though the entire organisational structure was built around the maintenance of distinctions of this kind.

These impressions of the practical difficulties of choosing strategically in organisations facing complex problems have been strengthened and extended by many other experiences since the conclusion of the Coventry project — not only in the world of local government but in other public sector organisations, in industry and commerce, in voluntary organisations, and in the increasingly wide range of problem situations where these different domains of decision-making tend to converge. On the strength of this broader experience, a view is presented in Figure 2 of five broad dimensions in which difficult choices of *balance* tend to arise in the management of a continuing process of strategic choice. There is a choice between:

— a more **focussed** and a more **synoptic** treatment of problem *scope*;
— a more **simplifying** and a more **elaborating** treatment of *complexity*;
— a more **reactive** and a more **interactive** treatment of *conflict*;
— a more **reducing** and a more **accommodating** treatment of *uncertainty*;
— and a more **exploratory** and a more **decisive** treatment of *progress* through time.

The practical task of choosing a position in each of these five dimensions is not one of making a firm and lasting commitment to one extreme or the other. It is more a task of maintaining an appropriate *balance* in continually shifting circumstances, shifting from time to time in one direction or another, according to the — often intuitive — judgements of those involved. In the chapters that follow, the picture presented in Figure 2 will be used as a point of reference in building more structured frameworks of ideas through which to expand further on the view of planning as a process of strategic choice. These frameworks will give deeper significance to the various contrasts which, at this stage, can only be indicated in outline terms.

In later chapters, fuller interpretations will be offered of other related aspects of the dilemmas of practice observed in Coventry and elsewhere, which are not brought out so clearly in the comparatively broad set of balances presented in Figure 2. In particular, later chapters will have more to say about the issues of urgency and incrementality, and about the relationship of the political arena to the technical domain. This is a dichotomy which, in Coventry City Council, could be seen as the fundamental organising principle on which the formal structures of accountability were designed; but it is a relationship with far wider implications for decision-making, even in contexts where such distinctions may become more blurred.

FIGURE

2

Judgements of Balance in Strategic Choice

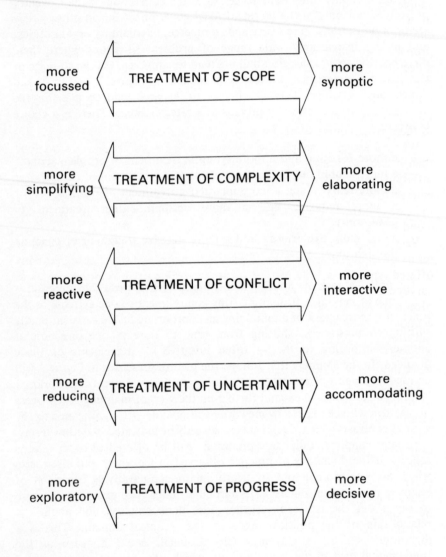

more
focussed ⟨ TREATMENT OF SCOPE ⟩ more
synoptic

more
simplifying ⟨ TREATMENT OF COMPLEXITY ⟩ more
elaborating

more
reactive ⟨ TREATMENT OF CONFLICT ⟩ more
interactive

more
reducing ⟨ TREATMENT OF UNCERTAINTY ⟩ more
accommodating

more
exploratory ⟨ TREATMENT OF PROGRESS ⟩ more
decisive

Responding to Difficulty in Making Decisions

The view of planning as a process of strategic choice is, above all, a dynamic one. However, in building up a view of the way this process works, it is useful to begin with a more static picture. This picture, which is quite simple yet also quite general in its application, has as its focus any situation in which one or more decision-makers are experiencing *difficulty* in choosing how they should act in response to some particular *decision problem* with which they are currently concerned. A snapshot view of such a decision situation is presented in Figure 3. The decision problem itself is depicted as a cloud, to indicate that its shape will often be in some degree obscure. However, what makes it problematic to the decision-makers is that they are experiencing some pressure to arrive at a decision, yet it is not clear to them what course of action they should choose.

Where a group of people find themselves collectively in such a situation, then it is often found that different members of the group will advocate different ways of responding; so some degree of conflict of opinion may emerge. Three types of response which are repeatedly offered in practice are indicated by the three different 'bubbles' shown emerging from the central cloud in Figure 3.

Very often, people will see the way out of their present difficulties in terms of explorations of a more or less technical nature. The suggestions offered typically include various forms of costing or forecasting exercises, surveys, technical analyses, research studies; or, in some circumstances, proposals for investment in more ambitious forms of mathematical or economic modelling. Whatever the form of investigation, however, the purpose is to reduce the difficulties of making decisions by investing in a process of *exploration* into particular aspects of the decision-makers' working environment about which it is felt that too little is currently known.

Other people, meanwhile, may see the way out of the difficulty in terms of other, less technical, kinds of exploration designed to establish more clearly what policy values should guide their choice of action. Typically, they may call for investment in activities designed to clarify goals, objectives, aims or policy guidelines, whether through formal or informal channels. In some situations, this may mean simply consulting decision-takers who bear more direct responsibility for organisational policy; in others it could mean deliberately seeking fuller involvement in the process by a range of affected interest groups or their representatives.

A third response is to seek the way out of the difficulty by moves to extend the current agenda of decision-making concern. People advocating this response will often argue that the decision problem currently in view is one that cannot realistically be addressed in isolation, because it is connected to one or more other decision problems which lie ahead. So the demand here is likely to be for some form of co-ordination, negotiation or

FIGURE
3

Three Types of Uncertainty in Decision-Making

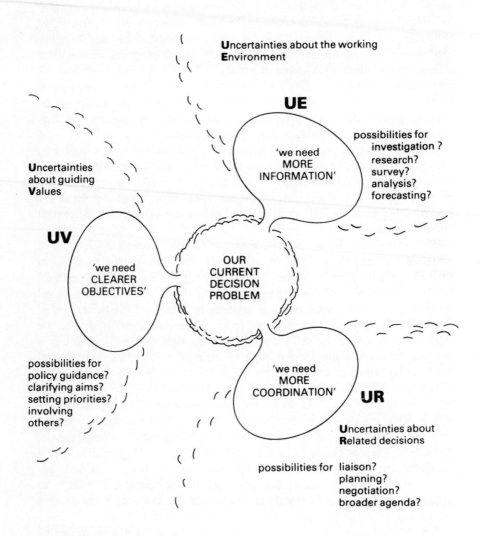

Uncertainties about the working
Environment

UE

possibilities for
investigation ?
research?
survey?
analysis?
forecasting?

'we need
MORE
INFORMATION'

Uncertainties
about guiding
Values

UV

'we need
CLEARER
OBJECTIVES'

OUR
CURRENT
DECISION
PROBLEM

possibilities for
policy guidance?
clarifying aims?
setting priorities?
involving
others?

'we need
MORE
COORDINATION'

UR

Uncertainties about
Related decisions

possibilities for liaison?
planning?
negotiation?
broader agenda?

planning exercise that will allow the current decision problem to be explored alongside others within a broader, more synoptic problem focus.

Each of the three kinds of demand — most typically expressed as demands for *more information*, for *clearer objectives* and for *more co-ordination* — can be regarded as a different kind of attempt to manage the current state of **uncertainty** over what should be done about the current decision situation. Indeed, it is possible to go on to identify three general *categories* of uncertainty along the lines indicated below, which are distinguished by the different forms of response that can be made. These three types of uncertainty play an important part in the philosophy of planning as a process of strategic choice; they can be formally described as follows:

Uncertainties about the working Environment: **UE** for short
Uncertainties about guiding Values: **UV** for short
Uncertainties about Related decisions: **UR** for short

It is important to stress that the idea of uncertainty in strategic choice is normally viewed in *relative* rather than absolute terms. It is treated as an attribute of particular situations and people rather than something with an objective reality of its own. In practice it is often far from easy for people to agree which of the three kinds of uncertainty are most crucial in a particular decision situation; and, therefore, how much attention should be given to each possible form of response. For instance, members of a city planning team, considering whether to recommend approval of an application to build a new hotel, might see possibilities either for calling for deeper investigation of its traffic implications; or for seeking clearer guidance on the Council's policies in relation to this particular kind of development; or for initiating a wider review of tourism possibilities within the city as a whole. They might of course want to move in all three directions more or less at the same time; however, this is not always possible where there are pressures to make a speedy decision. Nor will it necessarily be desirable to invest resources in all possible ways of responding to uncertainty — especially if some of them are expected to be less effective than others, in terms of reducing the feelings of uncertainty among the decision-makers involved.

Managing Uncertainty : A Dynamic View

So, in practice, it may be far from easy to judge how uncertainty is to be *managed* at any moment, even in situations where the sources of that uncertainty have been clearly identified.

To consider further the possible ways of managing uncertainty through time, it becomes necessary to move to a more *dynamic* view. Such a view is presented in Figure 4 which builds on the 'snapshot' picture of Figure 3 by

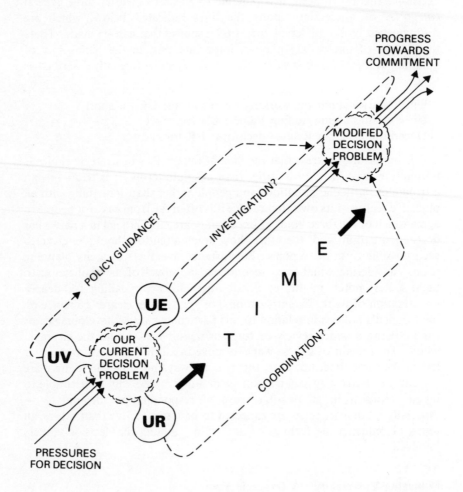

FIGURE
4
Opportunities for Managing Uncertainty through Time

PROGRESS
TOWARDS
COMMITMENT

MODIFIED
DECISION
PROBLEM

POLICY GUIDANCE?

INVESTIGATION?

COORDINATION?

UE

OUR
CURRENT
DECISION
PROBLEM

UV

UR

T I M E

PRESSURES
FOR DECISION

introducing the reality that any form of investigative, policy clarifying or co-ordinating initiative must take some time to carry through. Indeed, explorations in some of these directions may, in practice, take longer to carry out than others. However, the intended consequence of pursuing any chosen exploratory path is to make the decision situation less difficult to deal with once the outcome of the exploration is known — in other words, to lessen the feelings of uncertainty being experienced by the decision-makers, and thus to increase the level of *confidence* with which they can act. In practice, however, it will not often be realistic to expect that the feelings of uncertainty surrounding a difficult decision problem can be made to vanish altogether, however much effort may be invested in exploratory activities. In terms of the symbolism used here, the process can be pictured as one whereby the original cloud becomes smaller in its dimensions and, by implication, less obscure.

Sometimes, of course, feelings of uncertainty may be reduced through time without any conscious action on the part of the decision-makers. Expected events may or may not unfold; trends may become more apparent; the intentions of other parties may be revealed; policy positions may become more clear cut. In general, however, uncertainty can only be reduced at a cost — whether this be merely the cost of delay when there may be urgent issues to be settled, or whether it also includes more direct costs in terms of money, skills or other scarce resources.

So the management of uncertainty through time is rarely simple in the types of judgement it entails. It is the raising of these judgements to a more conscious level that is one of the most distinctive characteristics of the strategic choice approach.

Interconnected Agendas of Decision-Making

Of the three exploratory routes indicated in Figure 4, it is the co-ordinative (UR) route which is of most far-reaching significance in developing the idea of planning as strategic choice.

The demand to move in this direction arises when there is a sense that the present agenda of decision-making is too restricted — that the decision problem currently in view is significantly influenced by uncertainties to do with intended actions in other fields of choice. Such a concern for a wider view will also often lead to an extension in the time frame as well, because the pressures for decision may be less immediate in some of these related areas. The concern for co-ordination may also shift the process in the direction of some form of liaison or joint working with other sections or departments, and sometimes, also, with other decision-makers quite outside the organisational framework within which the current problem is being addressed.

FIGURE
5

Extending the Problem Focus

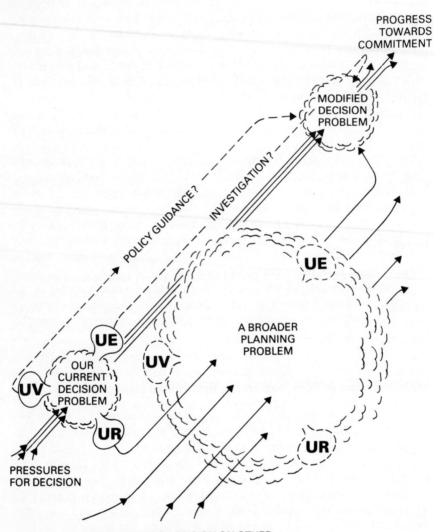

PROGRESS
TOWARDS
COMMITMENT

MODIFIED
DECISION
PROBLEM

POLICY GUIDANCE?

INVESTIGATION?

UE

A BROADER
PLANNING
PROBLEM

UV

UE

OUR
CURRENT
DECISION
PROBLEM

UV

UR

UR

PRESSURES
FOR DECISION

PRESSURES FOR DECISION ON OTHER
RELATED AGENDAS (varying time horizons)

The concern for co-ordination in dealing with related fields of choice does not, however, inevitably mean transcending organisational boundaries in this way. At a more modest level, it may simply be a matter of the same decision-maker recognising that an issue to be dealt with today should be considered in relation to some other issue to be dealt with next week. In the case of the hotel development mentioned earlier, for instance, it could be that a proposal to develop an indoor leisure centre is known to be pending on a neighbouring site, suggesting that either proposal could affect the other.

In general, the pursuit of the co-ordinative (UR) route implies forging a relationship between one decision process or planning process and others, in the manner indicated in Figure 5. The dynamic view is here taken a step further than in Figure 4, by showing the fuller implications of a shift from a more limited to a broader decision focus. The investment in 'more co-ordination' can be seen as shifting the focus, temporarily at least, from the original decision problem to a broader and more complex problem within which it is contained.

Incremental Progress in Planning

One of the most important points about this shift to a broader problem focus is that it does not automatically mean that those involved should be aiming for early decision in respect of all the related choices now brought into view. It is perfectly possible that the shift to a broader focus will help to reduce uncertainty in the original decision problem and so enable firm commitment to be agreed, without leading to simultaneous commitments in any or all of the other related areas. Indeed, the issue of balance between exploratory and decisive progress has already been highlighted (Figure 2) as one of the main areas of judgement in strategic choice; and it is a balance of critical importance in managing uncertainty through time.

The broader the focus of the problem within the larger cloud in Figure 5, the more it is likely to be thought of not simply as a decision problem but as a *planning problem* because it contains elements of both immediate and longer-term decision. But the distinction is not so much an absolute one as one of degree. This point is made in Figure 5 by showing the three kinds of uncertainty surfacing again at the broader level of the more complex planning problem. Indeed, if uncertainties of type UR again appear important at this level, this may trigger off concerns to move to an even broader level of concern, and to begin to explore the shape of an even larger and more obscure cloud. But this process of continually enlarging the scope of the problem will always have its limits in practice; and, if useful pointers to action are to emerge, then the focus of concern must be kept within manageable bounds.

FOUNDATIONS

It is not hard to see how planning procedures conceived with ambitions towards comprehensiveness can develop their own internal momentum. Such tendencies can be found in corporate planning procedures for the guidance of large and diffuse commercial enterprises, and also in exercises in the production of land-use plans or economic planning frameworks, through which public agencies endeavour to set a context for the actions of other parties. The danger is always that such activities will become separated from other management processes and so cease to exercise any real influence on the more immediate decisions they were designed to inform. This risk of disengagement between arrangements for planning and for management has already been suggested in the keynote diagram (Figure 1); it is a risk that can be confronted directly from the perspective of planning as a process of strategic choice.

Human Settings for Decision-Making

The shift from a 'snapshot' view of decision-making (Figure 3) to a more dynamic, multi-level picture (Figures 4 and 5) implies that the imagery of the cloud should itself be conceived in more realistic, multi-dimensional terms. To extend the metaphor, clouds in reality are not flat: they have length, depth and breadth; their edges may be blurred; they progress across the sky, changing shape as time passes; they dissolve, they merge, they break up; and, in so doing, they assume new and often unpredictable forms.

With such a picture in mind, it is possible to look more closely at some different kinds of human context for decision, as a step towards a closer examination of the processes of thought and communication which go on 'within the cloud'. Figure 6 begins by looking at an organisational context of the most simple and restricted kind: an individual sits on a chair (symbolising a defined organisational role), with successive matters for decision arriving in an 'in' tray on a table (symbolising an agenda). The matters are dealt with in sequence, agreed rules are applied, and decisions are then transferred to the 'out' tray one at a time.

If the rules are unambiguous in their bearing on the issue currently being dealt with, then the cloud representing the thought process of the decision-maker is a small one, and quickly evaporates, to be replaced by the next. Indeed, the symbolism of the cloud can be replaced by the more mechanistic image of the black box — and the decision-maker at the table is at risk of being superseded by an electronic counterpart. Of course, the cloud may sometimes become larger, when a more complex case arrives. The decision-maker now experiences uncertainty and, as in the case of the public official dealing with the application to build a new hotel, this uncertainty may be in part due to awareness of links to other related cases — as symbolised perhaps by some matters marked for further attention in a 'pending' tray.

Figure 6 then demonstrates another context of sequential decision-making, by contrasting the situation of a single decision-maker sitting at his or her small table with that of a collective decision-making body — a committee or management board — grouped around a larger table. Such a group will often have a pre-circulated agenda, presenting an ordered list of issues to discuss and where possible resolve, corresponding to the 'in' tray of the single decision-maker. Among the occupants of the roles symbolised by the chairs around the larger table, there will usually be someone in a 'chairing' role, responsible for ensuring that the business is dealt with in an orderly and expeditious way. In place of the 'out' tray, there will usually be a running record of decisions kept by a committee secretary or clerk; while the occupants of at least some of the other chairs around the table will sometimes be recognised as having different representative or expert roles to play.

The decision-making process is now not purely one of cogitation within an individual's head; it embraces processes of communication, verbal and non-verbal, among the members of the group. For the observer of the process, the elongated cloud above the large table in Figure 6 takes on additional substance, in that it becomes possible to follow the dynamics of information sharing, negotiation and — if decisions are to be reached — compromise between conflicting views. For instance, if the issue of permission to build a new hotel has been brought up on the planning committee's agenda, there may be a variety of financial, aesthetic, engineering and commercial considerations to be exposed and shared. Further, there may be various conflicts of interest to be managed; for instance, there could be conflicts between the committee's responsibilities to the local community and the relationships of some members with the developer, who could perhaps be a well-known and influential local figure.

However, many decision processes in practice fail to conform to either of the tidy, sequential models. If the issues are complex and their boundaries unclear, then organisational responsibilities too are likely to be diffuse and probably confused. Communications may take place not just around tables but on the telephone, in corridors, in small back rooms. The inputs and outputs can no longer be seen as falling into any clear sequence, and the image of the single cloud may have to be replaced by one of several separate clouds which continually come together, drift apart, coalesce or disappear. For instance, the hotel developer, in making his or her own investment decisions, may have a series of meetings with planners and other public officials, as well as finance houses, landowners and other commercial interests. The developer as well as the committee members will have uncertainties to manage in some or all of the three categories of UE, UV and UR; and the extent to which the different planning processes can be linked may begin to raise a host of difficult administrative, political, ethical and legal issues.

Modes of Decision-Making

In developing further the view of planning as a process of strategic choice, it is helpful to see the process within any 'cloud' as continually shifting between different and complementary 'modes' of decision-making activity. In the simple situation of sequential decision-making, where the nature of the problem inputs and the expected decision outputs is well defined, this movement can be seen in terms of only two complementary modes: the one concerned with *designing* possible courses of action, and the other with *comparing* them in the light of some view of what their consequences might be. This relatively simple view is indicated in Figure 7.

The process may not in practice be strictly linear because a comparison of the consequences of any pair of alternatives — for instance a straight 'yes' or 'no' to the application to build a hotel — may reveal that either response could have undesirable consequences and so trigger off a search for some other compromise solution. So it becomes necessary to allow for the possibility of a feedback loop returning from the comparing to the designing mode. So, in Figure 7 the single 'cloud' is shown as tending to change shape into two smaller clouds — clouds which may still not be clearly separable in practice, insofar as the interplay between designing and comparing may become rapid and difficult to trace.

This picture has much in common with other, more orthodox models of decision-making processes, which tend to present stages or activities in logical sequence, having a beginning and an end, while allowing for elements of feedback or recycling in between. However, the more diffuse, continuous kind of process which is characteristic of the making of complex decisions in practice involves coping with multiple problem inputs and multiple decision outputs, with no clear sequential relationships between the two. To represent this kind of process, it is necessary to move to a rather more elaborate picture of the process within the cloud, introducing two additional modes as shown in Figure 8.

The two further modes of decision-making activity which make their appearance in Figure 8 are both of a more subtle and political kind. One of these is concerned with the *shaping* of problems; a mode within which judgements about the possible connections between one field of choice and another can have a crucial role to play. The other, referred to as the *choosing* mode, is concerned with the formation of proposed commitments to action progressively through time. Here it has to be kept in mind that the more complex the shape of the problem, the wider the choices that have to be faced. There will be choices, not only about what courses of action are preferred, but also about what degree of commitment is appropriate at this stage; which decisions should be deferred until later; and what explorations could be set in train in response to different types of uncertainty.

So, instead of two partially overlapping foci within the cloud, there now

FIGURE

7

A Process of Simple Choice

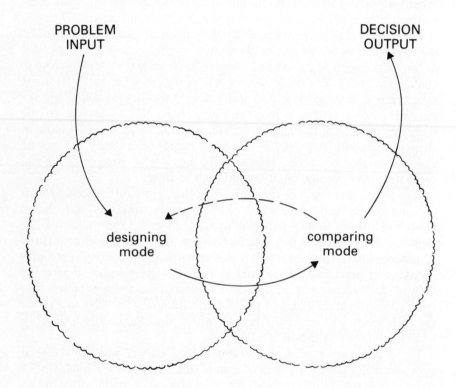

PROBLEM
INPUT

DECISION
OUTPUT

designing
mode

comparing
mode

appear four, with a variety of possible directions of movement between one mode and another. The most orthodox progression might appear to be from shaping problems, through designing possibilities, to comparing their consequences and then on to a final choosing of actions. However, such a progression is likely to be neither straightforward nor realistic, insofar as the process is to be seen as a continuous and incremental one, with no clear beginning and no single end. For the choice of actions to deal with some parts of the problem situation will leave other choices open for the future, creating opportunities for future reshaping of problems as unexpected events occur and new connections begin to appear.

Challenges to Management and Planning Norms

Already, the ideas presented here can be seen to pose some direct challenges to long-established management and planning norms: norms which have indeed been under sustained challenge from other sources, yet remain extremely persistent in the design of formal management and planning procedures — often for reasons of organisational stability and accountability which cannot be lightly criticised. Among the more deeply-established norms in any management system are those of *linearity, objectivity, certainty* and *comprehensiveness*. These can be summarised as follows:

aim for **linearity** — "Tackle one thing at a time";
aim for **objectivity** — "Avoid personal or sectional bias";
aim for **certainty** — "Establish the full facts of the situation";
aim for **comprehensiveness** — "Don't do things by halves".

Such norms may usually be adequate enough for the functionary sitting at a desk, working to highly constrained terms of reference. However, even here the system of rules can rarely be exhaustive in representing the situations that could arise; so feelings of uncertainty about how to act will sometimes surface and, with them, will arise difficulties in conforming to the norms of linearity and objectivity in their pristine forms. When a shift is made from decision-making to plan-making, the same four norms tend to show a remarkable persistence, even though the language may change. Yet the experience of working on difficult and complex planning problems is that the norms of linearity, objectivity, certainty and comprehensiveness keep on breaking down. So, in this book, they will be replaced by less simple prescriptions of the following form:

don't aim for linearity — learn to work with **cyclicity**;
don't aim for objectivity — learn to work with **subjectivity**;
don't aim for certainty — learn to work with **uncertainty**;
don't aim for comprehensiveness — learn to work with **selectivity**;

FIGURE
8

A Process of Strategic Choice

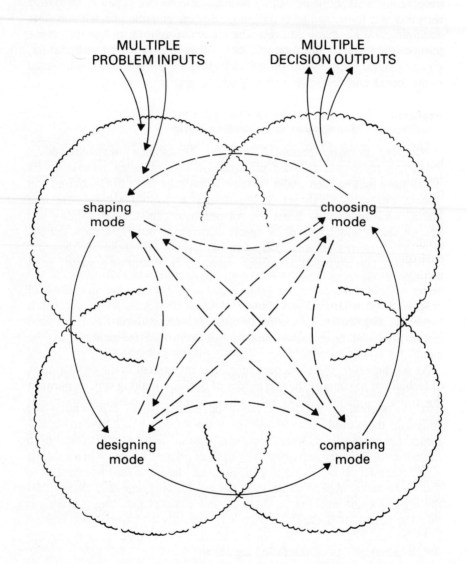

MULTIPLE
PROBLEM INPUTS

MULTIPLE
DECISION OUTPUTS

shaping
mode

choosing
mode

designing
mode

comparing
mode

These alternative prescriptions may appear to be less straightforward to interpret in practice than the more familiar norms. But experience demonstrates that they offer a much more effective guide for people in attempting to choose strategically in practice. What is more, once they are stated and developed more fully, they can help people cope constructively with any sense of residual guilt they may feel in failing to apply simple management and planning norms when they encounter problems of a more complex kind.

Implications for a Technology of Strategic Choice

There are many forms of management and planning technique which have been devised to help people deal with difficult decision problems. Indeed, systematic methods of designing courses of actions, and comparing their likely consequences, have reached a considerable level of sophistication in some professional fields. For instance, systematic methods have been developed for assessing investment proposals in the light of predictions of not only their economic but also their social and environmental implications, while there are various computer-aided methods which can help generate a range of alternatives within some of the better understood fields of technological design. Meanwhile, mathematical programming techniques can allow analysts to conduct a systematic search for better solutions within a complex, multi-dimensional field, provided certain stringent assumptions about the structure of the problem can be met.

As yet, however, there has been much less investment in the development of techniques to support the two modes of decision-making which appear in the upper part of Figure 8 — even though these two modes take on special significance in confronting decision problems of a less clearly-structured kind, where it becomes necessary to cope with multiple inputs and outputs in a highly flexible, cyclic and, necessarily, subjective way.

Just as a distinction can be drawn between the two lower, more technical, modes in Figure 8 and the upper, more political modes, so another kind of distinction can be drawn between the two modes to the left of the diagram and the two modes to the right. Whereas the former two modes are primarily addressed towards the task of opening up the field of choice facing the decision-makers, the latter two modes can be seen as addressed towards the complementary task of narrowing that field down again in order to work towards agreement on action.

This distinction will be used as a basis for the organisation of the next two chapters. These will introduce and illustrate a series of basic concepts and techniques which have been developed, tested and modified progressively

FIGURE
9

A Structure for Subsequent Chapters

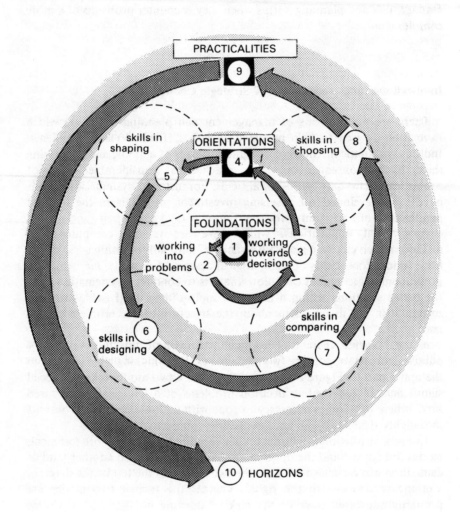

STRUCTURE

through repeated application to a range of applied planning problems. Together, these concepts and techniques can be seen as constituting an *appropriate technology* for strategic choice: appropriate in the sense that it is not intended as an advanced technology for use primarily by the expert. Rather the technology is designed to support the interactive work of groups of people who have different perspectives to contribute to a problem; who face quite daunting challenges in communicating with each other; yet who may appreciate the importance of working quickly and informally under the pressures of day-to-day events.

So, the concepts to be introduced in the next two chapters will only occasionally be worth applying with a high level of analytical sophistication by specialists in a back-room setting. Indeed, the more complex and unclear become the issues and their relationships, the more problematic become the more political modes of shaping problems and choosing actions, and the more vital it becomes that any technology of strategic choice be capable of use in a flexible and relatively non-technical way.

Implications for Chapter Structure

The emphasis in the chapters that follow will therefore be on quite simple and *transparent* concepts and techniques — most of them involving graphical forms of representation. These are intended to aid the processes of communication between people whose perspectives, attitudes and experiences may differ, as much as to help individuals in structuring their own personal thought processes. Working on these principles, Figure 9 presents a preview of the way in which the content of the nine chapters that follow will relate to the four modes of strategic choice which were distinguished in Figure 8. This picture can be used in conjunction with the Quick Access Guide at the beginning, by the reader who wishes to refer at any moment to the principles of structure on which this book has been designed.

Chapter 2, which is concerned with concepts and techniques for working into complex problems, will begin with the shaping mode, and will introduce some simple concepts which can help in structuring areas of choice and the interconnections between them. It will then move down to the designing mode, to introduce some further ideas to help in organising views about the options available and the patterns of compatibility or incompatibility between them. Chapter 3 is concerned with the complementary process of working towards decisions; it will begin with some concepts intended to help in comparing the foreseeable consequences of alternative courses of action, taking uncertainty explicitly into account. It then moves on to introduce further concepts addressed to the explicit management of uncertainty and the choice of incremental actions through time, drawing on the UE/UV/UR framework which has already been introduced. Together, the two chapters provide a foundation for the discussion, in later chapters, of the many different ways in which the basic concepts and methods can be brought into play in practice.

2
Working into Problems

Introduction

The aim of this chapter is to introduce a set of basic concepts and methods which, taken together, offer a means of helping people to structure complex decision problems in terms of inter-related elements of choice. These concepts and techniques are addressed in particular to the work of the shaping and designing modes as set out on the left hand side of the general process diagram (Figure 8). This means that they are concerned both with the shaping of problems and with the designing or formulation of possible courses of action in response to those problems. A further set of concepts and techniques for comparing those possible courses of action and for choosing between them will then be described in Chapter 3, to complete this introduction to a basic 'technology' for strategic choice.

The basic concepts to be introduced in this chapter will include those of the decision area; the option within a decision area; and the decision scheme, consisting of a set of mutually consistent options drawn from a set of interconnected decision areas. These and other concepts will be introduced in turn, illustrated by example and more formally defined. Taken together, they offer a quite general and flexible basis for the formulation of complex decision problems; and, more specifically, for the use of an analytical method known as Analysis of Interconnected Decision Areas — AIDA for short. The essentials of the AIDA method will be explained in this chapter, but some of the more important variations on it will be deferred for discussion in later chapters.

The approach to structuring of complex problems to be introduced here is quite simple in its essence. Yet, because it involves trying to express complex realities in simple and comprehensible terms, it can demand subtle and shrewd judgements of those participating in the process; judgements of a kind which are often made intuitively by individuals, yet are rarely exposed to argument in the normal course of debate. The nature of these judgements will become more apparent as this chapter unfolds.

For the purpose of introducing the basic ideas as simply and clearly as

27

possible, this chapter will begin to develop a case example to be known as the *South Side Story*. It is a story of a group of decision-makers faced with a set of linked investment and locational decisions which impinge on a residential community of around 7000 people, living on the fringe of a larger urban area long dominated by heavy industry, but now in a state of economic and environmental decline.* The story is one which will be developed gradually in this and later chapters, as further concepts are introduced and the skills and judgements involved in applying them in practice are discussed.

For purposes of exposition, the various concepts and techniques will at this stage be introduced sequentially and in an orderly way. However, it has to be kept in mind throughout that in practice the process of strategic choice is normally much more flexible and adaptive. The process can shift rapidly from one mode to another, with a continued readiness to 'recycle' through earlier stages of analysis as new insights emerge and the level of understanding grows.

The Concept of the Decision Area

The concept of a **decision area** provides the most fundamental element in the approach to problem structuring to be described in this chapter.

In essence, this concept offers no more than a means of describing and labelling any problem situation where people see an opportunity to choose between different courses of action. To begin with a simple example, you, the reader, may even now be thinking about a choice as to whether to read the remainder of this chapter or to skip ahead to the next. Or a person lying in bed may be conscious — even if only dimly — of a choice about what to do when a bedside alarm sounds: whether to get up, to ignore it, or to silence it by whatever means may be available. On a less personal note, a bank manager may encounter a decision area when judging what level of interest to charge a particular client for a loan; while the local authority planners mentioned in the last chapter found themselves faced with a decision area as to whether or not to approve the proposal for a new hotel. Meanwhile, the developer in question might face a range of decision problems, to do with timing, choice between alternative locations, scale, design, financial backing and other important commercial matters. These could either be expressed as a single, rather complex decision area or — as would be more usual when using strategic choice methods — as a set of different decision areas, the mutual relationships of which would have to be explored.

Implicit in each of these situations is an opportunity for decision-makers, whether alone or in association with others, to act in at least two alternative

* The South Side Problem as presented here is closely — though by no means exactly — modelled on one of the first successful experiences in applying strategic choice methods to urban development problems.

ways.* Also implicit in each situation is some sense of pressure or concern to arrive at a commitment to some preferred course of action amongst those believed to be available — even though it is only to be expected that some decision areas will carry a greater sense of urgency to act than others. It is this sense of pressure to act that creates a *decision problem* for those concerned — it being useful to distinguish the idea of a decision problem from that of other types of problem or puzzle which may be picked up and worked on casually as a diversion by anyone looking for interesting ways of passing their time.

To illustrate the concept of the decision area through the example of the South Side Story, it is now necessary to set the scene a little more fully, by describing how the pressures to act have arisen in this case. At this stage, the context will be taken as one in which South Side comes within the administrative boundaries of a large urban municipality — the city of Dockport, serving around a quarter of a million people in all. South Side itself is an old-established neighbourhood with a strong sense of community among the residents — though they have been steadily declining in number as older housing has been cleared and local employment opportunities have dwindled. This population base is likely to be reduced further over the next few years by the impending closure of the local steelworks, which has been a source of many jobs — but also of severe local air pollution that has lessened the attraction of South Side as a residential area. Although many of the older houses which remain in South Side are scheduled to be demolished in the next two or three years, others could have a prolonged life if designated for improvement, with financial aid from governmental grant aid programmes.

Suddenly, however, a new note of urgency has arisen for the municipality in considering what to do about South Side — and, in particular, in addressing the problem of how far to invest in its continued viability as a residential community. For a proposal has just been published by a transportation agency to route a new arterial highway carrying industrial and other traffic directly through the neighbourhood. As might be expected, this heightens the sense of anxiety about the future among the local residents and traders. In response, the municipality calls for an early report on the problem from a specially-formed internal working party of planners, engineers, accountants and legal and valuation experts. From their initial discussions, it will be supposed that a list of seven potentially important decision areas emerges, as indicated in Figure 10.

In this list, it will be noticed that each decision area has not only been

---

* Purists sometimes point out that the word 'alternative' applies logically to an 'either/or' situation, so it is not strictly correct to talk of a set of more than two different courses of action as 'alternatives'. However, this need not be treated as a serious source of difficulty here, as in the chapters that follow the *comparison* of alternatives will usually be treated as essentially a pairwise process.

FIGURE

10

SOUTH SIDE
EXAMPLE

The Concept of a Decision Area

DECISION AREA	LABEL
which route to choose to take the new arterial road across South Side?	ROAD LINE?
where to locate the local shopping centre for South Side?	SHOP LOC'N?
whether or not to declare West Street a housing improvement area?	WEST ST?
what land use to specify for the area of cleared housing in the centre of South Side	CENT'L SITE?
what level of investment to indicate for the continued life of South Side as a residential area?	DIST LIFE?
what land use to specify for the disused gasworks site?	GAS SITE?
when to schedule the closure of Griffin Road school?	GRIFF SCHL?

SHAPING

CONCEPTS

A DECISION AREA is an opportunity for choice in which two or more different courses of action can be considered.

described with some care, but also given a brief label for purposes of future reference. The question marks — though they can be treated as optional in practice — are here added as a reminder that each decision area is supposed to represent an *opportunity* for choice rather than any particular *outcome* of the decision process. This is a point that is also stressed in the more formal definition accompanying Figure 10.

As the example shows, any list of decision areas can be quite diverse in the types of opportunity for choice which it contains. The first decision area in the list concerns choice of alignment for a road; the second concerns choice of location for a proposed local facility; two others concern choice of land use for particular sites; while the last in the list concerns a choice of timing.

There can also be variations between decision areas in the level of generality at which they were expressed. Whereas the fifth decision area concerns choice of policy stance in relation to investment in South Side as a whole, the third concerns a much more specific choice of action in relation to one particular street. It is one of the inherent strengths of the decision area concept that it allows different types and levels of choice to be considered together within a common analytical framework.

Links Between Decision Areas

As soon as a set of opportunities for choice has been formulated as a list of decision areas — even if only in a tentative way — it will usually begin to become apparent that some of them at least can be viewed as *interconnected*, in the sense that there is a case for considering them jointly rather than attempting to come to decisions taking each of them one at a time.

For example, an appreciation of the local geography of South Side might make it apparent that it could be unwise to consider the choice of use for the central site without any reference to the choice of location for the future local shopping centre. This implies a belief that the choices made if the two decision areas were considered together could *differ* from those that might emerge if each were looked at in isolation, on separate 'agendas' of decision-making. This might be the case if the choice of particular uses for the central site made some conceivable locations for the shopping centre physically impossible, or vice versa: it could also be the case if certain choices in either decision area seemed likely to make some choices in the other less attractive in terms of costs, implications for local residents or other consequences with which the working party could be concerned. More obviously, there could be an interconnection between the two decision areas if one of the possible locations for the shopping centre were the central site itself.

However, not every pair of decision areas in a list is likely to be directly linked in any of these ways. For instance, there may be no direct reason for

FIGURE

11

SOUTH SIDE
EXAMPLE

The Concept of a Decision Link

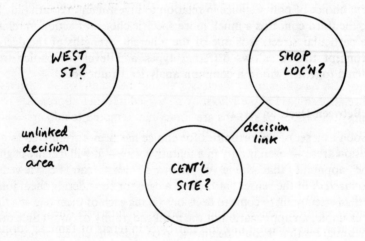

WEST
ST?

SHOP
LOC'N?

unlinked
decision
area

decision
link

CENT'L
SITE?

A DECISION LINK is a relationship between two decision areas expressing a belief that it could make a difference to consider them jointly instead of separately.

supposing that the choice as to whether or not to improve West Street cannot be arrived at independently from the choice of location for the shopping centre, or the choice of use for the central site.

Using labelled circles to represent the decision areas and connecting lines to represent the presence or absence of direct links between them, a picture of mutual relationships can be built up graphically as shown in Figure 11. Here the connecting line, or **decision link**, represents no more than a working assumption that, at least at the present stage of understanding of the problem, it makes sense to look into the mutual relationships between the two decision areas CENT'L SITE? and SHOP LOC'N?. Meanwhile, the absence of a link between WEST ST? and either of the other decision areas represents a working assumption that this choice can be dealt with independently from the other two.

The idea of a decision link forms a second 'core' concept in the strategic choice vocabulary, and is more formally defined in a statement appearing below Figure 11. The term *decision link* is usually abbreviated simply to *link* for working purposes, because it is usually clear from the context that the word is being used in this special sense. It is important to note at this stage that the concept of a decision link implies no particular view about the *sequence* in which the linked decisions should be taken, or about possible causal relationships. People who may be versed in other approaches to the mapping of decisions or systems are sometimes tempted to add arrowheads to decision links, to suggest directions of influence or precedence between one choice and another. However, it has not been found helpful to introduce such conventions into the approach being discussed here, which is purely concerned with the logic of *mutual* connectedness between one decision area and another.

Another caution concerns the tendency to interpret the concepts of decision area and decision link too narrowly in terms of familiar forms of relationships. In dealing with land use or locational problems in particular, there is a tendency for planners to focus on spatially defined decision areas and to look for links in terms of geographical adjacency or similar relationships. But decision areas and relationships between them can be used to reflect all kinds of non-spatial considerations as well, as the further unfolding of the South Side Story will make clear. For this reason, no physical map of South Side is introduced at this stage: but any reader who may find it helpful to form some view of the geographical layout of South Side may like to glance briefly at the sketch map at the end of this chapter (Figure 18).

The Decision Graph as a Representation of Problem Structure

In any situation where a complex problem can be expressed in terms of a set of several decision areas, some but by no means all of which may be

FIGURE

12

SOUTH SIDE
EXAMPLE

The Concept of a Decision Graph

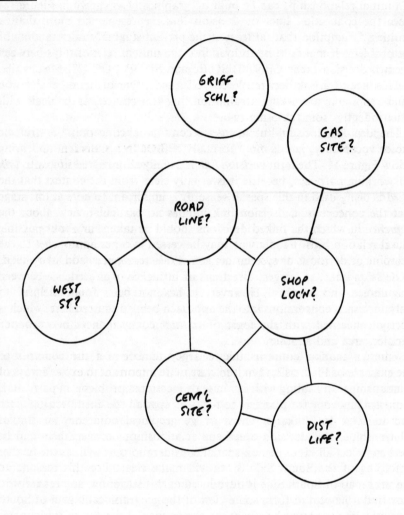

A DECISION GRAPH is a diagrammatic representation of a set of decision
areas and the relationships between them expressed as decision links.

directly connected by decision links, then it is possible to use the graphical connections introduced in Figure 11 to build up a wider view of the structure of that problem in the form of what is called a **decision graph.***

A decision graph is, in effect, no more than a two dimensional 'map' showing a set of decision areas and a set of links which connect some pairs but not others. Figure 12 gives an example of a decision graph for the set of seven decision areas so far identified within the South Side decision problem. This indicates that there are eight decision links in all, out of the total of 21 which would be theoretically possible if each of the seven had been directly linked to each of the other six.

This particular decision graph reflects an agreed view, among people who can be supposed to have specific knowledge of the realities of the South Side situation, that some decision areas are more directly interconnected than others. For instance, it shows several links connecting the four decision areas concerned with ROAD LINE?, SHOP LOC'N?, CENT'L SITE? and DIST LIFE? — even though ROAD LINE? and DIST LIFE? are only linked indirectly through the other two. The WEST ST? and GRIFF SCHL? decision areas, in contrast, are comparative outliers, each being directly connected to only one of the other decision areas. Indeed, had it not been for the sudden introduction of a choice to be made about the road line, as a result of a highway planning exercise over a wider area, the WEST ST? decision area would have been completely disconnected from the SHOP LOC'N? and CENT'L SITE? decision areas, as was earlier suggested (Figure 11). This is a relatively simple example of a common occurrence not only in urban planning but in other fields, where the introduction of new decision areas can introduce additional complexity into a hitherto much simpler pattern of decision links.

Where a decision graph includes a larger number of decision areas than the example of Figure 12, then it may be quite important to explore ways of rearranging it to bring out its underlying structure more clearly. It is important to note that there is no set rule to guide the positioning of each decision area on the graph: the map is a *topological* one, the meaning of which would not be changed if the relative positions of the decision areas were altered. The essential information conveyed by Figure 12 would be exactly the same if the WEST ST? decision area were shifted from the left to the right of the picture. However, it might then show some awkward crossovers between decision links, unless other decision areas were to be repositioned at the same time.

The value of any decision graph lies essentially in the picture it presents about the structure of relationships between elements of a complex problem; a picture which can be modified through time and challenged wherever there is disagreement between participants in the process. In this

---

* In some earlier writings this was referred to as a strategy graph.

FIGURE

13

SOUTH SIDE
EXAMPLE

The Concept of a Problem Focus

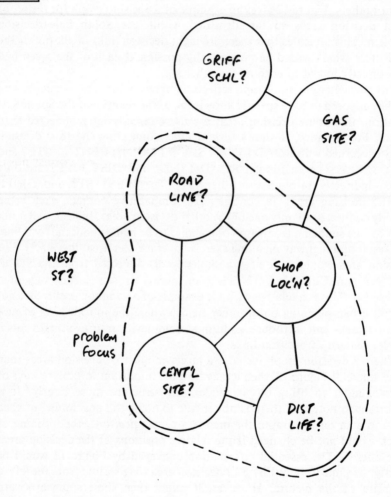

A PROBLEM FOCUS is any subset of the decision areas in a decision graph
which is selected for closer examination.

way the participants can proceed, through as many iterations as need be, towards deeper examination of possibilities for action and their consequences, either within the graph as a whole or within selected decision areas or clusters within its structure.

The Choice of a Problem Focus

The possibility of focussing on a selected cluster of decision areas within a larger decision graph offers an important field of judgement in a process of strategic choice. Indeed, it can mark a critical point of transition from the work of the shaping mode to that of the designing mode — especially where the decision graph is so large and complex in its structure that it is difficult to think of designing possible ways forward while keeping the full set of interconnected decision areas in view.

Any focus for the examination of possible ways forward which has been deliberately selected to include some but not all the decision areas in a decision graph can be referred to as a **problem focus**. It is important to note here that the scope of this problem focus can be changed, repeatedly if so desired, as work on the problem proceeds. There are many different considerations that can be taken into account in choosing a problem focus, and these will be discussed more fully in Chapter 5. At this stage it is the general *concept* of the problem focus that is important, as a means of managing the transition from the shaping to the designing mode.

In Figure 13, one possible problem focus has been selected for the South Side problem, by exercising a degree of selectivity within the decision graph of Figure 12. The comparatively isolated WEST ST?, GAS SITE? and GRIFF SCHL? decision areas have here been excluded, and a boundary indicating the limits of the resulting problem focus has been drawn around the other four. In the case of a decision graph of comparatively simple structure such as this, the step of choosing to concentrate on these four may seem a somewhat obvious one to take, working on the basis of the structural information alone (Figure 12). But it is not hard to see that the judgement could become more difficult if there were many more decision areas and connections to consider, and if it was thought important to take into account other reasons for focussing — such as the relative urgency and importance of different decision areas.

Even in this simple example, there are several other choices of focus that could have been made. It could have been decided to focus only on the triangular cluster of ROAD LINE?, CENT'L SITE? and SHOP LOC'N? decision areas, on the grounds that each has at least three decision links joining it to other decision areas, whereas DIST LIFE? has only two. It could also have been decided deliberately to keep all seven decision areas within the problem focus, or even to restrict it to only one decision area in the first instance — SHOP LOC'N? being one possible candidate because

FIGURE

14

SOUTH SIDE
EXAMPLE

The Concept of a Decision Option

DECISION AREA	OPTIONS	OPTION LABEL
ROAD LINE ?	- northern route - southern route	- NORTH - SOUTH
SHOP LOC'N ?	- Main Street - King Square - gasworks site	- MAIN - KING - GAS
CENT'L SITE ?	- industry - housing - open space	- IND - HOUS - OPEN
DIST LIFE ?	- 10 year horizon - 20 year horizon - 40 year horizon	- 10 YR - 20 YR - 40 YR

options in further decision areas excluded from problem focus:

WEST ST ?	- improve West Street - no action	- YES - NO
GAS SITE ?	- shopping - open space - housing - industry	- SHOP - OPEN - HOUS - IND
GRIFF SCHL ?	- schedule for early closure - keep open a few more years	- EARLY - LATER

DESIGNING

CONCEPTS

A (DECISION) OPTION is any one of the mutually exclusive courses of action
that can be considered within a decision area.

of its pivotal position on the graph. The narrower the focus, the less work there will be to do in the designing mode, especially if the alternatives within the decision area or areas concerned can be considered clear cut. So the more rapid can be the progress forward into the comparing mode. However, this is not to suggest that the case for choosing a broader focus will not re-emerge later, once the uncertainties involved in working within the narrow focus have taken clearer shape.

Options within Decision Areas

Despite all the information about the structure of a decision problem that may be contained within a decision graph, or even within a particular problem focus within a decision graph, this form of problem representation does nothing in itself to indicate what range of possible actions is likely to be open to the decision-makers. To make progress in this direction, it is necessary to move into the more technical domain of the designing mode, which takes its place in the bottom left-hand corner of the general process diagram (Figure 8). This is where the analytical method of *Analysis of Interconnected Decision Areas (AIDA)* begins to have an important part to play.*

The term **decision option** — usually referred to in practice simply as an **option** — will be introduced at this point to describe any one course of action within a decision area, out of whatever range of possibilities may be seen as available. In the South Side case it will be supposed, for the sake of example, that the members of the local working party are able to agree that the range of choice in each of the seven decision areas can be represented by a set of two or more possible options, as indicated in Figure 14.

In practice, of course, it may sometimes be necessary to list more options than indicated in this example if a fully representative picture of the range of possibilities within a decision area is to be presented. Indeed, there may be a good deal of debate about these options among participants who may have different appreciations of the problems before them. During such a debate, different perceptions could well emerge not only about the number of options in each decision area, but also about the terms in which they should be expressed. For instance, it could be asked why the set of options for public investment in the continued life of South Side as a residential district should be limited to the range of 10-year, 20-year and 40-year horizons. Why not 5 years, or 15, or 100? And why express the range of possibilities in terms of time horizons at all? Could not the alternative policies perhaps be expressed in some broader, more flexible but still

* The AIDA method was first developed in the course of a seminal IOR/Tavistock Institute project on communications in the building industry, conducted in parallel with the Coventry local government study. Fuller references will be found in the guide to further reading at the end of this book, but see in particular Luckman (1967).

FIGURE

15

SOUTH SIDE
EXAMPLE

The Concept of an Option Bar

COMPATIBILITY TABLE FOR OPTIONS FROM
FIRST TWO DECISION AREAS - ROAD LINE ?
& SHOP LOC'N ?

ROAD LINE ?

		-NORTH	-SOUTH
SHOP LOC'N?	- MAIN	•	✗
	-KING	•	✗
	- GAS	✗	•

[
• represents a COMPATIBLE combination

✗ represents an INCOMPATIBLE combination or OPTION BAR
]

EXTENSION TO INCLUDE A THIRD
DECISION AREA - CENT'L SITE ?

		ROAD LINE?		SHOP LOC'N?		
		-NORTH	-SOUTH	-MAIN	-KING	-GAS
CENT'L SITE?	-IND	•	✗	•	✗	•
	-HOUS	•	✗	•	•	•
	-OPEN	•	•	•	•	•

DESIGNING

CONCEPTS

An OPTION BAR is a representation of an assumption that two options from different decision areas are incompatible with each other.

meaningful way, such as a choice of short, medium and long term strategies?

It is also important to check that the options within a decision area are *mutually exclusive*. For instance, if industrial use of the central site did not necessarily rule out the possibility of housing or open space on part of the site, then mixed use options might have to be introduced; or perhaps the decision area itself could be reformulated in some way, to enable the options available to be expressed in a different form. Questions about whether the options within a decision area can be considered both representative and mutually exclusive can be well worth discussing if they help to focus critical attention on what is meant by the decision area in question, and to suggest possibilities for reformulation of the problem in more realistic ways.

Once the set of options within a decision area is agreed to be adequate as a base for further analysis, it can be a useful practical step to give them short labels, as in Figure 14. So long as these labels do not suppress too much of the information contained in their full descriptions, they can save a great deal of time and space when it comes to examining combinations of options from different decision areas.

Compatibility of Options in Interconnected Decision Areas

Once options have been identified, the question arises of what possibilities for choice are to be found not merely within each decision area taken separately, but within linked pairs or sets of decision areas within the selected problem focus. It therefore becomes necessary to introduce assumptions about how far options from different decision areas can be combined. For instance, the ROAD LINE? decision area in South Side contains two options while the SHOP LOC'N? decision area contains three; if each option in the first decision area could be freely combined with each option in the second, this would give a total of 2 × 3 = 6 possible combinations from which to choose. In practice, however, the range of possibilities may be more restricted, because of various kinds of *constraint* which may be encountered in trying to combine particular options in one decision area with particular options in other decision areas. For example, a knowledge of local geography in South Side might make it sensible to assume that the choice of the southern road line would rule out the choice of both the Main Street and the King Square shopping locations, because either would mean that the majority of residents would be cut off from their neighbourhood shopping centre. Such a combination could be seen as violating what might be recognised as an important design principle — if not altogether destroying the centre's economic viability. A similar check on other combinations of options from these two decision areas, followed by a testing of options in the CENT'L SITE? decision area against those in each

FIGURE

16

SOUTH SIDE
EXAMPLE

The Concept of an Option Graph

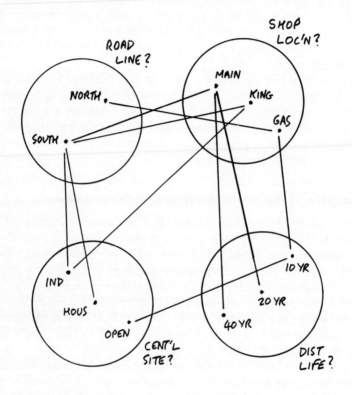

DESIGNING

CONCEPTS

An OPTION GRAPH is a diagrammatic representation of the compatibilities and incompatibilities of options within a problem focus.

of the previous decision areas, might generate further assumptions on incompatibilities as shown in Figure 15. Such a table is sometimes known as a *compatibility matrix*. When other decision areas are added, it can be extended further in a stepwise fashion to form a triangular array, until each pair of the decision areas within the present problem focus is covered. Each relationship of incompatibility between a pair of options from different decision areas, as indicated by a cross in any particular cell of the table, is known as an **option bar**. In the South Side example, there are altogether three option bars connecting the ROAD LINE? and SHOP LOC'N? decision areas, which rule out three of the six conceivable combinations of options; then there are a further three option bars ruling out certain further combinations once the CENT'L SITE? decision area is added.

As in the identification of options within a decision area, it is quite normal for different participants to hold different views as to which combinations of options are feasible and which are not. Again, such differences can be used as a point of departure in working towards a clearer shared view of the structure of the specific decision problem which the decision-makers face.

Building up an Option Graph

Where there are many decision areas and options to consider, and so the number of possible combinations is large, then it can become a correspondingly laborious matter to check each option in each decision area for compatibility with each option in every other decision area in a systematic way. This itself is one good argument for choosing a limited problem focus of no more than four or five decision areas within a complex decision graph. However, in building up a series of two-way tables such as those in Figure 15, it is usually found that crosses representing option bars appear in only a minority of the cells. This can greatly simplify the analysis of which combinations are possible and which are not.

The same kind of information can be built up by graphical methods, through an extension of the kinds of conventions used to develop the decision graph. This involves constructing what is known as an **option graph**, in which decision areas are represented by circles, as in the decision graph, but the set of options available within each decision area is specified within each circle as in the example of Figure 16. This allows the structure of relationships between specific options to be represented by drawing in connecting lines between those pairs of options from different decision areas where option bars have been identified.

It can avoid clutter in the option graph to use abbreviated labels for the options within each decision area, and also to write the name of the decision area itself outside, rather than inside, the circle. The pattern of option bars can then be built up gradually, scanning the whole graph for possible incompatibilities rather than working logically through the combinations one at a time — and concentrating on pairs of decision areas which are directly connected through decision links. This kind of approach can provide a more open means of building up a picture of incompatibilities than the matrix approach — especially where there are several participants with different kinds of insight to offer.

Although the picture of Figure 16 may look quite complex and hard to interpret at a glance, it is worth noting that it includes only ten option bars in all, as compared to the much larger number of combinations of pairs of options from different decision areas — in this example, thirty-five — which remain feasible. This observation helps to explain the convention of using connecting lines in an option graph to represent *incompatible* combinations rather than *compatible* ones. When first encountered, this convention can be found surprising and counter-intuitive. Nevertheless, a little experience soon shows that it is normally far more economical to use links between options to represent the few incompatible pairs of options than the many compatible pairs. Not only does this make the picture of criss-crossing lines less impenetrable to the eye; more importantly, it allows new option bars to be introduced gradually as new reasons for incompatibility suggest themselves, and makes it much easier to keep track of the logic within the option graph.

It is only to be expected that the pattern of option bars in an option graph will bear some resemblance to the pattern of decision links within the corresponding part of the decision graph — if only because one obvious way in which a pair of decision areas can be interconnected is through some restriction on the extent to which options within them can be combined. However, the correspondence will not necessarily be precise: for instance, a pair of decision areas may be seen as linked on the decision graph not because there are any combinations of options which are incompatible, but because there are some combinations which appear to bring particular advantages or disadvantages in terms of costs or other consequences. So decision links do not necessarily imply option bars. Nor is it inconceivable that option bars will be identified to connect pairs of options from decision areas which were not thought to have been linked when the decision graph was first drawn; it is always possible that deeper reflection will bring insights into the problem structure which were not apparent at first sight.

Generating Feasible Decision Schemes

At this point, the core concept of a **decision scheme** will be introduced, to describe any combination of options, one drawn from each of the decision areas within a problem focus, which is *feasible* in the sense that it does not violate any of the option bars included in the current formulation of the decision problem. Even where the number of option bars in an option graph is quite limited, it can be far from easy to see what range of possible decision schemes is available simply by looking at the option graph itself. Instead, it is necessary to embark on a logical procedure for testing the feasibility of different combinations of options from the decision areas, considered not just two at a time but in sets of three or more taken together.

This means first arranging the decision areas within the current problem focus according to some chosen sequence, and then proceeding logically through that sequence in the manner illustrated in Figure 17. Here the various feasible combinations of options from the four selected decision areas for South Side are built up by proceeding through a systematic branching process. The combinations are presented in the form of a tree-like arrangement, which is not dissimilar to the kind of *decision tree* used in other systematic forms of decision analysis. However, the object here is not to anticipate contingencies and calculate probabilities, as in classical decision analysis, but simply to list the set of available decision schemes so that they can be examined further.

In Figure 17, for example, the path through the tree which combines the NORTH road line with the GAS shop location is eliminated at an early branching point, because of an option bar linking these two options directly. At a later stage, the NORTH-KING-IND route is terminated because there is an option bar between the KING and IND options, while further on again, the NORTH-MAIN-IND-20YR route is ruled out because of an incompatibility between a 20 year district life and the main street shop location. So, in progressing along each branch of the tree, it is necessary to check the compatibility of each new option not only with the option in the immediately preceding decision area, but also with all the others further back. In this example, indeed, the entire branch which begins NORTH-MAIN-OPEN is eliminated, not because of incompatibilities involving any pair of these three options, but because of two different types of option bar which are encountered once the final DIST LIFE? decision area is added.

In this example, the systematic development of the tree shows that there are, in all, nine feasible decision schemes, each of which has been given an alphabetic label for reference purposes. Sometimes, there will be only a few feasible decision schemes, or even none at all: on other occasions, there may be so many that they become difficult to compare at all without some further filtering process.

The process of working systematically through the branches of a tree can provide important opportunities for learning. It can, of course, become time-consuming if the number of decision areas and options is much larger than in this example. In such circumstances, computer methods can sometimes be helpful, both as a check on the logic of the process and a means of testing rapidly the effect of different assumptions on options and option bars. There are various alternative ways of setting out the kind of information contained in Figure 17. In this example, the closed branches are

FIGURE

17

SOUTH SIDE
EXAMPLE

The Concept of a Decision Scheme

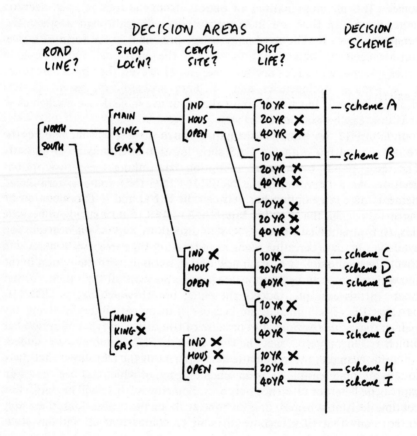

A DECISION SCHEME is any feasible combination of options containing one from each of the decision areas within a problem focus.

included and terminated by a cross to help demonstrate the logic of the process; they could however, have been omitted, so allowing the range of available choices to be presented in a more compressed form. If desired, the set of feasible schemes could have been presented as a straight list rather than in the form of a tree; the advantage of the branching format is essentially in the *structural* information it conveys. Also, the arrangement of the set of decision schemes could be changed, either by working through the decision areas in a different sequence or by introducing comparative considerations to bring to the fore those schemes which might be considered more desirable. But this latter possibility means moving on to the perspective of the comparing mode, and will be left for further consideration in Chapter 3.

Analysing Interconnected Decision Areas: Concluding Review

This chapter has introduced a set of basic concepts which provide a foundation for the general method of problem structuring that has become known as Analysis of Interconnected Decision Areas, or AIDA for short. The most fundamental concepts of the AIDA method — those of the decision area, the option and the option bar — together form the basic elements required as input to build an option graph as a representation of the structure of choices within a problem or part of a problem; and, from this, to find out what range of possible 'solutions' or decision schemes are available. Among the other ideas introduced in the earlier sections of this chapter were those of the decision link, the decision graph and the problem focus — all of these being intended to help people in debating the overall 'shape' of the problem before the more specific AIDA methods are brought into play.

The AIDA method of problem structuring does, of course, have its limitations in representing complexity of certain kinds; and these limitations will be discussed further in later chapters. In particular, it is not always easy to adapt the method to decision problems which are most naturally expressed in terms of adjustments to the levels of a set of more or less continuous control variables. However, decision problems can only be seen in terms of this kind of 'control model' in comparatively stable operating contexts, where the overall shape of the problem can be seen as more or less invariable through time. In such a case, it may be possible to use more sophisticated and specialised forms of analysis concerned with the systemic relationships among the decision variables particular to that operational setting. Nevertheless, even such 'well structured' problems can often be embedded in wider problem settings with a more volatile structure, to which a more open-ended approach to problem structuring, of the kind described in this chapter, can usefully be applied. For the strategic choice approach has no claims to be a 'systems approach' in the commonly accepted sense:

FIGURE
18

SOUTH SIDE
EXAMPLE

South Side: Some Local Orientation

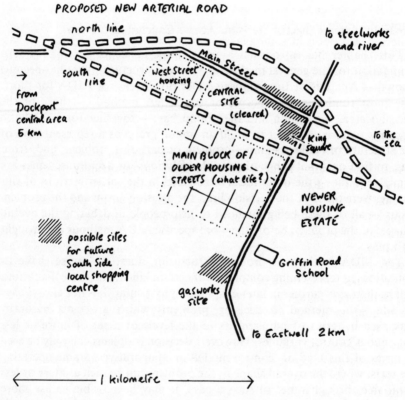

PROPOSED NEW ARTERIAL ROAD

north line

to steelworks
and river

→ south line

Main Street

west street housing

from
Dockport
central area
5 km

CENTRAL
SITE
(cleared)

King
square

to the
sea

MAIN BLOCK OF
OLDER HOUSING –
STREETS (what life?)

NEWER
HOUSING
ESTATE

possible sites
for future
South Side
local shopping
centre

Griffin Road
School

gasworks
site

to Eastwell 2 km

←——— 1 kilometre ———→

rather, it is a *process* approach in which the elements are choices which are normally supposed to be of a transient nature, and the relationships between elements are not therefore expected to assume any systemic form.

Relating the concepts and methods introduced in this chapter to the five basic dimensions of balance in strategic choice (Figure 2), the first of them — to do with the treatment of scope — has begun to be addressed by the concepts introduced to guide the work of the shaping mode: the decision area, the decision link, the decision graph and the problem focus. The second dimension of balance — to do with the treatment of complexity — has begun to be addressed by the general concepts of the decision option, the option bar, the option graph and the decision scheme, introduced to guide the work of the designing mode. But there is more to be discussed about the treatment of scope and of complexity in strategic choice in later chapters. Meanwhile, the treatment of conflict, uncertainty and progress — while touched upon in some places in this chapter and Chapter 1 — has scarcely begun to be discussed in terms of basic concepts and techniques. It is the introduction of such concepts and techniques that will be the purpose of Chapter 3.

Some Exercises

At this stage, some readers may be glad of an opportunity to test their ability to make use of the concepts introduced in this chapter. To this end, the chapter concludes with a short set of exercises, all of them based on simple variations in the formulation of the decision problem faced in the South Side story as described so far.

1. If every pair of decision areas in Figure 12 which is not shown as directly interconnected were to be connected up, how many additional decision links would there be?

2. Suppose in Figure 12 that two additional decision links were added, one to connect ROAD LINE? to DIST LIFE? and the other to connect WEST ST? to SHOP LOC'N?. Could the positions of the various decision areas be altered to make the structure of the decision graph clearer, in particular by avoiding any crossovers between the connecting links?

3. How many different ways can you see of choosing a problem focus within the decision graph as modified in Question 2, so as to include three fully interlinked decision areas?

4. Suppose the 40YR option for DIST LIFE? were to be eliminated as no longer available for some reason. How many of the nine feasible decision schemes in Figure 17 would this remove?

5. If an extra option bar were to be added to Figure 16, to rule out the combination of the 40YR option in the DIST LIFE? decision area with the OPEN option in the CENT'L SITE? decision area, how many of the nine

feasible decision schemes in Figure 17 would have to be ruled out as not feasible?

6. Which of the decision schemes in Figure 17 — *beyond* those eliminated by Question 5 above — would be cut out if option bars were to be added between the NORTH option in the ROAD LINE? decision area and *both* the 10YR and 20YR options in the DIST LIFE? decision areas.

7. How many additional decision schemes would be added to the list of nine in Figure 17 if the option bar ruling out the SOUTH option in the ROAD LINE? decision area in combination with the IND option in the CENT'L SITE? decision area were to be *removed*?

Finally, two more open-ended questions which, unlike those above, have no one answer. First, examine Figure 18, which shows the spatial relationships between the locations and alignments assumed in the formulation of decision areas and options in this chapter.

8. Do the spatial relationships shown in this map lead you to question the reasoning behind any of the decision links shown in Figure 12, or to suggest that any new ones should be included?

9. Do these same spatial relationships suggest that there could be a case for questioning the arguments behind any of the option bars shown in Figure 16 or for adding any further option bars?

3
Working towards Decisions

Introduction

The aim of this chapter will be to complement Chapter 2 by introducing a further set of basic concepts and methods, designed to guide work within the comparing and choosing modes. Taken together, the various core concepts introduced in the two chapters will form a skeleton for an *appropriate technology* of strategic choice: a skeleton which will be built upon further in Chapters 5 to 8, where a range of variations on these concepts and methods will be discussed.

The transition from the last chapter to this one involves a shift of focus; a shift from a concern with designing possible courses of action to a concern with discriminating among those possibilities in order to make progress towards decisions. As in Chapter 2, the intention will be to introduce a limited set of core concepts in as simple and basic a form as possible. However, they are concepts which address evaluative issues more directly than the concepts introduced to guide the work of the shaping and designing modes; and these evaluative issues can become quite subtle and complex.

The first three concepts to be introduced are those of the comparison area, the relative assessment and the advantage comparison. All of these terms have their counterparts in everyday use; but they are expressed here in a language which is designed to encourage a more explicit consideration of uncertainty than is found in some other approaches to evaluation.

These concepts apply generally to any situation where there are different courses of action to be compared, whether there be only two alternatives to consider or a much wider range of possibilities to be scanned. Also, the concepts are designed to apply whether or not there are numerical or other acceptable scales of measurement in view — recognising that consequences can often be subtle and far-reaching in their impact, so that an attempt to reduce assessments to a single unambiguous scale may not always be an appropriate way of dealing with the complexities and uncertainties encountered in practice.

The fourth concept to be introduced — that of the working shortlist —

does however mean introducing more simplified scales of assessment to narrow down the range of possible alternatives. This is especially useful when working with several linked decision areas, generating a wide range of feasible combinations of options to be compared. So it is at this point of the chapter that the basic concepts about comparing come together with those about designing feasible decision schemes through AIDA, which were introduced towards the end of Chapter 2. In the second half of Chapter 3, four further basic concepts will be introduced, designed to guide the work of the choosing mode: these are the concepts of the uncertainty area, the exploratory option, the action scheme and the commitment package. It is in introducing these later concepts that the emphasis on management of uncertainty through time will come directly to the fore, in the spirit of the view of planning as a continuous process of strategic choice which was presented in Chapter 1.

Formulating a Set of Comparison Areas

The task of comparing any pair of alternative courses of action necessarily involves forming some view of what the consequences, effects or implications might be if either course of action were to be pursued rather than the other. It is possible to conceive of circumstances in which it may be sufficient to consider implications in relation to only one dominant area of concern. For example, a person choosing a painting to hang on a bedroom wall might be content to compare and choose solely on the basis of personal aesthetic judgement — at least in circumstances where that person lived alone and the set of alternative paintings available were all offered at the same price, with the same physical dimensions. Or a developer, comparing competitive tenders for a building project, might conceivably be content to compare on the grounds of quoted cost alone — but only in the somewhat artificial circumstances that all tenders met the brief in an identical way and no other comparative information was available with which to discriminate between contractors in terms of their reputations for reliability or quality of work.

These two examples indicate how rarely in practice it is realistic to restrict attention to a single dimension of comparison taken on its own. Indeed, the more far-reaching the implications of a decision problem, the wider the set of participants likely to become involved. So the less practicable it can become to reduce their concerns to a single basis for comparison, whether this be expressed in monetary or other terms.

The approach to comparison to be developed here can therefore be described as essentially a *multi-criteria* approach — to adopt a phrase which has lately become fashionable in relation to more specific mathematical methods of comparison. The concept of a *criterion* is of course familiar enough, not only to decision scientists but also to many practising planners and managers. However, the word is one which can convey subtly different meanings to different people — for instance, it conveys to many people an expectation of a defined scale of measurement, even though dictionary definitions tend to suggest the idea of comparison with some preset standard or norm. For this reason, the concept of criterion will here be replaced by a more general concept of a **comparison area**, which will be more carefully defined within the context of the strategic choice approach.

In essence, a comparison area can be seen as simply a description of some area of concern to the participants in a decision process, within which they may wish to consider what the consequences of alternative courses of action might be. Figure 19 illustrates this concept by presenting descriptions of four different comparison areas which could be seen as important in addressing the decisions facing the South Side Working Party, in the planning situation that was outlined in Chapter 2. As in the earlier listing of decision areas, each of these comparison areas is specified in terms of both a brief label, for quick reference, and a fuller and more careful description of what it embraces. By convention, the brief label is followed by a colon (:), so as to distinguish a comparison area from a decision area, the label of which is followed by a question mark (?). The fuller description can serve an important practical purpose, as a means of checking that the same comparison area is being interpreted in a similar way by different participants; and it can of course always be modified later as understanding grows.

It is often helpful to include, within the fuller description of a comparison area, not only an indication of the *types* of effects or consequences that it covers, but also some indication of their *incidence* in terms of community sectors or interest groups, or perhaps over different time horizons. This can be especially significant where the participants see themselves as accountable to more than one 'constituency' of affected interests. Indeed, different participants in a decision process will sometimes be recognised as representing different sectors or groups. Questions of incidence and perceived equity can sometimes become quite crucial to the politics of comparing and choosing; and they can indeed emerge as major sources of uncertainty in the UV category, the management of which can become critical to the guidance of the overall decision process.

In order to keep the number of comparison areas manageable, they can if desired be formulated so as to bring together several different elements under a single more general heading. For instance, in Figure 19, the familiar heading of CAPITAL: is used to bring together expenditures on both construction works and property acquisition. In other situations, however, there might also be compensating capital receipts to consider, from the disposal of surplus land or buildings which, according to accounting convention, might be considered either within the CAPITAL: or the INCOME: comparison area.

P.U.P.—C*

FIGURE

19

SOUTH SIDE
EXAMPLE

The Concept of a Comparison Area

COMPARISON AREA	LABEL
differences in capital outlay on construction works and property acquisition :	CAPITAL :
differences in net flows of income to this authority :	INCOME :
differences in local employment opportunities :	JOBS :
differences in confidence and quality of life for South Side residents :	RESIDENTS :

A COMPARISON AREA is a description of any field of concern in which it is desired to compare the consequences of alternative courses of action.

Sometimes, too, different comparison areas can be combined. For example, it might be agreed that for working purposes the CAPITAL: and INCOME: comparison areas in Figure 19 should be combined into a broader comparison area simply called FINANCE:. These examples merely serve to demonstrate the general point that there may be much scope for *choice* in the way a set of comparison areas is formulated. Indeed, where there are several participants, it can be valuable to encourage open debate over this choice, leading to elaboration or simplification of the set of comparison areas as work proceeds and the level of shared understanding grows.

Assessing Consequences within Comparison Areas

Once a set of comparison areas has been chosen, it can be put to use as a framework for comparing alternative courses of action in the light of people's assessments of what their differing consequences might be. The idea of a **relative assessment** will be treated as another core concept in the strategic choice vocabulary; but it will often be abbreviated to the single word **assessment** so long as the context is clear. The idea of a relative assessment is intended to cover not only any consequences or implications of a direct and immediately foreseeable kind, but also any consequences or implications which may be more gradual, indirect and hard to pin down in any tangible way.

There are two important qualities to bear in mind in making a prior assessment of the consequences of some proposed future course of action, as opposed to a retrospective assessment of the consequences of some course of action already carried through. Firstly, any assessment of future consequences will always be to some degree *conjectural*, in that it will involve elements of speculation or guesswork as to what might follow *if* that course of action were to be set in train. Secondly, such an assessment will be essentially *comparative* in the sense that, whether explicitly or otherwise, it involves contrasting the consequences of pursuing that course of action with those that might follow from choosing some other course instead. This point applies even if that other course were to take a passive stance and aim to preserve the status quo — which is a common baseline for many kinds of assessment in practice.

Figure 20 presents some examples of relative assessments within each of the four comparison areas for South Side. Two different examples of relative assessments are presented here, both from within the range of nine possible decision schemes which was developed earlier (Figure 17). First, Scheme B is assessed relative to Scheme A — the difference between these two alternatives being only in the choice of option for use of the Central Site. Then, Scheme H is assessed also in relation to the same baseline of Scheme A, recognising that the comparison in this case is likely to be rather

FIGURE 20

The Concept of a Relative Assessment

SOUTH SIDE EXAMPLE

DECISION AREAS	DECISION SCHEME	COMPARISONS	
ROAD LINE? | SHOP LOC'N? | CENT'L SITE? | DIST LIFE?		COMPARISON AREA	RELATIVE ASSESSMENT

NORTH – MAIN – IND – 10YR | scheme A

A = baseline for comparison

1st comparison: B vs A

↓

NORTH – MAIN – HOUS – 10YR | scheme B

assessments of B relative to A:

CAPITAL: about 250k* less

INCOME: 10k-30k* less per year

JOBS: 100-200 local jobs fewer

RESIDENTS: probably more confidence

2nd comparison: H vs A

↓ ↓ ↓ ↓

SOUTH – GAS – OPEN – 20YR | scheme H

assessments of H relative to A:

CAPITAL: 200k* less to 400k* more

INCOME: 40k-100k* less per year

JOBS: 40-160 local jobs fewer

RESIDENTS: much less confidence

[↓ indicates change of option relative to scheme A]

[* k = 1000 units of this national currency - e.g. £, $, Fr....]

less straightforward because Schemes H and A differ in the options selected in each of the four decision areas.

It will be noticed in this example that the *forms* in which the relative assessments are presented differ from one comparison area to another. Even though the capital and income assessments are both expressed in monetary units, the capital assessments are expressed as lump sums and the income assessment as annual flows, in keeping with familiar accounting conventions.

Differences in jobs are also expressed in numerical terms, but this time expressed in non-monetary units of the net number of local jobs created. However, the assessments of the consequences for the South Side residents are expressed here purely in terms of words — illustrating a very common situation in practice where there is no accepted numerical scale to which to refer.

The example of Figure 20 also illustrates some of the different ways in which feelings of *uncertainty* can be expressed. In one case — the assessment of capital outlay for Scheme B relative to Scheme A — a single estimate only is presented; but the word 'about' is inserted to convey the information that there is felt to be at least some uncertainty over the extent of the difference. In other places, a range of figures is presented; this conveys additional information about the degree of uncertainty experienced — which may well differ between one relative assessment and another. By moving to a more elaborate format of presentation than that in Figure 20, it would be possible to go into these feelings of uncertainty in more depth, distinguishing between different contributory factors, spelling out underlying assumptions and indicating contingencies which could have a significant effect of the levels of assessment presented. These possibilities will be discussed further in Chapter 7; for the time being, it is enough to stress that there is a wide field of choice in the level of elaboration or simplification employed in presenting relative assessments in practice.

Judging Comparative Advantage between Alternatives

Because the set of comparison areas is designed to reflect fields of direct concern to decision-makers, any statement that one alternative differs from another within a particular comparison area will usually convey a sense of positive or negative *value* in the current decision situation; it will be seen as either good or bad, nice or nasty. For example, from the comparison of Scheme B with Scheme A in Figure 20, it will almost certainly count as an *advantage* to B that it should incur about 250 monetary units less than A in capital outlay, but a *disadvantage* that it should yield less income. Again, it is likely to be considered a disadvantage to Scheme B that it should create fewer jobs, but an advantage that it should generate more confidence among the residents of South Side.

FIGURE
21

SOUTH SIDE
EXAMPLE

The Concept of an Advantage Comparison

DECISION AREAS				DECISION SCHEME	COMPARISON	
ROAD LINE?	SHOP LOC'N?	CENT'L SITE?	DIST LIFE?		COMPARISON AREA	RELATIVE ASSESSMENT

NORTH — MAIN — IND — 10 YR | scheme A

A = baseline for comparison
assessments of B relative to A:

comparison B vs A (as in figure 20)

↓

NORTH — MAIN — HOUS — 10 YR | scheme B

CAPITAL: about 250k * _less_

INCOME: 10k-30k * _less_ per year

JOBS: 100-200 local jobs _fewer_

RESIDENTS: probably m**o**re confidence

ADVANTAGE COMPARISON B vs A

ADVANTAGE TO A ⟸   negligible   ⟹ ADVANTAGE TO B
                        marginal   ▤   marginal
                   significant   significant
              considerable   considerable
extreme   extreme

CAPITAL   ◇

INCOME   ◇

JOBS   ◇

RESIDENTS   ◇

[KEY: ◄─► = range of belief about comparative advantage.   ◇ = best guess]

COMPARING

CONCEPTS

An ADVANTAGE COMPARISON is a name for any statement of belief about
the balance of advantage between alternatives in one or more comparison areas.

Sometimes, there may be some conflict of opinion as to whether a relative assessment should be viewed in a positive or a negative light; and often, there will be some doubt as to whether advantages in some comparison areas should be seen as outweighing disadvantages in others. Such a state of doubt appears to surround the comparison of Schemes A and B for South Side, because the overall balance of advantage across the four comparison areas is by no means clear. However, Scheme H appears to offer no advantages compared to A in any of the four comparison areas, if the same sense of positive and negative values is applied — unless perhaps further investigation of the uncertainty about the CAPITAL: assessment could reveal that H has indeed an advantage over A in this one comparison area.

Various methods of economic analysis have been developed which allow assessments in different comparison areas to be brought together by being expressed in commensurate terms. For instance, annual flows of income can be converted to capital equivalents by forms of discounted cash flow analysis which reflect market rates of return. Some economists have also developed methods for computing monetary values for other quantitative indicators, such as numbers of jobs created. But such conversions can have the effect of suppressing underlying uncertainties of value judgement which, from a strategic choice perspective, it may be important to expose to debate.

It is more in keeping with the philosophy of strategic choice to turn to an openly judgemental scale of comparison, in which uncertainties of value judgement can be exposed alongside any other uncertainties that have arisen in assessing the nature or magnitude of the consequences in the various comparison areas. Such an approach is illustrated in Figure 21, which introduces a non-numerical scale of **advantage comparison** as a basis for translating relative assessments within diverse comparison areas into a common framework. The adjectives 'negligible', 'marginal', 'significant', 'considerable' and 'extreme' are intended to represent an ascending scale of advantage to the decision-makers in either direction. However, the way in which these words should be interpreted — and indeed the judgement as to what the relative widths of the various bands of the scale should be — can be left open to the discretion of the users in the particular organisational and political context in which they are working.

For example, Figure 21 interprets the assessment that Scheme B will involve 'about' 250 thousand money units less capital outlay than Scheme A as representing somewhere between a significant and a considerable advantage to B in relation to the decision situation currently faced in South Side. In another context, the judgement made might be quite different: for example a central government setting a national budget might well regard such a difference as negligible, while a small business, or an individual managing a family budget, would probably consider it extreme. In each row of Figure 21, the convention is adopted of representing the range of uncertainty over where the advantage lies by a pair of arrowheads, with the current 'best guess' marked in between — frequently, but not necessarily, positioned at the mid-point of the range. As the example suggests, this range of uncertainty can vary considerably from one comparison area to another.

It is important to recognise that the range is intended to embrace uncertainties encountered both in assessing alternatives *within* each separate comparison area and also in judging how these assessments should be transferred to the common advantage comparison scale. For instance, in the South Side case, there may be considerable uncertainty not only over how large the difference in local jobs created might be, but also over how much weight should be attached to any such difference in policy terms. Turning to the impact on South Side residents, uncertainty arises partly because there is no clear numerical yardstick for assessment of different levels of confidence in the future of the area, and partly because some decision-makers may place a higher policy value on residents' confidence than others.

The value of a common judgemental scale, however crude, is that it provides a framework within which assessments in different comparison areas can be balanced and merged. For example, taking the four 'best guess' points in Figure 21, it can be argued that a considerable advantage to Scheme B in terms of capital should outweigh a (merely) significant advantage to A in terms of income: and that the advantage of B to local residents should roughly balance out the advantage to A in terms of jobs, leaving a slight overall advantage to B when all four comparison areas are viewed together.

However, this overall balance of advantage can become more difficult to judge when notice is taken of the uncertainties that surround the various placings on the advantage comparison scale. In the illustration presented in Figure 21, the combined effect of these uncertainties is to make it by no means clear to which alternative the overall balance of advantage for the decision-makers will lie. Some approaches to the more careful analysis of how such uncertainties affect the balance of advantage will be discussed in Chapter 7. However, the most important point about the particular format of advantage comparison illustrated here is that it allows many different sources of uncertainty to be brought together in a common perspective: a perspective which is designed to reflect the political realities of the situation within which the alternatives in question have to be compared. This kind of advantage comparison between specific alternatives will, therefore form an important point of reference when it comes to considering methods of working in the choosing mode.

Restricting the Focus for Comparisons among Decision Schemes

Where there are only a few alternative courses of action to consider, it may not be difficult to compare each with every other, using the same kind of methodical approach to pairwise comparison which was illustrated in Figures 20 and 21. This is usually feasible enough when comparing a set of three or four options within a single decision area, or when the focus of comparison is limited to only a few feasible decision schemes.

However, this pairwise approach to comparison can become much more time-consuming where there are many possible combinations of options available. For example, there are 36 possible pair comparisons that might be made among the nine decision schemes for South Side (Figure 17), because each of the nine can be compared with each of the eight others — the resulting number of comparisons being reduced from 72 to 36 when it is remembered that pairwise comparison is a two-way process. If the number of possible schemes was doubled to 18, the number of possible comparisons would increase more than fourfold, to 153. In general, the longer a list of schemes grows, the more essential it becomes to choose some more manageable set of schemes within the list — in everyday terms, a shortlist — before attempting to compare alternatives more thoroughly in a pairwise manner. The term **working shortlist** will be added to the basic strategic choice vocabulary to describe any shortlist formed for such a purpose. In effect, it serves the same kind of simplifying purpose when people are working towards decisions as does the idea of problem focus when they are working into complex problems.

One way in which a long list of decision schemes can be reduced is to focus only on those which come within acceptable limits in terms of one or more chosen dimensions of evaluation which the decision-makers see as of particular importance. So it might be decided to place a constraint on the maximum level of capital cost — if capital is regarded as a scarce resource — or the minimum level of income to be generated by a scheme. Or it might be agreed, in the South Side case, to exclude any schemes involving a net loss rather than a gain of local job opportunities compared to the status quo.

Introducing such a constraint normally means resorting to a simplified scale of assessment, on which each scheme can be represented by a single point, with all information about uncertainty set aside for this purpose. This then allows the set of schemes to be rearranged, or ranked, in an unambiguous order of preference so far as that particular scale is concerned, allowing all schemes above or below the agreed threshold to be set aside. Often the chosen scale will be a numerical one, but this is not essential: for instance, a non-numerical scale with seven points labelled 'very high', 'high', 'fairly high', 'medium', fairly low', 'low' and 'very low' provides quite an acceptable scale for ranking purposes, because it is quite clear which assessment comes before which other in the sequence.

A simplified scale for purposes of ranking or shortlisting can be defined either within a single comparison area, or to span more than one comparison area where there is some common scale through which they can

FIGURE 22

SOUTH SIDE
EXAMPLE

The Concept of a Working Shortlist

DECISION AREAS				DECISION SCHEME	SCALE ASSESSMENTS with preference rankings	
ROAD LINE?	SHOP LOC'N?	CENT'L SITE?	DIST LIFE?		SCALE OF EXPECTED CAPITAL OUTLAY K = 1000 units of this currency	SCALE OF RESIDENTS' CONFIDENCE R ⟷ RRRRR lowest highest

expected capital outlay shown against each option

- NORTH 1400k
  - MAIN +100k
    - IND +450k — 10YR +0 → Scheme A : 1950k 2nd= | RRR 4th=
    - HOUS +200k — 10YR +0 → Scheme B : 1700k 1st | RRRR 2nd=
  - KING +400k
    - HOUS +200k
      - 10YR +0 → Scheme C : 2000k 4th= | RRR 4th=
      - 20YR +100k → Scheme D : 2100k 7th= | RRRR 2nd=
      - 40YR +150k → Scheme E : 2150k 9th | RRRRR 1st
    - OPEN +50k
      - 20YR +100k → Scheme F : 1950k 2nd= | RR 7th
      - 40YR +150k → Scheme G : 2000k 4th= | RRR 4th=
- SOUTH — GAS — OPEN 1350k +550k +50k
  - 20YR +100k → Scheme H : 2050k 6th | R 8th=
  - 40YR +150k → Scheme I : 2100k 7th= | R 8th=

schemes selected for inclusion in working shortlist on basis of rankings UNDERLINED

COMPARING

CONCEPTS

A WORKING SHORTLIST is any subset of a set of decision schemes in which it is intended to compare alternatives more closely.

be linked. For example, a monetary scale can be used to span both capital and recurrent costs, provided there is some agreed convention for converting running costs into capital equivalents or vice versa. In general, however, the use of any such composite scale as a shortlisting device can mean a considerable sacrifice of information in the interests of simplification. Indeed, any approach to shortlisting can mean sacrificing much information about *uncertainty* which could be important later on. For instance, potentially significant information about South Side was presented earlier (Figure 20) through the use of qualifying words such as 'probably' and through using lower and upper limits in place of single-point estimates. Any shortlisting process can also mean loss of much information about the *multi-dimensional* nature of consequences both within and between the chosen comparison areas. Such losses of information can be quite justifiable as a means of focussing the process of comparison where there are many schemes to consider; but only so long as the possibility is not forgotten of reintroducing that information at a later stage in the decision process.

The use of simplified scales in forming a working shortlist is illustrated in Figure 22. This example introduces two contrasting scales for the purpose of choosing a more limited focus for comparison within the set of nine schemes already generated for South Side.

In this example, the scale of expected capital cost is expressed in standard monetary units, defined as in Figure 20. The assessment for each of the nine schemes has here been built up by a straightforward addition of capital estimates for each option, each measured against the same baseline which supposes there to be no capital investment at all. An alternative approach would, of course, have been to make a separate estimate for each of the nine schemes seen as a composite entity. Indeed, this might have been judged preferable if there were believed to be significant capital savings or costs associated with particular *combinations* of options from different decision areas.

The second scale, relating to confidence among local residents, is developed in a different way. The lowest score is awarded to the scheme or schemes judged to have the most negative effect on residents' confidence — in this case Schemes H and I — while the highest score is awarded to the scheme or schemes judged to have the most positive effect — in this case Scheme E. Then intermediate numbers of points are awarded to each of the other possible schemes. Of course, these scores too could have been built up cumulatively by options, in the same way as the numerical scale of capital cost — but it has been supposed here that the scoring of each scheme viewed as a whole offers a more realistic alternative in the particular circumstances of South Side.

Figure 22 shows not only the scores of the nine schemes on each of the two scales, but also the two sets of *rankings* obtained in this way, with tied rankings in some cases. Inspecting this information, it appears that Scheme B shows particular promise, having a high ranking in terms of both indices. In choosing a working shortlist for closer comparison, other apparently promising schemes might also be included, such as Scheme A and Scheme E — which is the most promising in terms of residents' confidence, even if the least promising in terms of capital outlay. Another candidate could be Scheme C, which is moderately well placed in both respects. But a fuller comparison of B with A, C or E might throw up disadvantages in other comparison areas, which might suggest that the focus of comparison should be shifted yet again. Furthermore, some schemes which are apparently poorly placed according to the scales of Figure 22 might well be brought back into consideration later because of types of advantage excluded from the shortlisting process at this stage.

Exploring Areas of Uncertainty

All the time comparisons of alternatives are being made, the participants will usually also be subject to practical pressures, political and administrative, to move in the direction of decisions: or, in terms of the general process model (Figure 8), to shift upwards from the comparing into the choosing mode. At such times, attention will shift from the comparison of alternatives under uncertainty to the conscious management of that uncertainty from a decision-making perspective.

So it is at this point that the concept of an **uncertainty area** will be introduced. This will be regarded as another core concept in the strategic choice vocabulary; similar, in some respects, to the concepts of decision area and comparison area as already introduced. All three concepts can be seen as expressing *areas of concern* to the participants in a planning process, and as offering wide scope for discretion and judgement in the way they are formulated. Indeed, circumstances often arise where what was at first expressed as an area of concern of one type may with advantage be reformulated in terms of any one of the other types.

An uncertainty area can be formulated at any moment in a process of strategic choice where doubts arise over the choice of *assumptions* on which the designing or comparing of alternatives should proceed. Such assumptions can be of many kinds, but they can be grouped broadly according to the three categories of uncertainty that were introduced in general terms in Chapter 1: **UE** for Uncertainties about the working Environment; **UV** for Uncertainties about guiding Values; and **UR** for Uncertainties about Related decisions (Figure 3).

In the UE direction, participants in a process of strategic choice may experience personal doubts, or may differ among themselves, as to the assumptions they should make about external circumstances or trends. In the UV direction, they may experience doubts or disagreements as to the values that should influence them, especially when they are seeking to compare alternatives across different comparison areas which reflect the concerns of diverse interest groups. In the UR direction, they may have difficulties agreeing what assumptions to make about the choices that are expected to be made in future in other decision areas outside the current scope of the problem on which they are working: decision areas over which they might conceivably have some influence, even if that influence may be quite limited or indirect.

In Figure 23, the concept of the uncertainty area is illustrated through seven examples which reflect various doubts and disagreements seen as relevant by members of the South Side Working Party, at a moment when they are trying to judge the balance of advantage between the two decision schemes labelled A and B. This list of uncertainty areas might be part of a considerably longer list built up at successive stages of the process. Here, however, those listed are all seen as having *relevance* to the particular task of judging whether the overall balance of advantage lies to A or B. This is a judgement that can be approached by focussing on the information about uncertainty that was presented in the advantage comparison analysis of Figure 21 — though that analysis on its own gives no information about what the main *sources* of uncertainty are.

As in the listing of decision areas, and indeed also of comparison areas, the convention is here adopted of giving each uncertainty area both a fuller description and a briefer label for quick reference. The convention of placing the question mark before rather than after the label is intended merely as a means of distinguishing uncertainty areas from decision areas. Indeed, it allows either kind of area to be quickly transformed into the other whenever it seems sensible to do so.

The list in Figure 23 begins by identifying five uncertainty areas which are seen as between them creating difficulty in judging the balance of advantage between Schemes A and B in the JOBS: and RESIDENTS: comparison areas. These two comparison areas are examined first because they appear (Figure 21) to hold the widest range of doubt when all the four assessments are translated into terms of the advantage comparison scale.

Looking first at the JOBS: assessment, the range of 100 to 200 local jobs fewer for Scheme B relative to Scheme A may reflect in the main a feeling of uncertainty about the attractiveness of the Central Site to employment-intensive industries — which can be expressed as an uncertainty area of type UE. However, once the attempt is made to translate this assessment into terms of comparative advantage, a substantial degree of doubt may also arise as to what weight the participants should give to the creation of new jobs in this locality, relative to other consequences of the choice before them; so this is a doubt that can be expressed as an uncertainty area of type UV.

Turning to the RESIDENTS: comparison, Figure 23 again shows a

FIGURE
23

SOUTH SIDE
EXAMPLE

The Concept of an Uncertainty Area

UNCERTAINTY AREA	LABEL	TYPE	
? attractiveness of central site to employment-intensive industries	?SITEJOBS	UE	identified as major influences on advantage comparison of A and B in relation to JOBS: comparison area
? policy value to us of job creation	?VALJOB	UV	
? decision on future use of steelworks site	?STEELSITE	UR	identified as major influences on advantage comparison of A and B in relation to RESIDENTS: comparison area
? policy value to us of meeting residents concerns	?VALRES.	UV	
? decision on density of new housing developments	?HOUDENS	UR	
? future trends in regional housing market	?HOUMKT	UE	identified as influencing comparison of A and B in relation to INCOME:
? policy decision on level of infrastructure provision on new industrial sites	?INDINFR	UR	identified as influencing comparison of A and B in relation to both INCOME: and CAPITAL:

CHOOSING

CONCEPTS

An UNCERTAINTY AREA is a description of any source of uncertainty which is causing difficulty in the consideration of a decision problem.

substantial area of uncertainty of type UV, concerned with the policy value that the municipality should attach to meeting the concerns of local residents. However, the main uncertainties in assessing the actual impact on local residents of choosing Scheme B rather than A can in this case be seen as of type UR rather than UE, because they are to do with two related areas of decision outside the current problem focus. One of these is concerned with the future use of a nearby site, which is expected to be vacated soon by a major steel making corporation. Some residents of South Side have been campaigning for redevelopment of this site for light industry rather than other purposes; if this case is conceded, it is thought their concern about the use of the Central Site will be less acute than if the site is put to any alternative use. The other uncertainty area relates to the recommendations of the municipality's own housing planning team over density of any future housing development on the Central Site itself: if the density is high enough and the cost low enough to make homes on this site available to local people, then it is judged that residents' confidence in the future of their community will be increased.

Finally, the list of Figure 23 includes two further uncertainty areas which impinge on the INCOME: and CAPITAL: assessments — in one case impinging on them both. However, a glance back to Figure 21 suggests that these uncertainty areas will not be so critical to the overall comparison of Schemes A and B as those affecting the JOBS: and RESIDENTS: assessments. So no attempt need be made at this stage to look for further uncertainty areas which affect these two financial dimensions of the overall evaluation frame.

Identifying Exploratory Options

Once a list of uncertainty areas has been developed, the question arises of what, if anything, should be done about them. For each uncertainty area that seems to be relevant to a particular comparison of alternatives, there is always the possibility of *accepting* the current level of uncertainty over what assumptions to adopt, and looking for ways in which it can be accommodated. However, there may also be a possibility of initiating some kind of *exploratory action* which offers a hope that current feelings of uncertainty can be significantly *reduced* before decisions have to be made.

Any course of action designed to alter the current state of doubt within an uncertainty area can be called an **exploratory option**. The idea of an exploratory option is of central significance to the work of the choosing mode, so it will be considered as another core concept in the strategic choice vocabulary. In effect, the identification of any exploratory options that could be adopted in response to a particular uncertainty area can be seen as extending the problem formulation by introducing an additional decision area; a decision area concerned with whether or not any investment should

FIGURE
24

SOUTH SIDE
EXAMPLE

The Concept of an Exploratory Option

UNCERTAINTY AREA	EXPLORATORY OPTION	COMPARISON OF EXPLORATORY OPTIONS	
		COMPARISON AREA	RELATIVE *ASSESSMENT
? SITE JOBS (UE)	Commission consultants to do market survey	CONFIDENCE:	slightly more confidence in advantage comparison A:B
		RESOURCES:	estimated fee 20k
		DELAY:	allow 3 months from commissioning to reporting
? VAL JOB (UV)	informal soundings with leading members of policy group	CONFIDENCE:	much more confidence in advantage comparison A:B
		RESOURCES:	some demands on time of busy policy-makers
		DELAY:	allow 1-2 weeks to contact and discuss
? STEEL SITE (UR)	liaison with joint steelworks site planning team	CONFIDENCE:	more confidence in advantage comparison A:B
		RESOURCES:	perhaps ½ day spent in meeting: also preparation time
		DELAY:	allow 1 month

* relative to option of taking no exploratory action i.e. null option be made in the reduction of current levels of doubt within the uncertainty area concerned.

This point is illustrated in Figure 24, which gives examples of exploratory options relating to each of the first three uncertainty areas from the list in Figure 23 — supposing these to be judged the most important at the present moment in the decision process. In each case, one possible exploratory option is identified and is compared with the 'null option' of taking no exploratory action in relation to the uncertainty area in question. The nature of any exploratory action to be considered will tend to vary with the type of uncertainty area addressed. As originally suggested (Figure 3), uncertainty areas of type UE will suggest possibilities for exploration in the form of research, surveys, analytical work or forecasting exercises. Uncertainty areas of type UV will suggest possibilities for exploration in the form of policy soundings or exercises designed to clarify objectives or goals; while uncertainty areas of type UR will suggest possibilities for exploration in the form of liaison, negotiation, joint planning or co-ordinating initiatives to deal with relationships between the decisions currently in view and others relating to different agendas and decision-making powers.

Sometimes, it is not initially clear which of the categories UE, UV or UR describes a particular uncertainty area best. The step of considering possible exploratory options may itself help to make this classification clearer. However, there may be cases where two or more quite different kinds of exploratory options seem to be available. This may sometimes lead to the possibility of splitting the uncertainty area into two or more separate elements, which will be discussed further in Chapter 8.

In assessing the consequences that might flow from pursuing any exploratory option, there are in general three dimensions of evaluation which will be of importance to the decision-makers. Firstly, they will be concerned with assessing any changes in the level of *confidence* with which decisions can be made, arising from a reduction in the state of uncertainty surrounding key assumptions. Secondly, they will be concerned with assessing any *resources* which may be used up in pursuing that exploratory option; such an assessment might cover not only such tangible resources as money and scarce skills, but also less tangible resources such as personal energy and goodwill, which may also be in short supply. Lastly, they will be concerned with questions of the *delay* involved in pursuing any exploratory option; this may be a critical consideration where there are pressures for early action to be taken into account.

These three dimensions of evaluation can be viewed as different kinds of comparison area within which relative assessments of the impacts of different exploratory options can be made — the aim being to judge whether or not to invest any exploratory effort towards the reduction of doubts within any of the uncertainty areas currently in view. For example, the information presented in Figure 24 suggests that the proposed informal

FIGURE
25

SOUTH SIDE
EXAMPLE

The Concept of an Action Scheme

set of possible ACTION SCHEMES within more urgent decision areas		choices remaining open in other decision areas DECISION AREAS			COMPARISON of FLEXIBILITY for each action scheme	
ROAD LINE?	DIST LIFE?	SHOP LOC'N?	CENT'L SITE?	DECISION SCHEME	Total count of available decision schemes	ROBUSTNESS INDEX = count of schemes with residents' confidence score at least RRR *
NORTH-10YR I		MAIN — IND		scheme A	[3]	3
		MAIN — HOUS		scheme B		
		KING — HOUS		scheme C		
NORTH-20YR II		— KING — HOUS		scheme D	[2]	1
		— KING — OPEN		scheme F		
NORTH-40YR III		— KING — HOUS		scheme E	[2]	2
		— KING — OPEN		scheme G		
SOUTH-20YR IV		— GAS — OPEN		scheme H	[1]	0
SOUTH-40YR V		— GAS — OPEN		scheme I	[1]	0

* see Figure 22

An ACTION SCHEME is a course of action involving commitments within only some of the more urgent decision areas within a problem focus.

soundings among policy-makers, directed towards the UV-type uncertainty area ?VALJOB, could yield better returns in terms of confidence, for a lesser cost, than the commissioning of a market survey directed towards the UE-type uncertainty area ?SITEJOBS — and furthermore that they could do so with less serious consequences in terms of delay to the decision-making process.

Choices in the Timing of Decisions

Because exploratory actions invariably take at least some time to carry through — ranging perhaps from a few minutes in the case of a quick telephone call, to several years in the case of a major research study — the consideration of how to manage uncertainty also means confronting difficult choices about the *timing* of commitments within a continuous planning process. For there is little point in taking actions to improve the confidence with which decisions can be made unless those decisions are deferred until the outcomes of those explorations are known.

However, if the problem involves consideration of choices in several interrelated decision areas, it does not necessarily follow that commitments to decisive action must be deferred in *all* those decision areas until any agreed exploratory actions have been followed through. There may be some decision areas in which the participants' preferred course of action will be little affected, if at all, by the outcomes of these explorations; and, furthermore, there may be some decision areas in which the external pressures for early commitment are much more intense than in others.

So, in practice, a choice arises in relation to each decision area within the current problem focus, not merely as to which option should be pursued, but also as to whether commitment in that decision area should be made now, or should be deferred until some later time. This means that the *extent of commitment* within the present problem focus has itself become a matter of choice for the participants. So at this point they must strike a balance between a more exploratory and a more decisive approach to progress through time (Figure 2). This is a type of judgement which is often confronted in practice by decision-makers, even though it has as yet received comparatively little attention in the development of planning methods.

As a means of dealing with this element of choice in the timing of decisions, the core concept of an **action scheme** will now be introduced.* This term will be used to describe any course of proposed action in which commitment to a specific option is indicated in one or more of a set of decision areas, while commitment in others is explicitly deferred until later in the process. An illustration of the way in which this concept can be applied to the South Side problem situation appears in Figure 25.

* The term 'action set' was used in the same sense in earlier writings on strategic choice.

In this illustration, five possible action schemes for South Side are compared. Each is based on a different combination of options in the ROAD LINE? and DIST LIFE? decision areas — it being supposed that these are the areas of choice in which pressure for commitment is currently most intense. The patterns of subsequent choice associated with each action scheme are displayed by a straightforward rearrangement of the branching sequence through which the original set of nine decision schemes was developed. So the same set of nine decision schemes appears as in the original array (Figure 17), but this time in a slightly modified order because the DIST LIFE? decision area has been brought further forward.

Of the five action schemes, there are two which, in effect, leave no flexibility of future choice at all, because of the structure of option bars. The choice of either of these action schemes implies commitment in each of the remaining three decision areas as well; however, each of the other three action schemes leaves open a future choice of between two and three of the original nine decision schemes.

This illustrates the important general point that action schemes which embody the same level of intended commitment in the more pressing decision areas can differ from each other in terms of the *flexibility* of future choice which is retained. Such flexibility may be of considerable practical value to the participants, especially where they are beset with doubts about what course of action will be the most advantageous in the longer term. One simple, yet practical, means of comparing action schemes for flexibility involves the use of what is called a *robustness* index; a 'robust' action being seen as one which is preferable to others in that it leaves open a wider range of acceptable paths for the future. The underlying assumption is that the more paths are left open which meet some specified level of acceptability, as viewed under current circumstances, the better equipped the decision-makers will be to respond to unexpected circumstances should they arise in future.

This idea of robustness is not a difficult one in its essentials but its interpretation in practice can sometimes call for a considerable degree of care. This is firstly because the threshold of acceptability may not be easy to define and, secondly, because — in a strategic choice problem formulation — flexibility in some decision areas may be valued more highly than flexibility in others. These points can be illustrated with reference to Figure 25, where the five action schemes are compared in terms of two different indices of flexibility. The first is based on a straightforward count of all schemes still left open, while the second is based on a count of only those schemes which pass above a particular threshold of acceptability in terms of residents' confidence (Figure 22). Both these indices assume that flexibility in the SHOP LOC'N? and CENT'L SITE? decision areas are valued equally highly; an assumption which could, however, be modified by giving them different weightings if that was felt to be more realistic.

Developing a Commitment Package

To conclude this discussion of work within the choosing mode, a final core concept will be introduced, bringing together the various dimensions of the choices people face in considering how to move forward at any moment in a continuous planning process. This is the concept of the **commitment package** — conceived as a balanced assemblage of proposed steps forward which may embrace a set of proposed immediate actions; a set of explorations to deal with important areas of uncertainty; and a set of understandings about the ways in which any deferred choices should be addressed. Any commitment package will, therefore, contain a considered set of proposals as to how to move progressively forward towards commitment through time: a set of proposals which can be compared against other alternative sets of proposals and, if agreed, can be adopted as a basis for incremental progress in a continuous planning process.

Figure 26 presents an example of one possible commitment package that might be considered as a basis for making progress in the South Side problem situation. It takes into account not only the analysis so far presented in this chapter, but also the political realities of the situation in which the South Side Working Party is currently operating. The basic format that is used here — some variations and extensions of which will be discussed in Chapter 8 — involves dividing the overall tableau into rows corresponding to the various decision areas, and also into columns corresponding to the different types of proposal that could be included in relation to each.

In the format of Figure 26, the heading of **Immediate Decisions** is used to register not only the set of substantive *actions* to which commitment is now proposed — in other words, the proposed action scheme — but also any *explorations* which it is proposed should now be set in train to create an improved basis for future choice. Such proposals for exploration reflect a deliberate choice of exploratory options to deal with some but not necessarily all of the more important uncertainty areas which have been identified. So the set of immediate decisions is in effect conceived as an incremental step forward, not just in relation to the substantive decision problem, but also in relation to the associated problem of how to manage uncertainty through time.

Under the second main heading of **Future Decision Space**, the format of Figure 26 allows not only for an indication of which options in which decision areas are to remain open, but also for any further proposals relating to the arrangements by which future decisions should be made. In relation to these *deferred choices*, proposals may be made as to the future time horizons at which decisions should be made — proposals which may reflect not only the time scales involved in undertaking relevant exploratory actions but also any procedural considerations arising from the particular

FIGURE
26

SOUTH SIDE
EXAMPLE

The Concept of a Commitment Package

COMMITMENT PACKAGE

DECISION AREAS	IMMEDIATE DECISIONS		FUTURE DECISION SPACE	
	ACTIONS	EXPLORATIONS	DEFERRED CHOICES	CONTINGENCY PLANNING
ROAD LINE?	NORTH	—	—	IF recommendations not accepted, THEN appeal
DISTRICT LIFE?	10 YEARS	—	—	IF a major developer appears, THEN be ready to extend life
SHOP LOCATION?	MAIN STREET	—	—	—
CENTRAL SITE?	—	informal soundings with leading members of policy group AND liaison with joint steelworks site planning team	in 2 months: decide use of central site [industry OR housing]	—
WEST STREET?	—	investigate designs and costs for possible improvement scheme	in 6 months: decide whether to improve West Street [yes OR no]	—

CHOOSING

○ ●
○ ○

CONCEPTS

A COMMITMENT PACKAGE is a combination of actions, explorations and arrangements for future choice designed as a means of making progress in a planning process.

administrative and political context in which the participants are working. In South Side, for example, the proposed informal soundings and liaison activities, designed to cope with uncertainty in deciding a use for the Central Site, might be expected to take no more than a month; but it might be two months before the next scheduled meeting of the decision-making group at which a formal decision on this matter could be taken.

The practicalities of the organisational context in which decisions are to be taken can also play an important part in the second sub-division of future decision space, concerned with what is here called *contingency planning*. This heading recognises that it will often be important to prepare in some way for particular contingencies of a foreseeable kind, which could have a crucial effect on future decisions — including possibilities that particular assumptions which seem to offer a firm basis for proceeding in present circumstances might be overturned by subsequent events.

In considering what proposals to enter in the last two columns, it may become necessary to probe certain basic assumptions relating to the terms in which decision areas were formulated for purposes of analysis. For example, in South Side it could be important to realise that even a firm commitment now to the northern road line may be more in the nature of a *recommendation* to an autonomous highway authority than a matter to be decided on the authority of the municipality of Dockport alone; so some preparation might be advisable for the contingency of that recommendation being turned down. Also, it might be important to recognise that the option of declaring a 10-year commitment to the continued life of South Side as a residential community does not imply an irrevocable commitment to the demise of that community ten years hence; there might be the possibility of an extension in that life at some later time, given certain conditions which might be anticipated now, even if only in general terms.

It will be noticed that the example of an action scheme incorporated in Figure 26 differs from the examples compared earlier (Figure 25) in that it proposes current commitment in three rather than two decision areas. The scope for future choice within the problem focus is in this case reduced to the two Schemes A and B; so the proposals for exploratory action in this commitment package are focussed on the comparison of these two schemes, drawing on the earlier analysis of uncertainty areas and exploratory options (Figures 23 and 24).

A final point illustrated by Figure 26 is that the design of a commitment package offers a point at which aspects of a decision problem that were deliberately omitted from a problem focus or a working shortlist can be brought back into view. In the South Side case, it will be noticed that the West Street decision area has now resurfaced, even though it had been deliberately left out of the problem focus chosen for most of the designing and comparing work. Despite the judgement that this decision area can be treated in an isolated way, the same judgements about immediate or deferred choice arise in this case; and the same general ideas about management of uncertainty apply.

Choosing Incrementally under Uncertainty

Summarising at this point, this chapter has followed the same principles as Chapter 2 in presenting a set of core concepts and methods — this time designed to help when working in the comparing and choosing modes. As before, the aim has been to introduce these concepts and methods at as simple a level as possible. So the chapter began by introducing some core concepts about comparing alternatives, starting with the concept of the comparison area and then introducing those of the relative assessment, the advantage comparison and the working shortlist, before turning to other concepts to assist work in the choosing mode. These later concepts were those of the uncertainty area, the exploratory option, the action scheme and the commitment package, the last of these offering a general framework within which to build commitments incrementally through time.

As may already be appreciated, these ideas cannot always be applied in practice in such a straightforward way as in the South Side case example as presented here. But the difficulties encountered in practice lie not so much in the concepts themselves as in the realities of the situations to which they are applied; and these difficulties remain to be addressed whatever methods of working it may be decided to apply.

In principle, there is nothing in the concepts introduced here which should make them incompatible with more formalised methods of technical, economic or environmental evaluation of the kind sometimes employed on problems which are seen as of enough importance to justify the investment involved. The key point emerging from the strategic choice philosophy is that there are always *choices* open to participants in the way in which the processes of comparing and choosing are to be addressed. Referring to the five dimensions of balance that were presented in Figure 2, choices of scope arise in agreeing the range of comparison areas to be included; choices in the treatment of complexity arise in judging how much elaboration or simplification there should be in the assessment of consequences; choices in the treatment of uncertainty arise in judging how far to invest in exploratory actions; and choices in the treatment of progress arise in the design of a commitment package. Choices in the treatment of conflict arise too, in deciding how far people should work on these issues in an interactive, as opposed to a reactive, way; and this raises issues which will be discussed further in Chapter 4.

It is important to emphasise that these various balances need not remain unchanging though time within a continuously evolving process of strategic choice. It is found in practice that this means approaching the work of the comparing and choosing modes in a spirit of *dynamic comparison*, within which attention is continually fluctuating between comparison of many alternatives at quite a rough and ready level, taking little explicit account of uncertainty, and deeper comparison of a selected few alternatives within which issues of managing uncertainty can be more consciously addressed. The broader level of comparison leads to restricted shortlists of alternatives to be examined more closely at the deeper level: while the deeper level in turn affords opportunities to examine critically the simplifying assumptions introduced in any such shortlisting process.

In Chapters 7 and 8, the skills appropriate to management of such a process of dynamic comparison, and the conscious management of uncertainty within that process, will be examined more closely in the light of working experience in a range of different contexts. In particular, the concept of the commitment package will be developed more fully, with reference to organisational contexts where the participants cannot always be considered as a cohesive team, and the politics of incremental action can therefore become subtle and complex.

For simplicity of presentation in this chapter, the participants in a process of strategic choice have been assumed to share a common framework of accountability and a common view of the task they face. Yet the more difficult and far-reaching become the problems to be addressed, the wider and more diffuse the interests on which they are likely to impinge; and the more unrealistic it may become to think of those involved in the process as having the same level of internal cohesion as has been assumed in the case of the South Side Working Party. Therefore, the more it is to be expected that the choices to be made about the treatment of conflict will involve skilled judgements as to how the politics of organisational and inter-organisational relationships should be addressed.

Some Exercises

This chapter — like Chapter 2 — will conclude with a few simple exercises based on variations of the South Side story. These are designed to help the reader begin to develop a working familiarity with the basic concepts and methods introduced here, so most of the questions are of a quite specific and sharply-focussed form. However, some of them do call for elements of inventiveness as well as interpretation, in that the information about South Side presented in the text and the diagrams will not always be enough to give the required answer. This merely means that the reader will be faced with some realistic problems of managing uncertainty in addressing even some of the simpler of the exercises which appear below.

FIGURE
27

SOUTH SIDE
EXAMPLE

South Side: Some Considerations of Scale

administrative boundary

MUNICIPALITY

OF

DOCKPORT

Total
population
230,000

WEST STREET
HOUSING AREA
160 dwellings
c. 500 residents

MAIN STREET SHOPPING AREA
17 existing traders within area
identified in Figure 18 as a
possible future shopping centre *

MAIN BLOCK OF
OLDER HOUSING STREETS

800 dwellings
c. 2800 residents

NEWER
HOUSING
ESTATE

650 dwellings

c. 2400
residents

SOUTH SIDE NEIGHBOURHOOD AREA
- about 7,400 residents and 28 traders in all

EASTWELL NEIGHBOURHOOD AREA
about 18,500 residents and 70 traders in all

* profitability of several South Side
traders known to be in decline

1. Working solely on the information presented in Figure 19, which of the four comparison areas might be broken down into more narrow comparison areas covering different sub-categories of consequences within the general headings as defined?

2. Working from information in Figure 20, what set of relative assessments could you make for Scheme H if you used Scheme B rather than Scheme A as a baseline? (Where you are not sure how to express this assessment in any comparison area, try to find some way of expressing the uncertainty you feel.)

3. Suppose that the relative assessments for income and jobs were at the same levels as shown in Figure 20, but in favour of Scheme B rather than A. Could there then be any grounds for hesitation in expressing an overall preference between A and B? If so, what would these grounds be?

4. Turning from Figure 20 to Figure 21, could the value judgements implied in converting the four relative assessments to a common advantage comparison scale lead you to modify your response to Question 3?

5. Does the advantage comparison of Figure 21 suggest that either scheme is likely to be preferable to the other in terms of a strictly financial evaluation covering both capital and income assessments?

6. Suppose in Figure 22 that the expected capital cost index were +200k rather than +400k for the King Street shop location, and 1200k rather than 1350k for the south road line. How might this modify your choice of working shortlist?

7. Can you infer anything from Figure 22 about the way in which residents' confidence is expected to be influenced by choice of the location for the shopping centre?

8. Would you judge that any of the three exploratory options compared in Figure 24 has a clear advantage over any one of the others as a response to the difficulty of judging comparative advantage between Schemes B and A? If so, on what assumptions does your judgement depend?

9. In Figure 25, suppose the most urgent decision areas are now DIST LIFE? and CENT'L SITE?. Which combination of options in these two decision areas leaves open the widest range of choice of schemes, first in total and secondly when the constraint of at least RRR on the residents' confidence index is applied?

10. Can you modify the commitment package of Figure 26 to reflect the proposal that choice should be left open in the SHOP LOC'N? as well as the CENT'L SITE? decision areas, as in the first action scheme listed in Figure 25? Referring if you wish to the sketch map of Figure 18, can you make a guess as to the sorts of explorations that might be recommended to prepare for this deferred decision?

11. In Figure 27, some further information is introduced about the numbers of people, dwellings and traders affected by decisions on the South Side problem. In what ways might this extra information help you in

answering any of the questions posed above? What further types of information might you look for if you were a member of the South Side Working Party, assuming time is short and pressures of decision are intense?

Answers to these questions will be found at the end of the book.

4

Orientations

Building on the Foundations

Taken together, the first three chapters present a set of basic foundations for the approach to planning under pressure which has become known as the strategic choice approach. Chapter 1 presented a view of the realities that people face when attempting to choose strategically under the manifold pressures of organisational life. It was argued that the key to a realistic approach lay in the idea of conscious management of uncertainty through time; an idea which was seen as posing a fundamental challenge to the familiar, if sometimes implicit, norms of linearity, objectivity, certainty and comprehensiveness which have traditionally been valued in the design of formal management and planning systems. In Chapters 2 and 3, this approach was extended by introducing a set of core concepts which could be seen as laying foundations for a *technology* of strategic choice, with reference to a view of *process* in which four complementary modes of working — shaping, designing, comparing and choosing — were seen as interrelated in a dynamic way.

The aim of this chapter will be to pause and take stock of what has been covered so far. It will do this within a general framework for reviewing alternative approaches to decision-making and planning, in which the considerations of *organisation* and of *product* are given due weight alongside those of *technology* and *process* which were the main focus of concern in the introductory chapters. This will provide a broad base from which more pragmatic advice on the use of the strategic choice approach will be developed in Chapters 5 to 9. So, in essence, this chapter offers a philosophical bridge between the three introductory chapters and the five that follow.

Review of the Core Concepts

Before addressing this main task, it will be useful briefly to take an overall view of the set of sixteen core concepts which have been introduced

FIGURE
28

A Vocabulary of Strategic Choice

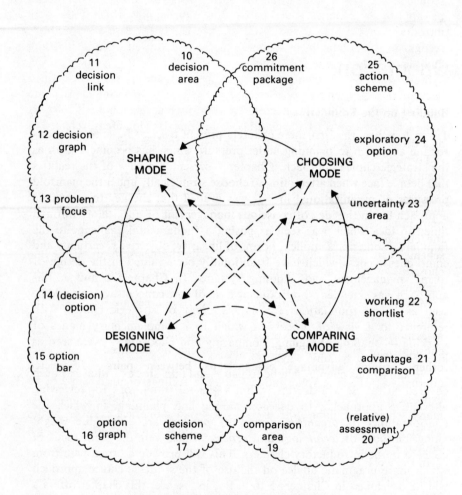

NUMBERS refer to earlier Figures in which
definitional statements and examples appear.

in the last two chapters. Figure 28 brings these concepts together and shows how they relate to the four complementary modes of shaping, designing, comparing and choosing presented earlier (Figure 8).

Because the essence of the process of strategic choice is that work should proceed in an adaptive and exploratory fashion rather than in a rigid sequence, there is no fixed order in which the sixteen core concepts should be applied in practice. The particular sequence in which they were introduced in Chapters 2 and 3 was chosen merely for ease of exposition, recognising that some linear sequence has to be followed when introducing any set of ideas for the first time.

Starting with the *shaping mode*, a complex and possibly ill-defined decision problem can be structured in terms of a set of **decision areas**, some pairs of which are directly interconnected through **decision links**. This leads to a picture of a network of relationships among decision areas, referred to as a **decision graph**, within which a choice of **problem focus** can be made.

Turning to the *designing mode*, a representative set of **decision options** is identified within each decision area, and **option bars** are specified wherever it is assumed that pairs of options drawn from different decision areas are mutually incompatible. The resulting **option graph** can be seen as a form of map, indicating which combinations of pairs of options are available within the current problem focus. The corresponding set of feasible **decision schemes** can now be developed by arranging the decision areas in some chosen sequence and then moving systematically through all possible branches in the resulting tree-like pattern.

Moving on to the *comparing mode*, **comparison areas** are formulated for comparing alternative options or schemes, and within these **relative assessments** are made, representing judgements as to what their consequences might be. Such assessments can be balanced against each other through **advantage comparisons** between pairs of selected alternatives, allowing value judgements and feelings of uncertainty to be expressed in a common decision-centred framework. Wherever there any many schemes available, the use of simplified numerical or other scales within some comparison areas becomes important as a means of choosing a limited **working shortlist**.

In the work of the *choosing mode*, sources of doubt are expressed in the form of **uncertainty areas**, leading towards the identification of **exploratory options** whereby some of these doubts might be addressed. Timing considerations are now introduced, leading to the consideration of **action schemes** which may contain proposals for early action in some but not necessarily all decision areas. Such proposals can be brought together with explorations in response to uncertainty, and arrangements relating to deferred decisions, within the framework of a **commitment package**, designed as an incremental step in a continuing process of decision-making through time.

FIGURE
29
Orientations and Guidelines in Strategic Choice

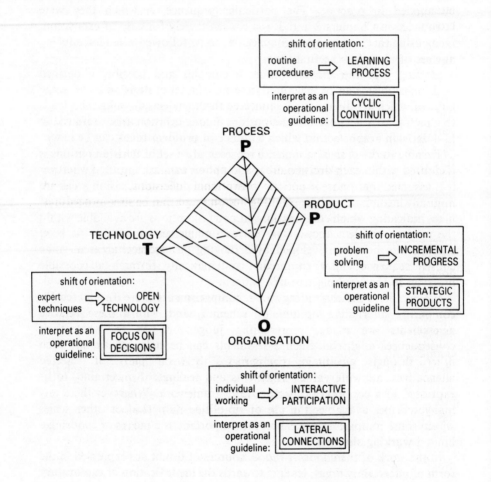

shift of orientation:

routine procedures ⟹ LEARNING PROCESS

interpret as an operational guideline: CYCLIC CONTINUITY

PROCESS
P

PRODUCT
P

TECHNOLOGY
T

shift of orientation:

problem solving ⟹ INCREMENTAL PROGRESS

interpret as an operational guideline: STRATEGIC PRODUCTS

shift of orientation:

expert techniques ⟹ OPEN TECHNOLOGY

interpret as an operational guideline: FOCUS ON DECISIONS

O
ORGANISATION

shift of orientation:

individual working ⟹ INTERACTIVE PARTICIPATION

interpret as an operational guideline: LATERAL CONNECTIONS

APPROACH

A TOPP

ORIENTATIONS

In distilling the essentials of a technology of strategic choice into this basic vocabulary of sixteen core concepts, the guiding principle has been to avoid specialised and esoteric words. Instead, words in common usage are linked together in pairs in such a way as to give them a heightened meaning. Formal definitions have already been recorded underneath the appropriate illustrations (Figures 10 to 17 and 19 to 26) — so the figure references attached to the sixteen core concepts in Figure 28 can be used as a quick cross-reference whenever clarification is required.

Technology, Organisation, Process and Product

In any approach to the challenge of addressing complex decision problems, people and their judgements become involved. In general, the wider the scope of the problem, the wider is likely to be the range of participants and of possible relationships between them. So the more it is to be expected that questions of appropriate organisation will come to the fore. Furthermore, if the process is to be effective for the participants and those to whom they are accountable, judgements will arise as to what the most appropriate forms of its product might be. These judgements too are likely to increase in complexity as the scope of a problem widens.

The four headings of **Technology, Organisation, Process** and **Product** together provide a useful framework through which to summarise at this stage the general *orientations* of the strategic choice approach. This will be done by contrasting them with the emphases of more traditional approaches to management and planning; approaches which still have a persistent influence on thinking in both commercial and governmental organisations. The mnemonic **A-TOPP** (Approach — Technology, Organisation, Process and Product) will be used here in referring to this framework for comparison, with the overall concept on an **Approach** seen as covering all the other four elements.*. It is not only the strategic choice approach that can be examined in terms of the four elements of technology, organisation, process and product: so too can any other approach, whether it is one which has been consciously designed with reference to particular principles or beliefs — such as the norms of linearity, objectivity, certainty and comprehensiveness described in Chapter 1 — or whether it has evolved pragmatically in response to particular local circumstances and constraints.

Orientations of the Strategic Choice Approach

The four elements within the A-TOPP framework — Technology, Organisation, Process and Product — are represented in Figure 29 as the

---

* This framework evolved from one first developed by Hickling; it was later applied to the comparative analysis of approaches in a study of methodologies of regional planning by a joint Birmingham University/Tavistock Institute research team (Hart, Hickling, Norris and Skelcher, 1980)

four vertices of a tetrahedron. The solid structure of the tetrahedron itself is intended to represent the idea of an overall approach viewed in a relatively complete, multi-dimensional way. The picture as a whole is intended to convey the message that each aspect of the approach can be selected in turn as the focus of attention — yet none of them can ever be viewed entirely in isolation from the other three. In Figure 29, the tetrahedron has been positioned so that the process vertex appears on top. But the whole structure stands on the base formed by the other three vertices, and the tetrahedron could just as easily be tipped over to bring any other vertex to the top, resting firmly on the base provided by the other three.

In Figure 29, the emphases which are characteristic of the strategic choice approach in each of the four 'corners' of the A-TOPP framework are first expressed in terms of general statements of *orientation*. This is to bring out the essential contrasts with more conventional approaches which tend to be well entrenched in decision-making arrangements set up to deal with comparatively clearly structured, bounded problems. There is no intention here to suggest that these well-tried methods should be abandoned altogether; it is more a case of advocating a shift of emphasis, so that a more appropriate balance can be struck.

In terms of *technology*, the strategic choice approach involves a shift away from a reliance on the kinds of *expert techniques* of solution-finding and evaluation which are characteristic of more routine decision-making arrangements. Rather, the orientation is towards what can be described as an **open technology** intended to be freely accessible to participants who have differing and complementary contributions to make. In situations where the very shape of a problem may be obscure and, indeed, a matter of possible controversy, the relevance of what may be called 'black box' technologies becomes considerably reduced. It is no longer enough to produce outputs of advice through the application of well-established methods the nature of which need not be disclosed, because they are considered so well validated by past exercises of a similar kind. Such 'black box' methods may still have their place; but it will be a place of limited significance in the wider process. For in problems of complex and ill-defined shape, it is likely that many different types of choice will become intermeshed — for instance, choices about finance, about timing, about location, about technological or marketing matters, about people and their roles and about contractual or procedural considerations. Such matters are, in turn, likely to cut across the preserves of many different experts; and it is only through an emphasis on open technology — a technology to support communications and interaction across these boundaries — that any momentum of joint working on complex problems can be sustained.

In terms of *organisation*, an orientation towards **interactive participation** is indicated as being characteristic of the strategic choice approach. This is in contrast to the emphasis on *individual working* on assigned tasks which is characteristic of organisational arrangements for working on more clearly structured, recurrent problems. There is, of course, a direct link between the emphasis on participative forms of organisation and that on open technology. Both stress the idea of people working together in an exploratory way, so as to transcend established boundaries of responsibility and specialist expertise. Again, the shift of emphasis is not intended to suggest that the clear assignment of tasks to specific individuals or organisational units no longer has its place. For this latter emphasis remains appropriate in situations where predictable types of issues have to be processed in a consistent and efficient way. So the question is not whether such organisational arrangements should be replaced, but how they can be complemented in circumstances where more challenging situations of strategic choice arise.

In terms of *process*, the shift of emphasis is from reliance on *routine procedures* for dealing with issues which fall into clearly recognisable categories, towards an acceptance that people should be engaged in a **learning process** about issues which no one person can claim to understand in full. Again, the emphasis on a learning process has a clear alignment with the emphasis on open technology and on interactive participation; for in responding to complex decision problems, people must be prepared to learn from each other, recognising that there may be a variety of complementary sources of insight and experience upon which to draw. Again the emphasis on a learning process is not intended to suggest that routine procedures no longer have a part to play: it is simply that they become less appropriate to the more complex challenges of a process of *strategic* choice.

Finally, in terms of *products*, the emphasis is shifted from the conventional idea of *problem-solving*, towards an orientation to **incremental progress** through time. Where problems are of a bounded nature, it is reasonable to look for equally clear and definitive 'solutions'. But there will always be some instances where it is not such a straightforward matter to decide what should be done. Action must sometimes be postponed, referred elsewhere, or entered into in a partial or qualified way. In a process of strategic choice, this kind of progressive commitment becomes more the exception than the rule.

Interpreting the Orientations into more Specific Guidelines

None of the four phrases used to describe the general orientations of the strategic choice approach — open technology, interactive participation, learning process, incremental progress — can be considered as exclusive to the strategic choice approach as presented in this book. Other people — practitioners as well as consultants and scholars — have argued for the adoption of these or similar orientations in responding to complex problems. So, as general prescriptions, such statements now have quite a familiar ring. In particular, the virtues of participative forms of organisation have been widely proclaimed, both in industry and the public sector, while the idea of public planning as a learning process has now almost passed into the realm of accepted conventional wisdom.

However, it has proved far from easy for people to give effect to such changes of orientation in practice. They can all too easily remain as pious exhortations, which evoke a cynical response from those who consider themselves to be realists in the art of decision-making under the practical pressures of organisational life. So the challenge is to find ways of interpreting the four broad orientations into more concrete operational terms. This is a challenge which is rarely faced in relation to technology, organisation, process and product considered *in combination*; however, it is the challenge to which the strategic choice approach is explicitly addressed.

In Figure 29, a first step in this direction is taken by interpreting each statement of preferred orientation into a more specific **operational guideline** which reflects more directly the philosophy of planning as a process of strategic choice. So the orientation towards an open technology is interpreted in terms of a *focus on decisions*; the orientation towards interactive participation is interpreted in terms of an emphasis on *lateral connections*; the orientation towards a learning process is interpreted in terms of *cyclic continuity*; and the orientation towards incremental progress is interpreted in terms of a guideline of *strategic products*.

Each of these guidelines calls for further explanation. This is done in the next four sections of this chapter, drawing on particular aspects of the philosophy of strategic choice as already presented. However, the value of these guidelines does not rest merely on their philosophical content. They are intended to give the statements of orientation a more practical slant; and they serve to draw attention to practical issues that arise in the *management* of the strategic choice approach, as applied to complex planning situations. So the next four sections will not only offer more precise meanings for the operational guidelines offered here under the four headings of technology, organisation, process and product; they will also indicate the nature of the practical management choices which they imply.

Guidance in Technological Choice

If any technology of strategic choice is to be truly *open*, then it must offer a means of bridging the differences in perception that can exist between participants who view the world from different professional, organisational or cultural perspectives. The adoption of a **focus on decisions** offers one pragmatic means of drawing the attention of participants towards matters which, individually or collectively, they feel to be important in their current planning task. It is only to be expected that they will frequently see the decisions before them in very different terms. They may disagree about the importance of one decision relative to another, or they may have differing views about the level of specificity or generality at which matters for decision should be expressed. Indeed, they can have different views about many aspects of decision-making; but such differences can provide a constructive focus for debate — with appropriate guidance — and thus help the participants in moving towards a more realistic sharing of views.

The centrality of the decision perspective is reflected in the focus on a current decision problem which was originally adopted as a starting point in developing a view of planning as a process of conscious management of uncertainty through time (Figure 3). In subsequent diagrams of Chapter 1, the symbolic shape of the 'cloud' representing this decision problem was variously expanded, pulled apart and examined from a range of contrasting perspectives. Then, in Chapter 2, the decision perspective was given more concrete expression by adopting the *decision area* as the fundamental unit of analysis, accepting that it could be used to represent choices about many different kinds of things — investment, location, alignment of roads, to mention only a few of the types of choice which were introduced in the telling of the South Side story. It is by the clearer articulation of such choices and their relationships that the form of the cloud representing a current decision problem can be made less obscure. So the adoption of a decision perspective offers one important means — now widely tested and adopted in practice — by which the orientation towards an open technology can be given practical expression, and the *transparency* of complex planning problems thereby increased.

It has to be recognised, however, that the focus on decisions is not the only possible emphasis that can be adopted in introducing an open technology. Other writers and practitioners have embraced with equal conviction the idea of a *systems perspective* as a key to a more effective approach to complexity in planning. However, in its more traditional forms, the adoption of a systems approach can be criticised as focussing attention on some forms of structural relationships at the expense of others, thus working against the spirit of an open technology. Such a comment could apply for example to the modelling of corporate planning problems in terms of systems of financial relationships only, or the modelling of cities in terms of systems of land-use/transport interactions alone.

Recently, some advocates of systems thinking have moved towards what is sometimes called a *soft systems* approach. This recognises that complex phenomena can be examined from many different perspectives, and that much can be learned by subjecting different views of the purposes, boundaries and inter-relationships of systems to structured analysis and debate.* So the adoption of a 'soft' systems approach offers an alternative means of giving expression to the emphasis of an open technology. It does, however, focus attention on relationships of a comparatively stable,

---

* See in particular Checkland (1981) and Ackoff (1974).

FIGURE
30
Technological Choice: Settings and Equipment

INTERACTIVE SETTING – EQUIPMENT: PAPER, COLOUR PENS . . .

REFLECTIVE
SETTING: HIGH
TECHNOLOGY

TECHNOLOGY

A–TOPP

ORIENTATIONS

REFLECTIVE
SETTING: LOW
TECHNOLOGY

enduring form, as opposed to the ever-changing relationships between decisions — expressed at various levels and carrying varying degrees of urgency — which provide the primary focus for the strategic choice approach. The approach developed in this book is, above all, intended as an instrument to help people plan under the pressures of the continuously evolving realities they face; which is not to say they cannot also benefit from standing back occasionally to reach out for a broader, more systemic view.

In pursuing the particular expression of an open technology presented here, it is important to see the scope of an *appropriate* technology for strategic choice as embracing not only a set of basic concepts and analytical methods, but also the choice of the physical settings in which people work, the equipment they use and the media through which they communicate with each other. In the more conventional settings of sequential decision-making (Figure 6) — the clerk sitting at a desk, the committee sitting around a long table — such aspects of technology are well established by convention and therefore rarely considered in a conscious way. Background information is presented verbally or in documentary form; while working on a problem, pens and paper may be used by individuals so that notes can be taken, and action points recorded. In the case of the individual decision-maker, dealing with relatively bounded and recurrent issues, the electronic work station has been beginning to change this familiar pattern. On the other hand, most *collective* decision processes continue to rely on the simplest of technological equipment: and there are good arguments for this, in so far as full rein can be given to peoples' capacities to interact with each other through verbal discourse and debate — freely augmented by those non-verbal signals through which a wider range of reactions and emotions can be expressed.

However, there are alternatives available to the technology conventionally used to support processes of communication and of interaction; and some of these have been found to give fuller expression to the orientation towards an open technology of strategic choice. One alternative setting which has been found to be particularly effective is reflected in the main sketch of Figure 30. This shows a group of people relating to each other not by sitting facing each other from fixed positions around a table, but in an alternative setting which allows them to communicate and interact in a more flexible way. The basic technology in this kind of setting consists of:

— large sheets of paper that can be arranged around the walls of a room, which has to be large enough for people to move around freely;
— a simple, non-permanent means of sticking paper to walls;
— a liberal supply of marker pens of several contrasting colours.

These materials are not, in themselves, very sophisticated; but many decision-makers are unaccustomed to their use, other than in relatively formal presentations. Used together, they have been found to play an important part in encouraging interactive working in groups. More specifically, they can encourage flexibility in use of the various graphical methods for expression of decision problems and their implications which have been introduced in earlier chapters.

It has to be recognised, however, that successful group interaction is not automatically assured merely by creating an appropriate setting and providing appropriate equipment and tools. It is always possible that one or two members of a group will tend to dominate the process, with others reacting by becoming alienated or withdrawn. Therefore, among the variations in strategic choice technology that will be offered in the next five chapters, some suggestions will be offered for helping members of a group to become more fully involved. For example, this can be done by creating opportunities for people to draw up individual lists of decision areas or uncertainty areas, before attempting to merge these into a shared picture on larger sheets of paper ranged around the walls of the room.

Figure 30 includes a reminder that it is not exclusively when they are working in groups that people can draw on the basic concepts and methods of the strategic choice approach. As several experienced decision-makers have found, ideas such as the UE/UV/UR classification of uncertainty can also be helpful to them when they are reflecting alone on difficult problems — as in the symbolic armchair — or when engaged in informal discussions with one or two colleagues who share an awareness of the basic language and ideas. It is in such individual or small group settings too that the electronic computer can sometimes provide a helpful adjunct to the basic technology of communication and interaction. For it can provide a means of guiding individual decision-makers through the various available paths of process choice in an exploratory but disciplined way.

It is important to stress however that, within the overall technology of strategic choice, a computer is merely an optional resource. Indeed, most of the effective applications of the approach to complex problems have made no use of computer technology at all. It offers a resource which, in general, should be kept firmly in the background when striving for creative interaction in a group setting, because the momentum of interaction can quickly be disrupted once attention is diverted to the images projected on a VDU screen. As the technology of human-machine interaction continues to develop, it is to be expected that new possibilities will emerge for combining group interaction and the computer in an adaptive, dynamic way. Some opportunities for research and experiment in these directions will be reviewed briefly in Chapter 10; what has to be stressed at this point is that computer methods are in no way part of the *essential* technology of the strategic choice approach.

In pursuing the emphasis on an open technology, the general rule is continually to aim for simplification rather than elaboration, so that high levels of effective communication and interaction can be sustained. However, it is important to remember that there are always choices of *balance* to be made in this and other dimensions of the approach (Figure 2). It is only realistic that the appropriate point of balance at any moment should be judged in the light of the participants' local appreciation of their own present problem situation, and the pressures within which they must work.

Guidance in Organisational Choice

Turning at this point to the organisational dimension of the A-TOPP framework, the recommended orientation towards **interactive participation** is by no means as straightforward to interpret in practice as might at first appear. For the wider the scope of the problem being addressed, the broader the range of organisational and other interests likely to have a stake in that problem. Then the harder it becomes to reconcile the desire that all these interests should be adequately *represented* with the desire to encourage interactive working. For the larger and more diverse the group, the more difficult it becomes for all to feel involved, and for progress to be sustained.

In addressing the choice of organisational arrangements to deal with complex planning problems, the conventional approach is to focus attention on the design of comparatively stable, clearly structured frameworks of hierarchical guidance. These usually incorporate elements of conscious forecasting and direction-setting as well as managerial control, and are shaped to fit closely the established management structure of the corporation concerned. The intention is — at least in theory — for historical inertias to be questioned; for people to come together to work across departmental boundaries on selected major issues; and often also to involve representatives of other significant interest groups, such as employees, residents or public service clients.

However, the basic management structures of most corporate organisations can still be seen as designed primarily as a means of responding efficiently to certain recurrent *categories* of decision problems, for which clear policy guidelines and rules of delegated responsibility can be defined. Where problems are of a more fluid, indistinct shape, experience shows that formal planning arrangements which reflect the established corporate structure can quickly break down. It is then that more informal, adaptive approaches take over — with the impetus usually coming from those points in the management system where the pressures for decision are most intense. It is in the face of repeated pressures of this kind that organisational arrangements for planning based on the hierarchical control structure begin to lose credibility, because their contribution to the making of key management decisions becomes increasingly hard to demonstrate.

FIGURE 31

Organisational Choice: Levels of Response to Uncertainty

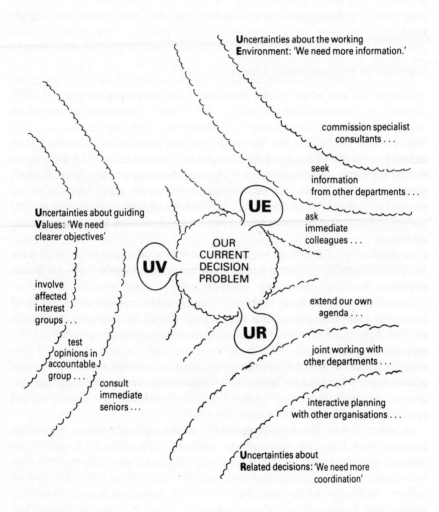

Uncertainties about the working Environment: 'We need more information.'

commission specialist consultants . . .

seek information from other departments . . .

ask immediate colleagues . . .

UE

OUR CURRENT DECISION PROBLEM

Uncertainties about guiding Values: 'We need clearer objectives'

UV

involve affected interest groups . . .

test opinions in accountable group . . .

consult immediate seniors . . .

extend our own agenda . . .

UR

joint working with other departments . . .

interactive planning with other organisations . . .

Uncertainties about Related decisions: 'We need more coordination'

ORGANISATION

ORIENTATIONS

So, to express the decision-centred philosophy of the strategic choice approach, an alternative guideline to the design of organisational arrangements is required. As an operational guideline, intended to reflect the orientation towards interactive participation as against individual working, the idea of a focus on **lateral connections** will now be introduced. The significance of this term in relation to a decision perspective is made more clear in Figure 31, which is an extension of the view of three contrasting responses to uncertainty in decision-making as first presented in Chapter 1 (Figure 3).

Figure 31 starts from the situation of an individual or working group currently concerned with some particular decision or planning problem — whether it be complex or more limited in scope — and experiencing some degree of *difficulty* in deciding what should be done. Different aspects of this current difficulty can be analysed in relation to the three basic categories of uncertainty — UE, UV and UR — and each of these types of uncertainty can be seen as having organisational implications of a somewhat different kind. In each direction, too, there may be various levels of investment to consider, reaching out increasingly far beyond the particular organisational setting in which the problem is currently being addressed. The possibilities may range from the level of quick and informal contacts with people who are relatively close in organisational terms, to the level of more deliberate, and possibly formal, approaches to others who are organisationally more remote.

When working outwards in the *UE direction*, the concern is essentially to acquire additional *information* relevant to the decision-makers' working environment. Some kinds of information can be acquired easily enough by means of informal enquiries from close colleagues; others may involve somewhat more formal approaches across departmental or corporate boundaries; while others again may mean initiating substantial survey, assessment or forecasting exercises, perhaps involving formal contractual arrangements with specialist consultants.

Turning next to the *UR direction*, there may again be several possible levels of investment in outward linkage to consider. However, the people approached now appear not merely in the role of knowledge providers, but also in the role of decision-makers in related fields. So any communication across boundaries will tend to take on a rather different flavour, involving more explicit elements of *negotiation* in so far as each party may be in a position to help the other in reducing some of the uncertainties that they face. The organisational options to be considered in the UR direction can range from occasional bilateral exchanges — whether by telephone or other means — to more interactive working arrangements calling for substantial time commitments by the parties concerned.

Turning finally to the *UV direction*, the most familiar and straightforward means of seeking to reduce uncertainty about guiding values involves referring upwards within a hierarchy to a superordinate point of authority. Beyond this, there may be a possibility of referring for guidance to a meeting of some collective body — a Board, Council or Committee — in which formal authority resides; accepting that at this level there may be many competitive pressures on its agenda and only limited discussion time available. Beyond this again, there may be opportunities to launch special consultative exercises to probe the value positions of interest groups which have a major stake in the present decision problem, whether by use of existing representative channels, by convening open meetings, or by some combination of the two.

The successive levels of response shown in Figure 31 are intended to give no more than a broad indication of the opportunities for working across organisational boundaries that might emerge at any moment in a planning process. Some more specific examples were presented in Chapter 3 (Figures 24 and 26), and further illustrations will appear in Chapter 8. Sometimes it will be appropriate to refer upwards or downwards within a hierarchy, especially as a means of addressing significant areas of uncertainty of the UV type. However, the main orientation in strategic choice is essentially towards building connections in a *lateral* way, working outwards from a specific problem focus rather than downwards from a point of central authority.

Often, there will be choices to be faced as to whether particular connections should be activated through formal or informal channels. In particular, there is always the possibility that conscious investment in building close working relationships with particular individuals will provide a foundation for quick and informal consultation later, when particular issues or circumstances arise. In managing a process of strategic choice, it is generally the choices about lateral working in the UR direction that pose the most subtle challenges; for, as was earlier indicated (Figure 5), it is in this direction that the boundaries of the decision problem itself become enlarged. So, the question now emerges as to how far the range of people involved in interactive working can be extended without the momentum of progress being lost.

Taking these considerations together, the significant areas of management choice in organisational terms can be seen as extending beyond the formal *structuring* of arrangements for internal co-ordination, as the hierarchical command perspective of planning organisation might suggest. For there are also important choices to be made about arrangements for bilateral *linking* and multilateral *grouping* in response to particular problems as they arise. The choices about linking relate to the informal cultivation and activation of networks of inter-personal working relationships by specific participants in the process. On the other hand, the choices about grouping relate to judgements as to when and how to initiate interactive group working with others, or to enlarge the boundaries of an existing interactive process. It should not be forgotten too that choices may arise as to when and how to disband a group which has outlived its usefulness, or otherwise to modify the lattice of arrangements through which a process of interactive working is pursued.

In confronting such choices, it has to be recognised that invitations to participate in interactive group processes will not always be welcomed without reservation. Resistances may be encountered because of fears about loss of autonomy, or straightforward time pressures, or conflicts of interests, or various other factors of a broadly political kind. Factors such as these can contribute to making the emphasis on interactive participation more difficult to interpret in practice than it might appear. The point to be underlined is again that there are always choices of *balance* to be considered. Not least, there is always a balance to be struck between the extremes of reactive and interactive working (Figure 2). This is a balance which must be expected to change through time in an adaptive, evolutionary way — and which can only realistically be judged by those directly involved in the process.

Guidance in Process Choice

To talk of a process of strategic choice as being essentially a **learning process** may seem to be no more than to repeat a statement which, applied to planning, has now become so widely accepted as to have become little more than a cliché. But this orientation, like the corresponding orientations towards open technology and interactive participation, has proved to be very difficult to put into practice in a satisfactory way. This is because the question of *what* it is most important to learn in relation to complex problems can be by no means easy to answer with any confidence in advance. Often, it is only after interactive work has begun on such a problem that the participants can begin to form any kind of informed, coherent view as to what the most serious obstacles to progress are, and therefore what course their learning process should take.

Most of the more conventional approaches to planning and complex decision-making have advocated a process based on clearly specified sequences of steps or stages, following the norm of linearity which is widely accepted in the design of procedures for dealing with more recurrent, clearly structured decision problems. Following this principle, specific timetables are laid down for consecutive stages of the planning process, covering such activities as survey, formulation of objectives, design of alternatives, evaluation and plan preparation. In those situations where the aim is to add a more purposive direction-seeking emphasis to an existing system of corporate management and control, such steps are then fitted into a periodic — often annual — planning cycle. Arrangements of this kind have

FIGURE
32

Process Choice: Opportunities for Movement Between Modes

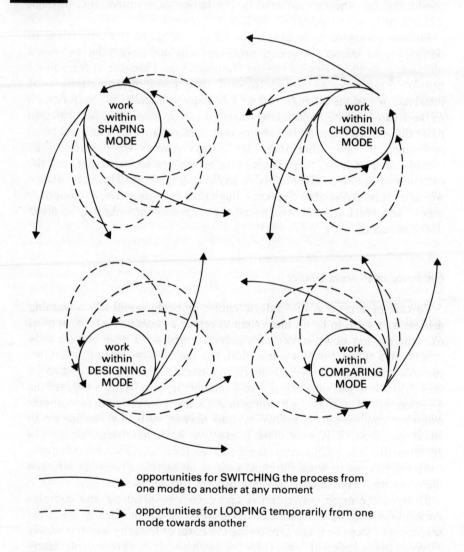

work within SHAPING MODE

work within CHOOSING MODE

work within DESIGNING MODE

work within COMPARING MODE

opportunities for SWITCHING the process from one mode to another at any moment

opportunities for LOOPING temporarily from one mode towards another

PROCESS

A-TOPP

ORIENTATIONS

the virtue of apparent predictability: this can be important in organisational settings where substantial human, financial or other resources are being committed to the planning task, creating a demand that their use be subject to due procedures of accountability. However, the risk is that the requirement to adhere to a pre-ordained sequence of activities will constrain people to concentrate their effort on learning the wrong things at the wrong times, so far as the more important pressures for decision are concerned. Instances frequently arise, both in business and in public planning, where lengthy and expensive exercises in survey, forecasting or evaluation are carried out to a prearranged timetable, yet turn out to yield results of little relevance to the more crucial problems of the day.

So, in describing the process emphasis of the strategic choice approach, the general orientation towards a learning process will be interpreted more specifically in terms of an operational guideline of **cyclic continuity**. In this, the conventional representation of a process in terms of a linear sequence of stages is replaced by a more flexible set of possibilities for movement between one *mode* of decision-making and another. It may be useful for some purposes to follow an agreed sequence of progression to ensure that all modes are considered in a methodical way; but to maintain the emphasis on a learning process in a complex and evolving problem situation, decision-makers must be prepared to adopt a much more flexible approach. Often the shape of a problem is only dimly perceived, and there are many partially-formed viewpoints to be exchanged. Then the participants have to be ready at any time to move 'backwards' to modes in which substantial work has already been done, so as to challenge and modify past assumptions. Equally, they must be ready to skip 'forwards' to modes where it might seem premature to work in any depth, according to a more conventional sequential view. Indeed, the very concept of a decision area implies a readiness to look ahead to what is *to be* decided at various points in the future, effectively skipping forward from the shaping to the choosing mode.

In Figure 32, the guideline of cyclic continuity is expressed more specifically in terms of the types of *process management choice* which it implies. Starting from the view of a process of strategic choice as involving a continuing interplay among four basic modes of activity, there are two types of choice that can be made in considering how to direct the learning process. First, there are choices about when and how to *switch* out of the primary mode of the moment and into any of the others, for a spell of deliberate working within that other mode. Then there are those more frequent, often informal, choices that people make about when and how to *loop* briefly outwards from the primary mode of the moment in the direction of another mode, to deal with some limited source of difficulty, before returning to pick up again the momentum of work already established in the primary mode.

Much of the advice to be offered in the next four chapters relates to forms of switching and looping judgement that people can consider when working in each of the four modes. Therefore, each of the next four chapters will end with a diagram which elaborates the relevant 'corner' of Figure 32 by summarising the types of switching and looping judgements that can be made when working in that particular mode.

The broader significance of the guideline of cyclic continuity is that, when people are consciously following the strategic choice approach, the conventional linear process of agenda control, as regulated through an appointed chairperson, no longer need apply. Instead, it becomes replaced by a more subtle, adaptive process of *route finding* with many possible paths among which to choose. In this process, both switching and looping judgements have to be made continually. Brief loops out of the primary mode of the moment towards another mode are often made subconsciously; however, in group working it can be a significant contribution to the learning process if they can be more consciously recognised and discussed. Switching judgements, on the other hand, have a wider significance in the management of the process as a whole. So it is all the more important that they should be openly debated within a group, if a conscious emphasis on an interactive learning process is to be maintained. More specific advice on how to manage such switches of mode in the course of interactive group working will be given in Chapter 9, reflecting accumulated practical experience as to how best to sustain the emphasis on *relevant* learning at all times.

The significance here given to switching and looping judgements does not mean that more conventional *scheduling* decisions can be ignored in the management of a process of strategic choice. Each participant in the process has inevitably to make at least some advance arrangements to organise his or her working life, in which there will usually be other relatively fixed commitments to fulfil. So periods of interactive working will often have to be scheduled in advance, even if the organisation of work within such a period is kept as flexible as possible by following the precept of adaptive route-finding in place of that of linear agenda control.

In practice, problems can arise in reconciling the demands of cyclic continuity with expectations of linear procedure, not only in the advance scheduling of work but also in accounting to other people retrospectively for the way in which any conclusions or recommendations have been reached. To argue that a particular set of proposals has been arrived at as a result of a cyclic, adaptive, learning process may be to do no more than describe the realities that underlie any process of working at complex problems. But it is only natural that those not directly involved should wish to see some kind of rational argument by which the conclusions offered can be justified, without becoming drawn into the full subtleties of the learning process. The requirement for some degree of 'post rationalisation' can be a vital one in some circumstances, and it will be the subject of further discussion in Chapter 9.

Guidance in Product Choice

The shift in orientation of the strategic choice approach in relation to the *products* of the process is expressed (Figure 29) in terms of a shift away from an emphasis on definitive resolution of problems at specified end points of the process, and towards a more subtle emphasis on making **incremental progress** through time. Where problems can be treated as simple and discrete, it may make sense to deal with them in accordance with some linear schedule or agenda, with the aim of settling each item of business in full before moving on to the next. When people encounter issues which are more interrelated and complex, the tendency is often to translate this desire for complete solutions into a concern with the production of *substantive plans* at as comprehensive a level as possible. The conventional wisdom is that such plans should be *implemented* in an equally complete manner through more specific operational decisions, budgets and programmes, after they have been steered through the required procedures of authorisation within the organisation.

However, it is a common experience for people to encounter very considerable difficulties in attempting to conform to such principles in practice. Indeed, the more comprehensively they may seek to view the scope of a strategy or plan in terms of the range of substantive issues it should cover, the more these difficulties tend to proliferate. It is in such circumstances that the alternative orientation towards incremental progress comes into its own.

Within the strategic choice approach, the operational guideline which is offered as a more specific interpretation of this idea is that of generating a balance between different kinds of **strategic products** through time. The spirit of this idea is captured in the concept of the commitment package, as introduced towards the end of Chapter 3 (Figure 26). The structure of the commitment package is designed to help people in thinking and talking about what level of *balance* between commitment and flexibility is appropriate at any moment of a continuous process. This entails their weighing up the various urgencies and uncertainties impinging on the choices with which they are currently concerned, and also considering how foundations for the making of future decisions can be built. Such considerations are of only marginal value in a conventional problem-solving approach, but are of profound importance in a process of strategic choice where the need for continuity is explicitly recognised.

The concept of the commitment package provides a particularly clear expression of the principle of treating *commitment as a variable* rather than as something to be conceived in all-or-nothing terms. Yet a commitment

FIGURE

33

Product Choice: A Classification of Strategic Products

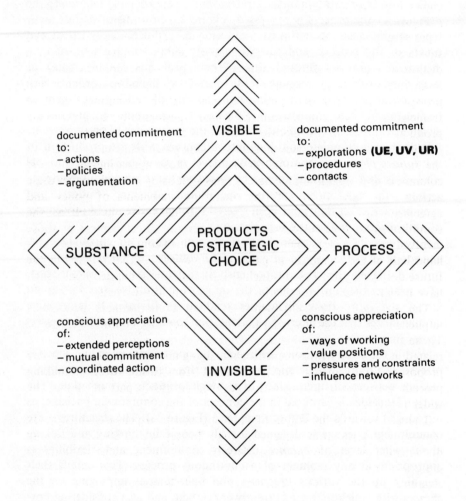

documented commitment to:
– actions
– policies
– argumentation

VISIBLE

documented commitment to:
– explorations **(UE, UV, UR)**
– procedures
– contacts

SUBSTANCE

PRODUCTS OF STRATEGIC CHOICE

PROCESS

conscious appreciation of:
– extended perceptions
– mutual commitment
– coordinated action

conscious appreciation of:
– ways of working
– value positions
– pressures and constraints
– influence networks

INVISIBLE

PRODUCT

A-TOP**P**

ORIENTATIONS

package is essentially a product of the work of the choosing mode; and it is important to recognise that there are also products of work in the various other modes of strategic choice which can make a direct contribution to progress in a broader sense. A wider view of the various types of strategic product which can contribute to the momentum of progress in strategic choice is offered in Figure 33.

Figure 33 presents a two-dimensional framework for identifying different types of strategic product, first in terms of a distinction between products of **substance** and those relating to the **process**; and, secondly, in terms of a distinction between **visible** products and those of a more **invisible** or intangible form. The essence of the distinction between substance and process can be illustrated by referring again to the commitment package framework (Figure 26), the aim of which is, essentially, to present the products of work in the choosing mode in a clearly visible form.

Within a commitment package, the products which relate most directly to the *substance* of the decision problem are those appearing in the first column, concerned with immediate actions — it being recognised that these actions may take various forms, including statements of policy and agreement on responsibilities, budgets and deadlines, as well as the commitment to here-and-now actions under the direct control of those involved in the process. There is also a substantive content within the right-hand half of the commitment package framework — that relating to the future decision space. For this includes information about decisions which have been deferred or are seen as contingent on future events.

The existence of *process* elements within a commitment package is implicit in its very nature as an incremental step in a continuing process. Those parts of a commitment package which are most directly process-related include the arrangements for managing uncertainty, along with any proposed arrangements for scheduling; for future decision-making procedures; and for linking with other people with a part to play in the wider process.

There are also other kinds of visible products which are not directly represented in the commitment package framework. These include any documented evidence of progress made through work done in the shaping, designing and comparing modes. Work done in these modes can lead to clearer expressions of the participants' shared views about:

— the nature of the decision problems they face;
— the range of options or schemes available;
— the consequences of different alternatives;
— the uncertainties that make it difficult to express preferences between them.

It is common in planning for such kinds of information to be assembled as part of a reasoned *justification* of recommended courses of action. There are various conventional forms — written, diagrammatic, numerical — in which such information about problems, opportunities, criteria, constraints and sources of uncertainty can be assembled and documented whenever important moments of formal commitment to policies and actions arise. But the various concepts and conventions illustrated in Chapters 2 and 3 are specifically intended to help people build up a visible record of progress in all modes in a more continuous way. This is of particular importance when work is proceeding interactively in groups. There is still a task of *interpreting* visible products expressed in such ways into forms which are intelligible to those not directly involved; but there are practical ways of addressing this task, and these will be discussed further in Chapter 9.

Important as these various visible products may be, it is vital also to recognise that any process of strategic choice generates *invisible products* which can have a profound influence in the longer term. First, in terms of the *substance* of problems, people can expect to extend their perceptions in ways that cannot be fully reflected in any documented evidence of progress that is produced. Such extended perceptions may embrace all aspects of substantive progress already discussed at the more visible level, including problems, opportunities, effects and uncertainties.

Such personal shifts in perception will generally be in the direction of increased *sharing* of views among those involved in interactive working; or increasing intersubjectivity, to use a term which others have found useful in relation to group processes (Eden, Jones, Sims and Smithin,1981). Moves in this direction can be of considerable significance beyond the boundaries of the group involved in the interactive working process; for they can affect the ways in which individuals seek to influence the views and behaviours of colleagues, superiors and associates within their wider working environment.

Also, more realistic perceptions of the external political realities surrounding a problem can be an important invisible product of a process of strategic choice. However, such a product must be seen as relevant as much to future *process* as to the substance of particular problems; so this leads naturally into the discussion of the final quadrant of the product classification of Figure 33. Among the important invisible products which relate more to process than to substance is fuller understanding of:

— other peoples' values;
— their ways of working;
— the pressures and constraints acting on them.

In most cases, this is backed up by extensions to the communications networks of individuals involved in the interactive working.

In interactive working, it is important to consider how far the full range of visible and invisible products can be expressed in more accessible forms, so that they can be better understood at a collective level. This raises important management choices in the areas of *recording* and *interpretation*. Recording is simply a question of keeping track of progress as it is made. Various methods for recording progress on the substance of problems — and the more visible aspects of progress on the process side — have already been illustrated through the telling of the South Side Story in Chapters 2 and 3; but recording of invisible progress in terms of process is often less straightforward. However, conscious efforts to document shifts in understanding of others, and in communication networks, can be important if these aspects of progress are not to become lost.

It is important to recognise that any conscious documentation of progress requires a process of *interpretation* as well as recording. This must involve the translation of jargon used in group working — whether verbal or graphical — if progress is to be reviewed in terms accessible to others rather than in terms which are intelligible merely to those directly involved. This is important enough in the documentation of visible products, but is even more essential in attempting to document progress at the more invisible level. It is especially important, from a longer term perspective, that people should be helped to recognise invisible products through explicit review of the directions in which progress is — or is not — being made. Some practical advice on these aspects of the management of strategic products will be presented in Chapter 9.

Orientations of Strategic Choice: A General Review

The various points made under the four headings of Technology, Organisation, Process and Product are summarised in Figure 34. This is intended to form a point of reference in following the more concrete guidance to be offered in the next five chapters. The first two columns do little more than present in a more compact form the contrasts in orientation which were highlighted earlier (Figure 29), where the structure of a tetrahedron was introduced to convey the essential unity of the A-TOPP framework.

So, in general terms, the strategic choice approach is interpreted in terms of shifts of emphasis from conventional ideas about technology, organisation, process and product towards the four preferred *orientations* of open technology, interactive participation, learning process and incremental progress. These comparatively general, exhortative statements are then translated in the second column of Figure 34 into the four *operational guidelines* of focus on decisions, lateral connections, cyclic continuity and strategic products. All these can be seen as linked to the more general guideline of the conscious *management of uncertainty*, which distinguishes the strategic choice approach as a practical means of responding to complex problems. Each of these four guidelines can be contrasted with more conventional guidelines for responding to complexity which, in practice, are

FIGURE

34

Technology, Organisation, Process and Product:
An Interim Review

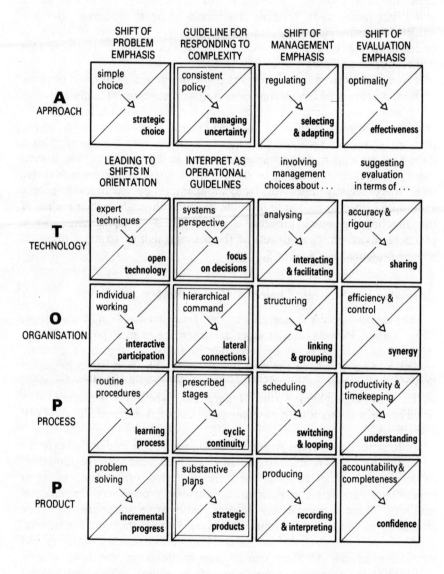

Figure 34 : Technology, Organisation, Process and Product: An Interim Review

ORIENTATIONS

often disappointing in their effects. These more conventional guidelines — systems perspective, hierarchical command, prescribed stages and substantive plans — have all been used as points of reference in discussing the strategic choice alternatives in the four preceding sections. So these too are brought within the comparative framework in the second column of Figure 34, linked to a more general guideline of consistent policy at the level of overall approach.

The third column of Figure 34 extends this framework to indicate the main areas of *management choice* which it is important to bear in mind when attempting to follow the recommended operational guidelines in practice. Again, these areas of management choice have already been introduced in the preceding sections of this chapter; but it will be helpful to gather them together here.

— In terms of *technology*, it is important to keep in view choices about ways of **interacting** and **facilitating** as well as about methods of analysis as such.
— In *organisational* terms, the important choices concern ways of **linking** and **grouping** across sectional or organisational boundaries, as well as about the design or more formal coordinating structures.
— In *process* terms, there are choices of **switching** and **looping** to be considered while working interactively, as well as the more familiar choices about scheduling of meetings and deadlines.
— In terms of *products*, there are choices to be made about ways of **recording** and **interpreting** progress, as well as the more familiar choices about production of formal reports which emphasise substantive actions and policies.

All these aspects of management choice can be seen as describing different facets of a more general task of managing the strategic choice approach. This means maintaining a spirit of *selectivity and adaptiveness* in planning and decision-making, as contrasted with a more familiar emphasis on the regulation of more simple decision-making tasks. Yet another level of contrast is added by the fourth and final column of Figure 34, which introduces a set of contrasting emphases in terms of the continuous *monitoring* of the quality of a process of strategic choice. In brief, the message is that judgements about the use of limited resources have to be approached not just in terms of any clearly defined criterion of optimality, but more in terms of a broader concept of **effectiveness**. In the successive rows of the framework, this concept is seen as embracing such concepts as *sharing, synergy, understanding* and *confidence*, in addition to more conventional indicators of success.

These evaluative issues will be discussed more fully in Chapter 9. They remain relevant whether the concern is to make quick prospective judgments about what to do next in the course of an interactive process, or to review progress in a more reflective vein. The important point is that it is not necessary to discard completely such traditional concerns as accuracy and rigour in technology; efficiency and control in organisation; productivity and timekeeping in process; or accountability and completeness in product. It is merely that other crucial considerations have to be explicitly considered as well. Indeed, this point applies to all the contrasts offered in Figure 34; to advocate a shift in emphasis from the top left section of each square towards the bottom right is not to be taken as implying that these more conventional emphases do not have their place. It has to be recognised that all organisations require a base of stability and predictability on which their more adaptive activities can be built; and the concern here is that this should be effectively complemented rather than undermined.

The concern with identifying areas of choice and evaluation which emerges in the third and fourth columns of Figure 34 may suggest that some of the core strategic choice concepts such as those of the decision area and the comparison area could be applied in structuring the management of the process of strategic choice itself. There is no reason in principle why this should not be possible. However, any explicit use of strategic choice methods for this purpose must not distract the participants from the real problems of substance that they face. So it is suggested that Figure 34 be treated as background rather than foreground in reading the chapters that follow. Working on the well-established principle that there is nothing so practical as a good theory, this framework can be referred to as and when required, as a broad philosophical context within which all the practical guidance offered in the next five chapters should make sense.

5

Skills in Shaping

Introduction

This chapter offers some practical guidance on approaches to the shaping of complex decision problems. It does so by building on the basic concepts of the shaping mode which were presented in the first half of Chapter 2 — the concepts of the *decision area*, the *decision link*, the *decision graph* and the *problem focus*. Each of these ideas is quite simple in its essence. Within the overall technology of strategic choice, they together provide a foundation for the more technical activities of generating options and exploring their mutual compatibility which distinguish the work of the designing mode.

The importance of work in the shaping mode arises from all the difficult and subtle judgements that can be involved in expressing practical problems in terms of decision areas and linkages between them, and then in agreeing a problem focus on which to work within the resulting decision graph. This can be an especially challenging task in situations where the nature and scope of the choices to be made are far from clear cut and where there are many participants in the process, each with a different understanding of what is at stake.

Experience has repeatedly shown that it can be worth while spending a substantial amount of group time working to achieve more satisfactory formulations of a decision graph. This may mean changing the 'map' of decision areas and their connecting links several times, as the level of shared understanding grows. Indeed, such a process of recycling is of value not only when a group of people is still in the early stages of working together. It can also be well worth while for the group to return and carry out further work in the shaping mode after they have consciously moved ahead and invested effort in the work of the designing, comparing and choosing modes. This point is inherent in the guideline of cyclic continuity in the process, which was emphasised in Chapter 4 and gave rise to the various switching and looping opportunities indicated in Figure 30. Taking a longer time perspective, the idea of the commitment package demonstrates how incremental progress towards commitment will usually mean deferring choice within some of the decision areas within a decision graph. Any such deferments will, in turn, create opportunities for the reshaping of decision areas and their relationships at future points in time — when other quite new areas of choice may possibly have come to the fore through the unfolding of external events.

In Chapter 2, it was suggested that the choice of problem focus within a wider decision graph marked an important point of transition between the work of the shaping and the designing modes. There are, however, many different considerations which can be taken into account in this process of 'cutting a problem down to size'. Some of these considerations — urgency, degree of importance, level of interconnectedness, degree of influence on the part of a particular set of decision-makers — may be much more important in some decision contexts than in others. Indeed, their importance can vary with the passage of time, even within the same decision context. So the whole process of problem-shaping can be seen as one in which a continuing tension must be expected between the desire to expand the boundaries of a problem to encompass all conceivable elements of choice, and the desire to keep its dimensions more manageable so as to secure a sense of progress towards action.

Approaches to Building up a Set of Relevant Decision Areas

Given some agreement to carry out work in a difficult but as yet unstructured problem field, the task of beginning to build up a set of decision areas to represent the choices within that field is one that can be organised either at an individual or a group level. It is broadly akin to the process of 'agenda building' which is, literally, no more than the construction of a list of things to be done, or matters to be addressed. However, in strategic choice, the task is not simply to arrange these things to be done into some appropriate order so that they can be tackled sequentially. This is because some of them at least are likely to be interrelated, in a way which implies that they should perhaps be grouped or clustered so that they can be examined together.

Wherever an individual or group is working to a reasonably well-defined remit, as in the problem of looking into the implications of the proposed new road through South Side, then it may not be too difficult to decide where the process of building up a list of decision areas should begin. For example, among the seven decision areas listed in Figure 10, it might be that the first four at least would suggest themselves fairly readily to anyone familiar with the local planning context. Yet in other circumstances, where the remit may be broader or looser, and the elements of choice less clear or less urgent, difficulties are to be expected in agreeing the way in which even the most basic elements of choice should be expressed.

Such difficulties may, of course, arise even where an individual is working alone: but where people are working as a group they can be expected to surface rapidly in the form of debates and disagreements between one person and another. Usually, the different members of the group will bring different kinds of perception to bear, rooted in different kinds of experience, different bases of professional or technical knowledge and different responsibilities to people outside the group, apart from any deeper differences in ways of construing the world around them. Such differences can be valuable in so far as they can help the group develop a more rounded appreciation of the choices which they face. In South Side, for example, it might be expected that any engineers in the group might see the relevant choices in terms of road alignments, construction techniques and other technical matters to do with elevations, access roads, surface drainage arrangements or bids for resources on capital programmes. Urban planners might see them in terms of opportunities to specify intended uses or other controls relating to particular areas of land; economists might see them in terms of investment levels, amortisation of fixed assets, balance between private and public expenditures and incomes. Then again lawyers, administrators, project co-ordinators, politicians and any other participants in the process might all have their subtly different perspectives on the range and content of the choices to be considered.

In a group setting, one good way to start the process of building up a set of decision areas is simply to begin with a large sheet of blank paper on the wall, on which an initial list of issues or matters of concern is recorded by one participant in such a way as to be clearly visible to all the others. Figure 35 gives an example of the kind of tentative list that might be built up by the South Side Working Party at the outset of its work, before any kind of sorting or grouping of decision areas has been attempted. What matters at this stage is primarily to encourage the involvement of as many participants as possible in the listing of an initial set of elements, however imperfect it may seem. The spirit called for is one of organised brainstorming, in which ideas put forward by one participant can trigger off new directions of thought by others.

An alternative way of starting is to ask each participant to spend a few minutes writing down a list of a few decision areas he or she believes to be important, before the interactive group process begins — or at least before it has built up a momentum of its own. If each individual uses a separate sheet of paper or card to record each suggested decision area — and if these sheets are not too large — then the results can be shared by spreading all the sheets prepared by the participants out on a table top or, perhaps, merely on a patch of clear floor space in the centre of the room. Wall space can, of course, be used for displaying these sheets of paper, provided there is a simple, non-permanent means of sticking paper to the wall.

This kind of approach can be helpful in generating an initial sense of involvement by all participants in a group. Of course, it is also likely to lead

FIGURE

35

SOUTH SIDE
EXAMPLE

Building up a Tentative List of Decision Areas

DECISION AREA	LABEL
road line across South Side ?	ROAD LINE ?
shopping centre location ?	SHOP LOC'N?
use of central site ?	CENT'L SITE ?
use of gasworks site ?	GAS SITE ?
closure of Main Street ?	MAIN ST ?
timing of construction of new road ?	ROADTIM ?
policy on rehousing ?	REHOUS ?
traffic management in South Side ?	TRAF MGT ?
West Street improvement ?	WEST ST ?
closure of Griffin Road school?	GRIFF SCHL ?
investment in life of district ?	DIST LIFE ?
re-routeing of local bus services?	BUS ROUTES?
cutbacks in municipal spending?	CUTBACKS ?
extent of further housing clearance?	HOUSCLEAR?
policy on housing repair ?	HOUSRPR ?
policy on contracting out design work?	DESIGN WK ?
procedure for property acquisition ?	PROPACQ ?

initial quick
listing by
group working
collectively

further
additions
suggested
after
individual
reflection

SHAPING

SKILLS

The building up of an unstructured list of decision areas such as this can be a
useful step when a group is just starting work. The list can be extended, altered
or restructured as understanding grows, with some entries transferred to lists of
comparison areas or uncertainty areas. Individuals can be invited to list their
own suggestions either at the start or later in the process.

to a degree of redundancy in the information generated, because some of the more obvious decision areas are likely to be thought of independently by different people. But this kind of redundancy may be no bad thing at an early stage in a group process, both because any area of choice which is identified by many people can be given more weight on that account, and because the elements of a problem may be perceived in subtly different ways by different participants. Such differences can then provide a focus for constructive debate when it comes to the point of formulating decision areas in more precise terms.

In this kind of activity, it is only to be expected that doubts will arise as to whether some suggested elements of a problem should be considered as decision areas at all. Some areas of choice may seem to lie largely outside the direct sphere of influence of the participants, in which case they might perhaps seem better expressed as uncertainty areas. Other 'decision areas' offered may seem more in the nature of statements or choices to do with generalised aims, criteria or desiderata, in which case there would be a possibility of reserving them to be introduced later as comparison areas. As will be seen later, comparison areas and uncertainty areas can always be transferred to separate sheets of paper on the wall, for further consideration when the process moves into other modes. However, there is no reason why they should not be included in a single unstructured list of problem elements in the first instance, with a view to further rearrangement when the group decides to move ahead.

Sorting Decision Areas by Categories and Levels

Where the problem to be tackled has no clear boundaries, and especially where many participants are involved, it is not uncommon for the process of generating decision areas to develop a momentum of its own. Each new addition to the list can then prompt further suggestions; so that the process begins to appear a never-ending one. But once the list of decision areas reaches around fifteen or twenty — as in the example of Figure 35 — then questions will begin to arise as to whether it is useful to continue any further in this way. Participants may then well begin to ask whether, before thinking of any further additions, those decision areas already on the list should not be sorted or rearranged in some way, to identify possible overlaps and gaps in the problem formulation as it has shaped up so far.

One obvious way in which to begin to restructure a list of decision areas is to introduce some framework of *categories* of choice which are felt appropriate to the present decision setting. In a setting such as that of the South Side Working Party, for example, it might be felt that the decision areas in the list could be rearranged into broad fields of choice to do with transport, with land use, with finance and, perhaps, with other familiar functional areas such as housing, education, legal or personnel matters. In

FIGURE

36

SOUTH SIDE
EXAMPLE

Sorting Decision Areas by Categories and Levels

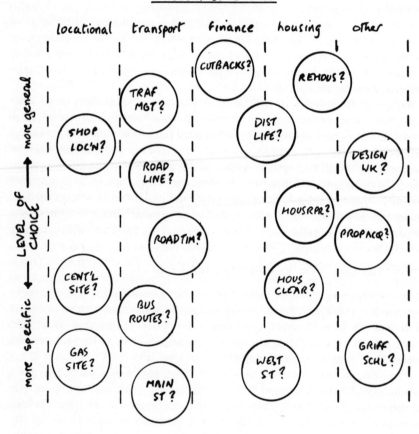

CATEGORY OF CHOICE

locational transport finance housing other

LEVEL OF CHOICE
more general
more specific

CUTBACKS?

REHOUS?

TRAF MGT?

DIST LIFE?

SHOP LOC'N?

DESIGN WK?

ROAD LINE?

HOUSRPR?

PROPACQ?

ROADTIM?

CENT'L SITE?

HOUS CLEAR?

BUS ROUTES?

GAS SITE?

GRIFF SCHL?

WEST ST?

MAIN ST?

SHAPING

SKILLS

It can be useful to rearrange decision areas by fields or levels — or both — whenever an unstructured list seems to be becoming too long or unwieldy. This can help in redefining or clustering similar decision areas; in considering the possibility of a multi-level problem structure; and in choosing a problem focus where there are many decision areas.

an industrial management context, the key functional areas might well be different, with categories such as production, marketing, purchasing, maintenance and product development forming the most natural frame of reference for the participants.

The differentiation of *levels* of choice offers another obvious means of sorting decision areas, especially where either the nature of the remit or the diversity of the participants leads to the generation of a list of decision areas some of which are expressed in more generalised terms than others. For example, in the list of Figure 35, the decision area about 'cutbacks in municipal spending' could be seen as impinging not just on South Side but on the population of the municipality as a whole; while that on investment in the continued life of the South Side district could be seen as clearly broader than that to do with the comparatively local West Street improvement issue.

Figure 36 illustrates one approach to the sorting of decision areas both according to category and to level of generality at the same time. Each decision area is here positioned, vertically, in relation to a spectrum ranging from the most specific operational choice to the most generalised choice of policy orientation. It is also located, horizontally, according to some set of functional categories which, for this purpose, need not be very precisely defined. These two dimensions can be marked out either on a large sheet of paper on a wall, or on a sufficiently large area of floor or table space, depending on the preferences of the group and the facilities of the room in which they are working. The use of floor or table space, with decision areas represented by movable cards, sheets of paper or discs, has the advantage that their positions can be shifted around easily, until the participants agree that the resulting layout represents a good enough 'map' as a basis for further shaping work. Of course, the same flexibility can be achieved on a wall, provided the technical problems of adhesion and easy re-positioning can be dealt with — but refinements in this direction are by no means an essential adjunct to the approach.

The main purpose of this sorting and positioning procedure is to build a broad picture of the overall *balance* of the set of decision areas so far generated; a picture within which it is possible to search for both overlaps and gaps. There may, for example, be very good reasons why, in Figure 36, there should be several comparatively specific transport decision areas, whereas the only financial decision areas seem to appear at the more generalised level: but at least it becomes possible to debate whether there are overlaps that should be eliminated or important gaps to be filled. Overlaps are, of course, especially likely to arise where some or all of the decision areas have been generated by individuals independently, rather than as part of a group process. Often, overlaps will point towards opportunities for more careful reformulation of decision areas, using the kind of guidelines to be discussed in the next section.

Where decision areas seem to be poorly balanced between levels, a useful way of proceeding is to review whether any of the comparatively specific decision areas can be thought of in terms of choices of *means* towards more general *ends*, or whether some of the more general ones can be thought of in terms of choice of ends, suggesting more specific choices of means. For example, the general CUTBACKS? decision area might, on reflection, suggest more specific choices to do with the relative severity with which any particular departmental budget or capital programme was to be cut back in a coming annual review cycle; while the specific issue of closure of the Griffin Road School might, on reflection, suggest broader areas of decision to do with educational re-organisation policy in a wider area.

This kind of ends/means investigation is likely, in practice, to cut across whatever divisions were agreed as a basis for organising decision areas into functional categories. For instance, choices about the closure of the Griffin Road School might be seen as leading towards broader policy choices beyond the field of education — especially if possible non-educational uses were being kept in view for the buildings or site, with implications for other policies and budgets.

Experience tends to indicate that categories are often simplest to distinguish in the middle range of the generality/specificity spectrum, while tending to converge both at the broad policy level, and in some cases at the level of specific local impact. So the vertical divisions in Figure 36 can be thought of as rather like lines of longitude on a globe, which gradually converge as they are extended upwards or downwards towards the polar regions where they meet.

As in the construction of an initial tentative list, one outcome of this process of sorting by levels and categories may be a growing recognition that some decision areas may be better expressed either as comparison areas or as uncertainty areas, so may be best set aside for later consideration in this light. Also, as in the preliminary listing process, it is important not to spend too long in re-sorting decision areas according to categories and levels; this is because of the connections *across* levels and categories which are of more fundamental importance to the work of the shaping mode.

Reformulating Decision Areas

For a group to establish momentum, it is good practice to formulate decision areas loosely and informally in the first instance, without worrying about the finer points of how they should be worded or the specific nature of the choices which may be available within each. However, this can mean bypassing definitional issues which can be of much importance in practical terms; and it can be well worth while returning to consider such issues more carefully once the participants in the process feel satisfied that they have built up a good enough set of decision areas to form the basis of an initial decision graph. This kind of pause for reformulation of individual decision areas will be particularly important where there appear to be overlaps between somewhat similar decision areas; overlaps which could be overcome by more careful formulation of what is meant, so that the decision areas can either be merged or else more clearly distinguished from each other.

There are two kinds of difficulty which often arise in the initial listing of decision areas, especially among people who have not previously been accustomed to thinking explicitly in decision area terms. One is that decision areas are confused with options within decision areas: for instance, the decision area described as 'West Street Improvement' could be read as the specific proposal to improve rather than the area of choice as to whether to improve or not. It is this kind of scope for misunderstanding that makes it useful to maintain the discipline of writing a question mark at the end of both the full description and the full label of every decision area.

The other source of confusion encountered in practice is a tendency to express decision areas in terms of choice of preferred state, rather than choice of preferred action. For instance, depending on the powers at the disposal of the decision-makers, it may be one thing to consider whether the vacant central site in South Side should be in residential or industrial use at some future time; yet quite a different thing to consider which zoning should be indicated on a local plan to be prepared and published as a guide to future development decisions. So 'choice of zoning' may be a more realistic phrasing than 'choice of use', when considered in relation to the levels of influence which the public decision-makers in South Side can actually bring to bear. The choice of *action* within their control may relate strictly speaking to the action of setting down a policy statement in print, accompanied by the action of shading a map in one tone rather than another; this act may have some influence over the way the land is used, but perhaps by no means the only influence once market pressures and other policy influences come to bear.

In some contexts, refinements in the expression of a decision area may not matter very much: but in others they may be crucial. In essence, the attempt to express decision areas in more careful and realistic terms involves looping outwards from the shaping mode towards the designing mode. It means thinking about options within decision areas, in order to arrive at a clearer view of the nature of the decision areas themselves. Figure 37 illustrates this point by offering some more careful formulations for five of the seventeen decision areas for South Side which were tentatively listed in Figure 35. These same five decision areas will also be found in the set of seven decision areas first presented to illustrate the general concept of a decision area (Figure 10). For that purpose, they were defined with more care than in the tentative listing of Figure 35, but with less precision than in Figure 37. This illustrates the general point that there is often considerable

FIGURE

37

Refining the Expression of Decision Areas

SOUTH SIDE
EXAMPLE

BRIEF INITIAL FORMULATION   MORE CAREFUL FORMULATION
(as in figure 35)

ROAD LINE?   which route to reserve on the South
                                   Side local plan map for the proposed
road line across South Side?   new arterial road?

SHOP LOC'N?   which site to designate in the South
                                   Side local plan as the location for
shopping centre location?   a more concentrated local shopping
                                   centre?

CENT'L SITE?   what type of land use to specify in
                                   the South Side local plan for the
use of central site?   central area of cleared housing land?

DIST LIFE?   what public statement to issue
                                   about level of intended investment in
investment in life   the continued life of South Side
of district?   as a residential district?

WEST ST?   whether or not to propose to the
                                   Housing Committee that the West
West street improvement?   Street area be added to the
                                   priority list for improvement
                                   area status?

SHAPING

SKILLS

It is worth giving some thought to the more careful formulation of particular decision areas if they appear to overlap with other decision areas, or if they appear at any time to be emerging as part of a problem focus for the design and comparison of alternatives. The operational meaning of decision areas can become especially crucial when it comes to the design of possible commitment packages.

scope for debate and judgement in the way any particular decision area is expressed.

The closer formulation of decision areas can be seen not just as a means of reaching a clearer understanding of problems, but as a check against wishful thinking — in particular, against the illusion that the participants are in a position to choose between end states, in situations where in reality they may have only limited opportunities for intervention or influence in relation to the decisions of others. So this kind of probing can lead into subtle distinctions between decision areas in terms of decision-making agencies and roles. In a situation such as that of South Side, for instance, there could be an important distinction between professional officers, who are expected to offer *recommendations* on particular matters, and a politically accountable council or committee, which has the power and the responsibility to accept, modify or reject these recommendations as a basis for executive *action*. Such distinctions can become crucial when turning to the work of the choosing mode, and when considering the design of commitment packages in particular. This means that any attempt to formulate decision areas more clearly in action terms can be seen as a form of looping outwards in the direction of the choosing mode.

Of course, too much reflection on such subtleties may inhibit progress in the construction of a decision graph. So again it is important to avoid becoming too deeply immersed in this kind of activity. However, in moving ahead it is important to record any progress which is made in the more exact formulation of decision areas — as in the example of Figure 37 — so that it is available for reference if and when required.

Introducing Links between Decision Areas

As was emphasised in Chapter 2, the drawing of a decision link between any pair of decision areas represents no more than a working assumption that it could make a difference if the choices available within those two decision areas were to be considered together rather than independently.

As in the generating of the decision areas themselves, it is useful to treat the introduction of decision links and the resulting build-up of a decision graph as a creative group process, in which one person begins by suggesting one or two obvious linkages, stimulating other participants to join in and suggest others. Where the number of decision areas is large, it can be advisable to defer this process until they have been arranged in terms of categories and levels, as in the example of Figure 36. However, it is more usual in practice to start from a set of decision areas which has not been arranged in this way, but can be extended and rearranged freely as the group interaction gathers momentum. Whichever approach is used, it is important to follow a *selective* approach to the introduction of decision links, omitting any which seem less significant than others. This is because a

FIGURE

38

SOUTH SIDE
EXAMPLE

Building up a Picture of Decision Links

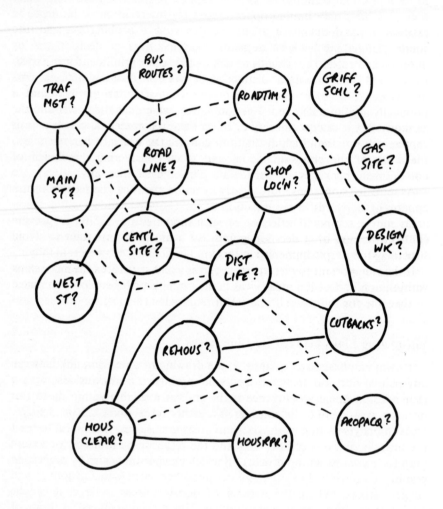

It is important to begin introducing links between decision areas at a comparatively early stage of work in the shaping mode, recognizing that many of the decision links will be only tentative at this stage. The pattern of decision links can if preferred be generated by using non-graphical methods, and the example from practice presented in figure 45 gives an example of an alternative matrix format.

decision graph can become hard to understand if it shows virtually every decision area as joined up to every other. Indeed, as soon as the pattern becomes as complex as this, it can quickly lose any value it might have had as a guide to the understanding of problem structure within the group.

Once the decision graph begins to take shape, a useful way to proceed is to look at each decision area in turn and ask which of the other decision areas — if any — are likely to affect it to a significant degree. It is only to be expected that doubts will arise from time to time over whether the connection between one decision area and another is clear enough or important enough to be shown as a link on a decision graph; and it is only to be expected that participants will disagree with each other over judgements of this kind. Where this happens, progress can be sustained by adding a broken line to the graph, to indicate an uncertain or debatable decision link, as shown in the example of Figure 38. Sometimes, indeed, it may be worth expressing more than one level of doubt about the status of decision links, for instance by distinguishing between broken lines and more tentative dotted lines which identify links of even more dubious status.

As more and more links are added to a decision graph, it usually becomes apparent that it would be helpful to redraw it with some of the decision areas moved across to different positions, so as to avoid or reduce the confusion caused by criss-crossing lines and thus to bring out the underlying structure of relationships more clearly.

If the aim were merely to represent the inherent structure of relationships within the graph — its topological structure to use mathematical language — there would be no need to spend time altering the positions of decision areas to avoid inelegant features of graphic design. However, because the purpose of the decision graph is primarily to facilitate communication within a group, the attempt to 'clean up' its representation can be well worthwhile in practice. A confused and untidy picture with many bent or intersecting lines can obscure aspects of problem structure which, with a little rearrangement, could be brought out much more clearly; and this in turn can help members of a group to identify possible clusters of decision areas which they might wish to explore more closely within an agreed problem focus. So it is worth at this point introducing some simple guidelines for rearrangement and clustering of decision areas within a decision graph.

Rearranging a Decision Graph

There are various working rules, some of them simple and obvious enough, which can be used as an aid to the reshaping of a complex decision graph. First, it is usually not hard to pick out any decision areas which have no more than one decision link connecting them to the rest of the graph, as

FIGURE

39

SOUTH SIDE
EXAMPLE

Rearranging a Decision Graph

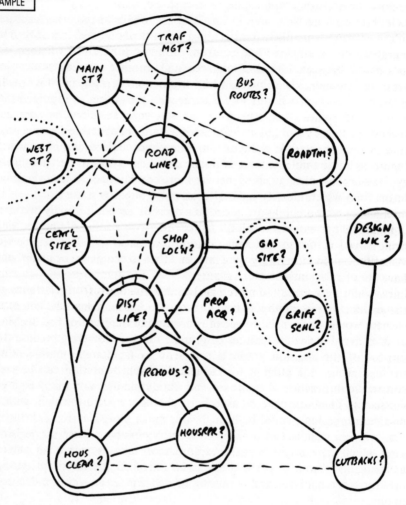

Where the structure of a decision graph is difficult to make out visually because there are too many decision links connecting decision areas which are far apart on the graph, it can be important to give time to the repositioning of at least some decision areas to bring out the underlying structure more clearly. It is useful to start by identifying more isolated decision areas and closely connected clusters.

in the case of WEST ST? in Figure 38. Sometimes, indeed, there may be one or two completely isolated decision areas which were originally seen as important when drawing up a preliminary list, but then turned out to have no links to other decision areas at all. There may also be 'chains' of decision areas — such as that connecting GRIFF SCH? and GAS SITE? to SHOP LOC'N? in Figure 38 — which have only limited connections with the rest of the problem structure. So a useful preliminary step in the restructuring of a graph is to identify such comparatively isolated parts and set them aside, as a step towards exploring more carefully the configuration of the decision areas that remain. Typically, there will be several 'triads' of three fully interlinked decision areas in a decision graph of any size. In Figure 38, for example, there are seven such triads, if only solid links are counted, and several more if broken links are counted as well. It will be less common to find totally connected clusters of four or more decision areas. However, in Figure 38 it is possible, with perseverance, to pick out three such clusters by eye, if broken as well as solid lines are counted. All three, it may be noted, incorporate the same ROAD LINE? decision area, which emphasises its importance to the overall problem structure.

Figure 39 presents the result of one attempt to re-draw the graph so as to bring out some of these structural features more clearly. Through the use of visual judgement and graphical dexterity alone, some of the decision areas have been shifted in position, mainly to reduce the number of criss-crossing lines, while preventing the more isolated decision areas from cluttering up the middle of the picture. Also, to identify closely linked clusters more clearly, boundary lines have been drawn round two clusters of four decision areas and one of five. Not all of these clusters include *totally* interconnected sets of decision areas, and there is no need to be rigid in this respect. What the clustering in Figure 39 does reveal is that there are three closely connected clusters which in this case connect up in a chain: an observation which offers an important aid in comprehending the overall structure of this particular graph.

It is not easy, nor perhaps too helpful, to try to codify more precisely the kind of rules to be used in this kind of structuring process. This is because any attempt to codify creates a need to agree more precisely what status a broken link should be given as compared with a solid link, and this may be to place too much meaning on what is intended as no more than a loose and informal convention for making assumptions about relatedness between decision areas. Yet it is always possible to develop and apply more precise codes of rules for the limited range of situations where this could be a worthwhile aid to the work of the shaping mode. For instance, decision links can always be formulated as yes/no or zero/one entries in a two-way table or *matrix* of mutual relationships between pairs of decision areas: and question marks or other symbols can then be introduced to represent doubtful links if desired. Then that matrix can be rearranged according to some set of logical rules which, in turn, may indicate how the decision graph could, with advantage, be redrawn.

Resort to such methods is most likely to be worthwhile in circumstances where a graph is so complex that visual inspection offers few clues to its underlying structure, so that any attempt to disentangle it without resort to a computer is likely to involve judgements of an arbitary and therefore misleading kind. In practice, experienced users of strategic choice methods usually stop well short of this level of elaboration in the size of a graph — not least because input of structural information to a computer can mean slowing down the pace of interactive working within a group.

Highlighting More Important Decision Areas

A decision graph may have to be rearranged more than once to bring out its structure as clearly as possible, and to draw attention to closely linked clusters without other decision areas getting in the way. However, this kind of structural information on its own cannot be expected to bring out all those characteristics of a problem situation which might be significant in choosing a more restricted problem focus or foci within which to switch to the work of the designing mode. In particular, the participants will often be aware that some decision areas are more important to them than others, in the sense that they represent choices where there is more at stake. Also, there may be some decision areas which may carry particular urgency even if they are not so significant in themselves — and it could be unwise to exclude these from any more restricted problem focus which the participants might choose.

It is always possible, however, to add information on importance, urgency or other considerations to a decision graph, by the simple device of introducing further symbols to highlight those decision areas which are believed to call for particular attention on any such grounds. Figure 40 illustrates how this can be done by simply adding to the graph various kinds of symbol to distinguish decision areas which the participants see as significant to them on different grounds. Here circles are marked in one way to indicate particular *urgency* of decision, and in another way to indicate particular *importance* in terms of their consequences. An asterisk is used to indicate decision areas within which there are thought to be comparatively *clear alternatives*, because these offer a prospect of straightforward progress when turning attention to the work of the designing mode. A different convention again is used in Figure 40 to highlight those individual decision areas which have a particularly high level of *connectedness* to other decision areas. The symbols chosen in this illustration are of a kind to allow them to be used in conjunction with each other, if necessary. So, for example, the CUTBACKS? decision area is identified as both urgent and important in its consequences; the ROAD

LINE? decision area is identified as both urgent and highly connected; the DIST LIFE? decision area, meanwhile, is identified as important in its consequences and also highly connected, if not thought to be so urgent at this stage.

The identification of highly connected or 'nodal' decision areas is of course one aspect of this process that can be carried out by working from the structural information contained in the decision graph itself. In the graph of Figure 40, it is not too hard to pick out ROAD LINE? and DIST LIFE? as the two most interconnected decision areas, as each has eight links to others, if the more doubtful links are included.

However, judgements about urgency and level of importance have to be made on the basis of information which comes not from the graph itself but from people's perceptions of the particular pressures and responsibilities that they face. It is, therefore, only to be expected that there will be differences of opinion as to relative urgency and importance where the participants are working as a group. There is no reason why different codings should not be used to pick out importance to different sets of interests; and when working with coloured marker pens, contrasting colours can always be used to build a richer picture than can be presented in a black and white diagram, such as that of Figure 40. For instance, one colour could be used to pick out decision areas of particular importance to local people in South Side, and another to pick out those of broader importance to the municipality as a whole, as a means of ensuring that neither perspective is lost sight of when it comes to choice of an agreed problem focus.

It is very much in the spirit of the strategic choice approach that differences of perspective should be debated openly within the group, while in the process of adding information on urgency and impact to the decision graph. In the course of such a discussion, specific arguments may emerge as to why one participant sees a decision area as urgent which another sees as not so urgent; or again, in the case of another decision area, it could emerge that one participant has foreseen that the choice could have serious importance for some sector of the community with which other participants were not so closely concerned. So the highlighting of more critical decision areas on the grounds either of urgency or importance can bring valuable benefits in terms of increased mutual understanding — involving as it does elements of anticipation of timing and evaluative considerations that the participants may wish to explore in more depth when it comes to future work in other modes.

Superimposing Organisational Responsibilities as a Decision Graph

A further type of consideration, which can be used to differentiate between decision areas within a decision graph, relates to the degree of influence or *control* which the participants expect to be able to exercise. In

FIGURE
40

SOUTH SIDE
EXAMPLE

Highlighting More Significant Decision Areas

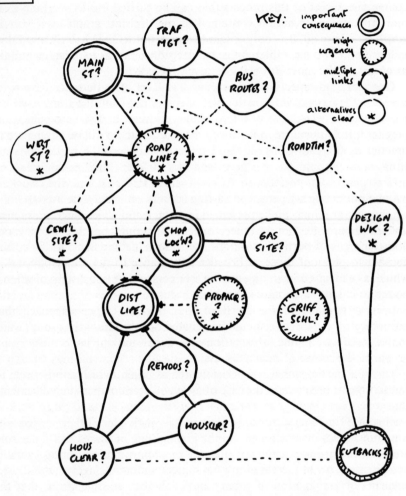

KEY: important consequences ◎
high urgency ⊙
multiple links ◯
alternatives clear ✳

Decision areas shown: TRAF MGT? · MAIN ST? · BUS ROUTES? · WEST ST? * · ROAD LINE? * · ROADTIM? · CENT'L SITE? * · SHOP LOC'N? * · GAS SITE? · DESIGN WK? * · DIST LIFE? · PROPNCR? * · GRIFF SCHL? · REHOUS? · HOUSCLR? · HOUS CLEAR? · CUTBACKS?

Where there are several possible problem foci within which work in other modes might be carried out, it becomes useful to use colour or other coding to highlight key decision areas on grounds of urgency, importance of consequences and any other such characteristics additional to those which are to be found in the structure of the decision graph itself.

South Side, for instance, the members of the working party might see themselves as collectively having a direct influence on the decision as to where the shopping centre for South Side should be located and, possibly, also on the choice of designated use for the central site. However, they might recognise that their influence was more limited when it came to recommendations on the line of the road; and their influence might be even more marginal in relation to the high-level corporate budgeting decisions which are implied by the CUTBACKS? decision area. Therefore, they might wish to discuss whether CUTBACKS? would be better reformulated as an uncertainty area instead of a decision area at this stage.

One means of reflecting judgements about relative influence or control is simply to designate another symbol with which to distinguish individual decision areas on a decision graph, along the lines of those used to indicate urgency and importance in Figure 40. This approach is indeed often used in practical applications of the strategic choice approach. However, in many situations it is useful to go further than this by distinguishing several different zones of *organisational responsibility* and influence, and to do this by superimposing a new set of boundary lines on the decision graph as a whole. For example, Figure 41 once more takes the overall decision graph arrived at for the South Side problem and superimposes three new sets of boundaries, to do with transport decisions; housing decisions; and financial decisions — each of these relating to a zone of organisational responsibility which is recognised in this particular decision setting. Such organisational boundaries will sometimes overlap; and both the patterns of overlap and the patterns of decision links across the boundaries can then reveal much about the issues of inter-departmental or perhaps inter-corporate co-ordination that would arise if any particular set of decision areas were chosen as a prospective problem focus.

The kind of information used to develop the graph in this way will often be similar to that used to sort a preliminary list of decision areas into functional categories, as illustrated in Figure 36. So the results of any earlier work in sorting decision areas by categories can be drawn on in the process of superimposing a map of organisational responsibilities onto a decision graph. However, it is important to stress that the decision graph is intended *primarily* as a picture of problem structure rather than organisational responsibilities. Its value in organisational terms is that it can be expected to highlight issues of co-ordination which could have remained hidden had the process of problem formulation been carried through in a more traditional way.

Of course, there is a danger that the introduction onto the same decision graph of information about organisational boundaries, on top of all the other information it contains, will present the participants with too rich and complex a picture for them to comprehend in its entirety. This is why Figure 41 — while highlighting particular decision areas as in Figure 40 — omits the cluster boundaries which appeared earlier in Figure 39. However, when

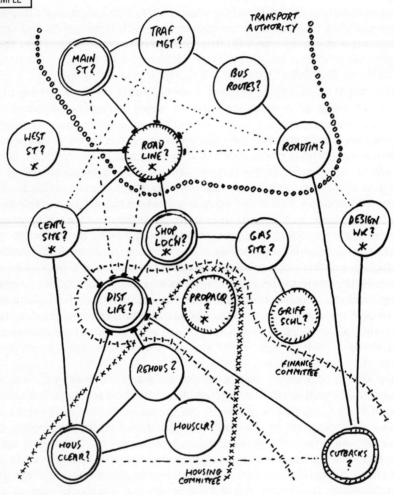

It is often important in practice to distinguish between different areas of
organisational or departmental responsibility in the manner indicated above,
using different coloured boundaries where possible. This can help in considering
who should participate in the work of other modes, and in what ways linkages to
the work of other parties might be maintained.

a decision graph is being built up on a large sheet of paper on a wall, the risk of confusion can again be much reduced through the use of contrasting colours to distinguish different sets of boundaries. For colour distinctions have a much clearer impact than distinctions among lines containing various patterns of dots, dashes and crosses, as used in Figure 41. Furthermore, they take less time to draw, which can be a significant factor where there is a momentum of group interaction to be sustained.

Considerations in Choice of a Problem Focus

The work done in adding all this further information to a decision graph can offer a basis either for further rearrangement and reformulation or — once the participants are satisfied that they have a good enough representation of the problems before them — for moving on to look more closely at choices within selected parts of the graph. It is only if the graph as a whole contains no more than four or, at most, five decision areas that a group — or for that matter an individual — is likely to find it useful to move into the work of the designing mode without limiting the problem focus in some way. To attempt to explore combinations of options within a set of more than five decision areas is to risk moving into a depth of analysis which can be very time-consuming and, as experience shows, only rarely productive in terms of the progress to which it leads.

Indeed, it is advisable to err on the side of too narrow a problem focus in the early stages of analytical work, by choosing a set of no more than three linked decision areas — perhaps two, or even only one. Alternatives can be carefully developed and compared within that focus before attempting to broaden the problem focus out again, possibly by introducing only one additional decision area at a time.

In the original example used to illustrate the concept of problem focus — Figure 13 of Chapter 2 — the choice of focus was a simple one. For there were only seven decision areas in all, and three of those clearly occupied comparatively outlying positions. But, when a set of participants is presented with a more complex picture, such as that of Figure 41, where should the process of choosing one or more foci for more intensive analysis begin? This judgement must inevitably depend on the context, as it is only the participants themselves who are in a position to judge what weight to give to decision areas they have marked as urgent compared to those they have marked as important or easier to influence; and it is only they who will be able to appraise the advantages to be obtained through working at clusters of issues which cut across departmental or corporate boundaries. Furthermore, it is only they who can weigh these advantages against any possible political difficulties they foresee, drawing on their own knowledge of the history of working relationships — good, bad or indifferent — between the individuals, professions or organisational units concerned.

FIGURE
42

SOUTH SIDE
EXAMPLE

Selecting Multiple Problem Foci

PROBLEM FOCUS
SELECTED FOR TECHNICAL
WORK BY TRANSPORT
SPECIALISTS

TRAF
MGT?

MAIN
ST?

BUS
ROUTES?

WEST
ST?
*

ROAD
LINE?
*

ROADTIM?

CENT'L
SITE?
*

SHOP
LOC'N?

GAS
SITE?

DESIGN
WK?
*

PROBLEM FOCUS
SELECTED FOR
FURTHER WORK
BY SOUTH SIDE
WORKING
PARTY

DIST
LIFE?

PROPACQ
?
*

GRIFF
SCHL?

REHOUS?

HOUSCLR?

HOUS
CLEAR?

CUTBACKS?

It becomes useful to distinguish more than one problem focus within a decision graph in any situation where it is possible to identify areas for more specialized analysis; where it is desired to define tasks for sub-groups of a large working group; or where there is a concern to schedule a succession of linked analytical task over a period of time.

In some situations, there is a case for adopting not just one problem focus but two or more, on which different groups of people can work simultaneously. This possibility is illustrated in Figure 42. Here it is supposed that it has been agreed in South Side to adopt two overlapping problem foci as a basis for deeper investigation. One of these contains four of the five linked decisions within the transport sphere of responsibility, so is likely to raise comparatively few organisational difficulties. Within this particular problem focus it is quite possible that the work of the designing mode can be treated as a purely technical exercise — though the work of comparing and choosing may still involve challenges of a wider political nature.

The second problem focus — which the reader may recognise as corresponding exactly to the set of four decision areas selected as the original problem focus in Chapter 2 — overlaps with the first focus in that it contains the ROAD LINE? decision area. It includes one urgent decision area and two of high importance, along with one other decision area which is connected to all these three. Three of the four decision areas are marked as containing reasonably clear alternatives; but the fourth, DIST LIFE?, is a broader policy-level decision area which presents more difficulties in this respect. This problem focus, in contrast to the other, does not lie entirely within a well-defined field of organisational responsibility; so it might well be agreed that the South Side Working Party, or some sub-group of those concerned, would afford the most appropriate setting for the next stages of the work.

It will be noticed in Figure 42 that some urgent and important decision areas are still omitted from either focus. So questions will, of course, arise as to what should be done about them — especially the more urgent ones. It may be agreed that some urgent decision areas such as PROPACQ? can best be explored further on their own at this stage, in effect forming a 'focus of one' in terms of the problem focus concept. And it may be that other decision areas such as HOUSCLEAR? and CUTBACKS? raise issues which can hardly be tackled without taking various wider organisational relationships into account. So it might be agreed that any deeper consideration of these issues should be set aside by the members of the South Side Working Party at this stage, accepting that they might wish to return to them in later work.

Summary: Process Judgements in the Shaping Mode

There is not much which is inherently difficult in the concepts of the decision area and the decision link, which have remained as the basic building blocks of the approach to shaping of problems throughout this chapter. Where the challenge lies is in applying these simple concepts to the representation of complex problems, in such a way as to capture as much as possible of the understanding of these problems which is to be found among the participants; to bring out differences of view wherever these are significant; and to help them find ways of moving forward towards an agreed collective view.

Because the concepts and tools used when working in this mode are simple in themselves, it is possible to take on board more complexity in the dimensions of the decision problems being looked at than would be the case with more sophisticated methods. So it can be quite realistic in practice to build up a decision graph containing twenty or even more decision areas, within which more limited foci for further analysis can be picked out, using some combination of the methods illustrated in this chapter. This is not, however, to say that it will invariably be useful to build up a graph of that size or complexity. If it is readily agreed that a problem can be represented in terms of only four or five important areas of choice — or indeed only one or two — there is no point in striving to make its representation more complex.

When working in the shaping mode, one of the few opportunities there is for moving to greater elaboration in analytical methods lies in the use of matrix conventions for representing the structure of a decision graph. Such methods were briefly touched on earlier in the discussion of ways of rearranging a complex decision graph and identifying clusters of closely linked decision areas. This kind of approach can occasionally be useful in a situation where a decision graph contains such a complex pattern of links that it is unclear from visual inspection alone how it could be rearranged to bring out its inherent structure more clearly; and where there are, therefore, dangers that human bias will play a significant part in its interpretation. In such cases, computer methods can be used to search rapidly for clusters and lines of partition according to whatever rules of structure it is desired to use. The results of such analysis will, however, often be sensitive to the choice of assumptions about where links do and do not exist. So there arises the possibility of using the computer as a means of *sensitivity analysis* in relation to changes in the structure of a graph, including the interpretation of doubtful decision links.

Here, as in other aspects of the strategic choice technology, the essential point is that depth of analysis can be treated as a variable to be controlled. Yet, experience shows that the creativity of the process of shaping problems is best sustained by keeping the level and methods of analysis as simple as possible, especially when working in groups. This is because it keeps the process open and transparent, and provides flexibility for changes in formulation as the work proceeds. For instance, it may be only after a comparatively complex graph has been gradually built up on the wall, by collective effort, that there is a shared basis for discussing what new decision areas might be added, and whether existing ones should be merged or expressed in different ways. The obvious next step will then be to start again on a clean sheet of paper, keeping the earlier version as a secondary record of the process rather than throwing it away. It is quite common for a group to go through many different formulations of a decision graph, before they can agree it offers a good enough basis for moving ahead. But such recycling of effort will only be creative if there is a shared sense that those involved are continually making progress in terms of mutual understanding of the underlying problem structure.

Figure 43 summarises the main points of this chapter, with reference to the concepts of *switching and looping* as explained in Chapter 4 (Figure 32). The types of judgements to be made within the shaping mode include not only choices of appropriate depth of analysis when working within that mode, but choices of when and how to move on into any of the other modes. Where some subset of linked decision areas has emerged as a useful problem focus, then the obvious next step is to move into the *designing mode* and, whether through AIDA or other methods, to search for feasible combinations of options among the decision areas concerned. But it is always possible that attention will be quickly drawn to just one crucial decision area, where the options are already clear cut; in that case, it may be possible to move directly to an examination of the consequences of those options within the *comparing mode*. Then, if there is little doubt which option is to be preferred, it may be possible to move almost straight away into the *choosing mode*, where a commitment to act on that particular option can be made. This describes the kind of fast route through a decision process which is often followed by an individual working on hunch or experience; but it is less characteristic of groups formed to work on difficult decision problems, the consequences of which for other interests may be profound.

If two or more different problem foci have been identified within a large decision graph, then the process can, of course, be carried forward by agreeing to move from the shaping mode into more than one of these other modes, more or less simultaneously — perhaps by sub-dividing the working group for this purpose, provided that the case for some continuing linkage between their activities is kept in view.

Apart from indicating the various possibilities for switching out of the shaping mode, Figure 43 also shows three shorter loops which represent brief excursions in the direction of the other three modes, while continuing to work primarily within the shaping mode. For instance, any attempt to formulate decision areas more precisely, in terms of the kinds of alternative actions likely to be available, involves a loop in the direction of identifying options — and therefore towards the task of the *designing mode*. Any attempt to balance a set of decision areas according to some framework of categories or levels, as in Figure 36, means looping in the direction of the *comparing mode*, because the broader levels of choice offer a potential evaluative framework. The highlighting of especially important decision areas within a decision graph can also be seen as a form of looping in the

FIGURE
43

Process Choices when Working in the Shaping Mode

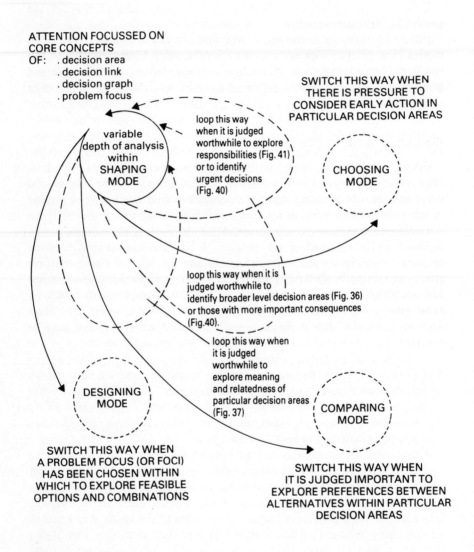

ATTENTION FOCUSSED ON
CORE CONCEPTS
OF: . decision area
         . decision link
         . decision graph
         . problem focus

SWITCH THIS WAY WHEN
THERE IS PRESSURE TO
CONSIDER EARLY ACTION IN
PARTICULAR DECISION AREAS

loop this way
when it is judged
worthwhile to explore
responsibilities (Fig. 41)
or to identify
urgent decisions
(Fig. 40)

variable
depth of analysis
within
SHAPING
MODE

CHOOSING
MODE

loop this way when it is
judged worthwhile to
identify broader level decision areas (Fig. 36)
or those with more important consequences
(Fig.40).

loop this way when
it is judged
worthwhile to
explore meaning
and relatedness of
particular decision areas
(Fig. 37)

DESIGNING
MODE

COMPARING
MODE

SWITCH THIS WAY WHEN
A PROBLEM FOCUS (OR FOCI)
HAS BEEN CHOSEN WITHIN
WHICH TO EXPLORE FEASIBLE
OPTIONS AND COMBINATIONS

SWITCH THIS WAY WHEN
IT IS JUDGED IMPORTANT TO
EXPLORE PREFERENCES BETWEEN
ALTERNATIVES WITHIN PARTICULAR
DECISION AREAS

SHAPING

SUMMARY

direction of the comparing mode. Meanwhile, the highlighting of more urgent decision areas on the decision graph tends to involve looping out towards the *choosing mode*; so does the superimposing of different organisational domains where responsibilities for action lie.

This brief review of relationships with other modes only serves to emphasise the underlying unity of the process of strategic choice. It is important to stress the value of making these choices of movement between modes in a flexible, evolutionary way, rather than feeling constrained to conform to any more rigid and prescriptive sequence of operations. Some practical guide-lines to help in managing this wider adaptive process will be offered in Chapter 9.

Illustrations from Practice

On the three double pages that follow, the reader will find a set of three contrasting *illustrations from practice* which have been chosen to supplement the points about skills in shaping which have already been made in this chapter with reference to the South Side problem.

The illustrations are taken from applications in very different contexts — in Brazil, in Britain and in the Netherlands. The first includes photographs of people in action, to give at least some impression of the way decision graphs can be built up and reshaped through interactive group working. The second illustrates some alternative ways of presenting information about the patterns of links between decision areas, while the third demonstrates how simple forms of ends-means mapping can be used to generate decision areas and to explore relationships between levels.

FIGURE 44

Illustration from Practice – Shaping 1

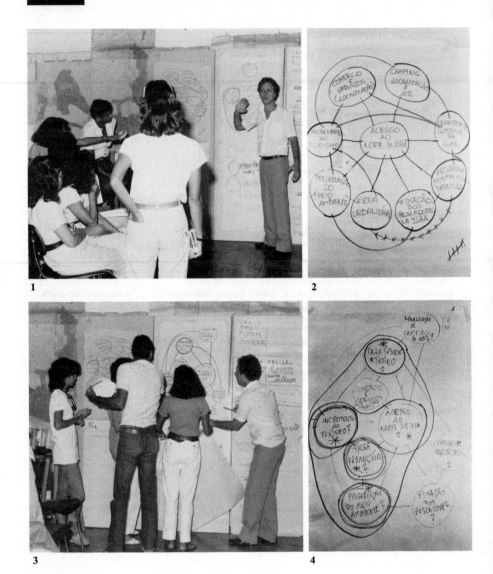

SHAPING / **PRACTICE**

Theme: Group Interaction in Problem Structuring using Decision Graphs to find a Working Focus.

Problem: Policy Formulation in a Comprehensive Development Plan for an Offshore Island.

Context: Five-Day Workshop with a Local Inter-Disciplinary Planning Team, Recife, Brazil, 1984.

COMMENTARY ON FIGURE 44

These photographs were taken during the second day of a five-day workshop held in November 1984 in Recife, in the tropical north-east of Brazil. The task was to apply strategic choice methods to the exploration of alternative land-use, economic, social and infrastructure policies for the offshore island of Itamaracá in the Recife Metropolitan Planning Region. This island, with an area of about 60 square kilometres and a permanent population of around 8,000, was connected to the mainland by a road bridge and had become subject to intense pressures for development, which had to be reconciled with concerns about the conservation of the natural environment and of the islanders' traditional way of life.

The group which participated in the workshop included members of an interdisciplinary planning team from FIDEM, the metropolitan planning agency, two of whom were attached to the island's local municipal council. The process was facilitated by two Brazilians who were already familiar with the strategic choice approach, with John Friend as visiting consultant. The workshop was jointly sponsored by FIDEM, the Federal University of Pernambuco, the State Transportation Department and the British Council.

The two decision graphs on the wall in the top left photograph are shown in detail to the right (2 and 4). The first was developed by focussing on a single important decision area selected from an initial set of about 60 — concerned with choice of road access to the undeveloped north of the island — then identifying and adding in eight other decision areas directly connected to it, and inserting the cross-links between these. On the second decision graph, this set of nine decision areas was rearranged to bring out clusters more clearly, and different colour codings and symbols were used to highlight decision areas of special significance on grounds of urgency and importance (the codings being listed on the wall on a sheet below the graph itself).

Of particular interest in this case was the use of different colours to pick out decision areas not only of metropolitan importance, but also those of particular local importance to the islanders themselves. This distinction was made in response to a concern among some members of the group that the analysis might ignore issues about which the residents themselves were concerned. There was a great deal of lively discussion over the choice of a problem focus for further analysis, as shown in the second group photograph (3) — where the second decision graph has just been replaced by a redrawn version showing the pattern of links rather more clearly.

It was later agreed to explore and compare alternatives within a focus of three decision areas chosen with both metropolitan importance and importance to the islanders in view. A later stage in the comparison of alternatives within this focus is illustrated in Figure 69 of Chapter 7.

FIGURE
45

Illustration from Practice – Shaping 2

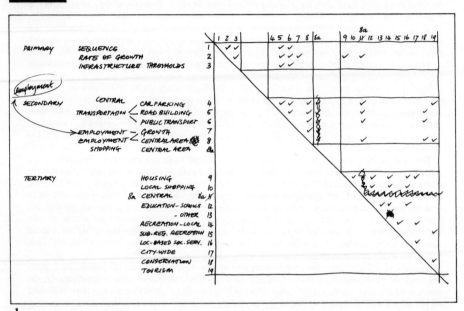

1

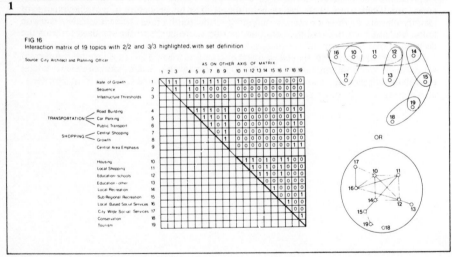

2

SHAPING

PRACTICE

Theme: Use of Alternative Forms of a Decision Graph in Sorting Decision Areas by Levels and Clusters.

Problem: Preparation of a Structure Plan as a Policy Framework for an Historic City.

Context: Planning Teams from the City of Worcester and the County of Hereford and Worcester, England, 1973 – 74.

COMMENTARY ON FIGURE 45

This illustration demonstrates some alternative ways of representing the pattern of links between decision areas, and also shows the emergence of different levels of concern. It is taken from working papers and documents produced by the policy planning team for the historic city of Worcester, England, with a population of 70,000 and problems of both congestion and expansion to be tackled. At that time — 1973/4 — responsibility for the City's first statutory Structure Plan was about to pass from the City Council to the newly-created County Council of Hereford and Worcester, but continuity was maintained because the same team now took on a similar role for the county as a whole.

Having previously investigated various systematic design methods, the team had come across the AIDA approach, and had contacted IOR for assistance. After initially working as consultants to the City Council, the IOR staff involved were able to launch a broader action research programme on Structure Plans with several participating counties, including Hereford and Worcester, and with development funding from the national Department of the Environment.

The first triangular table opposite, taken from a rough working document, illustrates a first attempt to explore the structure of links for a set of 19 decision areas which were then seen as relevant, sorted into three levels of generality labelled primary, secondary and tertiary. There is some evidence here of reformulation in progress — in particular, a judgement that the decision area on central shopping should be transferred from the tertiary to the secondary level. Only half the full 19 × 19 table has been completed, because the two-way nature of the concept of a decision link (reflected here by a tick or check) means that the full table would be symmetrical about the diagonal line.

The lower illustrations come from a more formal document, and show some further ways of presenting the same structural information. On the left, the triangular matrix is simply presented in a tidier form, with each cell marked either by 1 or 0 according to whether or not a direct decision link is assumed to exist. To the right of this matrix will be seen two different graphical representations for the set of internal links within the set of ten tertiary decision areas, numbered 10 to 19 for reference purposes. The upper picture uses set boundaries to identify clusters of three or more totally connected decision areas as well as other pairwise links, while the network representation underneath corresponds to the standard form of the decision graph as introduced in Chapter 2.

The Worcester Structure Plan work was the first application of strategic choice methods in which elected councillors were explicitly involved in the review of policy alternatives formulated in this way. After the project was completed, the strategic choice approach was also used for several other policy-planning projects within the county.

FIGURE
46

Illustration from Practice – Shaping 3

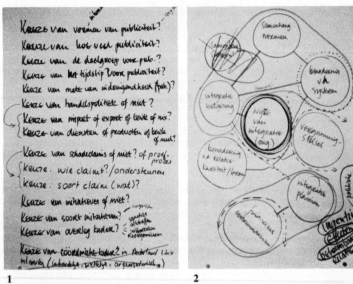

1

2

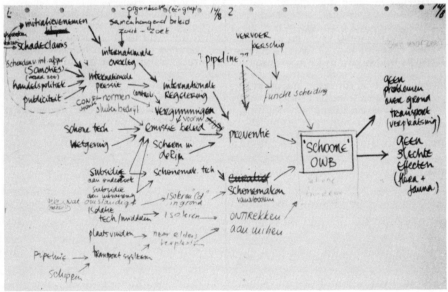

3

Theme: Use of Ends-Means Mapping to identify Decision Areas which are then analyzed to find a Problem Focus.

Problem: Disposal of Accumulated Polluted Silts dredged from the Rhine Delta.

Context: Inter-Ministerial Government Working Group, Den Haag, The Netherlands, 1985.

COMMENTARY ON FIGURE 46

These papers were made during one of the middle sessions in a series of exploratory workshops held in Den Haag, The Netherlands, in the period May to August, 1985. The project was set up to explore the extent of the problem, and the feasibility of inter-ministerial working in this case. It also formed part of an action-research project aimed at developing ways of managing uncertainty in environmental decision-making.

The problem centred on recent findings about heavy metals in the sediments lying under Holland's extensive water surfaces. Particular urgency created a focus on the Rhine estuary. Here a deep passage has to be kept clear to the harbour of Rotterdam. Unfortunately the sludge is replaced by the river currents almost as fast as it is removed. Thus to stop dredging is no solution — and there is an immediate need for a decision as to where to place the removed sludge. Sources of the pollution are known to extend far up the Rhine and its tributaries so there are international aspects to be taken into account also.

The working group was formed from various directorates of the Rijkswaterstaat (traffic, waterways and water supply) and the Ministry of VROM (housing, physical planning and environment), with Allen Hickling as Process Consultant.

The ends/means mapping (3) provided a way of helping the group to focus at several levels on what could be done to manage the situation. Thus, starting with "clean underwater soils" (in the rectangle), the first means to be identified included prevention, cleaning and isolation of the toxic sludge. Ends (to the right in the diagram) were very broad, including the elimination of bad effects on flora and fauna. The next level down (to the left in the diagram) brings out possibilities with respect to the technology for cleaning, policy over emissions, approvals — and, of course, the international dimension. These lead to more specific issues of law-making, subsidies, publicity, transportation and so on.

The list of decision areas (1) was one of those developed out of the ends-means activity. The two first words of each line demonstrate the discipline of using "choice of" ("Keuze van" in Dutch) as the opening phrase of all descriptions of decision areas. In this case they are mostly associated with publicity, claims for damages, various initiatives, and (at the bottom) one which is crossed out because it was thought to be too all-embracing and in need of working out in more detail.

This was done in the decision graph (2) next to the list of decision areas. The messiness of the chart is typical of work done when the learning process is going quickly. The analysis to find a working focus was by use of the basic decision-making criteria of urgency, impact, controllability and connectedness. Two candidates for such a focus can be identified — a cluster of three decision areas at the top of the chart, and a set of two at the bottom. In fact the upper one was chosen, together with the very important central decision area concerning different ways of integrating the organisations involved.

6

Skills in Designing

Introduction

In Chapter 2, the set of concepts for shaping complex problems led into the introduction of a further set of concepts for designing feasible courses of action within any selected problem focus. These further concepts together provided a set of foundations for a design method — Analysis of Interconnected Decision Areas, or AIDA — which could be applied quite generally to any problem that could be expressed in terms of multiple areas of choice, however diverse these might be.

This chapter will build on those foundations by discussing the challenges which can arise in applying the conventions of AIDA to untidy decision problems, and the types of judgement which are called for in meeting these challenges in practice. The chapter will draw on working experience in applying strategic choice methods to problems of many different kinds. Although a number of elaborations of the basic concepts and techniques will be introduced, it is not intended to suggest that these forms of elaboration are always either necessary or desirable: it is simply that they are available to the skilled user of the strategic choice approach, wherever they can be of help in overcoming practical difficulties as they arise.

The principal advantage of the AIDA method of problem formulation is that it can allow many different kinds and levels of choice to be expressed in the same general language. So it offers a means of opening up the process of problem structuring to participants who may see the elements of a decision situation from quite different professional or representative perspectives. Its strength is that it has no inherent bias towards any particular frame of reference, whether financial, locational, engineering, marketing, administrative, political — or, indeed, anything else.

This high level of generality is, however, only achieved at a cost. For it may be necessary to accept quite drastic simplifications when striving to represent complex design choices in terms of once-and-for-all decision areas, with a finite range of discrete options within each. There are, of course, other design methods which offer the possibility of overcoming these constraints — but usually these mean moving to a more specialised frame of reference, so as to view the problem primarily — for example — as one of engineering design; or of land-use planning; or of financial budgeting; or of scheduling a set of interconnected activities through time.

More specialised approaches to problem structuring can, of course, have an important place in practice, especially within management contexts where similar kinds of choice tend to arise recurrently over time. Choices can then often be expressed in terms of repeated adjustments to continuous control variables, rather than choices between discrete options within more transient decision areas. The AIDA approach to problem structuring was not developed with these comparatively well-structured management situations in view. Nevertheless, situations sometimes arise when it can be used to complement, rather than replace, more refined methods of problem structuring within particular specialist frameworks. Indeed, an initial quick analysis of options and relationships within the simplified conventions of AIDA can often form a useful prelude to deeper analysis by other methods. Its particular value can lie in opening up the debate about problem structure to a wider set of participants, and affording a clearer perspective of how far more specialist examination of particular parts of the problem may, or may not, be justified when set against the pressures for decision which the participants currently face.

Identifying Sets of Options within Decision Areas

In generating a set of options within a decision area, the most important consideration is that they should be mutually exclusive; that the choice of any one option should foreclose the choice of any of the others. In an idealised, analytical world, such a set of options should, where possible, also be exhaustive: in other words, it should be a complete list of all the possible courses of action available. But in practice, this may be quite an unrealistic condition to impose, and it is usually necessary to settle for a set of options which is agreed to be *representative* of the full range of choice available, rather than one which covers every conceivable possibility.

For instance, in South Side, it might be possible to think of other lines for the new road apart from the northern and southern routes which were identified earlier (Figure 14). It could equally be possible to conceive further locations for the proposed shopping centre, or other quite different uses for the central site. Turning towards the broader policy decision on level of public investment in South Side, this was expressed in terms of choice of time horizon; and the choice of time horizon is one which could, of course, be regarded as a continuous variable, to be extended more or less indefinitely into the future. So the question arises here of whether the particular horizons of ten, twenty and forty years are to be considered sufficiently representative of the full range of alternatives available in practice.

It may be that this is readily agreed to be so — perhaps because, in the municipality responsible for South Side, these represent familiar periods of amortisation for different kinds of capital assets. Yet any such assumption can always be challenged, debated and then modified if the participants agree.

Figure 47 illustrates the process of questioning which is involved in reviewing whether or not additional options should be included — a process which can be conducted either purely within an individual's head, or through interactive debate within a group. Whatever the method of search may be, it can be useful in practice to keep a record of possible options which have been considered but excluded, with reasons for the exclusion noted as in Figure 47. These options can always be reintroduced at a later stage if a case for doing so can be made.

The examples of possible additional options which appear in Figure 47 — relating to each of the four decision areas which were chosen as an inital problem focus (Figure 13) — illustrate various types of consideration which can arise in judging whether a proposed set of options is both representative and mutually exclusive. In the case of ROAD LINE?, for instance, the question arises of whether what is sometimes called a *null option* should be included, to reflect the possibility of building no new road at all. In this case, the null option is supposed to be excluded because of the particular brief given to the South Side Working Party: but of course this brief could, at any stage, be changed and the list of options modified accordingly. As will be seen later, the possibility of null options can arise again, more directly, when working in the choosing mode, when possibilities for deferring choice into the future begin to come to the fore.

Another question that can sometimes arise in practice is whether or not an option should be included when it is *uncertain* whether or not the conditions will occur which would make it possible. In Figure 47, this question arises in the case of the football ground as a possible location for the new shopping centre; and the assumption is recorded that this option should be excluded for now, possibly to be reintroduced at a later stage. Turning to the review of the DIST LIFE? decision area in Figure 47, it will be noticed that the 40-year option has been taken to *represent* the 60-year horizon, on the grounds that this possible additional option is believed to be broadly similar to the 40-year option in its consequences, and also in its pattern of option bars. Indeed, this latter test casts doubt on whether it is even necessary to distinguish between the 20- and 40-year options; for a glance back to Figure 16 will show that these two options are identical in their patterns of option bars within the chosen problem focus.

Reformulating Decision Areas containing Composite Options

Another situation often encountered in practice is that in which doubts arise as to whether the initial list of options can realistically be considered as

DECISION AREA	OPTIONS	FURTHER OPTIONS?	COMMENT
ROAD LINE?	-NORTH -SOUTH	-MIDDLE ROUTE?	not feasible without massive demolition, so EXCLUDE
		-NO NEW ROAD AT ALL?	possibility not at present being considered, so EXCLUDE (re-introduce later?)
SHOP LOC'N?	-MAIN -KING -GAS	-FOOTBALL GROUND SITE?	only possible if club decides to move. Looks unlikely, so EXCLUDE for now
CENT'L SITE?	-IND -HOUS -OPEN	-MIXED USE OPTIONS?	some possibility that housing in West of site could be combined with either open space or (light) industry in East. Possibly INCLUDE composite options in later design work
DIST LIFE?	-10 YRS -20 YRS -40 YRS	-LONGER SPAN? (eg 60 YRS)	similar to 40 YR option in consequences & option Bars, so EXCLUDE
		-SHORTER SPAN? (eg 5 YRS)	politically inconceivable because of promises to residents, so EXCLUDE

DESIGNING

SUMMARY

Both when first identifying options within decision areas, and at intervals thereafter, it is useful to question briefly whether any additional options should be included to make the set of options more representative of the full range of choice available. This is often done verbally and informally, but a record of arguments for exclusion or inclusion can provide a useful point of reference for later.

mutually exclusive — or whether, perhaps, some mixture of one option and another might be possible. For instance, in the case of the CENT'L SITE? decision area in South Side, the question could arise — as was suggested in Figure 47 — of whether it is possible to combine different uses on the same site and, if so, which particular combinations of use might be possible.

If the possibility of such 'composite' options arises, then it can be important to explore more carefully what the full range of possibilities might be. For instance, if it were possible to mix housing and industrial uses on the central site, could this imply an integrated design in which housing and light industry might be closely woven together throughout the site? Or would physical or other considerations suggest that housing should be sited towards one end and industry towards the other? Would different proportional mixes be possible, and how far could these different possibilities be reflected in the reformulation of options within the decision area?

The answers to such questions might sometimes depend on technicalities such as soil and drainage conditions, or on structural factors such as existing land uses on other or adjacent sites. Figure 48 illustrates one simple way of dealing with this kind of complexity, which involves simply dividing up the original decision area into two more specific decision areas. In this example, the composite options within the CENT'L SITE? decision area in South Side have been dealt with by defining two simpler decision areas covering the western and eastern parts of the site respectively.

Whether this is a realistic and a useful way of reformulating the choices available will often depend on an understanding of local realities. In this case, it is assumed that the site is such that a division into two parts along some east/west boundary line makes sense. The new formulation embodies an assumption — which can always be challenged and reviewed at any time — that industrial use in the west is incompatible with housing in the east. Whether the opposite combination is possible is supposed, in this case, to be more doubtful; and this is indicated by a broken line connecting the option of housing in the west to the option of industry in the east. So this example introduces a new convention: a tentative or *uncertain option bar*, represented by a broken line connecting the options in question. So, a broken line is used to express a feeling of uncertainty over the existence of an option bar — just as it was used to express uncertainty over existence of a decision link when working in the shaping mode.

The expansion of a decision area into two or more linked decision areas, in order to arrive at a clearer formulation of composite options, means re-examining any option bars which might have linked the original decision area to others in the wider problem focus. For example, it could be that those bars in Figure 16 which originally excluded the combination of industrial use on the central site with the option of the southern road line, and also with the option of the King Street shopping location, apply to industrial uses at one end of the central site but not necessarily at the other.

FIGURE

48

SOUTH SIDE
EXAMPLE

Reformulating Decision Areas with Composite Options

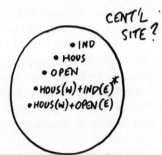

CENT'L SITE?

• IND
• HOUS
• OPEN
• HOUS(W)+IND(E)*
• HOUS(W)+OPEN(E)

* feasibility of this
option uncertain:
to be examined
further

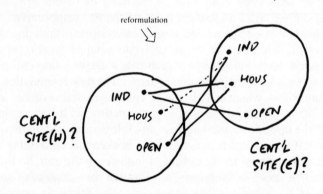

reformulation

CENT'L
SITE(W)?

IND
HOUS
OPEN

IND
HOUS
OPEN

CENT'L
SITE(E)?

--- indicates uncertain option bar

Occasionally, it is helpful to examine the possibility of breaking a decision area down into two or more separate but connected decision areas, especially if the number of possible options is large and some of them appear to be composite in form. Such a reformulation can help in examining whether the set of alternatives indicated is fully representative, and in exploring structural assumptions.

Recording Assumptions behind the Inclusion of Option Bars

There are many possible grounds for making a judgement that some pair of options from linked decision areas should be viewed as incompatible. Sometimes, the incompatibility will arise from the inherent logic of the situation. For instance, one option within the decision area about the use of the gasworks site (Figure 10), might relate to its development as the location of the new district shopping centre. This option would then be logically incompatible with any option in the SHOP LOC'N? decision area which involved locating the new centre in Main Street, at King Square or on any other conceivable site apart from the gasworks site itself.

Often, however, option bars are used to rule out combinations which are not so much incompatible in strict logical terms, but agreed to be undesirable on other grounds; perhaps because they may violate some agreed policy, or because they are thought likely to incur consequences which are agreed to be unacceptable. For example, there might be some design configurations for South Side which would present such severe engineering difficulties that they could only be overcome at unthinkable expense — for example, by the construction of a tunnel or deep cutting for the proposed new arterial highway.

The assumptions behind the inclusion of different option bars may be many and varied, and it is important to keep track of these assumptions so that they can be re-examined at any time. Figure 49 illustrates one simple way in which this kind of documentation of assumptions can be handled. This involves attaching a symbol to each option bar, whether as an addition to the information on the option graph itself or as a substitute for the simple cross used earlier (Figure 15) to register an incompatibility in the option compatibility table.

The symbols used in this example are simply letters of the alphabet, with an accompanying key to indicate the nature of the judgement involved in each case. Thus the two option bars marked 'a' are included because these combinations would both involve the unthinkable combination of locating a shopping centre where it would be cut off by an arterial road from its local residential catchment area. The combination marked 'b' is ruled out because it is judged not to be viable in economic terms; and the two combinations marked 'c' are excluded because they would mean permitting housing or industrial development on a restricted site unacceptably close to a busy main road. The more doubtful option bar marked 'd' reflects a more debatable assumption; the assumption that industrial use of the central site might erode the attractiveness of shops at King Square to local shoppers, who might then be able to take their custom to alternative shopping centres further afield.

While assumption 'd' has been picked out as more debatable than the rest, it may also be possible to distinguish in other ways between the levels

FIGURE

49

SOUTH SIDE
EXAMPLE

Recording Assumption Underlying Option Bars

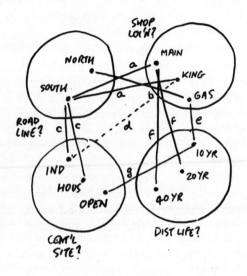

EXPLANATIONS FOR OPTION BARS:

a   shops would be cut off from homes

b   uneconomic combination

c   site too near road to be developed

d   industry on central site _might_ make King Square shopping uneconomic

e   shops on gas site not a short term option

f   main street shopping not a long term option

g.   open space use not possible in short term

ROAD LINE?

		–NORTH	–SOUTH	SHOP LOC'N?			CENT'L SITE?		
				–MAIN	–KING	–GAS	–IND	–HOUS	–OPEN
SHOP LOC'N?	–MAIN	•	a						
	–KING	•	a						
	–GAS	b	•						
CENT'L SITE?	–IND	•	c	•	d?	•			
	–HOUS	•	c	•	•	•			
	–OPEN	•	•	•	•	•			
DIST LIFE?	–10YR	•	•	•	•	e	•	•	g
	–20YR	•	•	f	•	•	•	•	·
	–40YR	•	•	f	•	•	•	•	•

The recording of assumptions behind the inclusion of particular option bars can be useful both as a record and as a means of challenging or justifying their validity in the course of interactive working. Cross-references to such assumptions can be included either on an option graph or a compatibility matrix. If some assumptions are deemed weaker than others, these can be removed on a trial basis.

of conviction with which option bars are to be regarded as imposing unacceptable constraints. This can be important if there are so many option bars as to seriously constrain the range of possible schemes that can be taken forward for comparison; in which case there will be an incentive to relax some of the less stringent of the option bars.

As a guide to this procedure, it is sometimes found useful to adopt a rough-and-ready judgemental scale to differentiate between option bars according to the relative ease or difficulty of breaking the constraints they imply. On a three-point scale, for example, the highest grading — perhaps indicated by three crosses — might indicate very strong grounds for an incompatibility judgement; the second grading, with two crosses, could indicate an incompatibility which might be broken if there were strong enough grounds for doing so; while the single cross grading could mark a weaker or more doubtful incompatibility. Such symbols for grading the strength of incompatibility could be used instead of more specific reference letters either in a compatibility matrix or an option graph. The procedure for developing a set of feasible schemes can then be repeated, either with or without the 'weaker' option bars, to test what effect different assumptions would have on the range of choice available. It should be emphasised, however, that the grading of option bars offers no more than a crude filtering device which can occasionally be helpful when working in the designing mode. It always carries the risk of suppressing deeper evaluative issues, of a kind which can be subjected to more explicit scrutiny when working in the comparing mode.

Introducing Multiple Option Bars

One of the basic simplifying assumptions of the AIDA design method is the assumption that the majority of important design constraints can be represented as simple option bars: as relationships of incompatibility between pairs of options drawn from pairs of interconnected decision areas. Indeed, it is this kind of simplification which makes AIDA such a versatile and transparent means of exploring complex problems. In most problem situations encountered in practice, design constraints can indeed be represented in this way, at least for working purposes. Sometimes, however, important design constraints arise which can only realistically be represented in terms of a more complex form of incompatibility, involving some combination of options from not just two decision areas but three or more considered together.

Where some combination of three or more options from different decision areas is incompatible, this can be formulated through an extension to AIDA conventions known as a *multiple option bar*. For example, in South Side there could be subtle economic arguments why it should be considered impractical to consider a district life as short as ten years if the particular combination of housing development on the Central Site and a

FIGURE

50

SOUTH SIDE
EXAMPLE

Introducing Multiple Option Bars

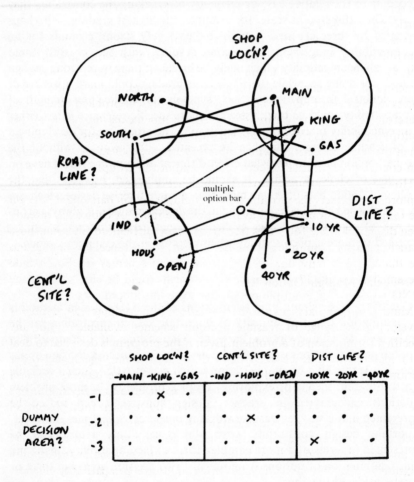

It is only occasionally in practice that it is worth trying to identify multiple option bars, to rule out particular combinations of options from three or more different decision areas. In practice, they can often be avoided by reformulation of the decision areas. The expression of a multiple option bar as a dummy decision area is useful mainly as a simplifying step were generating schemes by computer.

DESIGNING

SKILLS

King Square shopping location were chosen — even though a 10-year life might be quite conceivable in combination with either of these options taken on its own. So, a triple option bar could be formulated to connect the particular triad of options combining KING in SHOP LOC'N?, HOUS in CENT'L SITE? and 10YR in DIST LIFE?; and one quite simple means of representing such a triple option bar on the option graph is illustrated in Figure 50. Here, an unlabelled node on the graph is shown linked to each of the three options in different decision areas which are to be excluded in that particular combination.

It is usually not too difficult to add a limited number of triple or even fourfold option bars to a decision graph in the manner shown in Figure 50. But, in general, the introduction of multiple option bars tends to make the structure of a problem more difficult to comprehend, and is to be avoided unless it is clearly of pivotal importance to the present problem focus. It is, therefore, comparatively rare — though by no means unknown — for multiple option bars to be introduced during periods of interactive working, when the main concern is to develop a picture of problem structure which can contribute to mutual understanding within the group.

However, circumstances do arise in practice when it is important to explore what effects the introduction of multiple option bars might have on the range of decision schemes available. If the range of choice has already been displayed in the form of a tree, it is not too difficult to filter out those branches in which multiple option bars appear: for instance, it is not hard to see that there is only one of the nine decision schemes for South Side presented in Figure 17 — Scheme C — which would be eliminated if the KING-HOUS-10YR multiple option bar were introduced.

Multiple option bars can also be introduced into computer programs for developing the range of feasible decision schemes available within any specified formulation of a problem. Even if the program is designed to deal with incompatibilities between pairs of options alone, the higher-order option bars can be handled through the device of the *dummy decision area*.* The dummy decision area is defined to include as many options as the number of decision areas which are linked through the multiple option bar — three in the case of the multiple option bar introduced in Figure 50. Each of the options affected in these other decision areas is then excluded by an option bar linked to a different one of the options in the dummy decision area, as shown by the set of three additional compatibility matrices in Figure 50. The dummy decision area has the effect of excluding this particular combination of three options, but no other combinations of two among the three. The three simple option bars can then be used as computer input in place of the triple option bar, and the search for feasible routes through the tree can proceed in the normal way. The dummy decision area

* Introduced by Hunter in his early work on the development of an AIDA computer program.

FIGURE

51

SOUTH SIDE
EXAMPLE

Coalescing Closely Linked Decision Areas

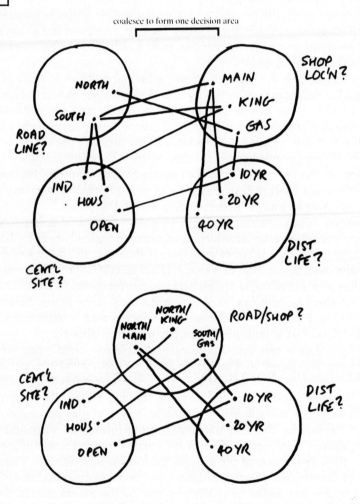

coalesce to form one decision area

It is usually only worth coalescing two or more decision areas into a single decision area in situations where the number of options and option bars can be significantly reduced by this step, and where the resulting set of composite options can be readily visualised and compared. In many cases, it will be possible to reformulate these composite options at a broader level of generality for subsequent reference.

can also, if desired, be shown directly on the option graph; in the example of Figure 50, this would involve replacing the unlabelled node by a full sized circle to represent a decision area labelled DUMMY?, including options labelled 1, 2 and 3, each with its appropriate connections to an option within one of the other decision areas. However, this kind of representation has little value in practice, as — unless the dummy decision area can be so labelled to draw out some deeper significance to the substantive decision problem — it is likely to serve more as a distraction than a source of illumination to the participants.

Coalescing Decision Areas

Wherever there is a pair or a cluster of decision areas with a high density of option bars connecting the various options within them, then the number of feasible combinations which remain available within that part of the problem focus is likely to be quite small. There may then be a case for *coalescing* two or more of the decision areas concerned into a single decision area containing a smaller set of composite options. This is, in effect, the converse of the device illustrated earlier (Figure 48), where a single decision area containing composite options was split up into two separate decision areas with option bars connecting particular options within them. An example of the device of coalescing decision areas appears in Figure 51 which is again based on the three closely linked decision areas for South Side considered in Figure 50. Here, there is a high density of option bars between the ROAD LINE? and SHOP LOC'N? decision areas, which has the effect of excluding three of the six possible combinations. Therefore, these two decision areas can be coalesced into one, here labelled ROAD/ SHOP?. This decision area includes the three composite options of NORTH/MAIN, NORTH/KING and SOUTH/GAS, each with its corresponding pattern of option bars linking it to options in the remaining CENT'L SITE? decision area.

In general, it is not likely to be worth coalescing decision areas where the result would be to create a decision area containing more than three or, at most, four composite options; as would be the case, for example, if the ROAD/SHOP? decision area in Figure 51 were to be further coalesced with either the CENT'L SITE? or the DIST LIFE? decision areas, creating a set of seven composite options in the first case, or six in the second. Nor are composite options of much value once they cease to be readily intelligible in design terms. In Figure 51, for example, it is not too hard to look at each of the three options within the ROAD/SHOP? decision area as a coherent physical option for the broad-scale design of a future South Side neighbourhood. But the ability of participants in the decision process to conceive alternatives in this way could easily be lost were any additional dimensions of choice to be introduced as well.

FIGURE
52

SOUTH SIDE
EXAMPLE

Estimating the Number of Feasible Decision Schemes

method of
estimation
(cumulative)

ROAD LINE?
- NORTH -SOUTH

SHOP
LOC'N?
- MAIN
- KING
- GAS

SHOP LOC'N?
- MAIN - KING - GAS

number of feasible combinations
of options in first pair of
decision areas [= 3]

↓

× number of options in   × 3
next decision area
↓
× proportions of feasible
combinations in new   × 4/6 × 8/9
compatibility tables

CENT'L
SITE?
- IND
- HOUS
- OPEN

CENT'L SITE?
- IND - HOUS - OPEN

↓
[= 5·3]
↓
× 3
↓

DIST
LIFE?
- 10 YR
- 20 YR
- 40 YR

[× 6/6] × 6/7 × 8/9

[= 9·5]

Comparison of estimates with actual numbers of feasible
combinations [as shown in figure 17]

	ESTIMATE	ACTUAL
FIRST 3 DECISION AREAS [ROAD LINE? SHOP LOC'N? CENT'L SITE?]	5.3	6
FIRST 4 DECISION AREAS [DIST LIFE? added]	9.5	9

DESIGNING

SKILLS

This kind of procedure for obtaining a rough estimate of the range of feasible schemes is rarely used explicitly in interactive working. It can however provide a useful quick aid to judgement when deciding whether or not to extend a decision tree by adding further branches — especially when a tree has grown to a point where it is beginning to become difficult to comprehend the overall range of choice it contains.

As soon as a first attempt has been made to identify options and option bars within a selected problem focus, various opportunities may be identified both for expanding some decision areas and for coalescing others. Changes in either direction will depend on the judgement of participants as to which aspects of their problems are of greater and of lesser importanace, as well as on more analytical considerations to do with the number of options within a decision area and the densities of option bars which connect particular pairs. In general, the aim will usually be to arrive at a design formulation which the participants feel to be *well-balanced* in relation to their current perceptions of the choices before them. In this respect, they are likely to find that their work within the designing mode yields changes in their perceptions of the decision areas and their links, and so contributes to a sense of progress in the work of the shaping mode.

Estimating the Range of Choice within a Problem Focus

Once a problem has been expressed in terms of a pattern of options and option bars connecting some set of decision areas, it becomes possible to work out the number of feasible decision schemes by arranging the decision areas in some chosen sequence and then working systematically through the branches of the resulting tree of possibilities, in the manner illustrated in Figure 17. However, it is sometimes useful to make a rough estimate of the number of schemes before embarking on this systematic process; and there is a rule of thumb which is sometimes useful in this respect.*

The basis of the rule is simply to work out a series of fractions, one for each pair of decision areas, representing the proportion of option combinations which remain feasible after any option bars are taken into account. Then the total number of combinations which would be available in the option graph, if there were no option bars, is multiplied by each of these fractions in turn. The outcome is an estimate — usually quite a close one — of the number of schemes that could be available were all the combinations to be worked through in full.

Figure 52 illustrates how this process works for the four decision areas in the original South Side option graph of Figure 16. The process of estimation is built up in a stepwise fashion, starting with only two decision areas and adding one more at each stage. At the first stage, the number '3' simply reflects the information that only three of the six combinations in the first small table are still available once the three option bars are taken into account. When the third decision area is added, the number of combinations available in the first two decision areas — three in all — is first multiplied by the number of options in this new decision area, which is

* This was first suggested by John Luckman and consequently became known as 'Luckman's Lemma'; a lemma in mathematics meaning no more than an unproved rule.

also three; the result is then multiplied by the two fractions 4/6 and 8/9 — representing the proportions of feasible combinations in the two additional option compatibility tables — to estimate the number of schemes now available for the three decision areas taken together.

The process of estimation indicates that approximately 5.3 out of the conceivable 18 combinations so far are likely to be feasible; this compares with the exact number of six as revealed by the tree of Figure 17. Figure 52 then takes the estimation procedure a step further, showing that the estimate remains quite close — 9.5 compared to 9 — when the fourth decision area is added. It is, of course, quite possible to work directly from the option graph when building up the estimates, if the information is not already set out in the form of compatibility tables. Wherever there are no option bars between a pair of decision areas, the appropriate 'multiplier' fraction is 1; a point which can greatly simplify the computations involved.

This kind of estimating procedure can be carried out by hand, as in Figure 52, or it can be built into an interactive computer program; it can be especially useful as an aid to deciding whether or not to add an additional decision area to a decision tree in which the range of feasible decision schemes so far has already been estimated or enumerated. The estimation process can also help in making quick assessments of the consequences of adding or removing option bars; if an estimate shows that a problem is so constrained as to be likely to leave open a very small number of feasible schemes, then this may suggest that certain of the more doubtful option bars should be removed in order to open up a wider range of choice. Where there is a large number of decision areas within a problem focus, the procedure can be used to estimate the likely number of schemes to be found either in the formulation as a whole or in particular branches of the tree. In other words, it is a flexible tool which is by no means essential to the strategic choice 'tool box' — but which can sometimes save time, and alter the course which further analysis may take.

Altering the Sequence of Decision Areas in a Tree

Figure 17 illustrated one kind of standard format in which it is possible to display the set of decision schemes that is feasible under any chosen set of assumptions about options and option bars. This format indicates those points where option bars have been encountered, by means of the device of displaying 'dead' branches wherever they arise in the development of the decision tree. However, various alternative forms of presentation are possible, including a format which simply suppresses information on dead branches, to make the resulting picture more compact (this simplified form was adopted in Figure 22). Another possibility is simply to list the set of feasible schemes in straight tabular form: or to list them using repeat signs wherever the same option in a decision area recurs on successive lines. This gives a presentation which is logically similar to that of the tree, but avoids any use of graphics; so it offers a useful alternative format in the production of typed reports.

A more fundamental choice that arises in developing a set of feasible decision schemes concerns the choice of *sequence* in which the decision areas should be considered. By bringing different decision areas to the fore, different structural features can be displayed. This point is illustrated in Figure 53, which begins by comparing just two of the twenty-four possible sequences available for arranging the four decision areas in the South Side problem focus. The first sequence is that originally used in Figure 17, with the information about dead branches omitted. It draws attention to the information that the majority of feasible schemes involve choice of the northern road line and that, of these, five out of seven involve choice of King Square as location for the shopping centre.

The second sequence illustrated in Figure 53 brings the DIST LIFE? choice to the fore — a rearrangement which might be decided upon in the light of the broad policy significance of this particular choice. To save space, options in the final decision area are this time listed horizontally, rather than vertically. This alternative sequence demonstrates that the three branches relating to the 10-, 20- and 40-year horizons all allow equal numbers of possibilities in the remaining decision areas. Furthermore, the combinations available under the 20- and 40-year life policies are otherwise identical — a point which might indeed have been spotted from the structure of the option graph, but is demonstrated more clearly in the structure of the decision tree.

The third example in Figure 53 illustrates another kind of format, in which a decision tree is developed in two directions, both to the left and the right of a selected 'pivotal' decision area. This can be particularly useful in circumstances where a decision graph can be partitioned into two parts which are only connected through a single decision area or decision link. In this example, just one decision area is introduced to the left of the pivotal ROAD LINE? decision area — the WEST ST? decision area, which was linked in the decision graph of Figure 12 to the ROAD LINE? decision area alone and, for that reason, was omitted from the original problem focus (Figure 13). It is supposed here that there is just one option bar which involves the WEST ST? decision area — an option bar which rules out the YES option in combination with the southern road line. This piece of information can be introduced quite simply when the new decision area is added to the left of the tree, adjacent to the only other decision area to which it is directly related.

The wider potential that may sometimes exist for developing a tree separately on either side of a pivotal decision area can be appreciated by glancing back at the larger decision graph of Figure 42, where the ROAD LINE? decision area forms the sole point of overlap between two potential

FIGURE

53

SOUTH SIDE
EXAMPLE

Altering the Sequence of Decision Areas in a Tree

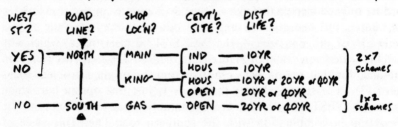

(a) sequence as in Figure 17, but closed branches omitted

ROAD LINE?	SHOP LOC'N?	CENT'L SITE?	DIST LIFE?	
NORTH	MAIN	IND — 10YR / HOUS — 10YR		2 schemes
	KING	HOUS — 10YR, 20YR, 40YR / OPEN — 20YR, 40YR		5 schemes
SOUTH	GAS	OPEN — 20YR, 40YR		2 schemes

(B) sequence altered to bring broader policy choice forward

DIST LIFE?	SHOP LOC'N?	ROAD LINE?	CENT'L SITE?	
10YR	MAIN — NORTH — IND or HOUS / KING — NORTH — HOUS			3 schemes
20YR	KING — NORTH — HOUS or OPEN / GAS — SOUTH — OPEN			3 schemes
40YR	KING — NORTH — HOUS or OPEN / GAS — SOUTH — OPEN			3 schemes

(c) sequence as in (a) but extended to left with ROADLINE? as pivot

WEST ST?	ROAD LINE?	SHOP LOC'N?	CENT'L SITE?	DIST LIFE?	
YES NO	NORTH	MAIN	IND — 10YR / HOUS — 10YR		2×7 schemes
		KING	HOUS — 10YR or 20YR or 40YR / OPEN — 20YR or 40YR		
NO	SOUTH	GAS	OPEN — 20YR or 40YR		1×2 schemes

At any moment when the range of possible decision schemes is set out in the form of a tree, it can be helpful to try changing the sequence of decision areas to explore different structural features. In particular, this makes it possible to focus on more urgent, important or controllable decision areas by bringing them further forward, or to develop combinations on either side of a pivotal decision area.

problem foci. If the pattern of option bars in the transport cluster of decision areas was an intricate one, then the range of possible decision schemes within the transport focus could be explored by developing another decision tree branching out to the left of the pivotal ROAD LINE? decision area.

Mention has already been made of the possible use of computer methods in developing sets of feasible decision schemes. This is by no means difficult, though it will not always be worth while to use a computer either to generate a set of schemes for only three or four decision areas or, on the other hand, for a set of decision areas so large that the computer has to plough through vast numbers of combinations and the resulting display is too large to be taken in by the participants. Where the computer comes into its own is not only in developing trees of intermediate size, but also in rapidly indicating the results of any changes that might be suggested, either in the sequence of decision areas, or in the specification of options and option bars. The introduction of changes in options and option bars is essentially a form of *sensitivity analysis*, which can be very valuable in testing whether or not the inclusion of more doubtful options or option bars makes any significant difference to the range of decision schemes available.

Exploring Consistency between Levels of Choice

There is another variation on the procedure for developing feasible combinations of options from several decision areas, which has been found particularly useful wherever there are some decision areas expressed at a higher level of generality than others. This is sometimes the case where a set of people are reviewing choices of broad policy orientation at the same time as more operational choices which might be consistent with some policy positions but not with others. In such circumstances, the options or combinations at the more operational level can be evaluated not merely according to their anticipated consequences in certain agreed comparison areas, but also according to their *consistency* with different policy orientations which could be adopted at a broader level. An example will help to illustrate how this analysis of consistency between two levels of decision can work in practice. Figure 54 shows an example of a consistency matrix (or table) relating to South Side, in which four of the seven decision areas from the original problem formulation — including the WEST ST? but excluding the DIST LIFE? decision area — have been regarded as forming together the more operational level of choice.

For purposes of exploring relationships between levels the DIST LIFE? decision area has been reformulated here as a broader policy-level choice of investment horizon with only two options — short and long. To this choice is added another choice at the broader policy level concerned with emphasis on public versus private investment — reflecting perhaps a well-recognised ideological difference on the municipal council. There are then four

FIGURE
54

SOUTH SIDE
EXAMPLE

Exploring Consistency Between Levels of Choice

LEVEL 1 DECISION AREAS (more general)

INVESTMENT EMPHASIS?
INVESTMENT HORIZON?

		PUBLIC		PRIVATE	
		SHORT	LONG	SHORT	LONG
		✓	✓	✓	?
ROAD LINE?	–NORTH	•	•	×	•
	–SOUTH	×	×	•	•
SHOP LOC'N?	–MAIN	•	×	•	×
	–KING	×	•	•	•
	–GAS	×	•	×	•
CENT'L SITE?	–IND	•	•	×	•
	–HOUS	•	•	•	×
	–OPEN	×	•	×	•
WEST ST?	–YES	•	•	•	×
	–NO	•	×	•	•

LEVEL 2 DECISION AREAS (more specific)

INVESTMENT ORIENTATION?   ROAD LINE? SHOP LOC'N? CENT'L SITE? WEST ST?

– SHORT TERM PUBLIC: – NORTH – MAIN – ⎡ IND —— YES or NO
                                              ⎣ HOUS —— YES or NO

– LONG TERM PUBLIC: – NORTH – MAIN – ⎡ HOUS —— YES
                                              ⎣ OPEN —— YES

– SHORT TERM PRIVATE: – no combinations feasible at level 2

– LONG TERM PRIVATE: – ⎡ NORTH – KING – OPEN – YES or NO
                             ⎣ SOUTH – GAS – OPEN — NO

DESIGNING SKILLS

Distinctions between broader and more specific levels of choice offer a valuable means of dealing with complexity where the number of decision areas is large. When exploring choices over many interrelated fields of policy, it can occasionally be helpful to introduce a hierarchy of three or even more levels of generality, using feasible combinations at the broader levels as a framework for evaluation at other levels.

combinations of emphasis at the policy level, which have been expressed as four columns in the matrix of Figure 54. In this case, it is judged that there is an element of doubt over whether a private investment emphasis can be considered compatible with a longer-term investment horizon in view of prevailing economic circumstances. So there is one possible option bar within the broader level of choice, which may possibly eliminate one of the four columns in its entirety.

The main cells of the matrix are then completed by entering a cross wherever an option within a decision area at the more operational level is judged *inconsistent* with a policy orientation represented by a *combination of options* at the broader level. As always, there can be scope for argument as to whether or not particular entries in the table should be included, and any such argument can yield useful products in terms of learning and mutual adjustment among the participants. Any incompatibilities between options among decision areas at the more operational level can also be displayed within this kind of format; and the triangular grid that appears to the left of the main matrix of Figure 54 offers one compact means of adding information of this kind.

The consequences of any set of assumptions about incompatibilities can then be worked out and displayed in terms of a series of separate decision trees covering the more operational decision areas, one corresponding to each broader choice of orientation. So it is possible to explore what range of choice is available for any one of the broader policy orientations, and to present the results in the normal branching form. It is often found that a particular choice of orientation will pre-determine the choice of option in some decision areas, while leaving open a range of alternatives in others. In Figure 54, for example, a choice of a shorter term public investment emphasis restricts choice of ROAD LINE? to the northern option, and choice of shopping location to Main Street, while leaving the WEST ST? choice completely open.

Where there are many decision areas it can be useful to draw out such structural features by varying the sequence of decision areas between one branch and the next, to bring any 'no choice' decision areas to the front and to set back any 'free choice' decision areas to the end of the sequence; this will sometimes leave a 'conditional choice' zone in between, the structure of which can be examined more closely. This kind of representation is sometimes referred to as a *decision stream*; it can be especially useful in displaying structural characteristics of problems which include a large number of decision areas, and then seeking reactions from policy-makers before going on to search for compromise schemes which may sometimes be consistent with more than one policy orientation.

This kind of analysis of consistency, between levels of choice, in effect takes the process of strategic choice in the direction of the comparing mode; for it introduces a form of evaluation which stresses the assessment of alternatives not so much directly in terms of their consequences, as in terms of their perceived consistency with different political orientations or aims. In effect, the comparison areas described in Chapter 3 are replaced by the broader-level decision areas — illustrating how one kind of strategic choice concept can be replaced by another in a flexible, adaptive way. This therefore provides a fitting point at which to conclude this chapter, and to review the various points made about skills of working within the designing mode.

Summary: Process Judgements in the Designing Mode

The various points made in this chapter have taken the process of strategic choice into a somewhat more technical domain than those made in Chapter 5 — reflecting a general shift of emphasis in moving from work in the shaping mode to work in the designing mode. It is worth first re-emphasising the general point that work in the designing mode may sometimes be very important, but at other times much less significant. In the extreme case, there will be little designing work to be done at moments where the problem focus has been restricted to a single decision area, and the options within that decision area are not too hard to identify. However, even in these circumstances, it may be difficult to choose between these options because of uncertainties of type UR relating to possible future decisions in related fields; so sooner or later other decision areas may be brought back within the problem focus, and the range of possible combinations may begin to broaden out again.

When working in the designing mode, as in each of the other modes, the choice of appropriate *level of analysis* is always a matter of judgement. In general, there is a case for inclining towards simplification in the first instance, and only then moving in the direction of further elaboration if or when there seems justification for so doing. In the work of the designing mode, simplicity generally means working within a limited focus of no more than three, four or five decision areas, usually with between two and four options in each. At this level, the number of option bars will usually be manageable and the process of developing a set of feasible decision schemes will not be too complex. The simpler the structure, the more practicable it will be to develop the set of schemes in a way which keeps all the participants involved. But when participants are working in the designing mode, as opposed to the shaping mode, there is more likely to be a case for handling at least some of the complexity in other ways. In particular, a computer can be used in checking combinations in terms of feasibility; in rapidly changing the sequence of a tree to display different structural information; and in testing the consequences of removing or adding option bars, or options, in terms of the overall range of choice available. But the computer can become a distraction in an interactive group situation; and its benefits in terms of speed and flexibility may be of little value if the momentum of group working is thereby disrupted.

Figure 55 shows the various directions of movement out of the designing mode towards other modes. One frequent direction of movement will be towards the *comparing mode*, to develop a basis of comparison among the various decision schemes that are available. But, as was explained in Chapter 3, there are different levels of comparison from which to choose. If there are only two or three schemes available in all, then it becomes possible to compare them all in considerable depth, taking uncertainty explicitly into account; but if there are many schemes, it may be more practicable to compare them first at a much broader level, to form a more limited working shortlist as illustrated in Figure 22.

Alternative directions of exit from the designing mode take the process into the choosing and the shaping modes respectively. Exit directly into the *choosing mode* will be possible where the participants agree that one course of action in a particular decision area is clearly superior to the others. For example, the participants in the South Side exercise might be so convinced by the advantages of the northern road line, after realising that it presents a far wider choice in other decision areas than the southern alternative, that they agree to make a recommendation for the northern line straight away, without conducting any further analysis. And there are also many circumstances in which an exit from the designing to the *shaping mode* will made sense. In particular, a very restricted range of alternatives within a problem focus may suggest that this focus might easily be extended, whereas a very wide range may suggest it should be narrowed down.

Also, as indicated in Figure 55, there are various ways in which the guidance offered in this chapter can involve more modest process 'loops' in the direction of the other modes. A loop towards the *shaping mode* is implied both in the coalescence of decision areas and in the breaking down of decision areas with composite options into two or more linked decision areas. A loop towards the *comparing mode* is implied in the step of separating out different levels of choice for the development of consistency matrices. It is also implied in the device of annotating option bars to indicate different kinds of arguments for introducing assumptions of incompatibility between options; arguments which in many cases will be grounded in value judgements of a debatable kind. Finally, the resequencing of a set of decision areas to bring more urgent decision areas to the fore implies a form of looping towards the *choosing mode*, where the pressures for action begin to dictate the direction in which the process moves.

Illustrations from Practice

Following the precedent set in Chapter 5, a set of three diverse *illustrations from practice* is presented on the pages that follow. They have

FIGURE 55

Process Choices when Working in the Designing Mode

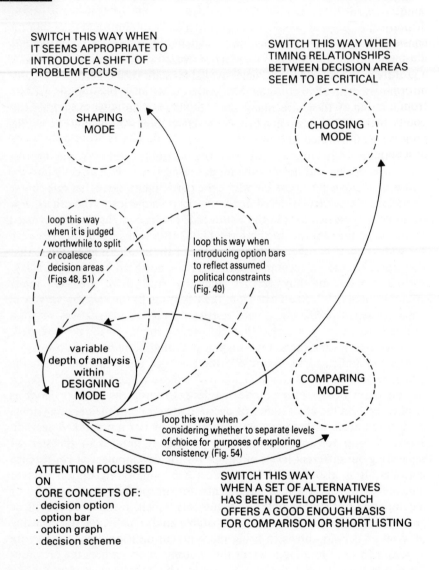

SWITCH THIS WAY WHEN
IT SEEMS APPROPRIATE TO
INTRODUCE A SHIFT OF
PROBLEM FOCUS

SWITCH THIS WAY WHEN
TIMING RELATIONSHIPS
BETWEEN DECISION AREAS
SEEM TO BE CRITICAL

SHAPING
MODE

CHOOSING
MODE

loop this way
when it is judged
worthwhile to split
or coalesce
decision areas
(Figs 48, 51)

loop this way when
introducing option bars
to reflect assumed
political constraints
(Fig. 49)

variable
depth of analysis
within
DESIGNING
MODE

COMPARING
MODE

loop this way when
considering whether to separate levels
of choice for purposes of exploring
consistency (Fig. 54)

ATTENTION FOCUSSED
ON
CORE CONCEPTS OF:
. decision option
. option bar
. option graph
. decision scheme

SWITCH THIS WAY
WHEN A SET OF ALTERNATIVES
HAS BEEN DEVELOPED WHICH
OFFERS A GOOD ENOUGH BASIS
FOR COMPARISON OR SHORT LISTING

DESIGNING

SUMMARY

been selected to illustrate some of the more important practical points that arise in relation to the work of the designing mode.

The first illustration, based on extracts from documents published in connection with a land-use policy plan for an English rural area, demonstrates one way in which information about options and their mutual consistency can be presented clearly for public discussion. The second illustration, from an application in the Netherlands, shows how members of a group can work together in developing a set of feasible schemes from the information contained in an option graph. The third illustration is taken from a group exercise in organisational choice, and anticipates some of the points to be made in Chapter 9 about systematic documentation of the progress made through interactive working on flip charts around the walls of a room.

FIGURE 56

Illustration from Practice – Designing 1

Figure 16: Employment Policies Compared with Choices for Other Policies

	Employment Policy	Population	Housing	Movement	Recreation	Settlement	Finance
1.	Increased commuting. (Relying for job growth on the expansion of existing firms in Rutland)	✓	✓	Concentration on roads incompatible as people will need to get to the few job centres in Rutland so some public transport necessary.	Inconsistent with major development for some new firms almost certainly generated by recreation development.	Incompatible with sub centres policy as people would have to live away from the few job centres	Trend acceptable.
2.	Current pattern. (Maintain the present ratio of 4 jobs to 5 workers in Rutland).	✓	✓	✓	✓	Sub centres policy difficult to achieve	Trend probably possible but limited finance could be needed for job growth perhaps through a change in service priorities.
3.	Job growth to match population growth. (The number of new jobs created would equal the numbers of new people seeking work).	Unlikely to be achieved if population growth is encouraged.	✓	✓	✓	Firms will tend to be attracted to concentrations of facilities. More finance needed.	Trend unacceptable. Mixture of change in priorities and private investment. Lead in long term to more job income.
4.	Reduce commuting. (Provide enough new jobs for population growth and to provide for some people at present commuting).	Unlikely to be achieved if population growth is encouraged or no population control.	Additional Council housing might have to be built to bring in key workers – therefore reduction in percentage rented.	Either public or private transport extremes incompatible as new employers would expect some road improvements and some bus services to bring in labour.	Inconsistent with restrictive attitude to further development at the Reservoir which could create more jobs.	Firms tend to be attracted to concentration of facilities/ labour etc., therefore dispersal incompatible and quality or sub-centre policies difficult to implement.	Large injection of finance needed involving higher proportion of budget and more private investment.
5.	Job balance. (Creating enough new jobs to provide for growth and for all existing residents).	Incompatible with encouraging population or present trends as enough jobs couldn't be created. Difficult even with restricted population growth.	Higher rate of Council house building almost certainly necessary for above reason.	As above.	Inconsistent with restrictive or limited development policies at Reservoir for above reasons.	As above.	As above but much more investment needed. Very difficult to attract sufficient funds.

REJECTED POLICIES

Population:—
Encouragement of further growth.

Employment:—
Trying to achieve a complete job balance (trying to provide enough jobs for everyone in Rutland).

Movement:—
Concentration of resources solely on roads.
Concentration of resources solely on supporting public transport.

Recreation:—
Major development of Rutland as a tourist area.

Settlement:—
Dispersal of growth throughout Rutland.

Finance:—
Much higher proportion of County Council resources.
Focus on revenue spending (spending more on running existing services and investing less in new facilities).

9.11 Although several of the remaining choices may be to some extent inconsistent with each

other, they nevertheless would allow a fair degree of freedom in choosing between different policies in other fields. This is not to say that all the remaining policies can be easily implemented or that there is no difference between them. Most of the choices would require some effort to be successfully implemented and in many cases choosing one policy instead of another will have considerable social and economic consequences. But decisions about the relative merits of policies for these choices are bound up with attitudes and values, as will become clearer in the following chapter. What the balance sheet analysis and the preceding chapters have established is that the remaining choices of policy for dealing with each problem appear technically feasible and are not obviously socially or economically undesirable.

9.12 This chapter has therefore shown which policies would not fit well together and in doing this has demonstrated the sort of inter-relationships which have to be taken into account in selecting policies for particular problems. It has illustrated the point that there is more than one way to put the puzzle together depending on what you want to achieve; the combination of policies eventually selected will depend to a considerable extent on these underlying motives and attitudes.

In the light of the above analysis the following policies are now put forward as the most reasonable options for further discussion.

POLICIES FOR DISCUSSION

Population:—
(i) No control (continuing present trends).
(ii) Some restriction (where although growth is still allowed, it is limited to less than current rates).

Employment:—
(i) Increased commuting (relying for job growth on the expansion of existing firms in Rutland).
(ii) Current pattern (maintain the present ratio of 4 jobs to 5 workers in Rutland).
(iii) Job/new population match (the number of new jobs would equal the numbers of new people seeking work).
(iv) Reduced commuting (provide enough jobs for new population and for some people now commuting).

TABLE 9 : MAIN CHOICES, SOLUTION STREAMS

	Population	Recreation	Settlement	Movement	Employment	Housing	Number of Alternatives
CONSERVATION	Some Restriction	Restrict	Concentration	Emphasis on Roads or Emphasis on Public Transport	Increase Commuting / Current Pattern	Maintain Rented Proportion / Maintain or Increase Rented Proportion	7
			Social Policy	Emphasis on Public Transport	Current Pattern	Increase Rented Proportion	
DORMITORY	No Control	Restrict or Limited Development	Concentration or Concentration (New Village) or Sub-Centres	Emphasis on Roads	Emphasis on Increased Commuting	Reduce or Maintain Rented Proportion	12
LITTLE POLICY CHANGE	No Control	Limited Development	Concentration	Emphasis on Roads	Current Pattern	Maintain Rented Proportion	1
SOCIALLY DIRECTED	Some Restriction	Limited Development	Sub-Centres or Social Policy	Emphasis on Public Transport / Emphasis on Public Transport	Job Match / Reduce Commuting	Maintain or Increase Rented Proportion / Increase Rented Proportion	5
BALANCED GROWTH	No Control	Limited Development or Recreation Focus	Concentration or Concentration (New Village)	Emphasis on Roads or Emphasis on Public Transport	Job Match	Maintain or Increase Rented Proportion	16

DESIGNING

PRACTICE

Theme: Presentation for Public Discussion of Policy Options, Incompatibilities and Choices within Orientations.

Problem: Preparation of a Structure Plan as a Policy Framework for a Rural Area.

Context: Planning Team for Rutland with Various Community Groups, County of Leicestershire, England, 1975 – 76.

COMMENTARY ON FIGURE 56

These three extracts are taken from documents published by the County Council of Leicestershire in central England as part of the process of preparing a first official Structure Plan for Rutland. Rutland is a predominantly rural district of some 30,000 inhabitants which at that time (1975/6) had recently lost its independent County status.

The table at the top is one of a series of six similar tables presented for public discussion in November 1975, as part of a consultation document entitled "Let's talk about Rutland". This particular table focusses on employment policy for Rutland, and lists in the first column a set of five possible options for employment, treated as a single decision area. Each row of the table contains notes on the incompatibility of that particular employment option with specific options in other decision areas concerned respectively with population change, housing, movement, recreation, settlement pattern and finance. For presentation purposes, the individual options in these other decision areas were not shown in separate subdivisions of the columns as in the standard format of option compatibility tables. This kind of simplification is most desirable in published documents. It will be noticed that the table does however briefly indicate the arguments on which particular option bars are based, so that the underlying assumptions can be challenged by readers.

Below the table appears an excerpt from a subsequent page of the same document (2), arguing for the exclusion of certain options on the strength of the foregoing analysis — among them the fifth of the employment policy options, excluded on the grounds of its excessive financial implications. After a description of the challenge of policy design and evaluation that remains (paragraphs 9.11 and 9.12), the report then goes on to list out the main options that remain in the various decision areas (only those for the first two decision areas, concerned with population and employment, being included in this extract).

The final illustration opposite is taken from a technical document written to present the analysis on which the submitted Structure Plan was based. The five "solution streams" had been developed to indicate the range of choice available in the six main decision areas (excluding the financial decision area) for each of five broad policy "orientations" or emphases which could be clearly envisaged by the County and District Councillors. It was indicated by the planners that the set of policies finally selected might be based on a compromise between orientations rather than the selection of any one orientation in its pure form; and the final decision was to go for a set of policies based on a position part way between the conservation and the socially directed orientations.

FIGURE 57

Illustration from Practice – Designing 2

1

2

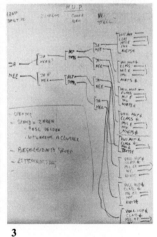

3

DESIGNING

PRACTICE

Theme: Deriving Alternative Schemes from an Option Graph and forming a Decision Tree.

Problem: Implementation Policy for the Law against Nuisances, in an Environmental Policy Plan for a Municipality.

Context: Action-Research with the Project Group, Municipality of Emmen, The Netherlands, 1982.

COMMENTARY ON FIGURE 57

These photographs were taken at a working session of the project group during the second month of a one-year project to produce a Municipal Environmental Policy Plan. This work was undertaken by the Municipality of Emmen in the Province of Drenthe in the north of Holland as part of an action research project sponsored by the Central Government.

The project group was drawn from various parts of the organisation and contained a mixture of administrators, planners, engineers and other professionals. The alderman responsible for the plan was often present for parts of such sessions. Allen Hickling and Arnold de Jong, who were conducting the research, acted as process consultants.

A high level of unemployment in this part of Holland, and around Emmen in particular, had led to the environment receiving very low priority in the recent past. This had been especially the case with respect to industry and commerce. Thus the need for an Environmental Policy Plan was a matter of debate. Environmentalists argued it to be essential if not too late, while others considered it not only unnecessary, but even harmful.

The focus of the work in this sequence of photographs is the implementation of controls of various kinds — legal, planning, and so on (1). It represents a good example of how different levels of choice can be combined in an option graph — although this may be only of value early in a project.

Here there are decisions about whether to produce detailed local plans for the industrial areas; whether to be involved in zoning and the setting of norms; and the thoroughness of the implementation plan to be made for the law about nuisances. At the same time there were more general considerations about the attitude to management of controls, and the relaxation of by-laws.

The process of deriving the decision schemes on the wall is important (2). In this instance there were three members of the group directly involved, and this helped to keep track of the logic. The decision tree itself (3) is typical in that an unexpected number of schemes had to be accommodated, leading to a very assymetrical layout. This does no harm to the learning process, and is corrected in the official loose-leaf record of the meeting. Here also the reasoning and assumptions underlying the option bars was recorded.

In this case recycling occurred soon after, and the whole problem was broken out into its constituent levels for further analysis.

FIGURE 58 Illustration from Practice – Designing 3

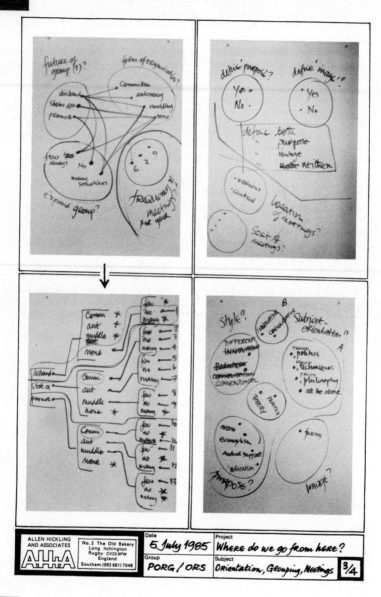

Theme: Documentation using a Photo-Record of Progress in Designing Alternative Decision Schemes.

Problem: Organisational Choice in Developing a Programme of a Study Group of a National Society.

Context; Process of O.R. Study Group, Operational Research Society, Birmingham, England, 1985.

COMMENTARY ON FIGURE 58

The four illustrations opposite show how even relatively quickly-drawn, exploratory flip charts produced in the course of a working session can be incorporated in a documentary record, to help the participants recall afterwards something of the spirit of the process in which they were involved. The flip charts are part of a set of 17 generated during a one-day workshop held at the University of Aston in Birmingham by a study group of the Operational Research Society of Great Britain. This study group, called the Process of OR Study Group (PORG) had been formed several years earlier by a set of members of the Society with an interest not just in the analytical techniques of operational research but in the wider process of carrying out operational research projects in organisations.

Nine members of the study group took part in the workshop, the task of which was to consider possible directions for the future of the group after a period in which its momentum seemed to have been slipping. Allen Hickling had agreed to act as facilitator to the workshop, of which John Friend was also a member. Because only a few hours were available, and because not all those present were familiar with the strategic choice approach, Allen Hickling did not involve the group as a whole in building up the record of progress on the wall; instead he combined the facilitator and recorder roles, attempting to capture the contributions of others on flip charts in a rapid, free-flowing way.

Quite early in the workshop, the initial concerns expressed by participants were structured loosely in the form of an ends/means diagram rather similar to that shown in Figure 46; from this, an initial set of seventeen decision areas was generated. The two wall charts on the right hand side reflect attempts to examine some of the broader decision areas more closely. It will be noticed that some questions arose in discussion about whether the labels of particular options should be changed, and whether or not options could be treated as mutually exclusive.

The more "finished" option graph in the top left corner includes a set of three key decision areas concerned with the future of the group; the form of organisation; and the question of expansion of its membership — a further decision area on frequency of meetings having been first included but then set aside. The analysis of this option graph indicated a choice of 14 decision schemes. A debate on preferences was centred on four comparison areas, some of which were treated as constraints; these were concerned with commitment, relevance to others, availability of enough willing people and effect on OR education.

The upshot of the meeting — corresponding broadly to scheme 10a in the tree — was the formation of a committee to work on a promotional strategy with a six-month deadline in view. The committee then went on to devise a programme of joint meetings with regional groups of the Society, thus opening up the debate about the practical process of conducting operational research projects to the wider membership of the Society.

7

Skills in Comparing

Introduction

In this chapter the aim will be to explore, more fully than was possible in Chapter 3, the subtle judgements that arise when working in the comparing mode. The relevant core concepts were introduced in Figures 19 to 22; they are those of the *comparison area*, the *relative assessment*, the *advantage comparison* and the *working shortlist*. These concepts are all very general ones, which can be adapted to guide the work of the comparing mode at a variety of levels, ranging from the most rough and ready appraisal of 'pros' and 'cons' of some proposed action, to the most elaborate exercises in quantification and predictive modelling.

However, experience so far in applying strategic choice methods to practical decision problems supports the view that it is only very rarely that the more elaborate forms of comparison exercise can be justified. In the first place, it will usually take an exceptionally weighty decision to justify the time and resources called for in collating and analysing large amounts of data; more fundamentally, however, the strategic choice philosophy draws attention to the question of whether extensive investment in analysis will produce a good enough return in terms of the level of confidence with which decisions can be taken, once the full range of uncertainties bearing on that decision has been considered.

So experience indicates that it usually pays to concentrate on quite simple, crude approaches to the comparison of alternatives. Yet it is important to stress that there is always scope for *choice* in the ways alternatives are to be compared. There are choices to be made in the formulation of comparison areas; choices in methods of relative assessment; choices in ways of presenting broader advantage comparisons; and choices in the extent to which simplified numerical or other indices are introduced to narrow down the full range of alternatives to a more limited working shortlist. The guidance offered in this chapter is intended to help users in addressing these choices of evaluative method and style in a more conscious and effective way.

FIGURE
59

SOUTH SIDE
EXAMPLE

Developing a Set of Relevant Comparison Areas

DECISION AREA [-options]	RELEVANT COMPARISON AREAS	check relevance to other decision areas within present problem focus :			
		ROAD LINE?	SHOP LOC'N?	CENT'L SITE?	DIST LIFE?
ROAD LINE? [-NORTH] [-SOUTH]	• CAPITAL OUTLAY • IMPACT ON RESIDENTS • FLEXIBILITY of future development opportunities	• • •	✓ ? ✓	✓ ✓ ✓	? ✓
SHOP LOC'N? [-MAIN] [-KING] [-GAS]	• INCOME from rents • CONVENIENCE TO SHOPPERS • CONTINUITY FOR TRADERS • ROAD SAFETY		• • •	✓ ✓	
CENT'L SITE? [-IND] [-HOUS] [-OPEN]	• LOCAL JOBS created • contribution to HOUSING POLICY • VISUAL IMPACT on local environment			• • •	✓
DIST LIFE? [-10 YR] [-20 YR] [-40 YR]	• CONFIDENCE of South Side residents				•

COMPARING

SKILLS

In building up a set of comparison areas which are relevant to a specific problem focus, it can be useful to start by examining each of the decision areas in turn, identifying the more important areas of difference between options as indicated here. When working interactively, this kind of activity is usually carried out verbally, and can be combined with the use of various brainstorming methods.

It is important to recognise that the work of comparing alternatives can become very *difficult* in practice, however simple or elaborate the chosen methods of evaluation may be. The difficulties encountered can be political as much as technical, especially where there are many different constituencies of interest which might be affected — some perhaps directly represented in the decision process and others not. Furthermore, the procedural setting itself may be far from simple, and may change as the problem focus shifts. For these reasons, the guidance in this chapter will be shaped according to the principle of *dynamic comparison*, which has already been touched upon in the concluding section of Chapter 3. This principle captures the evaluative implications of the wider view of planning as a process of choosing strategically through time: a process in which there may be a succession of 'evaluative moments' as the focus of comparison changes or as new information comes to light, whether through unforeseen circumstances or through explorations deliberately set in train.

Identifying Appropriate Comparison Areas

In general, a set of comparison areas should be chosen to be as relevant as possible to the scope of the decision problem currently in view, and also to the political domain within which decisions are to be made. With problems of any complexity, there is always a danger that these considerations taken together will draw the participants in the direction of quite an elaborate evaluation frame, with a longer list of comparison areas than can be conveniently managed when working under practical pressures. So, as with the definition of decision areas, it can be worth devoting some time and effort to the formulation of an appropriate yet manageable set of comparison areas. Yet again, as with decision areas, people's views on comparison areas may change as a group process builds up momentum and the level of shared understanding grows; so the formulation of comparison areas is better viewed as a continuing matter of concern than as something which should take up a great deal of time in the early stages of an interactive process.

Where a current problem focus is expressed in terms of a set of linked decision areas and a choice of options within each, one practical way in which to begin generating comparison areas is to take each decision area in turn — perhaps starting with those which are believed to be most important — and then to consider what kinds of consequences or effects are thought to be most relevant to the comparison of options within each. One way of organising such a process is illustrated in Figure 59.

In this example, the first question concerns the consequences of choosing between the northern and the southern road line through South Side. It might be immediately apparent that these options are likely to differ in terms of capital outlay and also in terms of impact on local residents.

Further discussion might then suggest that there is another important consequence to be considered, relating to the flexibility to pursue further local development options in the future. So the consideration of this one decision area has indicated a set of three different comparison areas straight away. These are listed in Figure 59 using brief and tentative definitions. Such definitions can always be extended later, in the manner illustrated earlier in Figure 19, and can be modified, if need be, as the work proceeds. Some of these comparison areas may, of course, also be relevant to other decision areas as well; this is indicated in Figure 59 by checking off subsequent columns in the table where this is thought to be the case, or where there is some doubt over this point.

Turning to the second decision area — that on location of the shopping centre — an additional set of comparison areas may emerge as important. These again are listed in a tentative way, using the options within the decision area as one source of guidance in reviewing what kinds of comparison areas are likely to be significant. As further decision areas are added, the list is extended further — though it becomes more and more likely that some at least of the relevant comparison areas will have already been generated at an earlier stage. In the example of Figure 59, it will be seen that a set of eleven tentative comparison areas has been generated once the four decision areas within the chosen problem focus have been considered in turn.

But a list of comparison areas generated in this way is unlikely to provide a well-balanced base for comparing alternatives, until some further work has been done on the *structure* of the list. For a start, the list may well be too long for working purposes; furthermore, it may contain a certain amount of repetition or overlap, raising doubts about the level of generality or specificity with which comparison areas should be expressed. For example, in considering the ROAD LINE? decision area, it was at first considered good enough to talk simply of 'impact on residents' without distinguishing one group of residents from another. Further down the list, in comparing options for DIST LIFE?, it was however felt to be appropriate to formulate a rather more specific comparison area concerned with the level of confidence of South Side residents in the future of the area. If the West Street decision area were to be added to the list, then a further question could arise of whether impacts on this more compact group of residents should be considered separately from those on the larger South Side community.

In many practical problem situations, questions will arise about *discrimination* between different affected groups, between different kinds of impact on the same group and, possibly, between different time horizons of impact as well. In the South Side situation, it might indeed be very important that the working party should debate what different *categories* of impact on residents there might be: whether, for instance, it could be important to distinguish the severe and immediate consequences for those few residents facing the possibility of physical demolition of their homes from the less severe but continuing nuisance to others from high levels of traffic vibration and noise.

Developing a Balanced Evaluation Frame

Participants in a decision process do not normally work entirely from scratch when building up a list of comparison areas relevant to each new decision problem that comes up. Usually, each member of a group begins with some preconceptions about a relevant *frame* of evaluation; a frame which may either have evolved as a purely intuitive response to felt political pressures, or may have been articulated more systematically as an expression of formal organisational policies or aims.

One of the more explicit forms that a frame of evaluation can take is a written statement of guiding *objectives* of the type often developed by those responsible for the management and control of large corporate organisations. Such a statement may sometimes be structured in a hierarchical form, with expressions of broad aspirations at one level and expressions of more specific policy intentions at another. In other situations the elements in the framework may be expressed in less aspirational and more pragmatic terms; perhaps in terms of broad problem areas to be addressed, such as poverty or unemployment, rather than in terms of idealistic aims to be achieved. Usually, however, a statement expressed in terms of amelioration of problems can be rewritten in terms of achievement of goals, or vice versa; the underlying sense of purpose may be quite similar in either case.

Underlying such statements of purpose, however, may be more subtle political pressures, relating to the structure of accountability within which the participants are operating. Sometimes, this sense of accountability will differ significantly from one participant to another: one member of the South Side Working Party, for example, might feel a special responsibility for the interests of South Side residents, and another for the interests of unemployed school leavers throughout the wider municipality. Such variations are likely to be influenced by some mix of personal commitments, respresentational roles and the principles of accountability on which the membership of the working group has been selected.

Figure 60 illustrates how it is possible to use more than one type of evaluation frame as a point of reference in the search to develop a more structured set of comparison areas for a process of strategic choice. In the first list, based on a more *purposive* approach, a set of broad headings and more specific sub-headings is used to develop a framework of *policy* appropriate to the South Side problem; in the second list, a different set of headings and sub-headings is used to identify relevant interests or

FIGURE

60

SOUTH SIDE
EXAMPLE

Building a Balanced Evaluation Framework

(1) FRAMEWORK OF POLICY CONCERNS (purposive approach)

ECONOMIC
- restrict municipal expenditure commitments
- increase local wealth / tax base
- create new local employment

SOCIAL
- avoid disrupting established communities
- reduce inequalities in access to welfare facilities

ENVIRONMENTAL
- segregate vehicles and pedestrians
- enhance quality of urban landscape
- reduce level of air pollution around steelworks

(2) FRAMEWORK OF INTERESTS TO BE CONSIDERED (responsive approach)

RESIDENTS
- Dockport urban area as a whole
- South Side district
- local neighbourhoods affected by particular proposals

UNEMPLOYED
- adults
- school leavers

LOCAL TAXPAYERS
- households
- businesses

EXTERNAL INTERESTS
- national taxpayers
- users of inter-city highways

COMPARING

SKILLS

Even where a set of comparison areas has been generated initially with reference to a particular problem focus, it can be useful to check the list for balance and coverage by cross-reference to broader evaluation frameworks. Different perspectives can emerge by referring to frameworks expressed in terms of organisational purposes and of political interests, so use of both types of framework can be worthwhile.

'stakeholder' groups, reflecting a concern to be *responsive* to varied political pressures. Either list would probably have to be extended quite considerably before it could be considered to be at all complete in its own terms. Nevertheless, these two examples of evaluation frames are both reasonably typical of their kind. The first is typical of the kind of hierarchically-ordered statement of objectives which is sometimes formally adopted as a set of central guidelines for the work of a corporate organisation; while the second is typical of the range of interests to which a set of publicly accountable decision-makers might see themselves as having to respond. If the setting were one of a commercial rather than a political organisation, the headings might, of course, be different - for example, the interests to be considered might include shareholders, employees, customers, suppliers - but the organising principles would be much the same.

Either type of list could, of course, be used directly as a set of comparison areas within which to evaluate alternative courses of action. However, in addressing any specific decision problem it will often be more helpful to generate comparison areas directly in the first instance, as illustrated in Figure 59. Then the tentative comparison areas generated in this way can be matched against whatever more structured lists of policy concerns and interests may be available, to help generate insights into ways in which the set of comparison areas to be used might be reformulated in a more logical and consistent way.

Although the two types of framework illustrated in Figure 60 are organised on different principles, there will often be more similarities between them than might at first appear. For example, a concern with employment appears in both lists, expressed in different ways, as does a concern with municipal expenditure levels. The value of this kind of cross-reference between contrasting frames of reference is that it illuminates the scope for *choices* in the way comparison areas are expressed. Among them are choices between different levels of specificity or generality, and between levels of aggregation or disaggregation which might be considered appropriate to a particular decision process and a particular 'evaluative moment' within that process.

One particular opportunity for evaluative choice concerns the possibility of reformulating some comparison areas as decision areas, relating to choices of policy orientation at a quite general level. This opens up the opportunity for an alternative approach to evaluation which was introduced in Chapter 6 (Figure 54), based on the exploration of *consistency* between different levels of choice. This can be particularly helpful where there is uncertainty or disagreement about choices of appropriate policy stance: for example, lack of agreement on whether corporate expenditure commitments should be held to their present level, allowed to increase to some degree, or perhaps deliberately reduced. Such matters can often be the subject of long-standing political controversy, which cannot always be addressed too explicitly in a process of strategic choice — but which even so can be accommodated in the analytical work.

Approaches to the Comparison of Alternatives in terms of Flexibility

Whatever the range of policy concerns or interests that may be relevant to a decision problem, there is one particular aspect of comparison that is of fundamental importance to the process of choosing strategically through time. This is the comparison of alternative courses of short-term action in terms of the *flexibility* of future choice which they allow. One approach to this aspect of comparison was illustrated in Figure 25, where five possible action schemes for South Side were compared in terms of the range of longer-term decision schemes left open by each. This range was first presented in terms of a straight count of schemes; but then a *robustness* index was used to indicate how many schemes in each case met a specified threshold of acceptability, reflecting the concerns of one of the more important of the various interest groups affected in this case.

In general, flexibility of future choice tends to be valued positively by decision-makers. This is because the more courses of action are left open for the future, the greater *in general* will be the prospects of successful adaptation to whatever changes in circumstances the future may bring.* However, it may not always be realistic to treat flexibility of future choice as one simple comparison area, because the value of such flexibility may differ between one area of future choice and another, and also between one set of interests and another. Indeed, flexibility to one party may sometimes mean restrictions of opportunities to others. In South Side, for example, the opportunities for residents to improve their homes, or to exercise other kinds of choices in their own domestic lives, might become more restricted if certain options for development on nearby sites were not foreclosed.

Where many alternatives are being compared in broad terms, it may be adequate to treat flexibility or some such term as a single broadly defined comparison area, as in the list of Figure 59. At other times, however, it may be important to relate this aspect of comparison more carefully to some evaluation framework which identifies a range of affected interests or policy concerns, as in the two examples of Figure 60. This finer level of flexibility analysis becomes practicable in any situation where opportunities for future choice have been structured in terms of decision areas and options, so that flexibility in some decision areas can be given greater weight than flexibility in others. For example, in the situation of Figure 25, the first of the five short-term action schemes could be regarded with particular

---

* This can be seen as essentially an expression of the cybernetic law of requisite variety, first enunciated by Ross Ashby in his 'Introduction to Cybernetics' (Ashby, 1956). At its simplest, the law states that 'it takes variety to control variety'.

favour as it is the only one to leave open the opportunity of developing the central site for industry — an aspect of flexibility which could be viewed as of particular importance to the local unemployed.

Another possibility — which will be discussed more fully in Chapter 8 — is that the preservation of options in some decision areas might be seen as of particular significance as a means of responding to certain specified *contingencies* that might arise in future. For example, the opportunity to zone the central site in South Side for industry might be seen as of particular significance if the contingency of closure of the local steelworks were to occur.

Circumstances sometimes arise in practice where another related aspect of flexibility has to be considered; the flexibility not just to choose between alternative courses of action in future but to *alter* courses of current action at some point in time after an initial commitment has been made. Where decision areas and options have been rigorously defined in terms of immediate action commitments of an irrevocable nature, this possibility should strictly speaking not arise. However, when people are working on problems under pressure, this kind of rigour is not always appropriate. This is a point that is of particular significance in relation to choices of broad policy orientation, which may be publicly adopted at one moment but can be modified or reversed later should circumstances change.

One means of approaching this question of flexibility to modify a policy position at some future time is illustrated in Figure 61. This example builds on the comparison of South Side policy orientations presented earlier (Figure 54). Figure 61 starts by presenting the courses of possible action at an operational level which are left open by each of the three possible policy orientations — omitting the short-term private orientation because no schemes at all at the operational level were found to be consistent with it.

Also, it was indicated in Figure 54 that a long-term private investment orientation was believed to be of doubtful feasibility. In such circumstances, one working assumption might be that such an orientation could not be adopted in the short term, yet that the choice of a short-term public investment orientation now could leave open the possibility of a later switch to a long-term private orientation, should a sufficiently interested and influential private investor appear. The full logic of this situation is represented in Figure 61, where POLICY NOW? and POLICY LATER? are formulated as separate areas of choice, in place of the composite decision area which was originally labelled INVESTMENT ORIENTATION?. The choice *now* of an orientation towards short-term public investment can then be compared to the choice *now* of a long-term public investment orientation — or, indeed, any other alternative — in terms of the additional flexibility it offers in terms of its *changeability* to a different policy position in future. However, it should be noted that, in this example, the flexibility available in the 'Level 2' decision areas may be

FIGURE

61

SOUTH SIDE
EXAMPLE

Expressing Interchangeability in Policy Choice

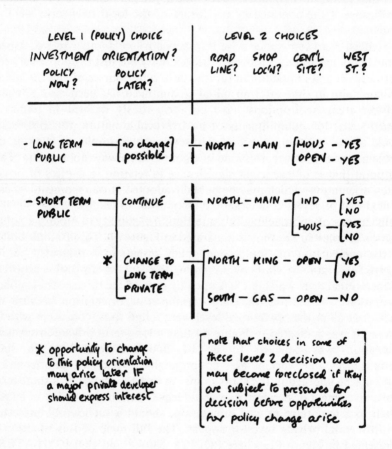

LEVEL 1 (POLICY) CHOICE	LEVEL 2 CHOICES
INVESTMENT ORIENTATION?	ROAD SHOP CENT'L WEST
POLICY POLICY	LINE? LOC'N? SITE? ST.?
NOW? LATER?	

- LONG TERM   ⎡ no change ⎤   NORTH - MAIN - ⎡ HOUS - YES
  PUBLIC   ⎣ possible ⎦   ⎣ OPEN - YES

- SHORT TERM —— CONTINUE   NORTH - MAIN - ⎡ IND — ⎡ YES
  PUBLIC   ⎣   ⎣ NO
                                                ⎣ HOUS — ⎡ YES
                                                         ⎣ NO

        ✱ CHANGE TO   ⎡ NORTH - KING - OPEN — ⎡ YES
           LONG TERM   ⎣   ⎣ NO
           PRIVATE   ⎣ SOUTH — GAS — OPEN — NO

✱ opportunity to change
to this policy orientation
may arise later IF
a major private developer
should express interest

⎡ note that choices in some of
these level 2 decision areas
may become foreclosed if they
are subject to pressures for
decision before opportunities
for policy change arise ⎦

Where decision areas relate to choices of policy stance or other positions which allow future modification, it can sometimes be useful to compare short-term alternatives in terms of the possibility of changing to other positions at some future time. Such comparisons are usually made informally and interactively, but this example of a more formal comparison illustrates the general principles involved.

limited if some of them are of high urgency, calling for commitment at or before the time the initial policy is agreed. This kind of difficulty will be considered further in Chapter 8.

Choice of Method of Assessment within a Comparison Area

Just as there are different ways in which alternative courses of action can be compared in terms of their relative flexibility, so more generally there are different ways in which alternatives can be compared within any other kind of comparison area. This means that there are always judgements to be made as to how any kind of comparative information should be *presented* to help people make comparisons between specific alternatives — not least where information from varied sources has to be compressed into a compact and intelligible form. Among the practical choices to be faced are choices relating to the use of different forms of language for communication such as words, figures and graphs, as well as choices about the ways in which feelings of uncertainty should be expressed. Some of the differences of approach that can be considered in both these directions were considered in Chapter 3 (Figures 20 and 21).

Underlying such choices of presentation, however, may be deeper choices about the actual techniques or *procedures* to be used in making assessments of alternatives, and the sources of information or judgement on which those procedures should draw. Such choices of assessment procedure can sometimes have an important bearing on the levels of effort and time to be devoted to different comparison areas, and also on the levels of confidence with which assessments can be expressed.

Some procedures of assessment are highly intuitive, while others involve precisely-defined sequences of calculation. For example, to form an assessment of the relative capital outlays involved in different development options for the central site in South Side, there could be a choice of either asking a single financial or engineering expert for a quick 'off the cuff' guess, based on accumulated personal experience; or calling for a more painstaking calculation taking several weeks, in which several different experts might be asked to play some part. However simplified or elaborate the procedure may be, it is important to remember that the range of underlying sources of uncertainty will be the same — the choice being one as to whether or not effort should be invested in exploring them in a conscious way.

Wherever a particular procedure of assessment is thought to be critical to the decisions currently in view, there is always the opportunity to pause and explore its structure in more depth, in a search for a fuller understanding of the pattern of elements and operations on which it is built. One systematic means of conducting this kind of exploration is illustrated in Figure 62. For illustrative purposes, this example is restricted to one comparatively

FIGURE

62

SOUTH SIDE
EXAMPLE

Uncovering the Elements in an Assessment Procedure

ELEMENTS IN ESTIMATION OF
CAPITAL COSTS OF SERVICING
CENTRAL SITE FOR
ALTERNATIVE USES:

CENT'L SITE?

- ind   - hous

	CENT'L SITE? -ind	CENT'L SITE? -hous
estimated cost of servicing this site	450k	200k
estimated usable site area	30 ha	25 ha
full area of site	40 ha	40 ha
⊖ estimated extent of buffer zone	-10 ha	-15 ha
⊗ estimated site servicing cost/ha	× 15 k/ha	× 8 k/ha
knowledge of unit servicing costs on other comparable recent sites	11-14 k/ha	6-7 k/ha
predicted rate of cost inflation for site servicing contracts	5% per year	5% per year
extent of any engineering difficulties expected on this site	not exceptional	not exceptional
policy on range of site infrastructure services to be provided by municipality	comprehensive for industrial sites	minimal for housing sites

[simple arithmetical operations]
marked ○

COMPARING

SKILLS

This kind of systematic exploration of the elements contributing to an assessment procedure is not usually worth carrying out unless and until the focus for comparison has been narrowed down to a few alternatives which differ critically in terms of assessments in particular comparison areas, making it important to explore key sources of uncertainty and alternative ways in which they might be managed.

tangible aspect of the assessment procedures in South Side — that of the relative assessment of capital outlays for two of the development options for the central site.

The breakdown of elements and operations in Figure 62 begins by taking two of the apparently straightforward numerical assessments of capital cost which were first presented in Chapter 3 (Figure 22); the estimates of 450k and 200k entered against the industrial and housing options for use of the central site.

The baseline for each of the assessments in Figure 62 is assumed to be the 'null option' of leaving the site in its present derelict state — an option which may be purely hypothetical in so far as it is not considered a realistic alternative within the present South Side problem formulation but, nevertheless, might offer a well-defined starting point for the application of standard cost assessment techniques.

In Figure 62, the assessments of capital outlay for the industrial and housing options are both shown broken down in a stepwise way into various contributory *elements* of assessment. Some of these take the form of other more basic estimates of a quantitative kind — for instance, estimates of the usable site area and the unit cost of site servicing per hectare — while others take the form of non-numerical statements of assumptions which are still worth recording explicitly, especially where they remain open to challenge. For example, one engineer might assume that engineering difficulties on the central site were 'not exceptional'; yet another might cast doubt on this assumption in the light of a somewhat different appraisal of drainage problems or geological conditions. Again, some participants might wish to challenge an underlying policy assumption that industrial sites should be provided with a comprehensive range of infrastructure services before being advertised for rental or sale, whereas only minimal infrastructure should be provided if housing development were being considered.

The breakdown of assessments into contributory operations and elements is a procedure that could, in theory, be pursued almost indefinitely, exposing more and more hidden assumptions all the time. However, this depth of investigation will not normally be justified unless it is suspected that it will expose new areas of uncertainty which might have a critical effect on work within the choosing mode. Under practical time and resource pressures, it is more usual to trust the judgement of the experts; however, the opportunity is always there to ask probing questions about the assumptions underlying any expert assessments, and Figure 62 illustrates one general procedure that can be used to probe systematically the range of assumptions on which particular assessments rest.*

Of course, the nature of the assumptions and the underlying procedure of assessment may be quite different in different types of comparison area.

---

* Other examples relating to actual planning studies carried out by Coventry City Council were presented in *Local Government and Strategic Choice* (Friend & Jessop, 1969/77 pp69-95).

For instance, any assessments of annual incomes for the two alternatives in Figure 62 could depend on judgements about the year-by-year build up of incomes over some fixed period of future years, with mounting levels of uncertainty as the time horizon extends. And, wherever there is no obvious numerical unit of assessment on which to rely — as in the assessment of the impact any course of action might have on existing residents of South Side — then the breakdown of contributory assumptions is likely to be a less straightforward matter. But the same principles apply; and the method of stepwise investigation of assumptions illustrated in Figure 62 remains valid even when most or all of the contributory assumptions have to be explored by interrogating an expert whose assessments are based purely on personal experience and informed judgement.

Expressing Feelings of Uncertainty when Assessing Alternatives

Because any assessment of the effects of pursuing a course of action involves at least some elements of conjecture, anybody who is asked to contribute towards the process of assessment must expect to encounter feelings of *uncertainty* — whether these feelings are addressed consciously or at a more unconscious level. Referring again to the example of an assessment procedure considered in Figure 62, it might be possible for a local planner to feel very confident about quoting a figure of four hectares for the full area of the central site, accepting that details of boundary demarcation could make a marginal difference. Yet the extent of the proposed buffer zone — assumed to be wider in the case of the housing than the industrial option, so as to provide a higher level of insulation from traffic noise — might be seen as a rather more debatable matter. And the assessment of site servicing costs per hectare might be expected to involve higher levels of uncertainty again — as was indeed suggested in Figure 62 by the fuller breakdown of this element into four different contributory elements, not all of them of a readily quantifiable form.

People who are asked to make assessments under uncertainty — even if they be professional experts in their field — do not always behave in a similar or consistent way. One expert, for instance, might prefer to quote a single estimate of 15k per hectare for industrial servicing costs, as if it were quite incontrovertible, treating any feelings of uncertainty as a purely personal concern. However, another expert might profess such a high state of uncertainty as to be reluctant to offer any figure at all — perhaps for fear of being called to account should any estimate offered later be falsified by events. To overcome such feelings of reluctance in quoting figures — or, conversely, to get a sense of the level of uncertainty which surrounds a single apparently confident estimate — it is often worth adopting a simple questioning procedure which has become known as the *surprise limit method*. This method is illustrated with reference to South Side in Figure 63.

The surprise limit method can be applied to any element within an assessment procedure which calls for judgements along some numerical or equivalent scale. It involves asking a series of questions of a person who holds information in that field — the *knowledge source*, in expert systems language — as to what levels on that scale would cause them *surprise*, starting with extreme levels at either end and gradually working inwards until a range of 'non-surprising' possibilities remains.

Figure 63 demonstrates two different levels at which this approach can be applied to the comparison of capital outlays for Schemes A and B in the South Side problem situation. In the first set of questions, it is supposed that an expert — in this case perhaps a civil engineer — starts from a position of reluctance to give any estimate of the capital cost per hectare of servicing the central site for industrial development. So the interrogator begins by taking what is likely to be an unrealistically low level — in this case 5k per hectare — and asking whether it would cause the expert any surprise if the servicing cost per hectare were as low as this. If the expert says 'yes' then the question is repeated with successively higher levels until a level which no longer causes surprise is reached. The same kind of question can also be asked, starting from what is initially judged to be an unrealistically high level and working downwards.

Usually, the questioner works from the two ends more or less alternately, accepting that there will be a tendency to 'overshoot' the limits of surprise from time to time. The process is, therefore, one of gradual narrowing down from both ends until a view is arrived at of the *range* of tenable assumptions in between. Such a procedure, of working by successive approximation towards a feasible range, can usually persuade even the most reluctant expert to give some expression to his or her 'limits of surprise', even when starting from a position of refusal to make any estimate at all. In the opposite situation, where an expert refuses to deviate from a single point on the scale, it becomes possible to test the limits of surprise by working outwards from that point rather than inwards from the extremes. In practice, the procedure is usually conducted purely through verbal questions and answers; it is mainly for illustrative purposes that Figure 63 sets out the successive steps in written form.

The second illustration in Figure 63 shows how the surprise limit method can be applied even when the scale is a non-numerical one. The scale here is the generalised one of degree of *comparative advantage* which was first illustrated in Chapter 3 (Figure 21). The process of asking surprise limit questions in relation to this non-numerical scale is essentially the same as before; this example demonstrates how relative assessments can be arrived at even within comparison areas where there is no basis for comparing alternatives other than in terms of some intuitive sense of level of advantage

FIGURE

63

SOUTH SIDE
EXAMPLE

Eliciting Limits of Surprise

would it surprise you if it were suggested that the CAPITAL COST
PER HECTARE to service industrial development on this site could be:

below 5 k/ha ?   (YES!)   above 30k/ha?   (YES!)
below 10k/ha ?   (YES)   above 20k/ha?   (YES)
below 12k/ha?   (NO)   above 18k/ha   (NO)

> So take range of assessments as [12k/ha to 18k/ha]
> point assessment (best guess) as 15k/ha

would it surprise you if it were suggested that the BALANCE OF
ADVANTAGE between schemes A and B in terms of the CAPITAL:
comparison area could be:

extreme in favour of A?   (YES!)   extreme in favour of B?   (YES)
considerable in favour of A?   (YES!)   considerable in favour of B?   (NO)
significant in favour of A?   (YES)
marginal in favour of A?   (YES)
negligible either way?   (YES)
marginal in favour of B?   (YES)
significant in favour of B?   (NO)

> So take balance of advantage in terms of CAPITAL:
> to be [significant to considerable] in favour of B

COMPARING

SKILLS

This kind of stepwise questioning process is usually carried out verbally, and can
be introduced briefly and informally at any stage of interactive working where it
is proving difficult to arrive at an assessment either on a numerical or a more
judgemental scale. It can be used either to overcome unwillingness to offer any
assessment at all, or to probe the level of uncertainty surrounding a point
assessment.

— marginal, significant or whatever — within the specific setting in which decisions are to be made.

There is, of course, no reason why surprise limit questions should not be addressed to more than one expert. Indeed, the possibility that there may be several different knowledge sources opens the way to the use of systematic approaches such as the Delphi method (Dalkey, 1969) for pooling the judgements of several individuals with differing kinds or levels of expertise to contribute. Such experiments, if used as a background for discussion rather than a substitute for it, can expose all kinds of hidden differences in the assumptions of different individuals. One exercise in which a surprise limit approach was used to explore differences in perception between colleagues in the same team — an adminstrator, a planner and an engineer — has been fully reported elsewhere (Friend, Power and Yewlett, 1974 pp140-158).

Combining Advantage Judgements Across Different Comparison Areas

It can be difficult enough at times to arrive at judgements of the balance of advantage between alternatives within any single comparison area: it can be even more difficult to judge the overall balance of advantage across a set of dissimilar comparison areas. This was illustrated by the comparison in Chapter 3 (Figure 21) of two alternative schemes for South Side across the four comparison areas of CAPITAL:, INCOME:, JOBS: and RESIDENTS:, each represented by a range of points on a common advantage comparison scale. It is at such moments of evaluation *across* comparison areas that major feelings of uncertainty about value considerations tend to come most directly to the fore, and have to be taken into account alongside whatever other feelings of uncertainty may have been encountered in making assessments within the separate comparison areas taken one at a time.

It is never an easy matter to bring diverse sources of uncertainty within a common analytical framework. But it is necessary to do so if it is intended to compare alternative approaches to the management of uncertainty within the choosing mode; and it was as a step in this direction that a broad-based method of advantage comparison under uncertainty was introduced in Chapter 3. The judgement was presented (Figure 21) that Scheme B had the advantage over Scheme A in terms of capital outlay and probably also in terms of impact on residents; but that Scheme A had the advantage in terms of income and jobs. But the levels of advantage were subject to much uncertainty — uncertainty deriving in part from the process of assessment within each comparison area and, in part, from the value judgements involved in conversion to the common advantage comparison scale. These uncertainties made it all the more difficult in that example (Figure 21) to

FIGURE

64

SOUTH SIDE
EXAMPLE

Combining Advantage Judgements Across Comparison
Areas

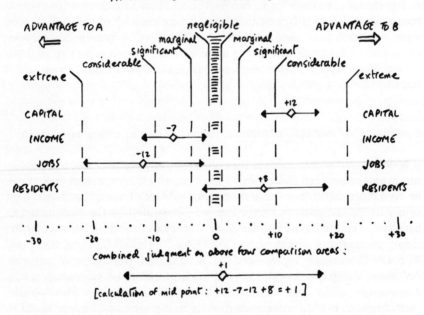

ADVANTAGE COMPARISON B vs A

combined judgment on above four comparison areas:

+1

[calculation of mid point: +12 -7 -12 +8 = +1]

EFFECT OF ADDING A FURTHER COMPARISON IN TERMS OF FLEXIBILITY

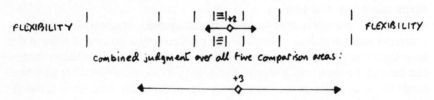

FLEXIBILITY   FLEXIBILITY

combined judgment over all five comparison areas:

+3

It is occasionally worth calibrating an advantage comparison scale numerically
as in this illustration, either to provide a firmer basis for arriving at judgements
of advantage across different comparison areas for a particularly important pair
of alternatives, or to carry out periodic checks for the types of bias that can arise
in combining judgements of ranges in a more informal and judgemental way.

judge where the overall balance of advantage lay when all four comparison areas were taken into account.

This kind of balancing process is one which people continually have to undertake in practice, if only in an intuitive way. However, once a comparative advantage scale has been used to record an explicit picture of judgements and assumptions, it becomes possible to supplement that intuition — and to carry out checks on its reliability — by resort to rather more systematic methods. One way of doing this is illustrated in Figure 64. In Figure 64, a numerical scale of advantage assessment has been introduced as a means of *calibrating* the distinctions between bands on the original non-numerical scale, and thus as a basis for combining judgements across the different comparison areas. The calibration of the scale is a matter of convenience: the particular numerical scale used in Figure 64 treats the point of no advantage either way as zero, and takes the boundary between the 'significant' and 'considerable' bands as ten points in either direction — one direction being treated as negative and the other positive so as to keep the arithmetic straight.

Such a scale allows the mid-point of the range for each comparison area to be expressed as either a negative or a positive number. These numbers can then be added together to arrive at a rough estimate of the mid-point of the *range of belief* about overall comparative advantage, for any set of comparison areas taken in combination. In the illustration of Figure 64, there is a total of 20 'advantage points' in favour of B to be counted by adding the mid-points of the CAPITAL: and RESIDENTS: ranges, against 19 points in favour of A obtained by adding the mid-points of the INCOME: and JOBS: assessments. The net effect is a marginal single point of net advantage in favour of B when all four comparisons are combined.

But then there is the influence of uncertainty to be considered, which is considerable in this case. A rough rule of thumb, which is good enough for most practical purposes, is that the range of belief for a combined advantage comparison will be a little wider than the range of belief for the most uncertain of the separate advantage comparisons within the individual comparison areas; if there are two comparison areas with an equally wide span of uncertainty, then a span about half as wide again as either of them can be assumed. In the illustration of Figure 64, it will be noticed that the range for both RESIDENTS: and JOBS: extends about 10 points on either side of the mid-point, whereas the range for both CAPITAL: and INCOME: assessments is significantly less. So the rule of thumb suggests that a range of about 15 points on either side of the mid-point will be roughly right as an expression of the total range of uncertainty when all comparison areas are combined. As shown in Figure 64, this means there could be a significant or even considerable advantage to either alternative when all sources of uncertainty are taken into account: so there is a case for some serious thought about how the overall range of uncertainty could be managed, before a preference in the direction of either alternative is expressed.

This kind of procedure for combining advantage comparisons can also be carried out in a step by step way, introducing one new comparison area at a time. This possibility is illustrated in Figure 64 by the introduction of FLEXIBILITY: as an additional comparison area; the range of positions on the scale being based, in this case, purely on a quick intuitive judgement about the relative flexibility of A and B. In the event, Figure 64 shows that this addition makes only a marginal difference to the mid-point and range arrived at for the other four comparison areas combined.

With practice, it becomes possible to use a non-numerical advantage comparison scale in a quick and informal way, either as a group activity or by asking people to work individually on pre-prepared sheets, then comparing and collating the individual judgements which they make. It usually takes a little experience to arrive at consistent interpretations of the different levels of significance within a particular working situation; for people have to learn to use the successive bands of a comparative advantage scale in a broadly similar way.

For example, in a particular context, it might seem to make sense to rate one alternative as having a 'considerable' advantage over another in each of two comparison areas, but little sense to regard their combined advantage as 'extreme'. In that case, it might be decided to extend the width of the 'considerable' band on the scale until such inconsistencies tended to disappear. Also, methods based on statistical theory can provide a check on any more intuitive rules of thumb by which ranges of uncertainty are combined.* However, in interactive group working, such checks are mainly of use on an occasional basis, as a means of building confidence that intuition is not generating results which are at too much variance with logic.

Applying Constraints in the Choice of a Working Shortlist

Where there is a large number of decision schemes to be compared, it will usually be quite unrealistic to subject more than a few of them to the kind of carefully structured pair comparison process under uncertainty which has just been discussed; so the need to choose a more restricted working shortlist becomes acute. One approach to the choice of such a working shortlist was illustrated in Chapter 3 (Figure 22), where all schemes which were estimated to come above a specified threshold of capital cost were set

* If a set of variables are independent and can be assumed to follow the normal (Gaussian) probability distribution, then the standard deviation of their sum can be taken as the square root of the sum of the squares of the separate standard deviations. So if the ranges shown in Figure 64 are assumed to represent two standard deviations on either side of the mean, the corresponding distance for the first four comparison areas combined would be the square root of (four squared plus five squared plus ten squared plus ten squared), which is about equal to sixteen.

aside, as were all those which did not meet a specified minimum level on the non-numerical residents' confidence index. The application of such minimum or maximum *constraints* on selected indices of assessment is a useful, if obvious, means of arriving at a working shortlist where there is a very large number of possible decision schemes to be considered. This is especially so where the options within the individual decision areas can be assessed separately on numerical or equivalent scales, and assessments for some at least of the combinations of options can be made simply by adding the option assessments together. In practice a monetary index is often used as a constraint, because there are many situations in which it is politically appropriate to apply some upper limit to the overall cost of a decision scheme. However, in other situations a constraint might be placed on the minimum number of jobs created, or the maximum number of residents to be displaced, or the minimum ratio of annual return to investment. In general, it will, of course, only be worth introducing a constraint on any scale if it corresponds to a concern which is important in the particular context in which the participants are working.

When applying a constraint to a large and complex set of decision schemes, it is not always necessary to work through all possible schemes in full. One means of simplifying the procedure is illustrated in Figure 65. Here, assessments of capital cost are indicated for the set of possible decision schemes for South Side, these being presented in the form of a tree as in Chapter 3 (Figure 22) — but with some adjustments introduced to illustrate particular points. First, the WEST ST? decision area has been added, which increases the total range of schemes. Secondly, the options within the SHOP LOC'N? and DIST LIFE? decision areas are assessed jointly rather than separately — because it is supposed now that there are certain costs associated with choosing options in particular combinations in these two decision areas — and the sequence of decision areas has been modified so as to bring these two decision areas together. Thirdly, the capital cost assessments in each column have been recalibrated so that the alternative with the lowest capital cost is taken as zero and the expected capital cost of every other alternative is assessed as a positive figure relative to this minimum amount. Such recalibration can be useful where it is desired to apply a constraint of expected *relative* cost — but of course in many situations cost limits may be conceived in more absolute terms.

Because only positive cost figures can now appear, it is possible to set a constraint on the maximum cumulative figure which is acceptable at any branching point in the tree. In Figure 65, a capital cost limit of 500k monetary units has been introduced. This has the effect of terminating the branches emanating from choice of the southern road line quite early on, and also closing some of the other branches before the full set of feasible schemes has been developed. In this example, only four feasible schemes remain which do not violate either the option bars or the cumulative capital

FIGURE
65

Applying Constraints in Generating Decision Schemes

SOUTH SIDE
EXAMPLE

expected capital costs in k [recalibrated with least cost alternative in each column = 0]

joint assessment

ROAD LINE?		SHOP LOC'N?	DIST LIFE?		CENT'L SITE?		WEST ST?	
– NORTH	50k	– MAIN	– 10YR	0	– IND	450k	– YES	150k
– SOUTH	0	– KING	– 10YR	300k	– HOUS	200k	– NO	0
			– 20YR	400k	– OPEN	0		
			– 40YR	450k				
		– GAS	– 20YR	650k				
			– 40YR	750k				

PROPOSED RULE FOR ELIMINATING HIGH-COST SCHEMES: close any branch when cumulative total for expected capital cost exceeds 500k

SCHEME:

```
NORTH ──50k── MAIN -10YR ──50k── IND ──500k── YES ──650k── X
                                              NO ──500k──── P

                                   HOUS ──250k── YES ──400k── Q
                                               NO ──250k──── R

              KING ─ 10YR ──350k── HOUS ──550k── X

                    20YR ──400k── HOUS ──600k── X
                                  OPEN ──400k── YES ──550k── X
                                               NO ──400k──── S

                    40YR ──500k── HOUS ──700k── X
                                  OPEN ──500k── YES ──650k── X
                                               NO X [option bar]

SOUTH ──0── GAS ─ 20YR ──650k── X
                  40YR ──750k── X
```

PROPOSED WORKING SHORTLIST: compare R, S, P, using R to represent Q.

COMPARING

SKILLS

Wherever options or combinations can be assessed in terms of a simplified scale, it becomes possible to cut down the range of schemes for closer comparison by introducing, on a trial basis, some constraint on the maximum or minimum acceptable level. It can save time and effort to close off entire branches at an early stage, and recalibration to make all relative assessments positive can facilitate this.

cost constraint of 500k. These four schemes have been given the labels P, Q, R and S for working purposes, and together they offer one basis for a manageable working shortlist.

If desired, the working shortlist can be further reduced by grouping together schemes which are rather similar in terms of their options, then using one of them to *represent* the other members of that group at this stage in the comparison process. In the example of Figure 65, the judgement has been made that Scheme R can represent Scheme Q within a more restricted shortlist of only three schemes, because the two schemes differ only in terms of the West Street option and R is the less costly of the two.

Often, it can be difficult to judge in practice at what level a constraint should be set, if the purpose is to develop a working shortlist which is neither too large nor too limited to serve as a base for more careful comparison of alternatives. The level of the constraint can, of course, always be raised or lowered in retrospect, if the level first chosen does not have the desired effect. However, where the procedure of working systematically through the tree is being carried out by computer, then these adjustments can be carried out automatically in accordance with specified rules. One possibility is to specify in advance the number of schemes required in the working shortlist, leaving the computer to adjust the level of the constraint accordingly. Another possibility is to specify the maximum level of difference to be considered between the least-cost scheme and any other scheme to be included in the list — recognising that, as in the example of Figure 65, the level of cost for the least-cost scheme cannot be known at the outset if there is a possibility that the combination of all the zero-cost options will be excluded by option bars.

Shortlisting Across Multiple Comparison Areas

The application of constraints in relation to numerical or similar indices can provide an effective way of reducing the range of schemes where this is very large. But this reduction can carry a cost, because it can mean ignoring for the time being any other comparison areas which cannot be treated in this way; and also because potentially vital information about uncertainty has to be temporarily set aside. So, it is often wise to view the use of constraints as only a crude filtering phase in the formation of a shortlist, leading to an intermediate list of schemes to which other methods of shortlisting can subsequently be applied.

As was also illustrated earlier (in Figure 22) the *ranking* of alternatives according to order of preference in different comparison areas offers another useful reference point in selecting promising alternatives for closer examination. Simple rankings can be deduced quickly wherever decision schemes can be compared in terms of numerical or equivalent indices, with tied rankings wherever the indices for two or more alternatives are the same;

FIGURE
66

SOUTH SIDE
EXAMPLE

Shortlisting Across Multiple Comparison Areas

RANKING OF 9 SCHEMES BY EACH OF 4 COMPARISON AREAS:

SCHEME	CAPITAL:	RESIDENTS:	INCOME:	JOBS:	dominated by:
A	2nd =	4th =	(1st)	(1st)	–
B	(1st)	2nd =	7th	8th	–
C	4th =	4th =	6th	6th	A
D	7th =	2nd =	4th	5th	–
E	9th	(1st)	2nd	4th	–
F	2nd =	7th	9th	9th	A, B
G	4th =	4th =	8th	7th	–
H	6th =	8th =	5th	3rd	A
I	7th =	8th =	3rd	2nd	A

RANK ORDERINGS OF 9 SCHEMES BY DIFFERENT COMPARISON AREAS:

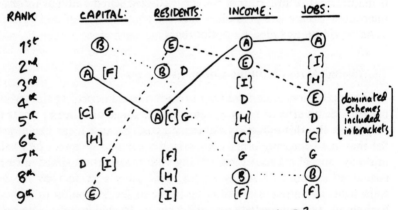

suggested working shortlist: A, E, B : possibly also D?

The ranking of alternatives taking several comparison areas separately offers a simple but useful aid to comparison where the set is neither too large to be readily handled in this way — in which case constraints can be introduced — nor so small as to make this step unnecessary. The setting aside of dominated schemes and the picking out of those ranking highly on several comparison areas can then aid the shortlisting process.

and it is not difficult to scan two or more comparison areas simultaneously once the information has been reduced to this form. But a set of alternatives can always be arranged in a tentative rank order in other comparison areas where assessments cannot be quantified — so long as there is some basis for judgement which allows one scheme to be rated, however hesitantly, as more desirable than, less desirable than, or roughly similar to any other.

Figure 66 develops this point by comparing the nine schemes A to I of Figure 22 in terms of their rankings on all four of the comparison areas which were originally introduced. The CAPITAL: and RESIDENTS: rankings are as earlier indicated in Figure 22; but the INCOME: and JOBS: rankings have been added on the basis of quick intuitive judgements about orders of preference within each of these two additional comparison areas.

On the basis of a set of rankings such as that in Figure 66, it may be possible to pick out one or more schemes which are *dominated* by particular others, in the sense that any dominated scheme is inferior to, or at least no better than, the other in each of the rankings in the different comparison areas. So, in South Side, there are four schemes — C, F, H and I — each of which is dominated by Scheme A in terms of this set of four comparison areas; and among them, Scheme F is dominated by Scheme B as well. So, it could be judged appropriate to exclude these four schemes from any shortlist selected as a basis for closer evaluation — accepting the risk that the excluded schemes might score quite highly in other comparison areas not considered at this stage, and also the risk that the rankings might change if major areas of uncertainty were to be investigated and new information uncovered.

As an alternative means of displaying the same information, it can often be useful to rearrange a set of rankings by reference to the principle of *rank ordering*, as shown in the second listing of Figure 66. Here the set of alternatives is arranged in four different orders of preference, each based on their rank order in one of the four comparison areas; so schemes which rate highly in terms of two or more comparison areas will tend to rise towards the top in the corresponding columns. It can be seen in this instance that Scheme A — which comes top in two of the columns — rates quite well also in the other two columns, while Scheme E — the most attractive from the residents' viewpoint — scores well enough in terms of income and jobs but is the least favourable in terms of capital cost. So, the comparison of A with E could be a promising one to explore more closely from the point of view of exposing underlying value issues; thus these two alternatives might well be taken forward to a committee of elected representatives for debate, perhaps after further assessment of their relative consequences has been carried out.

Further inspection of Figure 66 might suggest also that Scheme B be carried forward for closer comparison with A and E, in view of its high ranking in terms of both the residents and capital assessments — despite its

FIGURE
67

Process Choices when Working in the Comparing Mode

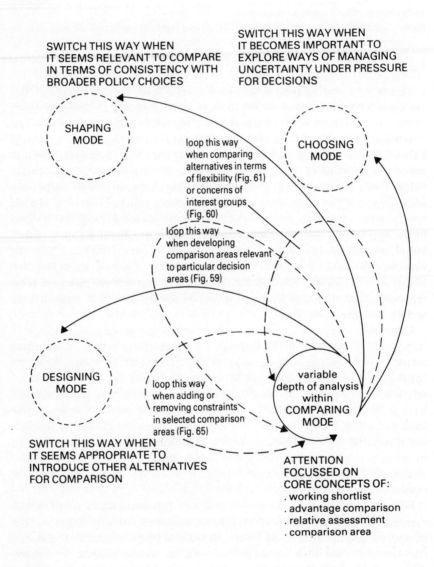

SWITCH THIS WAY WHEN
IT SEEMS RELEVANT TO COMPARE
IN TERMS OF CONSISTENCY WITH
BROADER POLICY CHOICES

SWITCH THIS WAY WHEN
IT BECOMES IMPORTANT TO
EXPLORE WAYS OF MANAGING
UNCERTAINTY UNDER PRESSURE
FOR DECISIONS

SHAPING
MODE

loop this way
when comparing
alternatives in terms
of flexibility (Fig. 61)
or concerns of
interest groups
(Fig. 60)

CHOOSING
MODE

loop this way
when developing
comparison areas relevant
to particular decision
areas (Fig. 59)

DESIGNING
MODE

loop this way
when adding or
removing constraints
in selected comparison
areas (Fig. 65)

variable
depth of analysis
within
COMPARING
MODE

SWITCH THIS WAY WHEN
IT SEEMS APPROPRIATE TO
INTRODUCE OTHER ALTERNATIVES
FOR COMPARISON

ATTENTION
FOCUSSED ON
CORE CONCEPTS OF:
. working shortlist
. advantage comparison
. relative assessment
. comparison area

COMPARING

SUMMARY

low ranking in each of the other two comparison areas. Conceivably, too, Scheme D could be carried forward as a possible compromise alternative, making a quite manageable working shortlist of four schemes in all — A, E, B and D — to be used as a basis for closer pair comparisons taking uncertainty more explicitly into account. And this in turn could provide a basis from which to switch into the work of the choosing mode.

Summary: Process Judgements in the Comparing Mode

This chapter has discussed various choices of method and emphasis that are continually encountered in practice when working in the comparing mode. They are choices which involve repeated judgements about the balance between simplification and elaboration in evaluation method; a balance which, as argued at the beginning of the chapter, is more usefully conceived in *dynamic* than in static terms. To maintain an appropriate balance through time can involve alternating between rough and ready comparisons among many alternatives, and closer comparisons of a selected few; however, this balance is one that has to be judged not only in the light of the application of broad guide-lines such as those offered in this chapter, but also in the light of political and administrative considerations which can vary from context to context. These will include the perceived importance of different decisions; the range of interests affected; and the nature of their representation, direct or indirect, in the processes by which comparisons and choices are to be made.

Underlying many of the evaluative choices to be made are questions of response to uncertainty — feelings of uncertainty being, in practice, inseparable from the necessary processes of conjecture about what the consequences of alternative courses of action might be. The concepts of relative assessment and of advantage comparison developed in this chapter have provided a way of coming to grips with these feelings of uncertainty, at least so far as their influence on comparative judgements is concerned. But the closer analysis of perceived areas of uncertainty, and the consideration of what might be done about them, is a matter that will be deferred for discussion in Chapter 8, as it is more germane to the work of the choosing than the comparing mode.

Figure 67 summarises the points made in this chapter, in terms of the various types of looping and switching judgements which centre on the comparing mode. Within the comparing mode itself, the idea of dynamic comparison, involving alternation between crude sifting of many alternatives and closer evaluations of a selected few, offers a key to the process judgements that have to be made. Considering first the brief loops that can be made out of the comparing mode towards other modes, Figure 67 indicates a loop in the direction of the *choosing mode* in situations where some rough and ready assessment of flexibility of future choice seems important; a loop in the direction of the *shaping mode* when developing a set of comparison areas relevant to a particular problem focus; and a loop in the direction of the *designing mode* whenever, for current working purposes, it is felt useful to reduce the range of alternatives by imposing additional constraints — or, for that matter, to extend the range by removing constraints previously assumed.

Turning to the question of less transitory switching into other modes, the normal progression in a conventional sequential process of decision-making would be from the comparing into the *choosing mode* — not necessarily to make a definitive choice among the alternatives that have been compared, but at least in order to make incremental progress in that direction. However, where a process is guided by the strategic choice philosophy, other directions of progress are possible. A move into the *shaping mode* will often be appropriate where the balance of advantage between alternatives across different comparison areas seems so problematic that choices of policy orientation should be brought more explicitly into the problem focus itself. At a more technical level, a switch back into the *designing mode* makes sense whenever it seems that a reformulation of options and option bars could lead to a clearer expression of the set of alternatives to be compared.

Illustrations from Practice

There now follows a set of three *illustrations from practice* illustrating some further practical points about the work of the comparing mode.

The first of these, from a planning exercise for North Holland, illustrates the merging of contributions from different members of a group in the building up of an initial set of comparison areas, and the collation of opinions about their relative importance. The second illustration, from north east Brazil, shows a variant of the advantage comparison method in which a list of uncertainty areas is built up as difficulties are encountered in arriving at group judgements. The third illustration is from an application in which ranking over several comparison areas was used in the formation of a working shortlist.

FIGURE

68

Illustration from Practice – Comparing 1

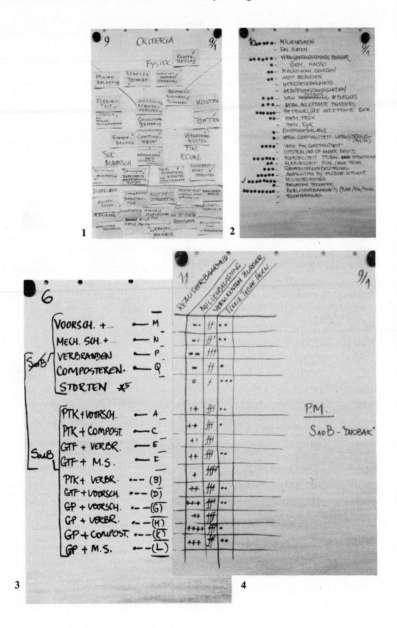

COMPARING

PRACTICE

Theme: Developing Key Comparison Areas for Exploring the Differences between Decision Schemes.

Problem: A Provincial Development Plan for the Disposal of Household Waste.

Context: Inter-organisational Planning Team, Province of Noord Holland, The Netherlands, 1986.

COMMENTARY ON FIGURE 68

These flip charts were drawn up during the final day of the first of a series of four ;
workshops, held to bring together the thinking of planners from the province of Noord
Holland, the central Government and the Municipality of Amsterdam on the problem of
disposal of solid waste. The workshops were held in Heemstede, the Netherlands during
January and February 1986, with Allen Hickling acting as process consultant to a team of two
facilitators from the Directorate General for the Environment.

A number of alternative decision schemes had already been formulated, and these were set
out in a list (3). A set of comparison areas ("criteria") was then composed in order to
differentiate among these. The first step in this procedure involved the use of cards on which
participants were encouraged to write their suggestions. All these were stuck up on the wall and
then sorted according to three categories: physical ("fysiek"); social ("soc. maatsch."); and
economic ("fin. econ."). Some cards naturally fell between categories, and were therefore
positioned so as to overlap sector boundaries; others were found to be duplicates
("dubbellen").

From this, a straightforward list was drawn up, in no particular order, defining each
criterion more clearly. Stickers were issued to the participants,who were asked to place them
next to the comparison areas which they thought most significant in relation to the range of
alternatives under consideration. The area of greatest concern emerged as practical feasibility
("realiseerbaarheid"), followed by environmental damage ("milieubelasting"), cost of
disposal to local citizens ("verwijderingskosten, burger"), and flexibility of waste disposal
method ("flexibiliteit techn. verwerking").

Assessments were then made by consensus in the group using very simple scales. A scale of
+ and − signs was used for the environment; the more plus signs the better. The Dutch
symbol for Guilders (f) was used for cost; the more symbols, the higher the cost. Spots were
used for flexibility; the more spots, the more flexible. The note by the side headed "PM" is
merely an elaborated definition, describing the system of separating the waste at source.

This work in the comparing mode was not taken further on that day, because it was felt to be
more important to explore further the uncertainties and assumptions which had been thrown
up; these were listed elsewhere on the wall. As is quite usual with work caried out in the early
stages of a strategic choice workshop, this particular part of the analysis was not resumed later.
By the time the group was ready to move back to work in the comparing mode, the formulation
of the alternatives and comparison areas had changed again, reflecting the further
understanding of the problem that had been gained in the meantime.

FIGURE 69

Illustration from Practice – Comparing 2

COMPARING

PRACTICE

Theme:	Generating a List of Uncertainty Areas during an Advantage Comparison of Shortlisted Decision Schemes.
Problem:	Policy Formulation in a Comprehensive Development Plan for an Offshore Island.
Context:	Five-Day Workshop with a Local Inter-Disciplinary Planning Team, Recife, Brazil, 1984.

COMMENTARY ON FIGURE 69

These two photographs were taken in Recife, Brazil, during the course of the workshop already described in Figure 44, concerned with policies for the offshore island of Itamaracá. At the moment when the first photograph was taken, attention had become focussed on a comparison between two sharply contrasted decision schemes, numbered 2 and 5, which had been picked out of a set of six feasible combinations of options from three linked decision areas. These covered respectively the choice of economic base for the island; the area chosen for urbanisation; and the access route to the undeveloped north. Scheme 2 involved retention of a traditional economic base, centred on farming and sea fishing, with a brake on any urban development beyond existing commitments; scheme 5 involved an emphasis on tourist development with additional allocation of land.

Initially, five comparison areas were chosen, concerned with fulfilment of metropolitan aims; with levels of income for the islanders ("renda"); with preservation of their way of life ("vida"); with conservation of the natural environment ("ambiente"); and with demands on a limited water supply ("agua"). A sixth comparison area was added later, concerned with internal transport for the islanders; it is interesting (Figure 44) that some of these comparison areas had earlier been viewed as decision areas.

In the top photograph, a member of the group has just filled in the top row of an advantage comparison chart, using a nine-point scale labelled (e c s m n m s c e). This is essentialy similar to that introduced in Figure 21 — the words extreme, considerable, significant, marginal and negligible all having close equivalents in Portuguese. On the first row in the photograph, excluded parts of the scale have been blocked out. So there was thought to be no possibility that the balance of advantage on the metropolitan benefit comparison area could be in favour of scheme 2 to any degree, or as much as considerable or extreme in favour of scheme 5. For the group to arrive at this judgement, they had to confront many areas of uncertainty; and a tentative list of uncertainty areas is being started up on another chart underneath. The three uncertainty areas encountered in debating metropolitan benefit are to do with which groups might benefit; with the actions of another agency; and with assessing how far investors would be attracted.

The second photograph shows the same two wall charts at a later moment when all rows of the advantage comparison table had been completed and the list of uncertainty areas extended accordingly. The various uncertainty areas have now been classified, the Portuguese equivalents of UE, UV and UR being IA, IV and IR respectively. Also appearing in the second photograph is a second advantage comparison chart, in which schemes 2 and 3 are compared. In this case, the process was carried out initially by each individual completing a smaller version of the chart. One member then collated the results and presented them to the group in the form of the mode and range of the frequency distribution for each row, as shown here.

FIGURE
70

Illustration from Practice – Comparing 3

1

Tabel 8.1.   Samenvatting van de beoordeling van de locaties ten aanzien van de aspecten bodem en hydrologie, natuur en landschap, landbouw en planologische inpasbaarheid.

locatie volgens nadere begrenzing	bodem en hydrologie		natuur en landschap		land- bouw	plano- logische inpas- baarheid
	effecten op bodem en grond water	effecten op opper- vlakte- water	effecten op natuur	effecten op land- schap		
2a Brunink	+	▢	▢	▢	—	▢/+
2b Usselerveld	▢	+	▢	+	▢	+
12a Sluitersveld	▢	+	▢	+/▢	—	▢
12b Kwinkelerweg		▢	▢	+/—	+	+
14 Hemmelhorst	+	▢	—	—(?)'	+	—(?)'
19 Elhorst	▢	▢	+	▢	+	▢
24 Westerachtermaten	▢	—	++	+/—	—	▢
25 Oelemars	—	—	—	+	—	—

') Het vraagteken geeft aan dat er onzekerheid bestaat over de beoordeling bij realisering van de uitbreidingen van Borne en Hengelo

2

3

Theme: Use of Rank-Ordering with Robustness Methods in Shortlisting by Multiple Comparison Areas.
Problem: Selection of an Alternative Dumping Site for Solid Waste Disposal.
Context: Multi-Disciplinary Consultant Team (Heidemij) under contract to the Gewest of Twente, The Netherlands, 1982.

COMMENTARY ON FIGURE 70

This illustration shows three stages in the comparison of possible sites for the disposal of solid waste in an area of the Netherlands covering the towns of Almelo, Hengelo and Enschede near the German border. The project was carried out in 1982 by a multi-disciplinary consulting team from Heidemij Adviesbureau of Arnhem, on behalf of the Gewest of Twente, a consortium of 21 Municipalities in this area.

The existing solid waste site for the area was at that time almost full and a new location had to be found. It was clear that none of the Municipalities wanted the dump in their area; so opposition could be expected to any recommendation, and it was important that the process of comparison should take a range of criteria carefully into account.

Agreement was reached relatively easily over an initial shortlist of eight possible sites drawn from a range of more than fifty. These eight are listed by code number (2a, 2b, .. 25) down the left hand side of the initial working matrix. Across the top are various comparison areas including impacts on soil and ground water; surface water; nature; landscape; and agriculture. Physical planning considerations are also covered, along with level of "achievability" and various types of costs.

In the case of some comparison areas, a simple form of robustness analysis was incorporated. Achievability (bereikbarrheid) and transport costs (transportkosten) were assessed explicitly in the light of alternative assumptions about the future administration of the area as one region (regio) or two. This form of analysis was later extended to cover alternative futures with regard to possible new technologies for town heating and recycling.

Assessments were made using a five point scale (+ +, +, □, −, − −). Explicit recognition of uncertainty can be seen in the use of question marks not only in the working matrix but in the presentation version, part of which is shown below (2). These uncertainties relate in particular to possible extensions of two of the towns, Borne and Hengelo.

Using the type of rank ordering approach illustrated in Figure 66, several cycles of comparison were undertaken to identify any sites which were consistently good or bad. From this, site 25 was soon eliminated while sites 12a and 12b emerged as leading alternatives. These were subdivided to allow comparison of more detailed local options (12a north, south; 12b east, west) (3). One scheme (12a north) was found to be dominated by another (12a south).

After making judgements about the relative importance of different comparison areas, site 12a south was selected from this set, and subsequently examined against three others (sites 2b, 14 and 19) within a final shortlist, from which it again emerged as the favoured alternative. It was later found that this location could not be made available in time; but the understanding gained through the analysis allowed site 12b west to be substituted, quickly and with confidence.

8

Skills in Choosing

Introduction

The work of the choosing mode calls for quite different kinds of judgements to the work of the comparing mode. In essence, they are judgements to do with the management of uncertainty and the development of commitment through time; for this is the mode in which the time dimension comes to the fore, and the pressures for urgent action have to be balanced against any concerns that the decisions faced may be too difficult to address before further explorations have been carried out.

The pressure for a switch towards the choosing mode can frequently be observed in the course of a conventional committee decision process. Typically, some participants start to become impatient, look at their watches and say 'isn't it time to reached a decision and moved on to the next business?', or 'isn't it time we brought the meeting to an end?' In practice, however, the issues involved in making progress through time become most complex and challenging where the problem under consideration is itself complex in structure, embracing many interrelated elements to which different urgencies and uncertainties apply.

Even though the challenges of making progress through time are readily recognisable from personal experience, they have received much less attention in the literature of planning and management methods than the more technical challenges of evaluation. This may be because judgements to do with choosing through time are much less easy to separate from the particular organisational or political context in which they arise than are judgements to do with comparison of specific alternatives, which scholars have generally been able to treat in a more detached, analytical way.

So in practice, the shift from the comparing to the choosing mode means a shift from the technical domain towards the political arena. But one political arena can differ sharply from another, in terms of the configurations of conflict, competition, consensus and coalition which influence the ways in which decisions are made; and such differences can reflect not only variations in the ways in which the participants themselves have shaped their own internal working relationships through time, but also deeper, underlying differences in their accountability to others with a stake in the decisions to be made. Even where progress is being sought towards action commitments by a set of participants who come together repeatedly in the same group setting — as has been supposed to be the case with the South Side Working Party — the members may differ from each other in terms of their external accountability. Indeed, in practice, the wish to include representation of all the most relevant departments, agencies or interest groups is often one of the explicit principles on which involvement in a decision process is designed.

So, in addressing complex issues, the working group in which all members share exactly the same accountability tends to be more the exception than the rule. Not only problems but also personal responsibilities may be perceived differently by different members of a group; and this in turn means that any guidance on the work of the choosing mode cannot always be addressed to all members of a working group as if they formed a single coherent team. There is no shortage of useful advice that can be offered in this chapter, at a generalised level, building on the four core concepts of the *uncertainty area*, the *exploratory option*, the *action scheme* and the *commitment package*. But readers should not be surprised when questions of whose uncertainty, whose exploration, whose action and whose commitment keep breaking through. Yet even in contexts where it is unrealistic to expect that views about these matters will be freely shared, there remains the possibility that individuals will be able to make good use of the concepts and methods offered here as a guide to their own personal contributions to a decision process.

Building a Working List of Uncertainty Areas

The concept of the uncertainty area can be used to represent any area where alternative *assumptions* can be made about matters which are of some importance to decision-making. Such assumptions may relate to various aspects of the *working environment* within which people are trying to make decisions; they may relate to aspects of the *policy values* to which they are expected to pay heed; or they may relate to other *related decisions* where commitments have not, at yet, been made. The labels UE, UV and UR, which were introduced in Chapter 1 to differentiate these three types of uncertainty, serve not only as a means of classifying particular uncertainty areas as they are identified, but also as a useful reminder of the broad scope of the uncertainty area concept. Such a reminder can be especially appropriate to participants of an analytical bent, who are often predisposed to view the management of uncertainty primarily in terms of prediction or survey exercises using established statistical techniques.

In Chapter 3, the concept of the uncertainty area was first illustrated at a point in the South Side story where the focus of comparison had been narrowed down to a particular pair of alternative schemes, A and B, for which the overall balance of advantage across comparison areas was far from clear cut. However, it is only to be expected that people will experience personal feelings of uncertainty at many moments in a decision-making process, and that these feelings will change continually as they are exposed to what other participants have to say. People may feel uncertain as to where the boundaries of their problem should be drawn; they may feel uncertain as to whether or not particular decision areas should be seen as interconnected; they may feel uncertain as to whether particular options or combinations of options should be considered feasible; and they may feel uncertain as to the terms in which particular comparison areas should be formulated. Then, when it comes to comparing specific alternatives, they are bound to experience feelings of uncertainty both in attempting to assess their consequences within particular comparison areas and in judging where the overall balance of advantage lies; and it is at such moments that it becomes most important to find ways to view all areas of uncertainty together as sources of difficulty in choosing — some of which may be more significant than others — using the methods which will be discussed in this chapter.

Because feelings of uncertainty may surface at virtually any moment in a process of strategic choice, it is often useful in group work to set aside a sheet of paper on the wall where a cumulative list of uncertainty areas can be developed, recognising that such a list can always be restructured, and the items within it reformulated, at some later time. An example of a relatively unstructured list built up gradually in this way is presented in Figure 71. This illustration follows broadly the development of the South Side Story as recounted in earlier chapters, so the listing of uncertainty areas follows the broad sequence of shaping, designing and comparing in a more or less linear way — after starting by registering one uncertainty area, to do with air pollution, that is in this case supposed to have been so clearly recognised among the participants that it could be placed on record even before the group activity of shaping problems began. In practice, however, the more work is carried out within a group, the more the group is likely to switch freely between one mode and another; so the longer a list of uncertainty areas becomes, the more mixed it will tend to become in the modes of activity from which successive uncertainty areas are drawn.

In a group process, the recording of each uncertainty area on the list implies a working assumption that the feeling of uncertainty it contains is shared among different members of the group. Sometimes, of course, one member may express a feeling of uncertainty which is promptly dissolved because of some piece of information which another member of the group can supply from a position of greater knowledge or authority in some particular field. Sometimes, too, there may be areas of uncertainty which

FIGURE
71

SOUTH SIDE
EXAMPLE

Building up a Working List of Uncertainty Areas

UNCERTAINTY AREA (tentative description)	TYPE	note on how/why this uncertainty first encountered
? RATE OF EXPECTED REDUCTION OF LOCAL AIR POLLUTION	UE(UR?)	preliminary discussion of problem
? TIMING OF CONSTRUCTION OF NEW ROAD	UR	early work on shaping of decision graph and selection of problem focus
? CUTBACKS IN MUNICIPAL EXPENDITURE	UR	
? POLICY VALUE OF JOB CREATION	UV(UR?)	
? FEASIBILITY OF OTHER ROAD LINE OPTIONS	UE	work in the designing mode
? AVAILABILITY OF FOOTBALL GROUND SITE	UE	
? FEASIBILITY OF COMBINING HOUSING ON CENTRAL SITE WITH SHOPS AT KING SQUARE	UE	
? SERVICING COST PER HA. ON CENTRAL SITE	UE	assessment of alternatives within particular comparison areas
? ATTRACTIVENESS OF CENTRAL SITE TO EMPLOYMENT-INTENSIVE INDUSTRIES	UE	
? STEEL CORPORATION DECISION ON FUTURE OF STEELWORKS SITE	UR	advantage comparison schemes A vs B
? POLICY VALUE OF RESPONSIVENESS TO RESIDENTS' CONCERNS	UV	
? EASTWELL DISTRICT SHOPPING COMPLEX – SCALE AND TIMING	UR	advantage comparison schemes B vs E
? POLICY VALUE OF MEETING TRADERS' DEMANDS	UV	

CHOOSING

SKILLS

It is useful to build up a rough-and-ready listing of uncertainty areas progressively in interactive working, as new areas of uncertainty can surface when working in any mode. The use of the UE/UV/UR typology helps in drawing attention to any under-represented types as well as borderline cases. Notes on origination are here included for illustrative purposes and would be omitted in practice.

remain largely *latent* until exposed within the group. For example, one member of the South Side Working Party may feel quite confident in assuming that the football ground will be available for redevelopment, only to discover in discussion that another participant is equally confident that it will not; and they may then discover that neither is in a position to refute the other's assumption on the grounds of superior knowledge. Whereas neither participant had feelings of uncertainty on this point before the group interaction started, both share a feeling of uncertainty after some communication has taken place; so a new uncertainty area is recorded, and the decision process has become the more realistic as a result.

Because a working list of uncertainty areas may be subject to considerable restructuring before it is put to operational use, it is usually not worth while assigning brief labels to the uncertainty areas at the time they are first recorded, in the manner that was illustrated in Figure 23. It can, however, be helpful to register from the outset whether each new uncertainty area seems to be of type UE, UV or UR, even if there remains some doubt over which classification is most appropriate. For the attempt to classify uncertainty areas in this way can provide a valuable check against any tendency to bias towards or against any one of the three basic types — a bias towards concern with uncertainties of type UE being a common experience among participants of a more analytical, apolitical cast of mind. Often there is a tendency in an initial list to include comparatively few uncertainty areas of type UR — most of them referring to decisions over which the participants feel they have relatively little control. This is natural enough at a stage of the process before a clear problem focus has emerged, because the tendency will have been to include most of the significant areas of choice within the decision graph itself. However, as soon as particular decision areas begin to be excluded from the problem focus, they become potential candidates for the list of uncertainty areas of type UR.

Finally, it is often helpful, as in Figure 71, to include brief notes against all the various uncertainty areas on the list, referring to the mode or moment in the process where each of them first surfaced. The value of this can be appreciated by noticing that some of the marginal notes recorded against particular uncertainty areas on Figure 71 — though not all of them — can help in making reference back to earlier chapters which covered other stages in the development of the South Side story.

Putting Uncertainty Areas into a Clearer Decision Perspective

Each uncertainty area on a working list, such as that of Figure 71, will have been recorded because at some moment in the process it appeared to have at least some relevance to the decision problems being addressed. However, the longer a list grows, the more it will usually become apparent that some of the uncertainty areas are more relevant than others — and that

FIGURE

72

Placing Uncertainty Areas in a Decision Perspective

SOUTH SIDE
EXAMPLE

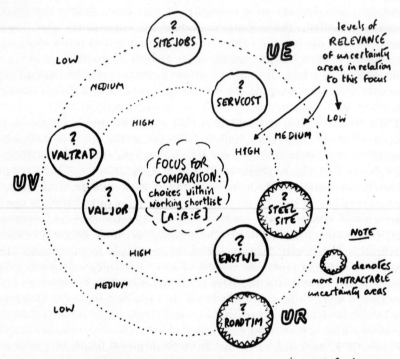

FULLER DESCRIPTIONS OF UNCERTAINTY AREAS in descending order of relevance

? VALJOB	? policy value of job creation	UV
? EASTWL	? Eastwell District shopping complex: scale and timing	UR
? SERVCOST	? servicing cost per ha. for development on central site	UE
? STEELSITE	? steel corporation decision on future use of steelworks site	UR (UE?)
? VALTRAD	? policy value of meeting traders' demands	UV
? SITEJOBS	? attractiveness of central site to employment-intensive firms	UE
? ROADTIM	? timing of construction of new road	UR

CHOOSING

SKILLS

This kind of radial uncertainty graph offers a useful way of putting the more important uncertainty areas into a decision perspective, and bringing together judgements about type, relevance and tractability. It is usual to start by plotting the more clearly-understood uncertainty areas, and position others with reference to these, reassessing the first few when this process is complete.

some of the less prominent ones might perhaps be set aside, or amalgamated with others to which they may seem closely related. So there will always be opportunities for the use of judgement and creativity in reformulating particular uncertainty areas, and in restructuring the overall list: opportunities of a similar kind to those already addressed in Chapter 5 in relation to the reformulation of decision areas.

Although a long and unstructured list of uncertainty areas can be tidied up at any time, where obvious opportunities for so doing can be seen, it is in practice usually worth saving any serious efforts towards restructuring until a moment arrives when there are pressures to explore preferences within a quite restricted working shortlist — perhaps a set of three or four promising schemes or, in many cases, only two promising alternatives — within which it is difficult to see where the overall balance of advantage lies.

The argument for leaving more detailed formulation and investigation of uncertainty areas until such a moment stems from the observation that in practice the relative prominence of different uncertainty areas can change quite dramatically as the decision perspective shifts. For example, some of the uncertainty areas listed in Chapter 3 (Figure 23) as relevant to the choice between Schemes A and B could well be overshadowed by others if some third scheme — such as Scheme E — were brought into the comparison as well. One way of picking out those uncertainty areas which are most relevant to a particular decision perspective is simply to use asterisks or some other symbol to pick out those in a longer list which are agreed to be most important in that particular light. However, Figure 72 illustrates one alternative form of presentation, which is sometimes found useful because it reflects the emphasis on creative use of graphics in communications which is characteristic of the strategic choice approach.

Figure 72 is an example of an *uncertainty graph* in which the more relevant uncertainty areas are represented by labelled circles, using rather similar conventions to those of the decision graph. But there is an important difference, in that the positioning of uncertainty areas on the uncertainty graph is judged in relation to a particular decision perspective that has been selected in advance. In the centre of the graph is indicated the current focus of comparison — in this case the set of three schemes, A, B and E, which was selected in Figure 22. Different directions of movement outwards from this central focus then correspond to the three basic categories of uncertainty, UE, UV and UR, occupying broadly the same sectors of the graph as in the general introductory diagram of Figure 3. However, the graph leaves the boundaries between the three sectors undefined, so that any borderline cases can be plotted in intermediate positions. In addition, the more *relevant* uncertainty areas are positioned closest to the centre of the graph; these being the ones which are judged to bear most closely on the difficulty experienced in making choices among the particular alternatives currently in view. As an aid to this aspect of positioning, two or three concentric rings can be drawn around the centre of the graph. When working with wall charts and coloured pens, these rings are best drawn in an unobtrusive colour, such as yellow, so that they do not get in the way of the other, more specific, information which the graph is intended to convey.

Working from an unstructured list such as that of Figure 71, it is usually best to begin by scanning it to pick out the most relevant uncertainty areas first. These can then be positioned within the innermost ring, working methodically outwards to add others of lesser relevance. Another approach is to begin by placing on the graph those uncertainty areas that are best understood and use these as points of reference in positioning others. It is not usually necessary to overload an uncertainty graph by attempting to locate within it *all* uncertainty areas, however insignificant relative to others; and it is rarely in practice worth going beyond a set of eight or nine uncertainty areas which are judged to be of particular relevance in relation to the current focus of comparison. Although the classification of uncertainty areas as UE, UV or UR may have been noted on the original working list, the act of plotting them on the uncertainty graph can provide a useful opportunity for second thoughts and for further debate on any doubtful cases.

Usually, some at least of the more relevant uncertainty areas will have come to the fore in the comparing of particular schemes — for example, the three uncertainty areas ?VALJOB, ?SITEJOBS and ?STEELSITE all emerged from the original comparison of Schemes A and B in Chapter 3 (Figure 23). However, other uncertainty areas may have surfaced while comparing other pairs of alternatives, or even in the work of the shaping and designing modes — for instance one or two of them might reflect doubts as to whether particular options should be considered feasible or whether particular options bars should be assumed.

Various additional kinds of information can be added to the basic information conveyed by an uncertainty graph about the type and relevance of different uncertainty areas. But too much elaboration can confuse rather than inform; so the only additional information introduced in Figure 72 is the use of a serrated ring to pick out particular uncertainty areas which are judged to be more *intractable* than others. The message is that there is thought to be very little that could be done to reduce the current state of doubt in each such uncertainty area, whereas in the case of other uncertainty areas it is possible to conceive of at least some form of exploratory action whereby current feelings of uncertainty might be reduced. In the case of these more tractable uncertainty areas, any decision to carry out this exploratory action will then have the intended effect of pushing that uncertainty area some distance further outwards from the centre of the graph; however, in the case of a more intractable uncertainty area, this possibility either does not exist, or is assumed to be realisable only at an unacceptable cost.

Restructuring Composite Uncertainty Areas

Once attention has been focussed on a few of the most relevant uncertainty areas — whether through use of an uncertainty graph or simply through picking out the most important uncertainty areas on a list — it is only to be expected that doubts will begin to arise as to whether they have been clearly enough formulated. In some cases, closer investigation will suggest that a particular uncertainty area is *composite* in form, and could with advantage be broken down into two or more separate elements for which different kinds of exploratory action would be appropriate. Some of these elements might then be found to be more relevant than others to the present focus of comparison; furthermore, the elements might occupy quite different parts of the uncertainty graph in terms of the UE/UV/UR classification. Therefore, the reformulation of composite uncertainty areas in terms of their more significant elements can sometimes lead to quite a radical restructuring of the content of the uncertainty graph, and a reappraisal of the picture of opportunities for managing uncertainty which it conveys.

It is possible to explore such possibilities for restructuring uncertainty areas by working directly from the uncertainty graph. But the graph itself can become overloaded and confused if too much information of this kind is added. Figure 73 illustrates a way in which the elements of composite uncertainty areas can be explored on a separate sheet, with a view to possibly modifying the graph at a later stage. The first example of a composite uncertainty area relates to the policy value of job creation; this is an uncertainty area occupying quite a central position on the graph of Figure 72, which was classified as of type UV. In Figure 73, this value uncertainty is broken down into two different value elements; one of them relating to the general priority given by the municipal council to job creation as against other policy aims; and the other relating to the more specific question of whether there is to be discrimination in favour of economically deprived neighbourhoods, such as South Side, in the attraction of new jobs to different parts of the municipal area. The meaning of each element is made more explicit in Figure 73 by spelling out, in parenthesis, a set of two or more alternative assumptions which can be regarded as representative of the current range of doubt. Such a set of alternative assumptions is exactly analogous to the set of options used to represent the range of choice within a decision area; indeed, within an uncertainty area, similar problems of how best to represent a complex or open-ended range of possibilities may sometimes have to be faced.

In this instance, it is possible that the participants will be experiencing doubts over whether the general priority attached by members of the municipal council to job creation has shifted upwards or downwards since its last written policy statement on this issue was agreed. But it may be

FIGURE

73

SOUTH SIDE
EXAMPLE

Reformulating Composite Uncertainty Areas

UNCERTAINTY AREA - elements	TYPE	RELEVANCE to [A:B:E] focus	PROPOSED RESPONSE - exploratory options
? VALJOB ? policy value of job creation	UV	HIGH	EXAMINE ELEMENTS
? value of job creation v. other policy aims [as stated; higher; lower]	UV	LOW/MID	• examine no further
? whether to discriminate in favour of low income areas in creating jobs [yes; no]	UV	MID/HIGH	• label as ? JOBDISC - refer to policy committee — consult leaders
?EASTWL ? Eastwell shopping complex scale/timing	UR	MID/HIGH	EXAMINE ELEMENTS
? scale of Eastwell shopping [as in plan; larger; smaller]	UR	MID/HIGH	• label as ?EASTWLSC - full analysis - brief liaison
? timing of Eastwell shopping development [sooner; later]	UR/UE	LOW	• examine no further
?SERVCOST ? cost of servicing central site	UE	MID/HIGH	EXAMINE ELEMENTS
? additional buffer zone in ha. if HOUS [3;5;7] *	UE	VERY LOW	• examine no further
? unit servicing cost in k/ha if IND [12;15;18] *	UE/UV	MID	EXAMINE ELEMENTS FURTHER
? geological/soil factors	UE	LOW/MID	• examine no further
? policy on range of services	UV	MID	• intractable: no action

* SENSITIVITY ANALYSIS : refer to Figure 62 for basic calculations

- additional buffer zone in ha [3;5;7] → | cost of site servicing | → [266;250;234] ±6%
- unit servicing cost in k/ha [12;15;18] → | difference IND + HOU | → [160;250;340] ±36%

CHOOSING

SKILLS

The splitting down of composite uncertainty areas into more specific elements is often carried out directly on the uncertainty graph, reassessing type and relevance in the process. Judgements about the relevance of different elements can be seen as a type of informal sensitivity analysis, and the more explicit form of sensitivity analysis illustrated here is used comparatively rarely.

judged that this element of uncertainty is not so important as the element of uncertainty relating to positive discrimination in favour of particular localities, about which there might recently have much political controversy. Therefore, Figure 73 shows the latter element rated as of medium-to-high relevance and so worth subjecting to further scrutiny straight away; while the former — rated as of only low-to-medium relevance — can perhaps be set aside for the time being. The latter element is assigned a brief label — ?JOBDISC — with a view to this replacing the composite uncertainty area ?VALJOB on the uncertainty graph. As a further step in analysing this more carefully defined uncertainty area, a note is made of the kinds of exploratory option which could be considered to reduce its relevance further. In this example, it is indicated that two alternative levels of policy soundings might be considered as possible exploratory options — the first of them more formal and the second comparatively quick and informal.

Turning to the second of the uncertainty areas in Figure 73 — labelled ?EASTWL — its original description in terms of 'scale and timing' of the proposed Eastwell shopping complex indicates that it also is composite in form. It is supposed here that further discussion of its content leads to the judgement that it is uncertainty over scale which is much the more prominent element. In the case of ?SERVCOST, it is supposed in Figure 73 that the analysis of elements can be taken further with the help of some more explicit *sensitivity analysis*, of a kind that only becomes possible in circumstances where assessments can be made on the basis of well-defined sequences of calculations or logical steps.

The particular procedure of sensitivity analysis used in Figure 73 can be appreciated more fully by referring back to Figure 62. This indicated a sequence of operations involved in estimating the costs of providing site services for either industrial or housing development. Some of these steps involved calculations of a straightforward arithmetical kind, but others depended on expert judgements — and the logical structure of these will often be much less transparent.

In the particular example of sensitivity analysis included in Figure 73, it has been supposed that it is the cost of servicing the site for industrial use rather than housing use which is the source of most of the uncertainty; and the relative contributions to this uncertainty of two contributory elements are explored. The difference in usable site area for the two alternative uses was estimated as 0.5 hectares (Figure 62) — the difference between 2.5 hectares for housing and 3.0 hectares for industry. In Figure 73 it is supposed that the range of uncertainty over this estimate has been assessed, through a process of surprise limit analysis, as extending from a minimum of 0.3 hectares to a maximum of 0.7 hectares. In the same way, a range from 12k/ha to 18k/ha has been assessed for the cost per hectare of servicing the site for industry (see Figure 63); the equivalent cost of servicing for housing being taken as a more predictable 8k/ha.

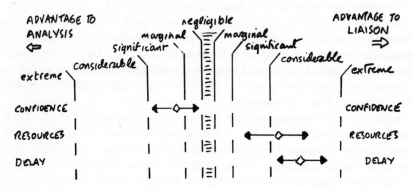

UNCERTAINTY AREA	EXPLORATORY OPTION	COMPARISON AREA	RELATIVE ASSESSMENT
? EASTWLSC (Scale of Eastwlk shopping complex) – as in plan – larger – smaller	– ANALYSIS (systematic analysis of alternative shopping configurations for Eastern sector of municipal area)	CONFIDENCE : RESOURCES : DELAY :	more confidence in judging balance of advantage E:B extensive survey & analysis work (c. 100 planner days) 4 months
	– LIAISON (brief exploratory discussions with leading staff of shops planning team)	CONFIDENCE : RESOURCES : DELAY :	somewhat more confidence in judging advantage E:B a few hours discussion 1-2 weeks to arrange meeting

ADVANTAGE COMPARISON [LIAISON vs ANALYSIS]

ADVANTAGE TO ANALYSIS ⇐   negligible   ADVANTAGE TO LIAISON ⇒

marginal   marginal
significant   significant
considerable   considerable
extreme   extreme

CONFIDENCE   CONFIDENCE

RESOURCES   RESOURCES

DELAY   DELAY

CHOOSING

SKILLS

It is only in the case of highly relevant and relatively intractable uncertainty areas that it is likely to be worth comparing different exploratory options in as much depth as illustrated here. Nevertheless, the general principles apply to any judgement about alternative responses to uncertainty, including judgements about whether to take no current action but prepare contingency plans.

Repeating the sequence of calculations in Figure 62 with the minimum and maximum figures substituted for the original estimates, first for the loss of site area and then for the servicing cost per hectare, Figure 73 shows that the former element causes very little variation in the estimated servicing cost for the site, while the latter element contributes considerably more.*

In pursuing this example further, it will be noted (from Figure 62) that this estimated site servicing cost per hectare can itself be broken down into four more specific elements of assumption — some expressed in numerical form and others not. So the process of breaking down elements of uncertainty can, in this case, be extended further. In Figure 73 this point is illustrated by indicating the two more important sub-elements of the uncertainty over industrial site servicing cost — the more significant of them in this case being of an intractable policy nature. This illustrates the general point that analysis of elements within an uncertainty area can lead to a revision of views about its classification within the UE/UV/UR framework.

Assessing Exploratory Options within Critical Uncertainty Areas

Once attention has been focussed on a few crucial uncertainty areas, attention can be turned to the question of what might be done about them. This involves examining more closely any exploratory options that are seen as realistic — whether they have already been identified or whether they only come to mind at this stage — and weighing up what the consequences of following these exploratory options might be.

In Chapter 3, one approach was illustrated (Figure 24) by which the implications of following any particular exploratory option could be compared with the consequences of not pursuing it. In this, the three comparison areas of *confidence, resources* and *decision delay* were used to represent the three most important dimensions of evaluation that normally arise when making judgements about how uncertainty should be managed. In practice, it is only rarely that it is worthwhile evaluating exploratory options in this explicit way. But the *principles* involved are crucial to the management of uncertainty in strategic choice; so Figure 74 illustrates how the comparison of exploratory options can be taken a step further in relation to any especially critical uncertainty areas where this deeper level of analysis may be justified.

Because the proposed scale of the Eastwell district shopping complex has emerged as an especially relevant uncertainty area (Figure 74), the implications of taking different exploratory actions in response are reviewed in Figure 74. The first exploratory option to be considered is that

---

* This is a contrast which can be quantified if statistical methods are used to calculate — on conventional assumptions of independence and normal distributional form — that the latter element explains some 97% of the combined variance.

of undertaking a full and systematic analysis of alternative combinations of district and more local shopping centres in the broader eastern sector of the municipality that includes both Eastwell and South Side. But, in addition, a more modest exploratory option is also considered, which might go at least some way towards reducing the level of doubt within this same uncertainty area; this is the option of engaging in some informal liaison with leading members of a specialist team of planners which the municipality has set up to look at shopping provision within its overall administrative area. This second option may mean relying on the specialist team's own expert judgement of the consequences of adopting different shopping patterns, rather than on any more rigorous methods of survey and analysis. Nevertheless, it could be well worth considering as a more modest — but possibly more effective — way of reducing the level of doubt in this same uncertainty area.

Figure 74 records the judgement that the first exploratory option — labelled ANALYSIS — is expected to lead to more confidence in judging the overall balance of advantage between Schemes E and B — this pair comparison being a more appropriate one to consider than A:B within the working shortlist (A:B:E) because A and B do not differ in terms of options within the SHOP LOC'N? decision area. But the more modest LIAISON option is also judged likely to lead to 'somewhat' more confidence in relation to the same pair comparison — and to do so at considerably less cost in terms of both demands on resources and decision delay. The call on resources for the ANALYSIS option is here assessed in terms of a rough estimate of the number of planner days required — although of course it could have other dimensions such as the use of computer time and the cost of origination of data, possibly involving the recruitment of interviewers through agency or other channels.

To weigh up whether it is likely to be worth pursuing the full ANALYSIS option as against the more modest LIAISON option, it becomes essential to take the urgencies and resource pressures of the current decision situation into account. In practice, this will usually be done intuitively. But intuitive appreciations of urgency may differ from one participant to another; so it can sometimes be a useful aid to communication, in the case of especially critical uncertainty areas, to introduce an advantage comparison framework as an aid to this kind of judgement. This possibility is demonstrated in the lower part of Figure 74.

In this case, the advantage comparison indicates a view that the additional gain in confidence from adopting the ANALYSIS rather than the simpler LIAISON response to the uncertainty about scale of the Eastwell shopping centre should be placed in the marginal-to-significant range. Yet Figure 74 shows that this benefit is likely to be outweighed by the considerable additional investment of resources required, along with the even more serious implications — in this particular decision situation — of a four-month's delay before the decision in question can be made. This example merely makes explicit the kind of judgements that are being made all the time in an intuitive way, when people have to decide how far to invest in any kind of exploratory action to improve the confidence with which important choices can be made.

This particular example concerns an uncertainty area of type UR; but the judgement of whether or not to invest in exploratory action can be expressed in a similar way whether an uncertainty area of type UE, UV or UR is involved — as was indeed demonstrated earlier in Chapter 3 (Figure 24). Quick and informed judgements of this kind can be debated with reference to the comparative information about the relevance of different uncertainty areas which is contained in an uncertainty graph such as that of Figure 72. As a general rule, it is rarely worth making major investments in exploratory action directed towards uncertainty areas of lower relevance, so long as uncertainty areas of higher relevance remain.

Relating Exploratory Actions to the Timing of Decisions

As was discussed in Chapter 3, the consideration of what to do about particular uncertainty areas can bring concerns about the *timing* of choices in different decision areas directly to the fore. For any exploratory action invariably take some time to carry through — whether this be measured in minutes, hours, days, weeks, months or even years — and can thus imply delays of a more or less serious extent in the taking of those decisions they are designed to inform.

The opportunities for taking immediate actions in some decision areas while deferring choice in others were approached in Chapter 3 through the core concept of the *action scheme*, chosen to cover some but not necessarily all of the decision areas within a problem focus. An example was then presented (Figure 25) of how action schemes could be compared in terms of the relative *flexibility* of choice left open; and various possible approaches to the comparison of flexibility were discussed further in Chapter 7.

There are, therefore, two types of timing judgement which have to be considered in practice. On the one hand there is the judgement of how far to invest in pursuing exploratory actions which imply delays in at least some decision areas; on the other hand there is the judgement of how far to make commitments to action in some decision areas in advance of others. This means that any consideration of the time dimension can make the structure of interconnected choices for the participants more subtle and complex; indeed, this is a reality that has to be faced whether or not the concepts and methods of strategic choice are being applied in an explicit way.

In dealing with these choices, a useful guide-line is to focus first on any decision areas where considerations of *both* urgency and uncertainty arise.

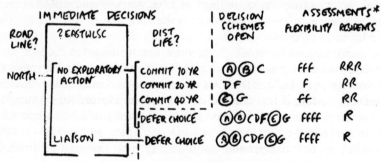

ROAD LINE?	DIST. LIFE?	ACTION SCHEME	CHOICES REMAINING OPEN IN OTHER DECISION AREAS		DECISION SCHEME [shortlisted schemes ringed]
			SHOP LOC'N?	CENT'L SITE?	
NORTH - [?]	10YR -	I	— MAIN — [?]	IND / HOUS	Ⓐ / Ⓑ
			— KING ———	HOUS	C
	20YR -	II	— KING ———	HOUS / OPEN	D / F
	40YR -	III	— KING ———	HOUS / OPEN	Ⓔ / G
SOUTH —	20YR	IV	— GAS ———	OPEN	H
	40YR	V	— GAS ———	OPEN	I

[?] indicates a critical branching point for comparisons within working shortlist [A:B:E]. Uncertainty area ?EASTWLSC identified as critical to urgent choice of action scheme I v. III so examine [explore/not]

IMMEDIATE DECISIONS

ROAD LINE?	?EASTWLSC	DIST. LIFE?	DECISION SCHEMES OPEN	ASSESSMENTS* FLEXIBILITY RESIDENTS	
NORTH ···	NO EXPLORATORY ACTION	COMMIT 10 YR	Ⓐ Ⓑ C	FFF	RRR
		COMMIT 20 YR	D F	F	RR
		COMMIT 40 YR	Ⓔ G	FF	RR
		DEFER CHOICE	Ⓐ Ⓑ CDF Ⓔ G	FFFF	R
	LIAISON	DEFER CHOICE	Ⓐ Ⓑ CDF Ⓔ G	FFFF	R

* KEY TO ASSESSMENTS :
flexibility index   F: minimum   FFFF : maximum
residents' satisfaction   R: minimum   RRR: maximum

In considering how far to defer decisions in strategic choice, it is useful to focus on any decision areas which may be urgent yet subject to major uncertainties which could be reduced through exploratory action. The judgement of whether to decide now or defer while explorations are carried through is usually made informally in constructing a commitment package, but the principle is as illustrated here.

This is illustrated in Figure 75, which takes as its point of departure the set of nine possible decision schemes first developed in Chapter 2 (Figure 17) for the four decision areas in the original South Side problem focus. In Figure 75, these schemes are arranged (as in Figure 25) with the two more urgent decision areas — ROAD LINE? and DIST LIFE? — brought to the fore; then, focussing more closely on the comparison of schemes within the more limited working shortlist of A, B and E, Figure 75 identifies the points of greatest *difficulty* in the decision process, by means of queston marks positioned at the relevant branching points of the tree.

It can now be seen that the DIST LIFE? decision area is the more urgent of the two decision areas in which there are differences between the shortlisted Schemes A, B and E; and it has already been discovered (Figure 74), that the ?EASTWLSC uncertainty area has an important bearing on the choice of routes at this branch point of the tree. So it could be especially important to explore how to deal with this particular uncertainty area if the urgencies of the problem situation are to be addressed. So, in the second picture of Figure 75, the first part of the decision tree is shown expanded to introduce, as additional branching points, a choice of two exploratory options within the ?EASTWLSC uncertainty area. The first is the 'null option' of taking no exploratory action at all, and the second is the quick option of a brief liaison exercise with the shops planning team — it being here supposed that the more costly and time-consuming option of fuller analysis has been ruled out after the kind of advantage comparison exercise illustrated earlier (Figure 74).

In Figure 75, the assumption is made that the DIST LIFE? decision should definitely be *deferred* if the exploratory liaison option is to be followed through. It is also supposed there may possibly be an argument for deferring choice of DIST LIFE?, as an alternative to early commitment to any specific option, if it is decided to take the 'no explorations' route; for such a deferment could make sense if there were any likelihood that some event might occur which could clarify the choice within DIST LIFE? without any specific exploratory action being taken. For example, it might be known that there was a meeting of a South Side community forum scheduled in a week's time to debate this very issue.

The introduction of an option to defer choice within the DIST LIFE? decision area has the effect of subtly altering the *meaning* of that decision area; for it now represents a choice as to what should be done *now* about the life of the district, rather than what should be done in any more timeless sense. However, the main point about the expanded decision tree in Figure 75 is that it displays five possible combinations of current choices and exploratory options that can be compared with each other as a basis for incremental progress; and these five paths can quickly be compared in terms of how many of the nine decision schemes remain available in each case. In Figure 75, the schemes remaining open are listed for each path, drawing attention in particular to the availability of the three shortlisted Schemes A, B and E.

In general, this analysis indicates that those courses of action involving immediate commitment in the DIST LIFE? decision area carry a risk of subsequent *regret*, through the foreclosing of particular decision schemes which might have been found to be advantageous had the explorations been followed through. For example, commitment now to a 40-year life for South Side might lead to regret if the work of the specialist shops planning team were to result in a proposal for a particular sector-wide shopping pattern which made it uneconomic to develop a new South Side local shopping centre on the King Square site; while commitment now to a 10-year life might lead to regret if geological difficulties on the central site were later found to be so severe that no uses other than open space could realistically be considered there.

In general, the choice of whether to opt for commitment or deferment in an urgent decision area involves some process, however intuitive, of weighing the risks of early commitment against the negative consequences of delay — including any political or professional penalties that might be incurred. In the particular circumstances of Figure 75, the deferment being considered is only a couple of weeks, so might well be considered worth while; unless, perhaps, there were an imminent meeting of the municipal council, or a closely fought local election, to introduce an added note of urgency over the commitment to district life, even within this otherwise insignificant time scale.

Accommodating Uncertainty by Preparing for Alternative Contingencies

Various approaches have now been discussed to the comparison of alternative courses of immediate action, in terms of the flexibility of future choice which they allow. At the simplest level, an intuitive judgement can be made that one alternative is likely to leave open more opportunities for future choice than another, without any analysis of what these opportunities are.* At another level, the patterns of future choice left open can be analysed and presented for visual comparison, or the comparison can be simplified by introducing some form of robustness index (Figure 25).

However, it is possible to go further in circumstances where there has been some analysis of the relative importance of different uncertainty areas, and where some attempt has been made to represent the more important of these in terms of the range of alternative assumptions that could be held. Where this is so, then it is possible to bring those alternative assumptions more directly into the comparison of current actions, and to explore how

* This was the kind of approach adopted when 'flexibility' was introduced as an additional comparison area in Figure 64.

far some such actions could have advantages over others in their capacity to respond to particular eventualities that could arise. One way of taking the analysis in this direction is illustrated in Figure 76. In Figure 76, two alternative action schemes for South Side are compared, each of which involves commitment to the northern road line and also to a particular option in the DIST LIFE? decision area. Referring to Figure 75, each such course implies that no exploratory action is being taken in relation to the important ?EASTWLSC uncertainty area. So the feelings of uncertainty over the scale of the proposed Eastwell shopping complex remains unchanged; and this uncertainty area has already been represented in terms of a choice of three possible assumptions labelled SMALLER, AS IN PLAN, and LARGER (Figure 73).

According to which of these assumptions is held, either the *feasibility* or the relative *attractiveness* of different courses of future action may be affected. In Figure 76, the judgement is made that the uncertainty about the scale for the Eastwell shopping complex is of such direct relevance to the choice of shopping location for South Side, that the King Square development must be ruled out on grounds of economic viability if the Eastwell complex is to be significantly larger than proposed in the current plan. Turning to the second of the action schemes in Figure 76 — Action Scheme III — this appears to allow no alternative to the King Square site; but it does afford protection against another contingency — the perhaps remote contingency of abnormal geological conditions being discovered on the central site, precluding the possibility of any use except that of open space.

However, another point in favour of Action Scheme I is that it leaves open the option of industrial use on the central site; provided geological conditions make this option feasible, Figure 76 shows that its attractiveness as a means of creating alternative local jobs could be enhanced should the contingency of early closure of the steelworks arise. So, the consideration of flexibility to accommodate different kinds of uncertainty can become more complex, the more contingencies are explored. Sometimes this kind of analysis can lead towards a searching re-examination of earlier assumptions. For example, the assumption that there is no possibility of using the central site for open space if a 10-year district life were chosen might now seem a rather unnecessary constraint. Referring back to the structure of the problem as reflected in the option graph (Figure 16), the reasoning behind this particular option bar could well now be challenged. The result could be an agreement that the option bar was no longer necessary, so removing an apparent advantage towards Action Scheme III on grounds of capacity to accommodate geological uncertainty.

Once the possibility is considered of introducing some of the more crucial uncertainty areas into the structure of possible paths through the problem situation, as illustrated in Figure 76, then it becomes possible to move in a

FIGURE 76

SOUTH SIDE EXAMPLE

Accommodating Uncertainty in the Future Decision Space

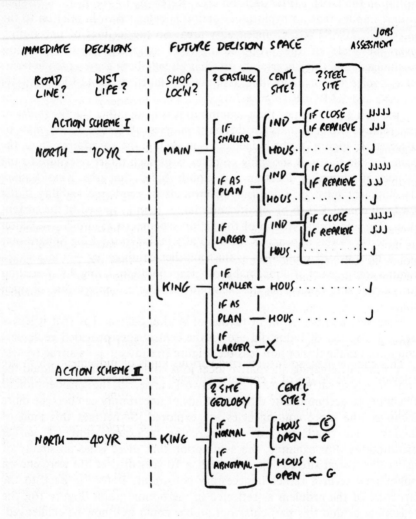

Uncertainty areas in which the choice of assumptions can have a critical effect on the choice of path through a tree may become an important focus for contingency planning. This consideration is usually introduced only when attention is turned to the design of a commitment package, but the extension of the tree to show contingencies as extra branching points can be a useful aid to communication.

number of different directions of further analysis, depending on whether these crucial uncertainty areas are of type UE, UV or UR. In the case of a UE-type uncertainty area — such as that over geological conditions in South Side — it may be important to ask whether the contingencies reflected in the alternative assumptions are of high or low probability: and questions then arise of how far it is worth safeguarding or insuring against specific *risks*. If these questions are of sufficient importance, then the analysis can be taken in the direction of the classical form of *decision analysis* in which numerical probabilities are assigned to different contingencies treated as alternate branching points in a decision tree.*

Any important uncertainty areas of type UV can, if desired, be absorbed into the analysis of decision areas expressed at a broader *policy* level — and such a step will open up the possibility of introducing the methods already illustrated for analysing relationships between *levels* of choice (Figure 54). Again, any crucial uncertainty areas of type UR can be absorbed into the problem structure as additional decision areas, thus in effect extending the problem focus. However, where these new decision areas relate to choices which are entirely or partially under the control of other parties — and where there are elements of conflict or competition in relationships with those other parties — then the decision situation may have to be considered as more like one of a *game* in which moves, counter-moves and points of potential stability might have to be explored: 'If they did this, we could retaliate by doing that'. This points to another direction of analysis — that of the analysis of conflicts and the theory of games — which will be touched upon further in Chapter 10.

Moving towards the Design of Possible Commitment Packages

This chapter has, so far, covered various kinds of judgement which are relevant to the design of a commitment package, conceived as a proposed incremental step towards commitment through time. The four basic sections of a commitment package were first illustrated in Figure 26: a set of immediate decisions covering both *actions* and *explorations* to reduce uncertainty; then a set of proposed arrangements for *deferred choices* and *contingency planning* within a future decision space. In any setting where decisions call for formal commitment of organisational resources, there will be moments when it is important to give careful attention to the design of *alternative* commitment packages. Yet it is important to emphasise that at other times, when there is a desire to move ahead informally, or to respond to particular urgencies of the moment, a commitment package may be much more skeletal in its content, and will not necessarily be recorded in written form.

In practice, important points of judgement can arise not only in

* See, for example, Raiffa, 1968.

FIGURE 77

Building an Appropriate Commitment Package

SOUTH SIDE
EXAMPLE

COMMITMENT PACKAGE IA
- based on **SHORT-TERM PUBLIC** investment policy

	IMMEDIATE DECISIONS		FUTURE DECISION SPACE	
	ACTIONS	EXPLORATIONS	DEFERRED CHOICES	CONTINGENCY PLANNING
SOUTH SIDE local planning	DISTRICT LIFE * - commitment now to 10 YEAR LIFE			IF a major developer can be attracted THEN consider extended life
	SHOP LOCATION * - no action	- leaders to arrange discussions with local traders	IN 6 MONTHS - decide Main St. OR King Square	IF scale of Eastwell complex increased, THEN reject King Sq.
	CENTRAL SITE * - no action	- commission quick geological survey	IN 6 MONTHS - decide industry OR housing IF Main Street shops stay (C2)	
	WEST STREET - no action	- initiate design and costing studies	IN 12 MONTHS - decide whether to improve West St.	
TRANSPORT	ROAD LINE * - recommend NORTH route through South Side			IF north route rejected, THEN appeal
	MAIN STREET - no action		WHEN road is in firm programme, THEN consider closing street	IF new road not to be built in next 5 years, THEN extend parking
ECONOMIC DEVELOPMENT		ask M.E.O. to approach steel corporation to discuss joint jobs initiative		

A   B   C   D

(right margin numbers: 1, 2, 3, 4, 5, 6, 7)

* identifies main set of interconnected decisions

SUMMARY OF COMPARISON with alternative package IIIA (LONG-TERM PUBLIC INVESTMENT)

CAPITAL: IA to cost 100k-300k LESS than IIIA
INCOME: IA likely to generate marginally LESS income
RESIDENTS: IA offers BETTER outlook
JOBS: LITTLE DIFFERENCE if B7 successful
FLEXIBILITY: IA preserves options in shop location

CHOOSING

SKILLS

The basic framework of a commitment package offers a framework for discussion in considering how to act which can be extended in a number of different ways, according to context. When working with large sheets of paper it is useful to add marginal notes against immediate decisions specifying agreed organisational responsibilities, resource commitments and deadlines.

developing the content of a commitment package, but also in judging the *format* in which it should be presented. This applies in particular to the rows as opposed to the columns of the framework. In the simple example presented in Chapter 3 (Figure 26), the problem structure was brought out by designating a separate row for each decision area. This presented no difficulty in that particular case, because each of the exploratory actions proposed to address uncertainty could be directly linked to a particular area of deferred choice. In practice, however, the number of decision areas to be brought together within the compass of a commitment package can sometimes be larger, and the relationships between explorations and deferred choices less straightforward. In these circumstances, it can be more practicable to group two or more decision areas together in the same row, perhaps relating to some designated sphere of responsibility. This way of presenting a commitment package is illustrated in Figure 77.

This example of a commitment package presents one coherent set of proposals which is, in effect, an expanded version of the first of the two alternative action schemes compared in Figure 76. The rows of the framework are organised into three broad spheres of responsibility, concerned respectively with local South Side matters, with transport issues and with economic development in the municipality as a whole. Only the first of these is within the direct sphere of responsibility of the South Side Working Party; and even then there may be procedures of formal authorisation or endorsement of proposals to be followed, requiring some consideration of contingency planning if any recommendations should be rejected or opposed. In the transport and economic development spheres, however, all the working party may be able to do is to make representations to other parties, and to use whatever influence or leverage they can exert to follow those representations through — perhaps again with some thought to possible contingency actions should the proposed representations or negotiations fail.

In Figure 77, asterisks are used to indicate the principal set of interconnected decision areas around which the commitment package has been built, as a reminder that it may be difficult to consider changing course in any one of these without considering what implications there might be for the others. However, there may be more scope for considering variations in other elements of the package; and the number of elements shown in this particular illustration, though quite large, is only a limited selection from those that could have been included if all the decision areas and uncertainty areas discussed in the course of the last few chapters were to be included. For example, extra spheres of housing or financial responsibility could have been included to reflect these other organisational interests in the South Side problem (Figure 41). Various other decision areas from this wider decision graph might then have been considered, in the shaping of either proposed actions or deferred choices. Further kinds of technical exploration could also have been suggested. For example, explorations could have been proposed into the feasibility of doubtful options, such as the possibility (examined in Figure 48) of combining some industrial with some housing development of the central site. Further explorations into policy values might also perhaps have been recommended: for example, into the issue of discrimination in job creation in favour or low income neighbourhoods.

So, however broad in scope it might appear, any commitment package is designed to be *selective* rather than comprehensive in its content, reflecting the various resource constraints, urgencies and priorities of the specific decision setting within which it is shaped. For it is intended as an incremental step in a continuing process of commitment, not as a conclusive response to the full range of problems that has been identified. Even so, there are many additional subtleties that can be introduced informally into a decision process while a commitment package is being designed, extending its scope beyond that of the analysis as so far pursued. For example, Figure 77 introduces for the first time the possibility that the uncertainty about the steelworks closure might not be so immune to municipal influence as earlier assumed, once the idea of a joint initiative to attract small business enterprises to the site has been conceived.

So, within the commitment package framework, a considerable amount of richness and complexity can be encompassed, even where a conscious effort is made to present its content in a form which is intelligible to people who may not have been involved in the analytical work which has gone into its presentation. Cross-referencing between elements in the package itself can be indicated by discreet annotations; in Figure 77, for example, row and column codes are used — sparingly — for cross-reference both within the commitment package and also in the brief statement of comparative information which appears below. The intention is that the format selected for the commitment package should offer a basis for structured debate about choices and assumptions; for closer comparison of alternatives, either within particular elements or on a broader scale; for modification to reflect new insights or representations; and — when the moment is ripe — for progress through commitment to decisive actions.

Helping Decision-takers to Choose

Even a carefully-organised and selective commitment package such as that of Figure 77 can present an overload of information for those decision-takers who may be called upon to authorise decisive actions. This problem of potential overload is of course not specific to the strategic choice approach; it applies equally to any form of decision technology, wherever actions have to be endorsed by busy people with multiple roles and responsibilities, who may not have the time to keep themselves closely acquainted with the progress of any analytical work.

However, if decision-takers are to exercise their right to choose *responsibly* in other than a token ritualistic way, it can sometimes be important that they be presented with more than one commitment package from which to choose. Judgements must then be made about how many alternative packages should be presented; how much back-up information should be offered in support; and what the balance should be between different forms of communication — text, graphics, numerical tabulations, verbal presentation — as opposed to documents circulated in advance. These are judgements which will depend on the particular decision context, and the way in which its opportunities and constraints are understood by those who carry the responsibility of presenting proposals to decision-takers.

Figure 78 gives one example of the way in which the members of the South Side Working Party might decide to present their initial recommendations to the policy committee to which they report. It is here assumed that the latter group, with many pressures on its agenda, is accustomed to acting mainly on the basis of written documentation of a condensed summary form — backed up, if need be, by fuller information introduced in the course of discussion.

Figure 78 therefore takes the form of a one-page summary report, presented in fairly conventional written form, offering guidelines which can be followed, questioned or challenged at the discretion of the decision-takers — in this case, the members of the municipal policy committee meeting as a group with the authority to commit resources to whatever course of action they may agree. To keep the report brief and readable, it is restricted in its focus to two main alternatives expressed in terms of contrasting policy orientations — one of these being a condensed version of the commitment package of Figure 77, and the other a contrasting package based on a 40-year horizon for the life of South Side as a residential area. In the interests of brevity, all but the most crucial characteristics of the two packages are omitted from the report; for the main aim of the report is to indicate what are the main differences in *structure* between the two.

It is likely that the main structural assumptions behind the alternative proposals will have been put to quite stringent testing well before this reporting stage; but it is important that they should be checked again carefully before the report is finally submitted. For example, if there were any serious residual doubts as to whether the 40-year life might, after all, allow the Main Street shopping centre to be retained, or whether industry on the central site might, in some circumstances, be compatible with the King Square shopping location, then the whole structure and emphasis of the report could be subject to challenge. The proposals might then either have to be redesigned in their entirety — or at least revised to allow this element of uncertainty to be acknowledged and an appropriate response prepared.

In any case, it will be only prudent that the working party members

FIGURE
78

SOUTH SIDE
EXAMPLE

Helping Decision-Takers to Make Progress

Meeting of Policy Committee, 10 June 1986

DOCUMENT 7 : Interim Report of South Side Working Party

ALTERNATIVES

The two most urgent decisions in South Side concern the alignment of the new arterial ROAD through the area and its continued LIFE as a residential neighbourhood. It is now clear that the balance of advantage lies with the northern road line; but the commitment to continued life of the district could range from the 10 years already pledged to a significantly longer horizon of around 40 years. The following alternatives have been examined in depth:

–a SHORTER TERM INVESTMENT HORIZON (committed life 10 years) would allow options of either consolidating the local shopping centre on Main Street or moving it to King Square. In either case the now vacant central site could be developed for housing – but industrial development would be an alternative were the shops to remain on Main Street;

–a LONGER TERM INVESTMENT HORIZON (committed life 40 years) would mean relocating the local shops in King Square, with the central site used for either housing or open space.

THE SHORTER TERM HORIZON offers advantages in terms of flexibility and response to the concerns expressed by residents, as well as in terms of nett expenditure by this authority. The following RECOMMENDATIONS are therefore put forward at this stage:

RECOMMENDED IMMEDIATE ACTIONS

(1) A case be formally submitted to the Transport Authority for adoption of the NORTHERN ROAD LINE (see accompanying map);

(2) A renewal of the pledge to residents of a 10–YEAR period before further housing demolition, with public investment in environmental improvements geared accordingly.

LATER DECISIONS

(3) A decision on the location of the LOCAL SHOPPING CENTRE be taken in 6 MONTHS, after consultation with local traders and consideration of the impending proposals of the shops planning team on the scale of the new Eastwell shopping complex;

(4) The use of the now vacant CENTRAL SITE also to be decided in six months, in conjunction with (3) above.

CONTINGENCY PLANNING

It is just possible that the recommendation of the northern road line will be rejected by the Transport Authority; in which case a formal APPEAL is recommended, backed by evdence from the working party's analysis to date.

It is also possible that a major private developer may be attracted to South Side at some time; in which case, an EXTENSION to the life of the district can be considered.

FURTHER EXPLORATIONS

Because there still remain some important areas of uncertainty affecting future decisions in South Side, the working party proposes to continue carrying through a programme of explorations and consultations with other bodies. Priorities for further work will be outlined verbally at the meeting.

CHOOSING

SKILLS

With ingenuity, it is often possible to present action proposals to decision-takers in forms which do not appear to deviate significantly from familiar forms of report, yet which reflect the underlying structure of a strategic choice analysis, as in this illustration. Use of diagrams should be viewed with caution and contingency plans may not be indicated explicitly where sensitive negotiations may arise.

should prepare themselves carefully for the sorts of debate that could conceivably develop at the meeting, on the basis of their prior knowledge of the responsibilities of committee members, their interests, their power relationships and the idiosyncracies or prejudices of particular members. As a first step, they could be well advised to prepare more detailed descriptions of each of the alternative commitment packages — perhaps using wall charts or other visual aids to present a broad picture of actions, explorations and future choices of the kind illustrated in Figure 77. They might also agree to come to the meeting armed with this kind of picture not only for the two contrasting packages highlighted in the report, but also for a 'compromise' 20-year package, to demonstrate how marginal the differences were between this and the 40-year alternative. Indeed, they might agree that it was a good move to prepare a further commitment package based on the southern road line, to indicate how limited a future it offers to South Side and what a strong case the Council has in recommending the northern alternative to the transportation authority.

Knowing the political inclinations of the committee members — which might cover quite a broad spectrum — the working party members might also feel it was important to prepare carefully the case for an emphasis on public rather than private development, in terms of the constraints presented by the local situation in South Side. They might, however, anticipate that the first contingency planning element of the package in Figure 77 offers a possible basis for helping the committee to converge on an agreed compromise view. They might also anticipate some surprise from committee members that this package is thought to offer local residents better short-term economic prospects than one based on a longer-term investment horizon. The explanation could be that a longer-term commitment to the future of South Side was expected to lead to rising house prices followed by gradual disintegration of the existing deep-rooted community structure; so they might have to be prepared for some challenging debate in the committee about the subtle issues of policy values this could raise.

The example of a commitment package given in Figure 77 is of a form which assumes that the decision-takers to whom it is addressed have significant influence not only in the sphere of responsibility of the Working Party itself, but also in their relationships with others. But this may not always be the case; and a decision situation involving negotiation between two or more autonomous or semi-autonomous parties may call for a different approach — especially if the parties are potentially in conflict, in which case it might not be thought tactically wise that all elements of the commitment package should be declared. For example, if the Working Party did not feel that the Council was in a powerful enough position to ensure that its recommendation of the northern road line would be accepted by the transportation authority, then it might have to re-think the whole commitment package in terms of a more subtle negotiating stance. To take another example, it might be thought more tactful — and more likely to yield results — if the idea of a joint small business initiative on the steelworks site were seeded informally in the mind of the Municipal Enterprise Officer, rather than suddenly presented to him in a background document during a formal committee meeting. So, the overt content of written proposals and background documents can be as much a matter of choice as any other aspect of the decision-making process.

To round off this particular episode in the South Side story, it will be supposed that some particular commitment package is accepted by the committee as a basis for action — whether this be Package IA as presented in Figure 77; or some variant of it which has attracted support in the course of discussions; or possibly some quite different package, perhaps embodying a higher level of commitment; or perhaps less. For it is the committee that has the final responsibility and authority to decide.

Whatever the outcome of the meeting, the use of strategic choice concepts and methods does not mean that the problems of the South Side community are now 'solved' in any final or comprehensive way, any more than it is ever realistic to expect in a case as complex as this. But progress has been made; and it is progress both in the direction of action and of learning. For both the decision-takers and their advisers should have gained valuable insights into not only the problem but also the process; insights which will help to lay foundations for more confident decisions when further chapters come to be written in the continuing South Side story.

Process Judgements in the Choosing Mode

Of course, not every moment of commitment in a continuous planning process need be approached as formally or with as much preparation as this last episode in the South Side story might suggest. Sometimes, a commitment package may consist of no more than a single action commitment on some aspect of the problem under consideration; and this action may fall within the personal sphere of responsibility of a single decision-maker. Perhaps this action may be accompanied by a decision to embark on some form of exploratory action to provide a clearer basis for other choices that have been deferred. Perhaps too — though not of necessity — that small step in the process will include some agreed arrangements for the making of those other choices at a later time.

But the latest episode of the South Side story does illustrate some of the subtle considerations of dialogue between advisers and decision-takers that can arise whenever a more formal moment of commitment arrives. And the story has at least touched on some of the complexities that can arise where there is more than one authoritative decision-taking body, and where different parties may be continually pulling in conflicting directions. In these circumstances, progress may well depend on quite complex negotiations across organisational boundaries — raising issues which will be discussed further in the next two chapters.

This chapter has shown how the work of the choosing mode can draw on prior work in any or all of the other modes — shaping, designing and comparing — sometimes in a very subtle way. Also, as summarised in Figure 79, the work of the choosing mode itself presents many opportunities either for looping briefly in the direction of these other modes, or for switching more deliberately to work for some time in a different mode, if it is judged that the moment for making commitments has not yet arrived. Then, even after a commitment package is adopted as a basis for immediate decision, there will remain the deferred choices to be dealt with at some later time. When this time arrives, all the various opportunities for shaping, designing, comparing and choosing will arise once again — perhaps in different forms, influenced by events and reappraisals over the intervening period. For the process of strategic choice is above all a continuing one which cannot be isolated from the processes of change within the wider environment in which it is set.

As in the concluding sections of the last three chapters, the content of Figure 79 will not be explained in detail. Rather, it is left as an exercise for the reader to reflect on the various switching and looping opportunities which it indicates. Indeed, the reader is encouraged to reflect on these not only in relation to the development of the South Side story in earlier sections, but also in relation to personal experience in choosing strategically in his or her own working life.

Illustrations from practice

This chapter again concludes with a set of three *illustrations from practice* selected to illustrate further points about the work of the choosing mode. All three illustrations are taken from applications in the Netherlands because, at the time of writing, it is in this context that the methods have been taken furthest in practical consultation work.

The first illustration shows how uncertainty areas can be mapped and sorted quickly and informally in a group setting. The next two illustrate diferent points relating to the construction and content of commitment packages; in the final illustration, the content of the commitment package for a major national policy issue is presented in a form indicating the wide range of actions, explorations and responsibilities involved in putting it into effect.

FIGURE
79

Process Choices when Working in the Choosing Mode

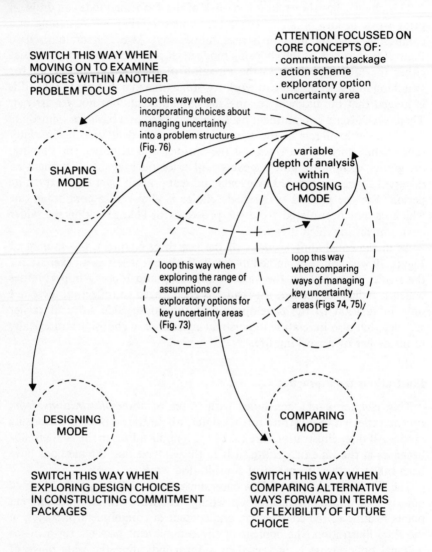

ATTENTION FOCUSSED ON
CORE CONCEPTS OF:
. commitment package
. action scheme
. exploratory option
. uncertainty area

SWITCH THIS WAY WHEN
MOVING ON TO EXAMINE
CHOICES WITHIN ANOTHER
PROBLEM FOCUS

loop this way when
incorporating choices about
managing uncertainty
into a problem structure
(Fig. 76)

SHAPING
MODE

variable
depth of analysis
within
CHOOSING
MODE

loop this way when
exploring the range of
assumptions or
exploratory options for
key uncertainty areas
(Fig. 73)

loop this way
when comparing
ways of managing
key uncertainty
areas (Figs 74, 75)

DESIGNING
MODE

COMPARING
MODE

SWITCH THIS WAY WHEN
EXPLORING DESIGN CHOICES
IN CONSTRUCTING COMMITMENT
PACKAGES

SWITCH THIS WAY WHEN
COMPARING ALTERNATIVE
WAYS FORWARD IN TERMS
OF FLEXIBILITY OF FUTURE
CHOICE

CHOOSING

SUMMARY

FIGURE

80

Illustration from Practice – Choosing 1

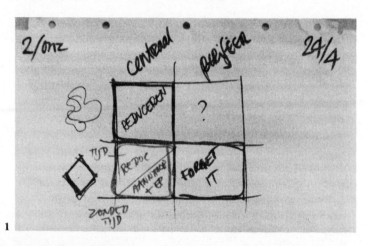

1

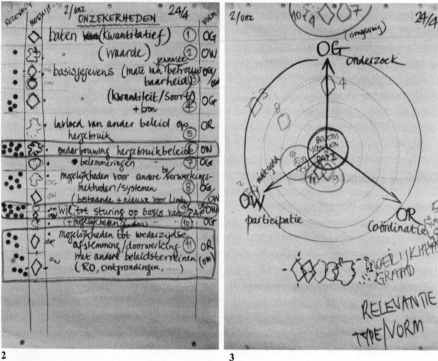

2   3

CHOOSING

PRACTICE

Theme: Putting Uncertainty Areas into Perspective through the Use of an Uncertainty Graph.

Project: Development of an Integrated Policy Framework for the Management of Solid Waste.

Context: Workshops with an Inter-Organisational Project Team, Province of Limburg, The Netherlands, 1986.

COMMENTARY ON FIGURE 80

These charts record work done by a project group at the end of the first day of a series of three two-day workshops, designed to get a more substantial planning project under way. The group consisted mainly of Provincial Government employees, and was charged with preparing a policy plan to integrate the management of different kinds of solid waste.

In the first instance, uncertainty areas were listed as they occurred to members of the group, drawing on their everyday experience and on understanding gained through earlier analysis (2). They ranged from the quite specific (quantity, type and source of solid waste) to the relatively general (basis for recycling policy). When this process slowed, the analysis proper was started, although the list was left open for additions if there were any.

Firstly, each uncertainty area was classified according to type, as can be seen down the left hand side of the list ("OG" = UE in Dutch, "OW" = UV, "OR" = UR). As usually happens, a number of the uncertainty areas were seen as falling between categories and so given dual classifications.

The second stage of the analysis then identified views about the difficulty or otherwise of reducing uncertainty in the various areas. A distinction between "diamonds" (hard to reduce) and "jellies" (easy to reduce) was adopted as a starting point. As might be expected, this quickly developed into a more subtle range which is shown just below the uncertainty graph (3).

The third stage of the analysis involved assessment of relavance to the plan. For this, use was made of stickers. Each member of the group was given four stickers and asked to place them next to the four uncertainty areas which they considered most relevant to the policy plan. The results appear down the left hand side of the list. The three boxed uncertainty areas emerged as more relevant than the others. They included the uncertainty over support for a policy of recycling; over level of commitment to making the plan work; and over possibilities for combining with other fields of policy.

All this information was then transferred to the uncertainty graph (3), which has as its centre the focus: "Beleidskeuzen in PAP II" (policy choices in the second Provincial Waste Management Plan). This was further analysed in line with principles outlined by means of a simplified 2 × 2 taxonomy (1). As a result the decision was taken to reduce uncertainty area number 6 about the level of support for a policy of recycling. However, because the project was still at an early stage, it was possible to give some more thought to ways of tackling the other central uncertainties which seemed more difficult to reduce. Had the process been nearer the end, they would probably have been tackled by making assumptions, perhaps backed up by some contingency planning.

FIGURE
81

Illustration from Practice – Choosing 2

1   2   3

Tabel IV AKTIEPLAN ○ – 22 – ○

4

keuzen \ onderdelen aktieplan	direkt te nemen akties	onderzoek	op termijn te nemen akties	eventualiteiten plan
reraffinage van alle afvalolie	aankondigen principe keuze voor reraffinage	– studie naar kosten/baten, invloed van marktsituaties	aankondigen definitieve keuze	ingeval van negatieve keuze, reaktiveren evaluatie op basis nieuwe inzichten
realisering installatie op basis van AVR-constructie	– benaderen betrokkenen – starten onderhandelingen	– studie naar basis voor onderhandelingen, incl. rijksbijdrage – uitwerken basis voor keuze vestigingsplaats – studie mogelijkheden monopolie	afsluiten "letter of intent" met betrokkenen vaststellen ontwerpbasis vaststellen financieringsstructuur	ingeval onvoldoende meewerken betrokkenen; terug vallen op de AVR, verhogen rijksbijdrage, samenwerking met slechts enkele betrokkenen
afbouwen bestaande bewerkingsaktiviteiten in de interimperiode	informeren betrokkenen van principe keuze	evalueren van de bedrijfs-economische consequentie van het niet verlengen van vergunningen	niet verlengen vergunningen	ingeval dreigende discountinuiteit verbranden in grote installaties met RGR overwegen schadevergoedings toezeggingen
voortzetten invoering regelgeving t.a.v. – verbranden in eigen beheer – inzamel vergunningen – inzamelen kca – importen	tegenhouden verlenen hinderwet vergunningen zelfverbranden ondersteunen EG-beleid voorbereiden wijziging brandstofbesluit voortzetten voorbereiding inzamel AMVB voortzetten projekt KCA	onderzoeken emissies kleinschalige verbranding onderzoek effekt direct te nemen akties onderzoek standaardspecificaties brandstoffen	invoeren nieuw brandstofbesluit invoeren EG-richtlijn opzetten inzamelstructuur kca verlenen inzamelvergunningen	ingeval onvoldoende effect maatregelen – verbreden Wca tot aktiviteiten binnen de bedrijven

CHOOSING

PRACTICE

Theme: Preparation of an Action Plan using a Commitment Package Framework.
Project: Continuing Policy Development on the Management of Waste (Used Oil).
Context: Ministry of Environment Project Team with a Process Consultant, Den Haag, The Netherlands, 1985.

COMMENTARY ON FIGURE 81

These working charts, and the excerpt from a typed policy document, were produced during a project carried out during the autumn of 1985 by the Environment Directorate General of the Netherlands Ministry of Public Housing, Physical Planning and Environment. This project was started as part of a preliminary action research programme to develop a method of continuous policy formation for waste management, based on the strategic choice approach. The project team was drawn mainly from the Waste Management Division, although other parts of the Ministry were also involved.

The problem under examination concerned policy on how to deal with used oil. The focus was initially on oil from cars, but was soon extended to cover all kinds of used oil. A solution based on re-refining was clearly favoured, but other issues — such as how to handle oil from the very many small sources — were less clear-cut.

The wall-charts (1), (2) and (3) show the first cycle in design of a commitment package. They were produced during a single half-day session, but based on a considerable amount of earlier work including explicit analysis of uncertainty. The framework is that of a standard commitment package, and it was filled in through interaction between the project leader and the facilitator, working partly in English and partly in Dutch. An accompanying note (foot of (3)) recorded explicitly the identity of the decision-taker; the intended life of the package; and its orientation towards re-refining. On the same chart (top of (3)) were recorded some key assumptions ("annamen") for which contingency planning was thought to be possibly relevant at a later stage.

The agreed commitment package, which was designed as much as an action plan as it is a policy statement, is shown in (4). It was finalised after the initial work had been discussed thoroughly in the project group, and bilateral consultations with others. Responsibilities and deadlines were not allocated explicitly; this is because the commitment package related to only one organisation committed to a regular cycle of review — which by this time had been extended from six to twelve monthly frequency. It was therefore well understood where the responsibilities lay, and the deadlines were implied by the review procedure. Other information was supplied in the supporting text to the document, which is not shown here.

This and other documents were produced and bound in loose-leaf form, as the whole process was designed to be cyclic and continuous. This means that statements such as (4) are never seen as definitive except to the extent that they are intended to stand as a guide to action until replaced by more up-to-date statements as part of the annual review cycle.

In 1986, as a result of the action research, a comprehensive loose-leaf handbook was produced as a working guide to all those involved in the management of different types of waste within the scope of the Ministry's programme.

FIGURE

82

Illustration from Practice – Choosing 3

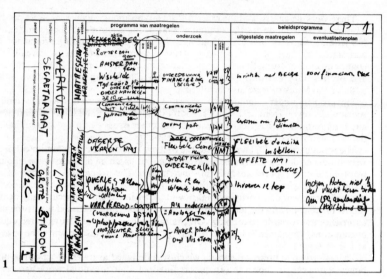

1

An excerpt of the commitment package for Dutch national LPG policy (1984)

Action set

Actions:
- traffic regulation: increase regulatory measures for LPG ships on the main national waterways;
- LPG inland tankships: adapt design and construction in order to effectively prohibit large LPG outflows;
- LPG railcars: large contingents should always be shipped in block trains; in case (for smaller contingents) of shunting some extra measures are specified;
- LPG road tankers: extra design adaptations are introduced to further decrease probabilities of LPG outflows;
- Stationary installations: specifications for zoning around such installations are given;
- Road transport routes: will basically be limited to the Dutch dangerous goods network. New stationary installations will be located in places compatible to this network.

Explorations:
- research into the safe domains around seaships will be done;
- the collision safety of seagoing tankers carrying pressurised LPG will be analysed;
- the possibilities of repressing fire around LPG inland tankers will be analysed;
- the further analysis with respect to effective and economic means of prohibiting Bleve's on LPG road tankers will be conducted.

Policy set

Delayed actions:
The result of the above mentioned analysis will be implemented in the relevant policy decisions and it will be introduced in national regulation and in international regulatory bodies.

Contingency plans:
- in case an LPG-terminal in Amsterdam is conceived then a refuge location for LPG tankers will be constructed;
- in case international regulatory bodies do not accommodate the proposed measures then the general character of such measures must be guaranteed along other lines;
- in case the analysis with respect to prohibiting Bleve in road tankers does not give satisfactory results then other means will be used to create an acceptable situation;
- in case measures with respect to LPG filling stations prove to be intractable due to local situations, then a decision will be made regarding other necessary measures or removal of the filling station.

2

Theme: Finalisation of a Policy Statement using a Commitment Package Framework.

Project: National Policy on the Handling and Distribution of Liquid Petroleum Gas (LPG).

Context: A Multi-Disciplinary Inter-Ministry Working Party, Den Haag, The Netherlands, 1983 – 84.

COMMENTARY ON FIGURE 82

This illustration is taken from a published case study (van de Graaf, 1985) of the application of strategic choice methods to the development of a new national policy in the Netherlands for the landing, transportation, storage and distribution of Liquid Petroleum Gas (LPG). The author of the paper is a civil servant in the Dutch Ministry of Economic Affairs who played a leading role in the project alongside representatives of other Ministries, with Allen Hickling and Arnold de Jong in the role of process consultants.

The situation was one in which the basic assumptions of the previously adopted policy had become eroded, because it had not proved possible to concentrate the landing of this economically attractive but hazardous hydrocarbon — of international importance as a fuel and chemical feedstock — at a single installation at the mouth of the Rhine, with distribution by pipeline. For two years, the search for an alternative policy had exercised the attention of civil servants from the Ministry of Economic Affairs, the Ministry of Transport and Directorates of the Environment Ministry concerned with land-use planning and environmental protection. Progress had been blocked by the well-known tendency to defend departmental positions. The explicit use of a more interactive approach based on strategic choice methods allowed rapid progress towards an agreed set of policies. However, the participants found it useful to switch back from time to time to a more adversarial mode of working, so as to appreciate more clearly the policy and other constraints they would have to contend with outside the context of the working group.

The working document reproduced here (1) was one of several in a set which were needed to cover all aspects of the problem. The printed framework adopted here is one that can be used large (A1 size) on the wall or small (A4 size) in a loose-leaf file. Notice the explicit accommodation of responsibility ("wie" = who), deadlines ("wanneer" = when), and budgets ("fl." = guilders (money)). The decision-taker is listed on the left ("secretariaat"), as is the orientation ("grote stroom"). Otherwise it is a standard commitment package framework.

The condensed extract from the final recommendations (2) is presented using the four headings of the commitment package framework — as was the actual set of proposals. These were formally adopted in February 1985 by the second chamber of the Dutch national parliament.

It will be noticed that the set of explorations are primarily of a technical and economic nature, reflecting concern with uncertainty areas of the UE type. However, the significance of uncertainty areas of type UR is clearly indicated in some of the proposals listed under the contingency plan heading — the other decision-makers identified ranging from international regulatory bodies to local agencies concerned with the siting and safety of filling stations. Uncertainties of type UV in the form of the conflicts between economy, safety and other criteria were accommodated in the design of the inter-Ministry working process.

9

Practicalities

Taking Stock

The last four chapters have completed a second and fuller cycle around the four basic modes of planning seen as a process of strategic choice. In contrast to the briefer, introductory tour made in Chapters 2 and 3, the emphasis has been on *appropriate* ways of drawing on the core concepts and basic methods of the strategic choice approach, in adapting to different working situations. Although certain elaborations of these concepts and methods have been introduced, it is important to stress again that moves towards elaboration should not necessarily be seen as moves towards 'better' use of the strategic choice approach. Simplification is usually a virtue when working under pressure; and in striking a balance between simplification and elaboration the most useful working rule is to favour simplification except where there are convincing arguments to the contrary.

At various points in Chapters 5 to 8 consideration was given to some of the *organisational* aspects of the strategic choice approach; to the switching of the *process* between modes; and to the forms that the more visible *products* might take. Also, those aspects of *technology* concerned with effective interaction and facilitation in a group setting were considered more closely than in the earlier introductory tour of core concepts and methods. But the exposition of the last four chapters has still followed the structure of the four modes in a sequential way. It has to be recognised that, the more effective a working group becomes, the more the process will tend to move freely and adaptively between modes through a succession of rapid switching and looping judgements. So the offering of operational advice on the management of the strategic choice approach cannot be organised according to the structure of the four modes alone. There is another level of practical advice which relates generally to the management of the approach as a whole. It is this kind of advice with which the present chapter is concerned.

The starting point for the advice to be offered here will be the general picture of the *orientations* of strategic choice presented at the end of

249

Chapter 4 (Figure 34). That diagram used the framework of technology, organisation, process and product to compare the strategic choice approach with more conventional approaches that could be regarded as quite appropriate in dealing with simpler problems. In successive columns, contrasts were drawn first at the level of general orientations, then at the level of operational guidelines, then at the levels of emphases in management choice and in evaluation. This chapter will interpret these last two aspects in still more concrete terms, reflecting the body of experience in *application* of strategic choice ideas that has been built up through working with many different people on a wide range of practical problems over a period of some fifteen years. First, this body of practical experience will be briefly reviewed. Then, the main lessons to be drawn from it will be presented; first in terms of the emphases on *selectivity* and *adaptiveness* which distinguish the overall approach, and then in terms of the four headings of Technology, Organisation, Process and Product, considered each in turn.

The Base of Experience

The advice that will be offered in this chapter is rooted primarily in the experiences of the authors, working with many other people over the years between 1970 and 1986, and the picture that has gradually developed through this experience of what constitutes 'good practice' in working with the strategic choice approach. This view of the current state of the art is one which is unlikely to stand still in the years ahead, as further experience accumulates. For the range of applications to different fields of decision-making seems likely to extend and, with it, both the variety of people and organisations involved, and the range of further adaptations made.

However, our current view of good practice is one which already has quite a broad base in terms of the range of planners, managers, specialists and lay policy-makers who have become exposed to the approach and played some part in its development. The people with whom we ourselves have worked have come from several different countries and decision-making cultures; and the types of working relationship through which we have collaborated with them have also been diverse. So, it will be a useful prelude to the advice of this chapter to indicate briefly what the range of these working relationships has been and, broadly, what has been learned through each type of experience. For this purpose, three broad headings will suffice — sponsored experiments, training events and consultancy projects. Each type of experience has complemented and reinforced the others: but the order in which they will be introduced here corresponds broadly to the historical sequence in which they first emerged.

Much of the early development work on the strategic choice approach took place through the medium of *sponsored experiments*, in which an organisation interested in the possibility of promoting new methods of planning and decision-making has been prepared to invest in a programme of one or more experimental applications of the strategic choice approach to 'on line' problems within its general area of concern. Leading examples included the initial LOGIMP experiment of 1970; the structure plan project of the mid-seventies; the Netherlands project on environmental policy plans in the early eighties; and successive projects in the states of São Paulo and Pernambuco in Brazil. References to some of these experiences will be found in the guide to further reading at the end of the book. Each exercise was sponsored not so much to help with specific decision problems, as to test the relevance of the strategic choice approach to a wider class of problems; yet success in helping with specific cases was quite central to this testing process. In each of the first three projects mentioned, between two and six 'live' planning problems were pursued in parallel, with the authors and other colleagues or associates acting as advisers to the local teams responsible for producing recommendations on these selected problems. The different teams would all meet together from time to time, to exchange experiences, review difficulties and provide mutual support — with representatives of the central sponsoring body maintaining oversight of the programme as a whole.

The overall style of working in these sponsored experiments has been one of *action research*, designed through negotiation with the dual aims of discovery and practical service to users in view. In contrast to more classical action research studies (Clark,1976), there was the added dimension that the action research team was engaged in collaboration with people not just from a single organisational context, but from a set of two or more local 'host' organisations together with a central sponsoring body, each with its own expectations of what the collaboration should achieve.

Inevitably, each sponsored experiment has involved elements of training in the strategic choice approach — partly in the form of 'on the job' training for the members of the local teams, and partly in the form of introductory lectures on philosophy and method. In addition, however, from 1971 onwards, free-standing *training events* have been arranged under the auspices of a wide range of other organisations, in various parts of the world. The duration of such an event has generally been short — ranging from as little as half a day to two weeks at the most — because those participating have generally been not full time students but decision-makers and planners with many other pressures on their time. The design formula for all but the shortest half-day events — a two- or three-day duration being most typical — has been for lectures to be interspersed with work in small groups on a realistic problem exercise. The aim is to move progressively through the shaping, designing, comparing and choosing modes, as in this book, with as much attention as practicable within the time available to the various opportunities for recycling that can be explored as understanding grows and circumstances change. The experiences of both sponsored experiments and consultancy projects have provided a rich source of case material for use in these training events, allowing the various facets of planning under pressure to be realistically reproduced. At the same time, the wide variety of management contexts and positions represented by those participating in the various training events has considerably enriched the process of feedback from practice through which strategic choice ideas and methods have gradually evolved.

Involvement in direct *consultancy projects*, where the primary aim has been to help with a specific planning or decision problem rather than to explore the relevance of the approach to some class of problems, has achieved momentum as the experiential foundations of strategic choice have become more secure. In almost all cases where we or others associated with us have been involved as consultants, arrangements for direct collaboration with people from client organisations have been treated as an important part of the project design, and opportunities for interactive working have been stressed.

The scale of such projects has varied from substantial engagements with national governments on national policy issues, to briefer assignments for commercial, public and voluntary organisations. Sometimes, too, brief exercises in mutual consultancy have been designed within short-term training events. Typically, an hour or two has been allowed for participants to talk about instances of specific problems which are currently concerning them in their own management situations.

While the various training and consultancy experiences have provided opportunities to experiment with many different styles in managing the process of strategic choice, the advice that follows is based primarily on one 'prototypical' style that has proved successful in many different settings and has been widely used both in sponsored experiments and in consultancy projects. It is a style that reflects the basic orientations and operational guidelines of Chapter 4, in that it is built around a programme of interactive group sessions of limited duration in the kind of working environment illustrated in Figure 30.

Within the group, the methods of strategic choice are used as an 'open technology', starting from some initial state of knowledge or uncertainty about the problem among the participants, that will gradually be revealed. The agenda is treated as flexible within the time constraints of the working session or sequences of sessions that has been arranged. Little or no backroom preparation is expected for the first session — though priorities for backroom work can build up as a shared view of issues and uncertainties develops within the group. Typically, a working session will cover two or three hours either in a morning or an afternoon, with the same kinds of pressures on time as in the more traditional committee setting depicted in Figure 6 — but with the important exception that there is no expectation of working through a pre-conceived agenda from start to finish as the session proceeds.

Selectivity and Adaptiveness: The Toolbox Analogy

It is most important that the strategic choice approach is not seen as a mere technique. The straightforward application of techniques, with some well-defined rules as to how and when they should be applied, has all the attraction of simplicity and is easily taught in a classroom setting. But such an approach has severe limitations, unless the problems being addressed are 'bent' to fit it — something which in practice happens rather more often than it should. The strategic choice approach has been developed in a way designed specifically to avoid this difficulty. This means that there is no one right way to use the approach. There can be no 'correct' sequence in which to do things, and no prescribed combinations to adopt — whether these be viewed in terms of technology, organisation, process or product. It is all a matter of judgement as to what is appropriate to the circumstances at that particular time. Every problem is different. Each must be tackled on its merits.

Use of the strategic choice approach has been likened to the use of a toolbox. The analogy is extremely apt so long as it is remembered that in strategic choice the tools are many and varied — including a wide range of concepts, modes, frameworks, techniques, activities and media.

Imagine taking a toolbox to mend a car engine. Having opened the bonnet and looked at the engine, it is likely that a start has to be made by undoing a nut. Reaching into the toolbox, one selects a spanner, takes it out and tries it on the nut. The first time, almost invariably, it does not fit. So one puts it back and tries another. It may be that the nut is still stubborn, in which case one dips down into the toolbox and chooses another spanner, using now the two in combination. It may be that this combination fails too. If so, they can be put back and another combination tried; or perhaps some penetrating oil is used in addition, thus using three items in combination; and so on, until it works.

As progress is made through the job in hand, different situations will emerge requiring different combinations of tools — and so on, until the job is finished. Also, the next time it is necessary to do the same job, it will probably be appropriate to use different tools, in different combinations and sequences. Imagine that the same car engine requires the same maintenance three months later. It may now be easier to shift that nut, which was once so difficult that several spanners had to be used to shift it; perhaps because it was greased before being tightened. This time, the tools needed may be different again. Perhaps a pair of pliers will be enough to get it undone — or it may be found to be only finger-tight in any case.

Meanwhile, however, other things might have changed; a bolt might have become rusted in, or broken off, or weakened in some way. So yet more different tools, sequences and combinations might have to be tried.

This analogy illustrates well the two key ideas which govern all the operational advice offered in the sections which follow. The first is the idea of **selectivity**. This follows inevitably from the wide variety of choice available in the use of the strategic choice approach. Indeed, it is clearly implied in the tool-box analogy; there are many tools which obviously cannot all be used on a specific task, even if they were all appropriate — which is most unlikely. Even more inconceivable is the idea that they could all be used at the same time. Thus it is necessary to be selective; to choose carefully what to do and what not to do — and how, with whom and when.

The second is the idea of **adaptiveness**. This follows from the feelings of uncertainty which are endemic to working with complex issues — uncertainty about what the problem is (and is not); what the alternative ways of dealing with it may be; how they rate one against the other; and, indeed, what to do about it. The idea that one can always, unerringly, select a good way of working in such a context is plainly unrealistic. It may serve some purpose to try to predict the course that the analysis should take; but to believe that it will be sensible to maintain that course whatever happens in the process is similarly far-fetched. So, there can be only one way of working; and that, paradoxically, is to be ready to work in many ways — in fact, to work adaptively via the explicit acceptance of the learning process, part of which is learning how to conduct that process. One's capacity to think about what to do; what not to do; how, when and in which context, is bound to evolve as one's understanding develops. It is only sensible, as long as time allows, to give that evolutionary process full rein.

Therefore, every opportunity has to be taken to promote that evolution — to keep the learning process going in a smooth and adaptive way. Referring back to the description of the toolbox analogy, there was an important moment when the first spanner selected proved to be the wrong one. This was not bad or inefficient — it was a vital step in the learning process. Being mistaken in this way is important because so much is learnt from it. Thus the second spanner was more likely to be right because the choice of it was so much better informed than the first. This is a classic example of learning from one's mistakes — a phenomenon well known in all cultures of the world, old and new. It leads to the idea of *learning by doing*. The only way to make mistakes is by doing something — so it follows that the more one does, the more mistakes will be made, and the more one will learn.

But this does not mean that selectivity is unimportant. Selections have to be made all the time, in order to keep the process going, and there are times when making a mistake can be costly. So it means that care must be taken in that selection; yet that too much time must not be wasted on it. Going back to the toolbox analogy again, a lot of thought could be given to the choice of which tool to use at any time. It is easy to hesitate when there are so many alternatives — not only which size of spanner to use, but also which sort of spanner, and, indeed, whether a spanner was an appropriate tool in the first place. The important thing is not to agonise too long over the choice of which to use; but to try one, drawing as much as possible on past experience, with an open mind and in a spirit of learning. As a rough-and-ready rule, it is worth bearing in mind that the time spent thinking about it should not exceed the time it would take just to try one out.

Naturally, experience is a vital help in selectivity. This in itself can lead to the idea of each user having his or her own individual *repertoire*. This is the sub-set of all the available tools which that person tends to use more freely and frequently than others — a form of behaviour which is systematically reinforced because it is the most frequently used tools that tend to stay at the top of the toolbox, thus being the first for consideration the next time. Tools from lower in the toolbox only get used when the earlier ones do not work so well, or when the specific task is very well defined. Different people's personal repertoires are likely to have a number of tools in common, and these may be expected to be those with the more general application; the equivalent of hammers, pliers and screwdrivers, though even these may be of various sizes and types. For users of strategic choice, among these common tools would probably be the basic concepts of AIDA; though even here such core concepts as the option bar and the decision scheme can be represented and used in different ways, as earlier chapters have shown.

So, even the experienced consultant or practitioner in strategic choice will have a personal repertoire, which will be similar but probably by no means identical as between individuals. These will reflect differences in their personal styles as well as in their work experiences in collaborative settings. The two authors, for example, recognise some clear personal differences in the emphases they give to particular concepts and methods in their respective repertoires.

Most people already have personal toolboxes of their own and, indeed, their own repertoires with which they are likely to feel quite comfortable. What is more, they are probably loath to abandon these just to take up what could seem to be a self-contained box of tools for strategic choice, such as that presented here. In most cases, this is not necessary. The strategic choice approach is intended to be open and flexible — and most of its tools can be used in combination with other ways of doing things. Indeed, mention has already been made of certain other tools of evaluation and design at particular points in the preceding chapters. There is also some development work under way which is likely to clarify the relationships between the tools offered here and others; and a brief synopsis of this at the time of writing will appear in Chapter 10.

Choosing Tools under Pressure

The most distinctive and significant feature of the strategic choice approach is that is has been developed directly out of practice, working with planners and decision-makers who are usually working under pressure. Consequently, it is under these conditions that strategic choice is most useful, and it is generally where deeper and more lengthy analysis is relevant that some of the other approaches come into their own.

In developing the strategic choice approach, it has been found helpful to distinguish between contrasting ways of handling work under pressure — especially pressure caused by the shortage of time. These are what is often called the *quick and dirty* way, and what may be called the *fast and effective* way. Taking up the toolbox analogy again, they can both be likened to types of screwdriver. The quick and dirty way can be likened to the 'Brummigem' screwdriver, whereas the fast and effective way can be likened to the 'Yankee' screwdriver. The 'Brummigem' (which is a corruption of the name Birmingham) is, in fact, a heavy hammer. Although designed for other tasks, such as banging in nails, it can be a very quick way of driving in screws. Of course, there tends to be a loss of effectiveness in the result, although the appearance may sometimes be satisfactory. The 'Yankee' (actually a trade mark) is a specially designed 'plunge'-type screwdriver which, by means of a helical thread inside the handle, turns the screw automatically as the tool is pushed on. It is very fast and, indeed, can be very effective. But the trouble is that it is not suitable for all situations and, unlike the 'Brummigem', it cannot be easily used for anything else.

Thus, it can be seen that there is no clear-cut recipe for the use in practice of the strategic choice approach. Selectivity and adaptiveness are both essential and, by definition, require that choices be made. And, as was implied in the toolbox analogy, these choices mean balancing ideas about effectiveness against ideas about the expenditure of effort, time and resources — whether the balance is struck in a conscious or sub-conscious way. Here it is worth mentioning the *Sutton Principle*, which many users of strategic choice have found helpful as a simple, light-hearted way of reminding themselves of the issues involved.

The Sutton Principle is named after Willie Sutton, who was an infamous American bank robber.* One day, when he eventually became available for interview, Willie Sutton was asked why he robbed banks. To this he came back with the now immortal reply: 'Because that is where the money is!'. His reasoning was very simple. Given a limited amount of time and effort (in Willie's case his own), these resources should be directed where the rewards are likely to be greatest.

Without examining Willie Sutton's logic too deeply, two important

* This principle was first enunciated as the 'Sutton Effect' by Robert E Machol in one of a series of brief, tongue-in-cheek articles on Principles of Operations Research (Machol, 1976).

lessons can be drawn. The first is that if one cannot deal with everything adequately then, rather than deal with all things inadequately, it is better to deal adequately with some things only. The second is that, in choosing which things to do, the process should always be steered in the direction where it is believed the greatest progress can be made. So it is also with deciding how to select tools from a toolbox — always remembering that in the strategic choice approach the toolbox includes modes, concepts, frameworks, media of communication and ways of working, as well as analytical techniques. The costs are generally the demands which the use of each tool places on the available *resources*; and, in the management of a process of strategic choice, the resources in question tend to take many forms. They include elapsed time; the skills and experience of relevant people; access to relevant information; and access to the capacity to process such information by electronic or other means. The effectiveness of alternative ways of proceeding has to be weighed against the demands they make on resources of all these kinds and, as such resources tend to be limited, they can become constraining, limiting the range of choice. Or sometimes, of course, they can be bought in from elsewhere.

Money has not been mentioned yet as a resource because it is rare for the selection of a tool from the toolbox to carry a direct financial cost. Where such costs do arise is in trying to make up for shortfalls in resource supply. This means giving consideration to improvement, support or, in some cases, replacement of the resources already available, in such forms as:

— more and/or more effective people (eg training and consultants);
— more and/or more relevant information (eg surveys and research);
— better and/or faster technological support (eg computers and software).

However, this is always assuming that there is enough calendar-type time available — and this is often the most inflexible constraint of all.

The effectiveness side of the resource-effectiveness balance is difficult to judge in advance because it is so intangible and uncertain. It is concerned essentially with the *potential* of the tool; in particular, the potential progress it might generate in terms of those broad and comparatively subtle dimensions of evaluation which were indicated in the final column of Figure 34. Progress in the directions of sharing, synergy, understanding and confidence can be difficult enough to assess in retrospect, let alone to judge with any clarity in advance.

So far, this chapter has discussed the practicalities of working with the strategic choice toolbox in rather general terms. The aim has been to explain more fully the broad management emphasis on selectivity and adaptiveness which appeared in the top row of Figure 34, and also to develop further the idea of effectiveness as an evaluative principle. To move to a more concrete level in this discussion of the practicalities of strategic choice, it will be necessary now to consider the overall approach in terms of the four components: technology, organisation, process and product.

Technology: Managing the Open Technology in Practice

In Chapter 4, it was argued that the technology of strategic choice was designed above all as an *open technology*; as a means of assisting and encouraging effective communication and interaction within a working group and not just as an aid to backroom analysis by experts. It is because of this emphasis on sharing between participants with diverse perspectives to contribute that the technology of strategic choice can be considered an *appropriate* technology for group working on issues the very shape of which may be both complex and confused.

The emphasis on an open technology was interpreted in Chapter 4 into an operational guideline of a *focus on decisions*. This guideline finds more specific expression in the set of core concepts to do with decision areas, decision options, decision schemes and the various other linked concepts which were introduced in relation to the work of the comparing and the choosing modes. In addition, an impression was presented of the kind of interactive work setting in which the spirit of an open, decision-centred technology can be achieved in practice (Figure 30). It was argued that choices about the use of rooms, furniture and equipment were just as much a part of the management of the strategic choice technology as were matters to do with the application of specific concepts and techniques. So there are various practical matters to do with these *physical* aspects of technological choice to be discussed in this section; after which, some further points will be made about the kinds of *social* technology that can be helpful in stimulating productive forms of interaction within a working group.

Some of the advice to be offered on effective use of walls, paper and pens may seem quite trivial and mundane. However, long experience in using the strategic choice approach with groups does indicate that the quality of group communication and interaction can be quite severely impaired by failure to pay heed to such considerations, especially in the early stages of group working, when patterns for future interaction are being set. It is important, firstly, to choose a room which is not so small in relation to the number of participants that their freedom of movement is restricted, constraining them to sit in fixed positions in relation to each other, as they would in the familiar committee setting. For the same reason, it is important to avoid creating a situation in which a table becomes the centrepiece. Indeed, a first step in preparing a room is usually to push any tables to one side, where they can still be used as required, for documents, refreshments, materials or note-taking, but do not create barriers between the participants as they move around. It is a matter of comfort and convenience to provide enough chairs for participants to be able to sit down whenever they desire. However, they are likely to spend much of their time standing and moving around when the process of interactive working is in full swing; and at such times the focus of attention will normally be on the ever-changing pictures of decisions and their relationships which are building up around the walls.

Fixtures such as blackboards or whiteboards do not allow this to happen. This is simply because the information they contain has to be eradicated once they are full; this is not consistent with effective working in a cyclic process, which requires the ability, at any moment, to go back to a previous point and to pick up where one left off. Nor do 'flip chart' boards on easels by themselves serve the purpose, because of their limited surface area.

It is important in strategic choice to display as much of the work as possible at any one time, thus encouraging instantaneous, ad hoc *looping* to take place. Participants should be able to compare the focus of the moment with previous work, skipping backwards and forwards through the process as freely as possible.

So, *walls* are important; and the interactive process can be impeded quite seriously if people are working in a room where the wall space is broken up by too many windows, or projecting panels, paintings or shelves; where access to the available wall space is restricted by too much furniture; or where the walls are uneven or richly decorated in a style which is designed to impress. This means that conventional boardrooms or council chambers do not make an ideal environment for this kind of interactive working; for tensions can often arise with other people who wish to preserve such rooms as settings for more orthodox meetings. Such tensions can usually be avoided by choosing to work in a more sparsely furnished and plainly decorated space. To work effectively on walls, plentiful supplies of *paper* of generous dimension are required. Continuous rolls of paper have sometimes been used; but pads of flip chart sheets of international A1 size have been found to be more flexible when it comes to rearranging and consolidating information as the work proceeds.

The more sheets of paper accumulate around the walls of the room, the more important the practicalities of *paper management* become. Sheets of paper can be affixed to the walls either by masking tape or by a re-usable putty-like substance such as 'Blu-tack'; pins only provide an acceptable substitute where walls are covered with cork or some similar soft surface. Blu-tack has been found to provide high flexibility in removing and repositioning sheets of paper quickly and, if properly handled, leaves no permanent marks on most types of surface. It is generally quite sufficient to fix each sheet by the top two corners only, placing the Blu-tack a centimetre or two in from the corner; each new sheet should be positioned with its upper edge a little above head height, for purposes of writing and of visibility. As wall space at this level becomes more scarce, sheets recording past work can either be moved down to a lower level or overlaid by others.

However, in doing so, it is important to avoid hanging paper on paper —
for the additional weight is then likely to pull the original paper away from
the wall, usually to the distraction of all concerned.

It is not always possible to keep the papers on the wall neatly arranged —
evenly spaced and vertical. However, well ordered walls can help a group
overcome the strangeness of working in this way and give a sense of
organised purpose. Architectural features, such as joints in walls, door
frames and even wallpaper patterns can be used for guidance — not only
with hanging the papers but also with setting up lines, grids and matrices on
them. Paper over-printed with a feint grid is also helpful in this respect.
Large sheets of paper with pre-drawn frameworks, such as:

— compatibility and consistency matrices;
— concentric circles for uncertainty graphs;
— advantage comparison charts;
— commitment package frameworks;

not only make the work look more organised; they also promote faster,
more effective working. Drawn on tracing paper, they can be copied quite
easily by the same processes that architects and engineers use. In this way,
one can have a large enough supply not to have to worry about running out.

The paper used need not be of high quality, so long as it is not too porous
when put to the test of being written on with coloured marker pens. The
pens themselves should be sufficient in number for participants not to have
to compete with each other when they feel moved to add something to the
'maps' of problems that are building up around the walls; and they should
be sufficiently varied in hue to allow colour differentiation to be used freely
as an aid to communication.

Experience has shown that some brands of marker pens are much more
reliable than others in terms of ink flow. Those using water-based coloured
ink have been found to provide the best service; and those with a wedge-
shaped felt tip, three to five millimetres wide, allow a variety of line
thicknesses, and clear visibility in most interactive environments. Many
experiences in group working have been impoverished by reliance on pens
which can only make thin, pale lines; which squeak in a jarring way; or
which are prone to dry up at important moments. However, this is not to
say that pale colours are never useful. In particular, a barely visible yellow
makes a good colour with which to pre-enter frameworks for guidance in
adding more substantive information; for example, it can be used to draw
up the rows and columns of a grid or matrix, or the concentric rings of an
uncertainty graph. In drawing up an option graph for a selected problem
focus, one useful 'trick' is first to draw a faint yellow ring intersecting each
of the decision areas, then to space out the options within each decision area
at intervals around this ring.

There are also more general points of calligraphy and style which regular users of flip charts have tried to cultivate — points about holding the pen, about drawing freehand lines and circles, about positioning of information on a new sheet of paper in a way that anticipates the further information that is still to come. Practice and discussion can lead to gradual improvements in these directions; but it is important above all that concern with the quality of the graphics should not be so pervasive that participants who feel they have few graphic skills should feel inhibited from taking part.

It is not to be regarded as a sign of failure to make mistakes, or to revise earlier views; it is a vital part of the learning process. So it is important to make corrections quickly and move on, rather than go to pains to erase any signs that a change has been made. Trivial mistakes can be covered up by self-adhesive labels; but less trivial changes or corrections are better left as part of the record on the wall, in so far as they represent a significant step in the learning process which people may wish later to recall. A decision graph or similar picture which has become too untidy and confused can always be re-drawn and the new version placed over or alongside the old, treating the original as a secondary record only. Every now and again, too, it may be sensible for the participants to pause and rearrange the total set of flip charts around the walls, perhaps grouping together those to which they expect to refer most frequently in the course of subsequent work.

Turning to what has been called the *social* technology of strategic choice, there are further management choices which arise when working with a group of participants in which there is little or no prior experience of this style of interactive work. It is appropriate for the person or persons acting in a facilitating role to take the lead in the use of pen and paper in the early stages, if only to demonstrate the general method of working and set a style for others to follow. Yet, in training courses which include small group exercises, it is usually found that most people start working on the walls spontaneously enough, provided they have had at least a brief demonstration of the art of paper management beforehand.

How quickly and energetically moves are made to open up the process of writing on the walls to wider participation is a matter which has to be judged according to the situation and the sense of how well a group momentum is developing without active steps to promote it. Sometimes it will be easy to encourage people to start using the walls, paper and pens in an interactive way; sometimes, they will be more inclined at first to sit and talk and leave any writing to the facilitator, unless they are explicitly offered a pen and encouraged to use it. In a brief exercise with inexperienced users with only an hour or two to run, it may be acceptable that the facilitator continues to play the main recording role, concentrating on capturing what other people have to say; but the longer the time available, the more feasible it becomes to build up pictures around the walls in which the draughtsmanship of many participants has been merged, so that the sense of common ownership can take on a visible reality of its own.

FIGURE

83

Management Check-list: Technology

PHYSICAL SPACE for interactive working
- ● check provision in advance [with hosts] for main group and any subgroups
- ○ **Large** enough ROOM to accommodate participants
- ○ enough uncluttered WALL SPACE (ideally to take about 20 A1 flip charts at two levels)
- ○ lack of OBSTRUCTIONS to free movement [e.g. central tables]
- ○ enough CHAIRS [moveable]
- ○ one or more SIDE TABLES for documents, refreshments

TECHNICAL RESOURCES – materials
- ● check supplies before session
- ○ PAPER – ample supply of large sheets for wall work (ideally about 50 A1 flip charts) – smaller sheets (e.g. A4/A5) for individual use/records cards/coloured stickers for use individual contributions
- ○ PENS – ample supply of marker pens in varied colours (preferably wedge tip, water base)
- ○ ADHESIVE – non-marking/removable (e.g. Blu-Tack, masking tape)
- ○ CAMERA (& film) for recording
- ○ RECORDS/DOCUMENTS as required: including records from earlier sessions (see figure 87)

continuous management of interaction and communications in this session

TECHNICAL RESOURCES – personal
- ● check one or more participants can bring
- ○ knowledge of relevant working methods/ concepts (e.g. chapters 1, 2, 3)
- ○ skills in applying these selectively and adaptively (e.g. chapters 5, 6, 7, 8)
- ○ process management skills (see Figure 86)
- ○ substantive knowledge in this problem area and related fields

SUPPORTING SERVICES
- ● check access in advance
- ○ TELEPHONE – ideally just outside room
- ○ COMPUTER HARDWARE/SOFTWARE [not essential]
- ○ REFRESHMENTS – preferably continuous supply of coffee, tea, juice to avoid interuptions between meal breaks
- ○ ROOM CLEANING etc. – staff alerted not to remove/ throw away work in progress

Mention has been made in earlier chapters of the advantages of punctuating interactive group working with brief opportunities for individuals to work on their own. It can help to ask participants to write down their own ideas about relevant decision areas, uncertainty areas or other elements in their own words, using cards or small sheets of paper. These individual contributions can then be compared and merged in such a way that each participant feels he or she has participated directly in building up the shared pictures that are taking shape around the walls. The use of floor or table space to sort and re-group the various individual contributions can itself help to build up a spirit of interactive working.*

There is a related technique, which can be especially helpful in bringing invisible products to a conscious level. It involves the use of small circular coloured stickers (about 2cm diameter), for the structuring of informal interactive evaluation. For example, if it is thought a good idea to review the growth of joint commitment in the grouping, each participant can be asked to place one sticker on a scale from good to bad which has been drawn on the paper. And much the same sort of process can be used for identifying the most important items in a list — such as comparison areas or uncertainty areas. The resulting pattern is then used as the basis of a creative discussion of the subject, often leading to consensus in the group.

It can pay to introduce brief opportunities for individual working from an early stage in a group process, with further such opportunities whenever the momentum of interaction appears to be flagging or dominated by a sub-group. In order to be ready when such opportunities occur, it is recommended that a supply of cards and stickers be on hand at all times — in addition to the pens and the paper. All these techniques can be adopted without them — sheets of paper can always be cut or torn into smaller pieces and marked with coloured blobs — but there is no doubt that cards and stickers in several sizes, shapes and colours give the process an air of professionalism which can be reassuring to some participants.

In Figure 83, all these practical points about the management of the technology of strategic choice are drawn together, in a form intended for quick reference, both when preparing for an interactive group session and while reviewing progress subsequently. The key distinctions made are betwen choice of the physical *setting* which usually has to be negotiated in advance; the provision of adequate *supplies* both for interactive participation and individual working, not forgetting refreshments; and,

---

* Working on paper on the wall is not exclusively a strategic choice style. There are others who adopt a similar style of working (Doyle and Straus, 1976); but very few have a structured approach to the use of the papers themselves. One such approach, which has much to offer, originated in Germany in the early seventies. It is called 'Metaplan', and is based on the use of shaped coloured cards (oval, circular, rectangular) on which the participants write, before pinning them onto special screens (Schnelle, 1973). There are some close parallels with the use of cards in strategic choice group processes, which started about the same time.

finally, the requisite *techniques* and *skills* to allow these resources to be used to good effect once the group process is under way.

Organisation: Managing Interactive Participation in Practice

It is neither practicable nor useful to attempt to draw a firm line to define where the management of technology ends and the management of organisation begins. There are some further points to be made about ways of managing the *dynamics* of a working group, and about opportunities for forming sub-groups and subsequently bringing them together. These points will be touched on briefly here, leaving some deeper points about the understanding of group dynamics to be opened up in Chapter 10. However, it is most important to recognise that any working group has to be seen as embedded in a wider organisational environment in which many other people may have a part to play. So important practical questions have to be asked about what levels and forms of participation — and of interaction — will be appropriate for other people beyond the confines of the present working group; and these questions too will be dealt with in this section.

The larger a working group, the more difficult it becomes to sustain a spirit of interactive participation through time. To make progress in such circumstances, it is useful at times to suggest that the group breaks into smaller sub-groups to pursue complementary aspects of the overall task. There are many possible grounds on which such a sub-division of work can be made. Conventionally, work is sub-divided by disciplines, professions or organisational units; but once some shaping of problems and their implications has been recorded on the walls of the room, other possibilities become available. The conceptual frameworks of strategic choice provide a rich source of logical ways for defining sub-groups. The four different modes of work taken individually, or in looped pairs, provide one useful division. And there are many other possibilities such as different problem foci, separate working shortlists, or commitment packages based on alternative orientations. Some such tasks for sub-groups may require considerable time, and so should be scheduled to be done in the periods between the main interactive sessions of the working group. However, there are many ways in which strategic choice structures can be used to identify briefer tasks for sub-groups within a working session. Examples of such tasks include designing options within decision areas separately; assessing alternatives by individual comparison areas; and exploring different areas of uncertainty. Such divisions of labour can be most helpful, but it is important:

- to use the structure of the analysis as the basis of the division;
- to set, and keep to, a strict time limit;
- to allow plenty of time for the sharing of results afterwards;

— to use the structure of the analysis to integrate the various contributions.

Of course, in suggesting which people might be assigned to which sub-groups, the skilled facilitator should be able to take into account which participants work well — or not so well — with each other, and which individuals can be looked to in order to provide stimulus and leadership for the more reticent members of the group.

The more complex the problem, the more difficult it may be to agree without any sense of doubt what the *composition* of a working group should be. Any strategic choice based working group can be seen as benefitting from recognition of the various roles which its participants can take. The distribution does not require one role per person, nor indeed that all roles be filled; but they should all at least be considered explicitly when a group is being formed. They can be labelled as follows:

— *Leader*: responsible for the substantive work, controlling the quality and quantity of the analysis and information input;
— *Co-ordinator*: responsible for process rather than substance, making sure that the right people are at the right place at the right time;
— *Facilitator*: responsible for internal group relations, guiding interactive sessions and helping with grouping and linking;
— *Recorder*: responsible for the visible results, co-ordinating the continuous output from the process and its distribution in appropriate forms;
— *Regular Participant*: responsible for general substantive input, and team member functions;
— *Occasional Participant*: responsible for a specific area of specialised substantive input, and general team member functions when present.

Then, if it is intended that there should be not just one working session but a series of sessions — whether concentrated within a few successive days or spread out over a longer period — it is likely that the composition of the group will alter at least a little from session to session, whether by design or because of restricted availability on the part of some participants. Such changes can, of course, affect the momentum and patterns of interaction within the group. This means that there is a balance to be struck between a desire for continuity of membership, with the advantage that everyone is working from the same basis of shared group experience; and a desire to keep the membership open, so that new participants can join and others drop away.

This desire to keep the group boundaries permeable can be especially important where ideas about the shape of the problem are initially unclear. Where this is so, the focus of attention may shift in unexpected ways, suggesting that others should be involved who were not seen as relevant earlier on. But it is important to keep in mind the point that extending the boundaries of a working group is not the only way of extending the processes of communication and interaction: and this is where a whole range of possible ways of *grouping and linking* can be considered. For any complex problem which impinges on many different organisational interests, it is only to be expected that participation also becomes a complex matter, with many people becoming associated with the process in one way or another.

It is quite easy to think of good reasons for involving many and various people interactively in the process of decision-making. But it is not so easy to make a case for the meetings that this entails. It is regularly argued that meetings are a waste of time; that there are too many of them; and that the decisions made as a result cannot be proven to be better. This is entirely justified and will continue to be so, as long as meetings are organised in the conventional manner. Therefore, in using the strategic choice approach, changes have to be made. Already, in the last section, ways in which the conduct of meetings can be changed have been dealt with at some length. In this section the concern shifts to questions about how the meetings should be set up, especially with reference to who should meet with whom.

The form of association will vary from person to person and from time to time. Of all the people who might be involved, only some may wish to be; others may be content to be involved occasionally, and in a reactive rather than an interactive way. It has to be remembered that interactive working, for all its advantages, is demanding in terms of time and energy; and people in practice must always find ways of distributing their personal resources of time and energy effectively, depending on the overall range of responsibilities they carry.

The general picture of three kinds of uncertainty was used in Chapter 4 (Figure 31) to indicate some of the main ways of initiating connections with other people, whenever it was found difficult to deal with a current decision problem in the present working context — whether it be that of individual work or an interactive working group. However, there are various types of relationships which can be distinguished, with different implications for the grouping and linking decisions that have to be made. They reflect different roles people can play in relation to an overall decision *process*, as contrasted to the roles they might play in relation to the work of a particular *group*. Nevertheless, in discussing these roles and relationships, it is useful to take as a reference point the task of a particular **working group** — a group which, in the prototypical decision setting being considered in this chapter, may be constituted as a more or less formal *project group* charged, like the South Side Working Party, with working on an issue of some importance over a period of several months. However, most of the points to be made here are also relevant to briefer, more informal exercises.

It is helpful to think of people in five prototypical *roles* in relation to the decision-making process:

— those who are *accountable* for the decisions to be taken in a broadly political way;

— those who are directly *responsible* for guiding the conduct of the decision-making process, at a managerial or senior professional level;

— those to whom periodic *reference* should be made because they have roles in other fields of decision-making which are instrumental in this case;

— those who fill a *representative* role in relation to specific interests which may be affected by the decisions;

— those who are *stakeholders* in the sense that they will be directly impacted by the decisions.

It is important to recognise that in any given decision process the exact way in which people in such roles should participate is a design question in its own right. This means that some of the roles — though not necessarily all of them — will be played by groups or semi-formal *groupings*. There will often be overlapping memberships and/or vacancies; and, in some cases, sub-divisions may be recognised. For example, it is common, in public agencies, to distinguish between internal and inter-agency reference groups.

The typical relationships between these groupings, one to the other and all to the working group, are illustrated in Figure 84. Broad distinctions are superimposed between those groupings which have a role to play in the technical domain and those with a role more in the political arena. In addition, a distinction is drawn between groupings which are internal and those which are external to the main locus of responsibility for the decisions being addressed. At the centre is shown a small *core group*, which has the role of continuous process management, looking after the day-to-day co-ordination of all the various activities and groupings, in ways which will be described later in this chapter.

First to be described will be the set of people who are formally **accountable** for the decisions with which the working group is primarily concerned. These can be thought of as the *decision-takers* in relation to a wider, more diffuse set of *decision-makers*, if the distinction is made between decision-making as a continuous process and decision-taking as something that happens at comparatively rare moments when formal authorisation of actions or policies is required. In the classical management hierarchy, decisions are taken at most levels throughout the process; but there is often a level of importance at which authorisation by some accountable group, such as a Board or Council, is required. In the public sector as opposed to commercial organisations, the stakeholders are usually more diffuse, so the principle of group accountability is rather more widespread. Sometimes, accountability is vested in joint organisations —

FIGURE

84

Organisational Responsibilities in Strategic Choice

HEAVIER BOUNDARY LINES indicate
direct responsibilities in this field of decision
BROKEN BOUNDARY LINES indicate
less continuous involvement

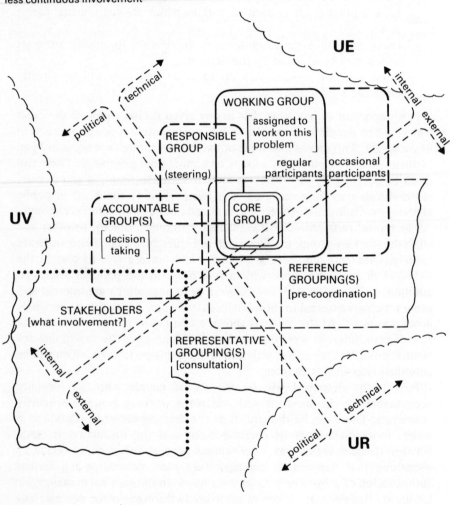

ORGANISATION

PRACTICALITIES

joint committees or 'standing conferences'. In general, the more complex the problem, the more complex will be the politics of accountability; so a working group may have to relate to more than one accountable grouping in some cases.

There have been a few applications of the strategic choice approach where decision-takers in such accountable roles have become involved in interactive working with members of a working group.* This can bring powerful benefits both in terms of the level of awareness with which formal decisions are taken and in terms of the direct input of political considerations into the work of the working group. However, it has to be recognised that senior decision-takers — whether appointed or elected — are often subject to multiple and severe pressures on their time. Their inputs can be particularly significant in the work of the shaping and choosing modes and, given limited opportunities to involve them in interactive working, it is important that their involvement should be focussed in these areas.

Often, a link between a working group and a set of accountable decision-takers is made by means of a project *steering group*. Meeting more or less regularly, guidance is provided on the directions and priorities of the work, progress is reviewed and any difficulties discussed, especially so far as the handling of external relationships is concerned. In multi-accountable decision settings, such a **responsible** grouping will often have been deliberately designed to bring together representatives of different organisations or departments involved in sponsorship of the project work. The membership can be relatively small; leading members of the project group may be directly involved either as members or in a reporting capacity; and there should be opportunities between scheduled meetings to work through informal links with individual members.

So, a great deal of informal *negotiation* about difficult or contentious matters can take place through the channels offered by the responsible grouping, both during and between meetings; and there will be opportunities here to use various aspects of the strategic choice approach. It is also through this set of relationships that members of the working group can retain the sanction of their departmental heads to continue acting on their behalf; and that changes in the membership of the working group can be discussed and approved. So the responsible grouping offers a channel through which the highly cyclic, adaptive work process of the working group can be adjusted to the more formally structured procedures and political realities of the wider organisational environment. It is, therefore,

---

* Members of the accountable grouping tend to find such a role shift easiest through involvement in the responsible grouping, and there is extensive experience of this. However, there have been some examples of their involvement in the working group. This occurred during preparation of the Structure Plan for the County of Hereford and Worcester in England, and more recently in the Netherlands, in Emmen, Venlo and Amersfoort.

important to allow the time and resources for this element of the wider participative process to work in an effective way.

What is referred to in the prototypical working context as a **reference** grouping consists of delegates or representatives of all those other organisations whose co-operation will be important if proposals arising from the work of the project group are to be put into effect. Where the project group's task is to produce a relatively generalised 'plan' or set of policies, the application of which depends on actions of many other agencies, it is important that there should not only be co-ordination during some eventual 'implementation' stage. A realistic framework for *pre-coordination* is also recommended, by which these other organisations or departments can have the opportunity to participate at an appropriate level throughout.

Even in comparatively simple contexts of inter-agency or inter-departmental working, an element of pre-coordination can be important so that duplication, omission or contradiction in the provision of services can be anticipated and avoided. However, when working on broader problems of strategic choice, pre-coordination can involve more complex issues of adjustment of values and perceptions. In larger-scale exercises of policy planning it is sometimes appropriate to invite representatives of all related agencies to participate in occasional seminars. In these some of the spirit of interactive working can be generated — even though given time pressures it might not be feasible to introduce the strategic choice methods in an explicit way.

There are two further types of grouping which it is important not to overlook; both fall into the external political arena. They are the **representative** grouping through which the political interests of specific sections of the population, such as car owners, conservationists or small businesses, are protected and promoted; and the wider **stakeholder** grouping of those directly impacted by the decisions, such as residents, consumers, or employees. They involve those who are concerned directly from time to time through exercises in direct public or employee participation.

Conventional attempts at a more general sort of participation, involving 'the public at large', tend to end up being conducted with members of these groupings. Unfortunately, because such exercises are aimed at a broader audience, they most often take the form of seeking reactions to well-formulated proposals, which it is too late to influence in any fundamental way. A more sensitive appraisal of which people in which roles are being addressed — and are willing and able to contribute — is the key to selective design of participative frameworks in which a high level of creative feed-back can be realised.

So the way in which all these types of relationships evolve through time forms part of the broad concern with *management of organisation* in a process of strategic choice. This applies not only in the prototypical project group situation that has been discussed here but also in other more modest working situations. Sometimes, in such cases, it can be more realistic to relate to those in other roles through more familiar patterns of bilateral contact and negotiation. So this is where patterns of *linking* through personal networks can play an important part in supplementing any *grouping* arrangements of a more formal kind. The extent to which strategic choice ideas can be used to guide such interactions will depend on the judgement of the user and the extent to which support has already been established.

Thus, the whole task of *managing the organisation* for strategic choice can be seen as a process of dynamic grouping and linking, in which there are many variables. It is not only a question of which people in which decision-making roles should be active, but of how frequently; in which combinations; and in what relationship they should be to each other and the current decision situation. A summary of the considerations which arise in these areas of choice is put forward in Figure 85. This is intended as a guide for those faced with the task in practice — probably in the core group role. The key emphasis in evaluation of such organisational choices will be not so much on efficiency and control, as in a classical hierarchical structure, as on the creation of *synergy* which can be realised through the orientation towards interactive participation.

Process: Managing the Learning Process in Practice

In the *process* aspect of the A-TOPP framework, the practical choices which people face are primarily to do with the effective use of time. Choices about the use of time have to be faced continuously during an interactive working session; and these have already been described at the end of Chapters 5, 6, 7 and 8, in terms of the various switching and looping judgements that have to be made in moving from one mode of work to another. This section will offer some further practical advice on how this switching and looping process can be managed within an interactive working session.

However, in a longer-term project, where there can be a commitment to a series of such working sessions over the project period, there are also important choices to be considered about the management of time in the intervals between one working session and another. During these periods, there will usually be backroom and investigative work to be done by at least some of the participants, individually or in sub-groups, and there will often also be various activities of a consultative or co-ordinative nature involving other people.

There are two interrelated tasks which are often overlooked, but which

FIGURE
85

Management Check-list: Organisation

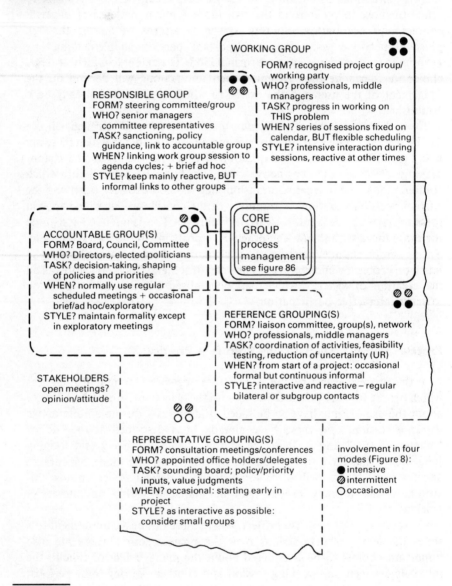

WORKING GROUP
FORM? recognised project group/
working party
WHO? professionals, middle
managers
TASK? progress in working on
THIS problem
WHEN? series of sessions fixed on
calendar, BUT flexible scheduling
STYLE? intensive interaction during
sessions, reactive at other times

RESPONSIBLE GROUP
FORM? steering committee/group
WHO? senior managers
committee representatives
TASK? sanctioning, policy
guidance, link to accountable group
WHEN? linking work group session to
agenda cycles; + brief ad hoc
STYLE? keep mainly reactive, BUT
informal links to other groups

ACCOUNTABLE GROUP(S)
FORM? Board, Council, Committee
WHO? Directors, elected politicians
TASK? decision-taking, shaping
of policies and priorities
WHEN? normally use regular
scheduled meetings + occasional
brief/ad hoc/exploratory
STYLE? maintain formality except
in exploratory meetings

CORE
GROUP
process
management
see figure 86

REFERENCE GROUPING(S)
FORM? liaison committee, group(s), network
WHO? professionals, middle managers
TASK? coordination of activities, feasibility
testing, reduction of uncertainty (UR)
WHEN? from start of a project: occasional
formal but continuous informal
STYLE? interactive and reactive – regular
bilateral or subgroup contacts

STAKEHOLDERS
open meetings?
opinion/attitude

REPRESENTATIVE GROUPING(S)
FORM? consultation meetings/conferences
WHO? appointed office holders/delegates
TASK? sounding board; policy/priority
inputs, value judgments
WHEN? occasional: starting early in
project
STYLE? as interactive as possible:
consider small groups

involvement in four
modes (Figure 8):
● intensive
⊘ intermittent
○ occasional

ORGANISATION

PRACTICALITIES

are of crucial significance — especially in situations where there are conflicting interests. These are the need for participants to:

— report progress made in the working group to their home organisation;
— and gather feedback as input to the group process in return.

If these activities are neglected, or given too little time, the results can be, at worst, that the work loses all credibility; or, at best, that there is a withdrawal of the backing that is necessary if the recommendations are going to be carried out.

Some of these tasks may have emerged directly from the activities of the working group, as a ways of dealing with important areas of uncertainty; while some of them may have been explicitly recorded in the format of a commitment package. But of course, not everything that happens between sessions flows from the work done in this interactive setting. All participants will have competing claims on their time between sessions, some more than others. They may have to respond to unexpected events of quite separate origins: some of them may be involved in more than one interactive process or have pressing outside deadlines to meet. So there is a fine balance to be struck between adapting to these pressures and maintaining the momentum of progress in the agreed common task.

In the typical project situation, this role of maintaining continuity is usually handled by a small subset of all the people who form the main working group. The task of this process management grouping, or **core group**, is to promote the effectiveness of the wider process in which members of all other groupings shown in Figure 84 may at different times be involved. It is a small group — generally two or three people — because it must have the capacity for extremely flexible behaviour, especially in its arrangements for meetings. It normally embraces the four specific intra-group roles identified earlier — leader, co-ordinator, facilitator and recorder — and, ultimately, it is sometimes seen as a function which can be handled by one person. When this occurs, that person is often described as the *project manager*. Unfortunately, neat as this arrangement may seem, all four roles are very difficult to play together — in particular the facilitator role sits uncomfortably with the other three. Also, it is often the case that the co-ordinator and facilitator have little direct knowledge of the specific problems being addressed. In such a case it is important to recognise the vital contribution which the leader can make. Thus, there are distinct advantages when such a project management function is given over to a small group. While any one person can take on any one role, there is a limited number of combinations of roles which any one person can play. These are the combinations of:

— leader, co-ordinator and recorder (project manager);

— leader and recorder (substantive content manager);
— co-ordinator and facilitator (process manager).

Another dimension which occurs in the choice of core group membership concerns the introduction of external consultants. While a capable process consultant should be able to take on any of these functions or roles, there are some to which they are better suited than others. For example, in many cases the facilitator role can be better performed by someone from outside the immediate organisational framework. Basically, there are two reasons, in addition to the extra manpower, why help of this sort can be useful. The first is that strategic choice skills may be lacking and need to be developed in the team; and the second, where several organisations are involved, is that an independent view may be required. In either case, it is important that the external consultant is given a *counterpart* from within the client group, to provide the detailed knowledge and experience of the problems, the people involved and the culture within which they work.

The core-group task embraces all the mundane jobs associated with organising meetings: tasks which range from the time-consuming job of getting people together at the same time and in the same place, to the provision of appropriate spaces to work in and adequate sustenance for the participants. However, in addition, it involves proper preparation for and steering of the interactive working sessions themselves; and it can take continual effort to keep those not involved in these sessions in touch with what is going on.

One of the greatest cultural difficulties encountered when introducing the strategic choice approach to organisations is that most of these tasks are not conventionally considered to be 'real work'; or at most they are considered as simple administrative tasks which can be delegated to clerical staff to be dealt with in a routine way. Some aspects of the arrangement of meetings can, of course, be dealt with as a matter of routine; but experience has repeatedly shown that the time involved between meetings on the part of those who carry the main core group responsibilities should not be underestimated. Many negotiations about involvement in meetings and related matters have to be handled informally on the basis of the rapport which is developing through interactive working; and a failure to allow time for this can soon begin to erode the quality of the process as a whole.

Even where there are several members of the working group who are committed to the project for much or all of their working time, some element of advance scheduling of meetings is essential. For example, the same day of the week can be scheduled for a number of weeks in advance, with the understanding that members of the working group will normally meet for two and a half to three hours in the morning and a similar period in the afternoon. Where possible, some flexibility should be built in by an understanding that, if necessary, the afternoon and/or evening before a session might also be used — or perhaps the morning of the next day. In some cases it may be necessary to use two or more days together; while, in other cases, less time may be necessary, allowing sessions to be cancelled. At intervals, other types of meetings may be fitted into this kind of schedule. In particular, allowance can be made for meetings of the responsible grouping, which involves senior managers in a steering capacity, and of the reference grouping through which working liaison is maintained with other departments and agencies. This *flexible scheduling* approach means arranging in advance a series of meetings, in which there are some basic and fairly firm expectations about time commitment and participation in meetings, with the understanding that either may be extended or curtailed should circumstances require.

Between sessions, the core group should arrange to meet every few days, although such meetings need not be very lengthy. The periods immediately before group sessions, and also immediately after, are also important times to exchange notes on progress and ideas on how the dynamics of group interaction can be maintained in the current situation. Laying out the room, setting targets for the day, monitoring progress towards them, analysing the results, recording wall charts; these are among the vitally important activities which the core group must undertake during such sessions. Without them, progress and direction can quickly become lost. It is better than nothing to get together in the main working room a few minutes in advance of the others — but that is really not enough. On the other hand, it should not be necessary to organise such meetings formally — they should happen spontaneously — but is is important that they should not be so squeezed out by other pressures. It is also important that the core group meetings should not be seen as secretive. If other members of the working group happen to come into the room while the core group is discussing process management issues, it is important that they should not feel excluded from the discussions but should be explicitly brought in.

It is not recommended that a half-day working session be formally broken, for instance to go to another room for coffee or tea at some appointed time. For the loss of momentum can be serious and it is much preferable that coffee, tea or other light refreshments be available in the working room itself. Lunch breaks, on the other hand, are more essential; they can be important not only as respite for the participants and as consultation time for core group members, but also for other informal purposes. In particular, process consultants working for the first time on a problem, in an organisation of which they have little or no inside knowledge, will often find themselves being briefed during the lunch hour on aspects of the internal political background which are well enough known to most of the participants yet cannot be openly discussed during the course of a working group session. Also, of course, social interactions in the evenings and weekends can play an important part in the cultural acclimatisation of all concerned, especially those who come from a distance to an unfamiliar organisational setting.

The facilitator role is of particular importance because it is concerned with the *group process*. The role is one with many parts and is sometimes handled flexibly between two or more people who are experienced in process management. This sort of *team facilitating* can be most effective, with the active facilitator role changing hands from time to time. It allows the benefits of active facilitating to be combined with simultaneous reflection on it, which improves the effectiveness of the review process. In many cases, it can enable process issues to be be discussed openly between members of the group, with the input of two or more independent views of what is happening at any one time.

The facilitator has always to be ready to aid communication between the participants, especially where they may have difficulty in sharing their different perceptions, concepts, assumptions and priorities. The task is to prevent progress being blocked whenever possible, and to unblock it when it is. It means keeping all the participants feeling involved by creating opportunities for all to make their contributions effectively. It includes active guidance of the interactive work of the group and, in particular, guidance of the judgements associated with switching and looping between modes of work. In making switching and looping judgements, the main evaluative emphasis is on seeking always to move in directions where the growth of *understanding* is expected to be greatest in relation to the time and energies of the participants. It is not, of course, easy for anyone, however skilled, to make judgements in advance as to whether more will be learned by a shift of mode in one direction rather than another. These are, essentially, judgements about where the rate of *potential learning* is likely to be greatest; and here the idea of the *learning curve* is of value.

When starting work in any mode, there is usually an initial period of quick learning, the duration of which will depend on how much is already known — and shared among the participants — at that time. When little is known about a problem, it can be some time before the rate of learning — the learning curve — begins to level off. But where there is an established base of understanding, a 'tailing off' effect in learning is soon experienced, so more rapid switching and looping is to be expected. A group which starts with little experience in strategic choice is likely to be dependent on a process manager or facilitator for judgements of this kind; but as a group becomes accustomed to this way of working, so the breadth of participation in active process management can increase. What is important is that people should be conscious of the mode in which they are currently working, and of the opportunities for switching and looping which exist at any particular moment. For this reason, it is a useful guideline that any group which includes members who have never worked with strategic choice before should have at least some experience of work in each mode during the course of the first working day. A flip chart showing the four modes (as in Figure 8) can be posted on the wall as a point of reference to which such people can refer; and occasional reference to the 'Sutton Principle' will help people to be conscious at any time of the opportunities to switch to the mode where they think the greatest rewards will be found.

But switching judgements can be difficult, especially if there is a sense of leaving work *unfinished* when moving into another mode. Part way through a lengthy analysis, the feeling often develops that there is little more to be learned by going on — so the learning curve is now becoming flatter, but nonetheless there is resistance to a switch because the analysis is incomplete. At this stage, a relaxed approach is recommended and the switch should be made. The analysis can always be completed later if, in coming back to it through the cyclic process, that seems a helpful thing to do.

A somewhat different form of this is experienced when people find themselves labouring to define some aspect of the problem, often in terms of a decision area, comparison area or uncertainty area the meaning of which is ambiguous, or the wording of which is difficult to agree. In such situations, the device of *temporary labelling* has been found very helpful in maintaining the pace of learning. The idea is that a name is given to whatever is unfinished; it is put on one side; and then it can be picked up later if it is still relevant. This device has become known as the 'Rhubarb Principle',* and around it has developed the informal shorthand of putting unfinished work 'in the rhubarb sack'. In practice, the rhubarb sack is usually an open-ended list of unresolved items built up on a separate flip chart on the wall. This is then used during review, and as input to agenda building exercises for future sessions.

To summarise at this point, process management choices are vital to effective progress, though not often recognised adequately in conventional practice. It is important that they be made explicit wherever possible, and that adequate time be allowed for them. As an aid to this, a summary of relevant process issues is presented in Figure 86. Some of the most important aspects of process to be considered are those associated with judgements about switching and looping within and between group sessions, combined with the passage of time. In evaluating the use of time through process choice, it is important to be guided by considerations of growth of understanding rather than just good time-keeping or productivity in terms of substantive plans; and these are judgements to which all members of a group can contribute, once they have become conscious of the considerations which arise.

---

* This name arose during early work on the formulation of policy choices for the Avon County Structure Plan, where the working group was struggling with the definition of a decision area about the quality of life. The impasse was resolved by one member suggesting that they label this decision area 'rhubarb' for the time being and pressed on to something else.

FIGURE
86

Management Check-list: Process

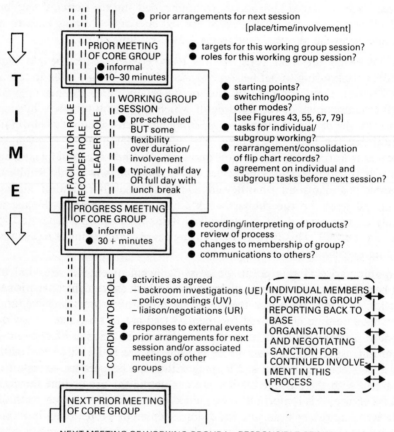

ADVANCE AGREEMENT ON SCHEDULE OF MEETINGS FOR WORKING
GROUP AND ASSOCIATED GROUPINGS (RESPONSIBLE, REFERENCE . . .)
WITH UNDERSTANDINGS ABOUT FLEXIBILITY TO EXTEND/CURTAIL . . .

SET OF PROCESS MANAGEMENT
ROLES represented in core group

T
I
M
E

● prior arrangements for next session
  [place/time/involvement]

PRIOR MEETING OF CORE GROUP
● informal
● 10–30 minutes

● targets for this working group session?
● roles for this working group session?

FACILITATOR ROLE
RECORDER ROLE
LEADER ROLE

WORKING GROUP SESSION
● pre-scheduled BUT some flexibility over duration/ involvement
● typically half day OR full day with lunch break

● starting points?
● switching/looping into other modes?
  [see Figures 43, 55, 67, 79]
● tasks for individual/ subgroup working?
● rearrangement/consolidation of flip chart records?
● agreement on individual and subgroup tasks before next session?

PROGRESS MEETING OF CORE GROUP
● informal
● 30 + minutes

● recording/interpreting of products?
● review of process
● changes to membership of group?
● communications to others?

COORDINATOR ROLE

● activities as agreed
  – backroom investigations (UE)
  – policy soundings (UV)
  – liaison/negotiations (UR)
● responses to external events
● prior arrangements for next session and/or associated meetings of other groups

INDIVIDUAL MEMBERS OF WORKING GROUP REPORTING BACK TO BASE ORGANISATIONS AND NEGOTIATING SANCTION FOR CONTINUED INVOLVE-MENT IN THIS PROCESS

NEXT PRIOR MEETING OF CORE GROUP

NEXT MEETING OF WORKING GROUP (or RESPONSIBLE GROUP or . . .)

PROCESS

PRACTICALITIES

Product: Managing Incremental Progress in Practice

In a process of strategic choice, there are both invisible and visible products. Various forms can be identified (Figure 33), taking the substance-process dimension as well as the visible-invisible into account. The management emphasis is placed on the *recording and interpreting* of these products as well as the act of producing them (Figure 34).

In any interactive working session, visible products will be continuously building up on flip charts around the walls of the room — apart from any notes that may have been made by individuals. At the end of a session, the choice arises as to what should be done about these products. At one extreme, they can be thrown away, while at the other extreme, they can be left intact as a starting point for the next session, provided the space is not required for other purposes. But there is a range of other more practicable possibilities in between; and this is where the task of *recording* becomes important.

Flip charts can, of course, be saved at the end of a session; and where this is the intention it is useful that somebody charged with the recorder role should number them in the sequence they were first written on — and add a date — at the end of the session. But flip charts are bulky, and to save too many can be to create both a storage problem and potential information overload, with severe difficulties of access and retrieval.

One of the most useful and simplest means of recording is simply to *photograph* the set of flip charts around the walls of the room at the end of a session — and possibly also at critical moments during the course of a session, especially at any moment when the information on the wall is being reorganised, breaking up a pattern of relatedness between flip charts which has become familiar to the participants and which they might later wish to recall. Colour prints are recommended to capture the way in which coloured pens have been used; but such niceties often have to be given up for the purposes of speed and effective sharing of information. For example, it is important that the information in the *photo-record* be easily retrievable, and that closely related parts of the work are kept together — a pile of separate prints does not do this. However, mounting sets of three or four prints together on A4 sheets of paper has been found to serve such purposes well, especially if they are suitably coded, dated, labelled and indexed (Figure 58). It is important that all members of a working group have a copy of the photo-record; and, unfortunately, it can be too time-consuming to make many such sets. Thus photocopying becomes essential, even though the added dimension of colour is lost and care has to be taken with the use of particular colours — such as yellow and pale blue. If pictures are required for immediate use, a polaroid-type camera producing quick prints can be useful — even though the prints are small. It is sometimes found useful to take pictures of people working as well — both as a reminder to the participants of the process, and as an indication to others of the general style of working within the group.

Another way of recording is to write up the key aspects of visible progress in the form of a *loose-leaf* record in a ring-back or similar file, which can provide a more accessible set of reference points for the participants when they reconvene for another working session. This can of course be supplemented by photographs of the flip charts in groups on the wall — in which case, some or all of the charts themselves can be scrapped, or the reverse sides written on again where the paper is of sufficient quality.

Any act of recording — even one of mere photographic recording — involves some element of *interpretation* of information into another form — usually a more condensed form appropriate for later use. If the intended use is reference by the same working group at a later meeting, the extent of the interpretation may be quite small, because those concerned have become used to the language of strategic choice — the graphical conventions, the vocabulary, the abbreviated labels by which they have learned to communicate with each other. But it is important to remember that this sort of recording can easily become, in effect, another cycle in the process. In some cases this may not be too serious; in others it can be interpreted by other participants as an attempt by the recorder to manipulate the results. It is hardly necessary to point out that this could have very negative effects on the group process. Where there is a danger of this, and when there is time enough, it is better to make recording the explicit subject of another group session — perhaps using a photo-record as a starting point. Another way, if time is short, is to allow the recorder to go ahead, but also to allow a reasonable amount of time for questioning and clarification at the start of the next group session. This can be usefully combined with circulation of the record in a reactive style between sessions.

It is only to be expected that the members of a working group will develop their own form of *jargon* — graphic as well as verbal. This can be extremely useful insofar as it helps them talk about problems rapidly and effectively among themselves. But such jargon, of course, can be of little value in communicating with others and, indeed, it can have the effect of confusing more than it informs. In practice, there is always a temptation for members of a working group to try to communicate with others in such terms, presenting decision graphs or lists of alternatives described in terms of brief labels which have acquired significance to them through the process of interaction within the group. But such information cannot have the same significance to others not so intimately involved. There is a danger that findings and supporting information presented in terms of apparently esoteric jargon will annoy and alienate rather than bring any sense of involvement to those only intermittently involved — such as members of accountable, reference and representative groupings (Figure 84). So, in reporting progress to others, and in providing a basis for interactive discussions with those who are only occasionally involved, some more substantial form of interpretation into plain language is required.

A general impression of the progressive build-up of visible products is presented in Figure 87. This shows the development of a loose-leaf record drawn from the flip charts relevant to each mode and, from that, the further development of documents suitable for use outside the group. The process of production is one of *incremental documentation*. In practice, the loose-leaf record builds up and evolves gradually, providing at any one time a statement of the latest findings and possible recommendations coming out of the work. Whenever it is necessary to produce a formal statement or recommendation, it is then a matter of taking the relevant leaves out of the loose-leaf system; assembling them in an appropriate order; and considering how to present the result. The remainder of the loose-leaf system provides the basis for any *reasoned justification* for the choice; a source of supplementary information; and a starting point for future cycles.

It is important in building up a loose-leaf record that it should reflect the products of work in all four process modes. It will, of course, be vital to record the content of a commitment package where the work of a session has culminated in a product of this form; but information on decision areas, decision graphs, problem foci, options, decision schemes, assessments, advantage comparisons, shortlists, uncertainty areas and exploratory options can be vital for future reference as well. On some major strategic choice projects, standard pre-printed forms have been used to record some of these kinds of information, so that it can be retained in as organised and immediately accessible a form as possible. What is most important is that the decision-takers should be in a position to question and challenge the presented argument; and that their advisers, when challenged, should be able to retrieve further information from the loose-leaf system wherein the fuller records of their work are stored. So the outer rings of Figure 87 are linked by loops which indicate a two-way flow of questions and responses. It is in this way that decision-takers, with many pressures on their time, can become interactively involved in the process — and can do so on their own terms, as it is they who set the questions on which the dialogue is based.

In taking a view of planning as a decision process in which uncertainties are managed continuously through time, it is vital to recognise the importance of process-related products. Nonetheless, it is the recommendations about the *substantive* problems which will be the focus of attention when the time comes for formal decision-taking. Even where they have been developed using a commitment package framework, these may differ little in visible form to recommendations made without the use of

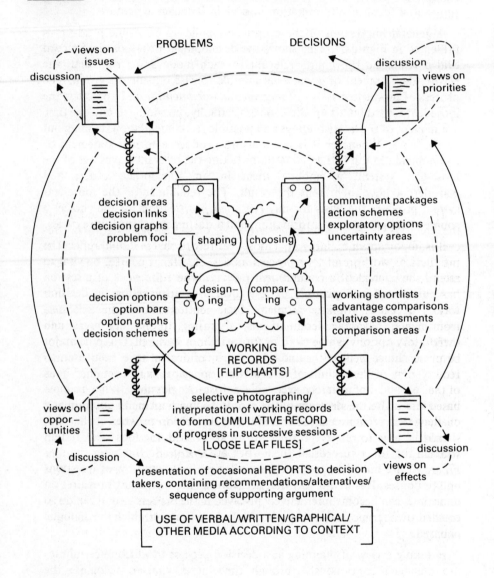

FIGURE 87 — Recording and Interpretation in Strategic Choice

PROBLEMS   DECISIONS

views on issues

discussion

discussion

views on priorities

decision areas
decision links
decision graphs
problem foci

shaping choosing

commitment packages
action schemes
exploratory options
uncertainty areas

decision options
option bars
option graphs
decision schemes

design–ing compar–ing

working shortlists
advantage comparisons
relative assessments
comparison areas

WORKING RECORDS
[FLIP CHARTS]

views on oppor-tunities

discussion

selective photographing/
interpretation of working records
to form CUMULATIVE RECORD
of progress in successive sessions
[LOOSE LEAF FILES]

discussion

views on effects

presentation of occasional REPORTS to decision
takers, containing recommendations/alternatives/
sequence of supporting argument

USE OF VERBAL/WRITTEN/GRAPHICAL/
OTHER MEDIA ACCORDING TO CONTEXT

PRODUCT

A-TOP**P**

PRACTICALITIES

strategic choice methods.* But it has to be recognised that such recommendations may include many partial and interim actions, to complement those which are explicitly deferred or made contingent on future events.

Although what decision-takers are being asked to sanction may be primarily the products of work in the choosing mode, the provision of some supporting information on the work of the other modes is essential if they are to feel that:

— the advice they are offered is soundly based;
— their advisers have explored the shape of the problem in a realistic way;
— they have looked at a wide enough range of alternatives;
— they have taken all the most significant consequences into account;
— they have attempted to deal with uncertainties in an adequate way.

To demonstrate these things can mean a degree of *post-rationalisation* of the highly complex and adaptive processes of switching, looping and recycling through which members of the working group in reality arrived at the findings they present; processes which could seem quite chaotic if any attempt were made to present them realistically in full.

As suggested in Figure 87, it is possible in strategic choice, as in other ways of working, for a reconstructed argument to follow a linear course from shaping, through designing and comparing, to choosing — though there is no reason why one or two feedback loops in the process should not be presented as well, if they are sufficiently critical in their implications. However, in strategic choice, such a linear framework is not essential. Free of the constraint of a retrospective process-based logic, the reasoning can be based instead on the structure of the problem — with an increased emphasis on the *prospective* aspects of the continuous decision process.

Indeed, this kind of 'prospective process-based logic' is essential in strategic choice, where the decisions are structured over time. Future *procedures* form an important part of most commitment packages. Not only is there explicit provision for various forms of exploration to reduce uncertainty, but statements in the 'future decision space' are likely to be couched in terms of procedures to reach decisions, rather than definitive plans. Such recommendations are likely to be needed in order to:

— keep track of how proposed actions turn out, and review the need for adaptive planning;

* This was particularly evident in the English Structure Plan project. However, some of the participating teams made use of structured frameworks of 'policy management information', to interpret commitment package concepts into forms of presentation which indicated how policies might be adapted through time. Assumptions were clearly stated, together with contingencies which would warrant change, and constraints which would limit that change.

— monitor the performance of assumptions so that critical misjudgements can be managed;
— provide for decision-making on a regular basis, as well as prepare for cases of emergency and/or unforeseen circumstances;
— allow for participation by individuals and relevant groupings with respect to expected and unexpected future decisions;
— maintain progress in implementation programmes related to time schedules and budgetary cycles.

In addition, documentation in relation to future processes is likely to include potential sources of information, as well as key individuals and organisations who are particularly relevant to the case in hand.

However, it is often difficult to define procedures exactly — and especially uncertain is the behaviour of the individual people who will ultimately enable them to work. Therefore, it can be very helpful to have developed a high level of understanding between the participants during the decision-making process, so that there is a foundation of shared perception, mutual respect and trust which can be built on in the future. This entails not only knowledge of others' ways of working, but also extended networks of communication within which these *invisible* products can be put to effective use.

Such products, which are continuously developing in a process of strategic choice, emerge from work in all modes and take shape in many ways. They take shape in the minds of individuals, as peoples' limited perceptions of problems, possibilities, implications and uncertainties gradually become replaced by richer perceptions through the sharing of views within an interactive group setting. Indeed, it can be said that invisible products build up in the 'hearts and souls' rather than just the minds of individuals, insofar as they come to share values as well as perceptions and to develop a sense of shared commitment to common directions of action or policy. These somewhat nebulous products can have an immediate value through the production of better integrated and more strongly supported decisions. But, in most cases, their full worth is experienced over time — paving the way for more effective working in the longer term future. However, they are likely to escape unnoticed unless explicit efforts are made to help participants:

— first of all to become conscious of them;
— and then to find ways of harnessing them.

Invisible products can be brought to a conscious level most effectively as they happen; and the facilitator will be trying to do this. Unfortunately, this is no easy task; so it becomes important also to try to capture the invisible products retrospectively. Most commonly in a strategic choice exercise, this is done at the end of sessions, through allowing opportunities for reflection at that time. A quick recognition of the visible work done during the session is followed by evaluation not only in terms of progress on the wall, but also in terms of the growth — or lack of it — in understanding, consensus and commitment. Peoples' ideas about matters of process as well as substance are likely to change; and these can also have profound implications for the quality of decision-making in the longer term. So these also can be usefully included in any end-of-session sharing of views.

Taking a more extended view, it is worthwhile to suspend business for slightly longer after a series of working sessions, so that participants have an opportunity to consider the cumulative growth of invisible products — increments of which may easily slip by without comment during more frequent evaluations. Longer, more formal surveys can be most effective at the end of a project.* Questionnaires can be focussed on the *potential* of invisible products and ways in which participants intend to capitalise on them. Retrospective questions paired with prospective ones, addressing the same issue in different words, reveal changes in attitudes. These changes may have been perceived at an individual level but become much more powerful when they are seen as part of a group development. Naturally, as with any survey of this kind, feedback of the results to the respondents is essential.

But all of this emphasis on process-oriented products — visible and invisible — is to no avail if nothing happens as a result of the work. What is required also is a convergence of view towards a common understanding about what has to be done — or not done, as the case may be. For this sort of joint commitment, there must be a degree of sharing of perceptions about what the problems are; the solutions which are available; and their likely consequences. All of which can build up to a well co-ordinated set of feasible recommendations with the backing of all concerned — especially given a framework for structuring them over time.

Where a working group has an inter-departmental or inter-organisational membership, there is a need for a framework which will enable the actions required of the various participants to be brought together. In the strategic choice approach, this can be achieved via a *mutual commitment package*. Each set of participants in a working group will have their own separate commitment packages, within their own spheres of responsibility — which may be expressed in a variety of forms. Parts of each such commitment package can however be merged to form a composite statement of the way forward — or mutual commitment package. But how much should be

---

* Evaluative questionnaires were used for this at the end of the LOGIMP experiment (Friend, Wedgwood-Oppenheim et al, 1970) and, more recently, in a number of environmental policy projects in the Netherlands. On two occasions, follow-up studies have been carried out by means of interviews with participants three or more years after the event, and the findings presented in internal papers.

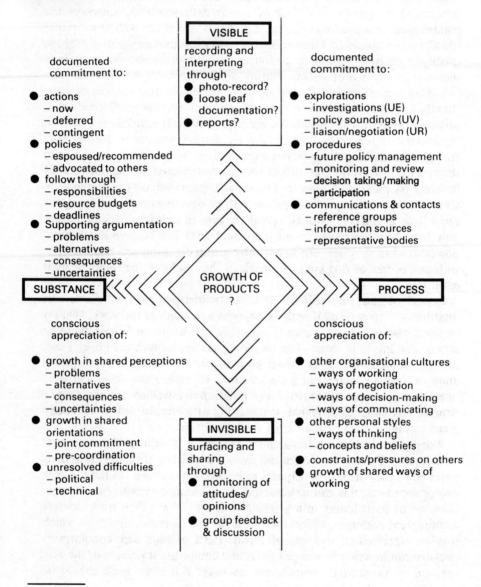

Management Check-list: Products

FIGURE 88

VISIBLE

recording and
interpreting
through
- photo-record?
- loose leaf
  documentation?
- reports?

documented
commitment to:

- actions
  - now
  - deferred
  - contingent
- policies
  - espoused/recommended
  - advocated to others
- follow through
  - responsibilities
  - resource budgets
  - deadlines
- Supporting argumentation
  - problems
  - alternatives
  - consequences
  - uncertainties

documented
commitment to:

- explorations
  - investigations (UE)
  - policy soundings (UV)
  - liaison/negotiation (UR)
- procedures
  - future policy management
  - monitoring and review
  - **decision taking/making**
  - **participation**
- communications & contacts
  - reference groups
  - information sources
  - representative bodies

**GROWTH OF
PRODUCTS
?**

SUBSTANCE

PROCESS

conscious
appreciation of:

- growth in shared perceptions
  - problems
  - alternatives
  - consequences
  - uncertainties
- growth in shared
  orientations
  - joint commitment
  - pre-coordination
- unresolved difficulties
  - political
  - technical

conscious
appreciation of:

- other organisational cultures
  - ways of working
  - ways of negotiation
  - ways of decision-making
  - ways of communicating
- other personal styles
  - ways of thinking
  - concepts and beliefs
- constraints/pressures on others
- growth of shared ways of
  working

INVISIBLE

surfacing and
sharing
through
- monitoring of
  attitudes/
  opinions
- group feedback
  & discussion

PRODUCT

A-TOP**P**

PRACTICALITIES

expressed in this form will be a matter for negotiation, as there may be various political sensitivities to keep in mind.

In such a multi-organisational group, the range of uncertainties encountered in agreeing how to move forward at any time may include areas of recognised conflict, which cannot be resolved at that point. But a decision process, structured within a commitment package framework, provides opportunities for the management of such conflicts. It allows decisions over which there is conflict to be deferred, whilst others over which there is agreement can be put into action. In many cases, when the time comes for the deferred decision to be taken, the conflict will have dissolved. Options can become infeasible over time, while new ones, over which there is more agreement, can emerge. In any case, even if the conflicts have not disappeared, at least those involved will by then have a better chance of understanding their consequences. Another source of conflict arises from uncertainty over events which may — or may not — occur. The commitment package includes space for contingency planning which can be used to handle this sort of uncertainty. Provision can be made to reduce the impact of adverse circumstances and thus remove the fear which is causing the conflict.

Of course, there may be times when it will be necessary to recognise deep-seated conflicts of interest, reflected in divergent pressures from different members of the group. Such conflicts are not often such as to block the opportunities for progress in a group using strategic choice methods; but where this happens, resort may have to be made to other means of resolution, such as external arbitration or mediation. Sometimes, where there is not one accountable grouping but two or more, conflicting interests may have to be reconciled in an incremental way, through a process of gradual mutual adjustment over time.* Even here, the commitment package framework can still provide a dynamic structure to aid collaborative negotiation.

Figure 88 contains a summary of the range of products which might be considered — structured as in Figure 33, along the dimensions of substance/process and visible/invisible. Naturally, it is necessary to be selective in the choice of products as in the other aspects of strategic choice. The evaluative emphasis which is most appropriate to the consideration of products is an emphasis on *confidence*; the gradual accumulation of confidence among participants that they are moving towards decisions which are soundly based, at least so far as a realistic appraisal of uncertainties and time and resource pressures allow. This is the emphasis which was contrasted with the more conventional emphases on accountability and completeness of products (Figure 34), important as these more tangible considerations remain. And the evaluation of growth in

* See, for instance, the case of Droitwich Town Development — Friend, Power & Yewlett (1974) or Batty (1979).

confidence is a matter not just for the working group itself, but for all those other participants who may be involved in other process roles.

Continuity and the Individual

In the prototypical working situation where substantial human and other resources are being committed to a major planning study, the rate of progress towards a more *continuous* way of working becomes an important test of the extent to which the philosophy of strategic choice is becoming diffused; especially so where there remains the expectation that the main substantive product will take the form of a fully integrated 'master plan', delivered by some appointed deadline. This shift in the direction of continuity has been called the *continuisation* of a planning process (Hickling, 1982) and it becomes an important evaluative emphasis in process terms, to accompany the emphasis on growth of confidence in the more substantive products.

But the shift towards continuity has its limits, especially when combined with the emphasis on interactive working. People cannot work interactively all the time and, indeed, practical ways of managing the process and products are essentially to do with the management of those *discontinuities* that inevitably arise when people can only come together periodically and for limited lengths of time. Two expressions that are often heard from people involved in complex planning tasks are 'let's start from scratch ...' and 'at the end of the day ...'. In real life planning, there is no such thing as 'scratch' and people never do reach 'the end of the day' in that final sense. Yet successive working days will come to an end and new working days will begin — whether the new day is spent working on the same problem or on another. And these are the realities against which moves towards continuity of process and incremental products must be judged.

Inevitably, it is at the level of the individual that the *experience* of continuity finds its fullest expression. For individuals exist continuously, in states of consciousness punctuated by more or less regular periods of sleep. While conscious, they make choices of many kinds, some of them in a more or less programmed and automatic way. They make choices about eating, drinking, moving from place to place; about small-scale social interactions and economic transactions. Indeed, one of the first examples of a decision area quoted in Chapter 2 was of the choice facing an individual as to how to respond to an early morning alarm, as the first choice of all at the start of another decision-making day.

Some personal choices, of course, call for more deliberation — either through a process of *simple choice* (Figure 6), with work concentrated in the designing and comparing modes — or through a more subtle process of *strategic choice* such as that exercising the individual depicted earlier (in

Figure 30) relaxing in an armchair and contemplating how some set of uncertainties should be managed — in which situation one possible response could be to rise out of the chair and to discuss it with someone else.

Choices for the individual arise over where to direct his or her attention at any moment; where to look; what to read; to whom to listen; and, indeed, how to use any of the various sensory mechanisms with which the body is equipped. These choices about *scanning* are continuously being made, more or less consciously, and are accompanied by choices in the realm of action, or *doing*, through the motor mechanisms of the body. So any complete model of individual decision-making must include some representation of these motor and sensory mechanisms which provide connections to the physical world outside. Indeed, various authors (Beer, 1966; Faludi, 1973) have built on this kind of cybernetic modelling in the attempt to develop more complete models of a planning process.

Following this line of argument, any complete representation of a process of strategic choice should include **scanning** and **doing** modes in addition to the four already considered in depth in this book. A more complete six-mode representation appears in Figure 89. The two additional modes are shown as embedded in a *world of operations* in contrast to the *technical domain* of designing and comparing, and the *political arena* in which the shaping and choosing work are done. So what has been called the process of simple choice (Figure 6) in effect by-passes the political arena — unless and until difficulties are encountered which mean moving in the direction of increasing complexity and, therefore, increasing interactions with others whose values and perceptions may conflict.

Of course, organisations as well as individuals have their 'worlds of operations' which tend to provide the strongest strands of continuity and predictability in their work. Individuals who are employed by organisations will spend parts of their conscious lives making choices within the framework of their employer's field of operations, and other parts of their lives making choices within more personal settings. Many of these choices will be simple, others more complex — possibly involving not just one technical domain or one political arena, but several, which may be inter-related in intricate ways. So the six-mode diagram of Figure 89 provides no more than a conceptual reference point in attempting to follow activities within a set of processes which may, in practice, have a very rich and complex texture — with threads of continuity provided by the scanning and doing activities of all the various individuals who may become involved.

The six-mode model of strategic choice will not be further developed here, but it can be used as a base from which to explore further what is involved in work in any of the four main process modes, with reference to the others. In particular, Hickling (1985) has developed a view of evaluation as a five-finger exercise, in which the comparing mode is treated as the palm of the hand, with the five 'fingers' of designing, shaping, scanning, doing

FIGURE
89

Strategic Choice as a Continuous Process

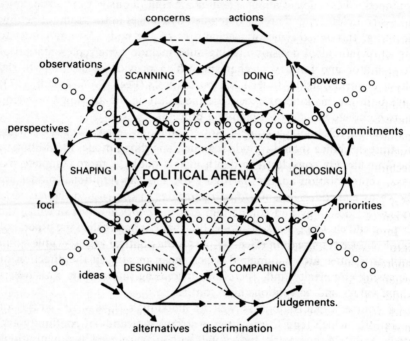

FIELD OF OPERATIONS

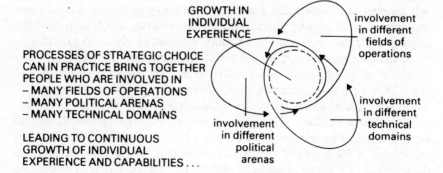

PROCESSES OF STRATEGIC CHOICE
CAN IN PRACTICE BRING TOGETHER
PEOPLE WHO ARE INVOLVED IN
– MANY FIELDS OF OPERATIONS
– MANY POLITICAL ARENAS
– MANY TECHNICAL DOMAINS

LEADING TO CONTINUOUS
GROWTH OF INDIVIDUAL
EXPERIENCE AND CAPABILITIES . . .

PRACTICALITIES

and choosing being used in various sequences and combinations as the pianist consciously works to extend his or her skills.

Keeping it Simple

The emphasis of this chapter has been on practical guidance in managing a process of choosing strategically through time. Attention has been given in turn to the four aspects of technology, organisation, process and product. These together comprise a coherent approach — or merely a 'way of working' if these aspects are developed in an informal rather than a conscious way. In the use of the strategic choice approach, these four aspects have provided a structure for the design and management of comparatively large-scale exercises. In some cases, governmental bodies have committed substantial human and other resources over a period of months to work on important national, regional or local problems. It is in such settings that deliberate attention has been paid to the finer points of technological choice (Figure 83); to the relationships of different groupings (Figures 84 and 85); to the scheduling arrangements for meetings (Figure 86); and to the systematic documentation and interpretation of products (Figures 87 and 88).

Important as these practical points are, they cannot, of course, be taken into account so consciously in every application of the strategic choice approach. The most important guideline of all is to keep things simple wherever possible. Problems vary and pressures vary. If an opportunity suddenly emerges to draw on strategic choice ideas in the heat of working with a few other people on an urgent problem, the setting and materials may not be ideal; the working group may have to be treated as given; and the time constraints may be severe. So the immediate products might have to be simple and direct. But a consciousness that there *are* management choices involved in each of the four aspects of technology, organisation, process and product can provide a valuable background to the snap judgements that have to be made, even in such informal working situations — and a framework for reflection once the moment of creativity has passed.

10

Horizons

State of the Art

It would be rash indeed — and quite contrary to the philosophy offered here — to suggest that this book should be regarded as presenting some ultimate state of development in the strategic choice approach. What it does present is a broad view of the approach which has been put together at a particular moment, following a sustained effort over several months to *consolidate* the lessons learnt through application to an increasing range of decision and planning problems. So, the view of strategic choice at the time of writing is different to — and we hope significantly clearer than — any that could have been put together ten, five, or even two years earlier; but, equally, the view is one that must be expected to change further in the years ahead.

This chapter is about horizons for future development; horizons which are themselves bound to shift as events unfold and new opportunities for adaptation and learning emerge. The events which have contributed to the historical development of the strategic choice approach have already been alluded to in the authors' preface; in the references to the seminal Coventry local government project in Chapter 1; and in the review of subsequent experiences in application at the beginning of Chapter 9. This historical view is one which some readers may wish to extend through selective reference to other sources; and the Guide to Further Reading which follows this chapter has been written with that end in view.

Even though the approach originated in a conscious attempt to bring together the approaches of operational research and applied social science, its evolution has always been more directly influenced by exposure to the *practice* of planning and collective decision-making than by established theories. There are a few writers, such as Vickers (1965), Lindblom (1965), Etzioni (1966), Miller and Rice (1967), Schon (1971), Emery and Trist (1972) and Faludi (1973), who have had a significant influence on the development of strategic choice ideas. But Faludi himself comments that the work of what he calls the IOR School has evolved with little reference to other recent developments in planning thought; and in his recent work

(1986,1987) he has set out to link the strategic choice more clearly to the ideas of other theorists in the urban and regional planning field.

Yet there are others in the broader world of management and social sciences who have been pioneering interactive approaches to the treatment of complex and ill-structured decision problems; and Bennett (1985) reports on some recent attempts in Britain to explore ways of linking some of these approaches more closely, through a programme of experimental activities involving collaboration between schools which have been pioneering different styles of 'soft' operational research. The horizons for further development which have been emerging through these activities will be touched on briefly in this chapter; so too will the opportunities for development arising from advances in the understanding of group dynamics, in decision analysis and in the information technology field.

The chapter will then conclude with some views of the challenge of education and training in strategic choice: a challenge which has, to date, been relatively neglected, but is seen as vital if the approach is to realise its full potential as an aid to interactive working on complex and important problems.

So, this chapter will range over many important topics — but it will touch on them briefly, with more generous references to the work of others than in earlier chapters. For horizons will continue to change — rapidly and sometimes unpredictably — and whatever is said here must be regarded as ephemeral to some degree. What does seem predictable is that the primary emphasis on advance through applications will remain; so this chapter begins with a review of three broad realms of application — in public policy, in corporate strategy and in inter-organisational working — where significant opportunities for *adaptation* of strategic choice methods can be seen. These opportunities will be reviewed within a perspective that embraces all four aspects of the approach — technology, organisation, process and product — and will lead naturally into a review of development opportunities in the fields of research and education.

Applications in Public Policy

At the time of writing, most of the development work on the strategic choice approach has taken place within the realm of **public policy**. This is in marked contrast to other innovative approaches to the management of complexity in decision-making, which have developed from private sector experience and then sometimes adapted, with varying degrees of success, to governmental settings.

Within the broad realm of public policy, the range of applications of strategic choice methods has been extending well beyond the field of urban and regional planning — which provided the context for most of the development work in Britain during the seventies. In particular, there has been a shift in the Netherlands towards applications to the development of national policies in such fields as energy investment, environmental pollution, waste disposal and social security. One of the first applications to national policy issues in the Netherlands has been reported in a paper by van de Graaf (1985). This describes a process of inter-departmental collaboration in policy-making for the landing, storage and transportation of liquid petroleum gas. It is significant, however, that the idea of using strategic choice as an aid to interactive working between departments of state had been foreshadowed in the Federal German Republic several years earlier (Scharpf, 1972).

The realm of public policy is, in many ways, more complex than that of decision-making within the corporate organisation. For the range of stakeholders is generally wider; many of the ways of influencing action are more subtle and indirect; and the arrangements for representation, accountability and consultation are correspondingly more elaborate. Many of these forms of complexity can, of course, be observed in the private sector too: it is simply that in governmental settings they tend to be more pervasive and impossible to ignore.

Most of the adaptations in strategic choice methods which began to emerge from the applications to British Structure Plans during the seventies (Bather, Williams and Sutton, 1976; Hickling, 1978) have been proving relevant in this subsequent policy work and are being refined and extended accordingly. These adaptations have already been mentioned in earlier chapters; they include the methods for exploring consistency between more general and more specific levels of decision, and the disciplines used to record the structure of policy statements and set down guidelines for continuous policy management.

In parallel with these adaptations in method, a number of more basic research projects have been carried out into the *dynamics* of public policy change, both in physical planning and other fields (Friend, Power and Yewlett, 1974; Friend, 1977; Friend, Laffin and Norris, 1981). In these projects, strategic choice methods have been applied in a descriptive rather than a prescriptive way, and have helped draw attention to aspects of policy change in practice which seem, as yet, to have received little attention in the burgeoning literature of policy science. Concepts which have emerged from this work include the phenomenon of *policy stress* — a state in which two or more conflicting policy guidelines impinge on the same decision-maker — and the related phenomenon of *policy erosion* through time which, once identified, can be seen as one of the main dynamic forces underlying the more widely discussed activities of policy formulation and review. These concepts have a bearing on the adaptation of strategic choice methods to problems of inter-organisational working at local level, which will be discussed in the next section but one. However, it is first appropriate to make some observations on the scope for adaptation of the approach to decision-making in the corporate strategy field.

Adaptations to Corporate Strategy

It is already apparent that strategic choice methods, in their basic form, have application to decision problems of an *ad hoc* kind which arise either in smaller commercial enterprises or in sections of larger organisations — especially where the shape of the problem is poorly understood. There have indeed been some applications in Britain and the Netherlands to problems of reorganisation, relocation and diversification in which the patterns of alternatives, consequences, uncertainties and relationships to other associated decision problems are initially unclear.

What is less clear at the time of writing is how far, and in what ways, strategic choice methods can complement more orthodox methods of **corporate planning** which are shaped to the guidance of large and complex organisations from positions of central authority. In such organisations, the very word 'strategic' tends to be used to refer almost exclusively to the choices that arise, at boardroom level, as to how the enterprise as a whole should adapt to powerful external forces. This usage is indeed reflected in the somewhat different interpretation of the term 'strategic choice' which has emerged through the work of organisational analysts such as Child (1972).

The prototypical context into which formal systems of corporate planning are introduced is one of a large organisation, in which divisions or departments are seen as subject to inertial tendencies or competitive claims for resources which must be counterbalanced by a more cohesive view of desired future directions. In an organisation geared to direct supply of goods or services in particular markets, the problem of corporate guidance is often interpreted primarily in terms of the forward *control* of various flows and balances — production, sales, stocks, market shares, cash, capital — with financial models and forecasts providing the integrating structure for the planning system as a whole. There are some approaches to corporate planning (Ackoff, 1970) which call for a broader process of adaptation to change in terms of objectives, human and material resources and redesign of organisational forms. Yet — for understandable reasons — in many large organisations the concern remains to develop a framework of corporate planning which can be institutionalised in terms of periodic review cycles, designated planning roles and budgetary adjustments.

The orientations of many corporate planning systems are, therefore, somewhat different to those of the strategic choice approach. In terms of the dimensions discussed in Chapter 4 (Figure 34), the formal emphasis is on a systems perspective rather than a focus on decisions; on hierarchical command rather than lateral connections; on prescribed stages rather than cyclic continuity; on substantive plans rather than strategic products. Of course, the reality may be more adaptive and more selective than these emphases suggest; indeed, it may have to be so, if formal planning systems are to have any real influence over the processes of choosing strategically in an often volatile working environment, whether at boardroom level or elsewhere.

The issue on the horizon can be viewed as one of how far, and in what ways, strategic choice methods as presented here can be adapted to *complement* systems of corporate planning and control which are shaped to the structures of particular organisations. Any developments in this direction must be seen as experimental at this stage and perhaps focussed on particular problem areas. One such area that is concerning policy-makers in most corporate organisations, large and small, is often referred to as that of *information technology strategy*. Here, complex relationships arise between decisions about acquisition and replacement of hardware, including balance between mainframe, mini and micro computers; about telecommunications networks; about integration of data and text processing; and about arrangements for software development. These choices in turn have implications for centralisation versus decentralisation; for training and job design; for industrial relations; and for dependency on particular manufacturers and software houses. Even though the desire may be to develop a comprehensive information technology strategy, the rapidity of technological and other changes is likely to mean that such a strategy can only realistically develop through incremental commitment; and the strategic choice philosophy suggests that the pace of commitment must be geared to the continuous management of uncertainty through time.

At the time of writing, exploratory workshops have been held with senior managers in a few large organisations, to test the potential for interactive use of strategic choice methods in this field, recognising that it cuts across many areas of corporate responsibility. But there is also the prospect that specific aspects of the strategic choice approach can be drawn on by corporate planning staff in a more piecemeal way. For example, Ormerod (1983) draws on the UE/UV/UR categories of uncertainty to review the activities of the British Coal Board's Central Planning Unit, concluding that efforts have been roughly evenly divided between the three.

Applications to Inter-Organisational Working

In the management and planning literature, much less attention has been directed towards approaches to inter-organisational working than towards the development of methods for decision-making and planning within the corporate setting. This is scarcely surprising for, even where the commitment to collaborative working exists, the actual *methods* of working have to be negotiated across the boundaries between organisations; they cannot be imposed according to any unified corporate view.

The development of the strategic choice approach has, however, been accompanied by a considerable amount of research by members of the 'IOR School' into problems of inter-agency working that arise at local and regional levels in various public policy contexts, including town expansion (Friend, Power and Yewlett, 1974); regional planning; community health and welfare; urban deprivation; alcohol problems; countryside conservation; and more recently the criminal justice system. The practical and theoretical outcomes of these studies are to be found detailed in project reports to the sponsoring government departments and research councils. Many of the findings and insights are also reported more briefly in the periodical *Linkage*, which was published by the Tavistock Institute between 1977 and 1983 and was specifically concerned with issues of inter-organisational working. Some especially relevant articles are listed in the Guide to Further Reading that follows this chapter.

At the time of writing there have been some encouraging results from the introduction of strategic choice concepts, at a quite basic and simple level, into training events designed for people in public service and voluntary organisations who operate at local community level with relatively few resources of direct authority and influence at their disposal (Jago and Norris, 1981; Jago et al, 1983). Such people can only extend their influence through effective negotiation and joint working across organisational boundaries; but conventional ideas of corporate planning and management are found to be of little help in this respect, even though they may be well entrenched within the hierarchical structures of some of the agencies concerned.

It is in such contexts of inter-organisational working that the idea of planning as *responsible scheming*, introduced at the start of Chapter 1, is being found helpful in providing an alternative model of planning which relates more directly to the dilemmas of practice experienced by both professional and voluntary workers. In a training context, it is found helpful to introduce exercises in mutual consultancy, in which each participant selects some specific decision problem of current concern and another acts as consultant in enquiring into alternative courses of action; organisational and other actors; range of consequences; and sources of uncertainty in choosing, drawing on the UE/UV/UR framework. Such exercises repeatedly throw up issues of interconnection with other problems, of negotiation across boundaries and of the management of policy stress.

The conclusion at this stage is that the development of strategic choice methods as a means of facilitating effective scheming by decision-makers with relatively few resources will have to focus on the provision of personal support for individuals, as well as on creating settings for interactive group working. The interactive use of strategic choice methods can, however, be important in a training context, as well as in any local contexts of inter-organisational working where the commitment to interactive methods can be negotiated. This conclusion has its relevance for the theoretical developments to be discussed in later sections of this chapter; for the review of the role of the computer in strategic choice; and for the discussion of the educational challenge.

Partisan Strategic Choice

Approaches to decision-making which assume partisan rather than consensual behaviour have been under development for several years in the management and social sciences, and have gradually been adapted to contexts in which patterns of conflict and coalition become quite complex. The strategic choice approach as presented in earlier chapters recognises that differences in value systems are an inescapable feature of most complex planning situations; and it approaches this partly through the inclusion of uncertainties in guiding values among the uncertainties which must be continuously managed; partly by advocating a focus of the decisions to be made; and partly by stressing the progress that can be achieved through an interactive style of working, wherever agreement on this can be achieved.

Although it has been recognised, at several points in this book, that different decision areas can come within the influence or control of different decision-makers (Figures 41 and 77), such differences have not so far been treated as central to the analytical methods of strategic choice. In the discussion of contingency planning in Chapter 8, the possibility was recognised that the structuring of the future decision space could lead towards representation of the decisions of other parties within what is sometimes called a *game-theoretic* framework, allowing the moves and counter-moves open to parties with potentially opposing motives to be systematically analysed; indeed, this is one of the directions in which there are possibilities for future adaptations to the strategic choice approach.

One point of departure is offered by the work of Nigel Howard (1971) on a theory of *metagames* in which — departing from more classical forms of conflict theory — the patterns of options available to different parties in a conflict situation are analysed and a search is then conducted for points of local *stability* in which no party is in a position to adopt unilateral improvements which bring disadvantages to others. This kind of approach has been further extended by Bennett and Huxham (1982), who allow first for the mapping of interdependent arenas of partisanship and conflict and, secondly, for a recognition that the options available in the 'game' may, in practice, be perceived differently by different 'players'.

Preliminary explorations with Bennett, Huxham and other associates (Bennett, 1985) have indicated some of the possibilities for linkage between strategic choice methods and these methods of conflict analysis. What strategic choice has to offer is a means of addressing the dynamics of incremental decision-making under uncertainty; while what conflict analysis has to offer is a more structured approach to issues of partisanship in situations where these are crucial in making progress towards decisions.

Meanwhile, there have been other lines of development in the management sciences, in the United States and elsewhere, which have focussed on the *behavioural* aspects of partisan decision-making. Among these are the work on mediation of Susskind (1987), and the work on effective negotiation of Fisher and Ury (1982) and Hawkins and Hudson (1986).

The approach of Fisher and Ury is entirely consistent with the strategic choice approach to the extent that it emphasises collaborative styles of negotiation; the invention of options for mutual gain; and, indeed, the use of paper on walls as an aid to interactive working. The belief is that, given the will, the application of some basic insights and skills can lead to win/win outcomes even where these could not be readily perceived at the outset. Within the strategic choice toolbox, the idea of the commitment package — and, in particular, that of the mutual commitment package, discussed in Chapter 9 — offers a framework in which it becomes possible to express such possibilities in a more dynamic form, as an aid to any process of continuous negotiation through time. So, in combination, conflict analysis methods and effective negotiation ideas suggest some important directions in which strategic choice methods can be adapted to partisan settings, with relevance in particular to applications in public policy and inter-organisational working.

Eliciting Problem Perceptions

Reference has already been made, with illustrations (Figure 46), to the use of simple forms of ends/means analysis in strategic choice as a means of sorting out preliminary views about relationships among loosely-formulated areas of concern, at a stage prior to the identification of decision areas. It is, however, possible to take this kind of approach to the preliminary 'mapping' of perception much further through an approach which is now being widely applied in Britain. This is the *cognitive mapping* approach, developed in the School of Management at the University of Bath (Eden, Jones and Sims, 1983). This approach draws on the work of cognitive psychologists and, in particular, on the personal construct theory developed by Kelly (1955,1972) in the context of clinical work.

Working usually with individuals in the first instance, Eden, Jones and their colleagues set out to elicit *personal constructs* which are meaningful to people within their own frames of reference. This they do either through informal discussion or, occasionally, by the use of more structured methods such as Kelly's repertory grid, in which concrete entities — for example known people, or makes of cars, are systematically compared in triads to elicit views on which any two of the three are perceived as similar and the other different (Eden and Jones, 1984).

Personal constructs are generally expressed in terms of pairs of opposites such as (assertive — passive) or (old-fashioned — up-to-date). These 'bi-polar' constructs are then used to build up *cognitive maps* of relationships between constructs, using graphical conventions in which such relationships are sometimes shown as directed and sometimes not: so the result is a graph in which some but not all links between nodes appear with arrowheads pointing in a particular direction. From this graph, clusters, loops and other structural features can be identified as an aid to further problem structuring and interactive learning.

The initial construction of maps may involve intensive interaction with individuals; but this is usually seen as a prelude to interactive working with groups, on the basis of a 'merged map' in which the views of different individuals are combined. This kind of approach has been used successfully in working both with organisational clients (Eden, Williams and Smithin, 1986) and community groups (Jones and Eden, 1980) to explore the complexities of the problems they face. Also, some effort has now been expended in the search for practical ways of linking cognitive mapping and strategic choice approaches within the broader initiative to explore connections between interactive decision aids already mentioned (Bennett, 1985).

The main similarity between cognitive mapping and strategic choice is to be found in the informal and interactive use of simple graphical methods to structure group working on complex problems: among the differences are the more explicit concern with personal perceptions in cognitive mapping, and the more explicit concern with management of uncertainty and incremental progress in strategic choice. In future development work, the hope is that these complementarities can be built on further, with cognitive mapping offering to strategic choice the possibility in particular of bringing deeper levels of insight to peoples' perceptions of problems, especially but not exclusively while working in the shaping mode.

The Dynamics of the Working Group

In Chapter 9, various forms of practical advice were offered on ways of achieving effective interaction within a working group engaged in applying strategic choice methods to a complex planning problem; and also on ways of handling the group's relationships with other participants in the wider decision process. The advice covered such points as choice of room; use of materials when working on the walls; creation of opportunities for individual working; the role of facilitator in process management; and the role of core group members in maintaining relationships beyond the boundaries of the working group.

All these pieces of advice reflect cumulative experience on ways of achieving effective working within and between groups. However, it is important to recognise that relationships within and between groups can be influenced not only by such design considerations but also by the dynamic interplay of many other forces — unconscious as well as conscious — which may have either a destructive or a constructive influence on the behaviour of those involved.

The theme of group and inter-group relations has itself been the subject of considerable study, much of it from a psychoanalytical perspective (Bion, 1963; Rice, 1965). Based on these insights, programmes of group relations training have been developed within the Tavistock Institute of Human Relations and various related institutions. Within the 'temporary institution' of a group relations event, participants are presented with a variety of opportunities to interact in both smaller and larger group situations; to assume various roles and to discover their authority within such roles; to address conflicts as they emerge; and to undertake negotiations across inter-group boundaries, Members of the course staff themselves assume a range of directorial, administrative and consultant roles — and in the consultant role are available to offer working hypotheses about what is happening, grounded on their own observations and experience.

Such insights and skills can clearly be of help to those involved in interactive group working on complex problems, especially to anyone operating in a facilitating role. The specific technology of strategic choice can be seen as creating a rather different context for interaction to that of other, more conventional forms of group working, especially in so far as it allows much of the group's attention to be focussed on the shared visible product which is building up around the walls. So there are opportunities to be explored for combining group relations and strategic choice perspectives in the *design* of interactive working sessions, whether in a decision-making or a training context. One training exercise designed on these principles has already been mentioned in the section on inter-organisational working (Jago and Norris, 1981). Also, it is possible to introduce questions relating to changing perceptions of group effectiveness into the continuous monitoring of invisible products in a process of strategic choice. At the time of writing, this is being treated as an important aspect of governmental and other policy projects in the Netherlands.

Developments in Operational Research and Decision Analysis

The strategic choice approach — and indeed also the cognitive mapping approach developed at the University of Bath — emerged from experiences in addressing complex problems within the tradition of operational research, as enriched by insights from the social sciences. But there have been many other developments over this same period in the field of operational research and the closely related field of decision analysis; so it has to be asked what relevance they could have for the future development of the strategic choice approach.

The approach to complexity which is generally regarded as most characteristic of operational research — and which is most widely taught in academic schools — is based on quite sophisticated methods of mathematical modelling and systems simulation. These methods are generally at their most successful in dealing with well-structured problems in which uncertainty can be dealt with through statistical distributions based on past frequencies, and the structural relationships of the decisions to be addressed can be seen as relatively unchanging through time.

However, these are not the forms of complexity that have been found to be most important to decision-makers in the contexts where strategic choice methods have been applied, especially in the fields of public policy and inter-organisational working. Here the most daunting complexities facing decision-makers have been found to be non-systemic in form: in other words, the structure of relationships between problems may change from month to month, as urgent problems are dealt with and quite different ones take their place within the wider fabric of interconnected issues to be addressed. So the question arises of whether there can be any complementarity between strategic choice and systems modelling methods in practice. One area of complementarity may be found in the use of the relatively crude methods of problem structuring offered by the strategic choice approach. For these can be used to identify particular foci of concern where more sophisticated forms of systems modelling are likely to be justified. From a strategic choice perspective, systems modelling can be treated as just one means of responding to uncertainty, which can be compared to other, perhaps simpler, means in terms of its cost-effectiveness in any particular decision situation.

Meanwhile, there may be more direct possibilities for adapting strategic choice methods to reflect some of the advances recently made within the field of *decision analysis*. Methods of decision and risk analysis which set out to explore contingencies and responses in a systematic way have gradually moved beyond the foundations laid by decision scientists such as Raiffa (1968); and increasing attention has been paid to methods of interactive working with decision-makers through which their underlying value structures can be elicited (Phillips, 1982; Thomas and Sampson, 1986). Methods of eliciting value structures progressively through successive pair comparisons have been developed by scientists such as Saaty (1980) and have been incorporated into interactive computer software. Meanwhile, Mason and Mitroff (1981) have developed a structured approach to the surfacing and testing of alternative planning assumptions which could make an important complement to the basic methods for analysing and managing uncertainty discussed in earlier chapters. In the public planning field, too, there have been some significant developments in interactive evaluation methods, which recognise the political complexity of evaluative processes in the public domain (Hill, 1968,1985; Lichfield, 1966,1985; Lichfield et al, 1975).

In reviewing the scope for using such methods in combination with those of the established strategic choice toolbox, it is important to keep in mind the adaptive nature of the strategic choice approach and, in particular, the precept — reflected in the Sutton Principle, as introduced in Chapter 9 — that energies should normally be invested in those directions where, at any moment, the most important opportunities for learning seem to lie. In general, the use of comparatively elegant methods of decision analysis will tend to mean lingering longer in a particular mode — whether it be shaping, designing, comparing or choosing — so the more important it becomes that this investment of time should be justified in relation to the pressures of the current decision process.

The Electronic Resource

In this and earlier chapters, occasional reference has been made to the potential for use of the computer as a resource in strategic choice. In general, the computer has been projected as a more marginal resource than in other approaches to complex decision and planning problems; and this can be explained in terms of the emphases on open technology and interactive participation which distinguish the strategic choice approach. For — as a glance back to Figure 30 may suggest — it is easy to imagine even the most user-friendly of microcomputers as a distraction when the main task is one of sustaining the momentum of interaction within a working group.

Yet the development of electronic information technology has been proceeding at an accelerating pace, with increasing convergence between the fields of data processing, text processing and telecommunications; with microcomputers becoming increasingly accessible, even to children in the home; with advances in computer graphics and other aids to man-machine interaction becoming widely available; and with prospects of even more radical changes to come through fifth and subsequent generations of information processing power. At the time of writing, the development of software for strategic choice has been largely confined to the combinational aspects of the use of AIDA in the designing mode, extending into the comparing mode only in so far as it allows sorting and filtering of the resulting combinations in relation to simple numerical scales. Uncertainty is dealt with only through those forms of sensitivity analysis which become possible through introducing exploratory changes to options, option bars and assessments. This kind of software, originally developed in FORTRAN IV in the early and mid-seventies, is easily enough adapted to the more flexible user-interactive potential of the microcomputer with direct keyboard input and VDU display.

There are some academic planners who have been involved in software development along lines broadly parallel to these (Openshaw and Whitehead, 1986). However, it is clear that the economy, accessibility and versatility of the desk top microcomputer open up much wider possibilities for helping users of strategic methods choice to work within and between all modes of the approach as presented in this book. In particular, there is a role for software which can:

— help people take explicit account of uncertainty in comparing alternatives;
— help people in identifying uncertainty areas and considering how they might respond;
— help people to assemble, modify and compare commitment packages;
— help people to explore the shape of complex problems through decision graphs.

Because use of the strategic choice approach in practice calls for rapid switching and looping *between* modes, it becomes especially important that any software for strategic choice should also help users in the difficult process of *route-finding* which is involved in applying the approach adaptively to complex problems, in the spirit of a learning process. In a group setting, the main source of guidance in route-finding is the facilitator or process consultant. Yet in *individual* decision settings the experience is that even the most skilled user of strategic choice methods finds it difficult to follow this kind of disciplined process of route-finding without help from someone else. So, a software package spanning all four modes and helping the user to address the various types of switching and looping judgements which were drawn out in earlier chapters (Figures 43, 55, 67 and 79) offers a means of making the strategic choice approach more accessible to individual decision-makers, whether working within organisations or between. In essence, the design concept for such a software package is the same as the design concept of this book. The task that remains, at the time of writing, is one of translating that design concept into reality.*

One important question that arises is that of how far such software can also facilitate the work of groups, without inhibiting the spontaneity of group interaction and the build-up of a clearly visible record of progress around the walls of the room. Advances in this direction can be predicted

---

* Up-to-date reports on the availability of strategic choice software can be obtained by writing to either of the author addresses as given in the Enquiries section on page 315.

with confidence enough; however, it is likely that the approach here will have to be more exploratory and experimental because it cannot be seen in isolation from the pace of future development in new forms of human-machine interface technology which can be adapted to interactive working within a group. But then the synthesis of group interaction with human-machine interaction poses daunting design problems, which are not likely to be resolved by technological invention alone: the challenge must be seen as essentially one of adaptive *socio-technical* design (Trist et al, 1963).

The Educational Challenge

In the development so far of the strategic choice approach, Faludi (1987) has pointed out that the resources of the academic community have been somewhat neglected, despite the valuable association of a few academic planners, operational researchers and political scientists with the work of the IOR School. The momentum of the work has been sustained primarily through interaction with practitioners in positions of responsibility in non-academic organisations; and this has had an important influence on the way the approach has evolved and been tested in practice.

This pattern of development has brought real gains; but it has also had its costs in developmental terms. In particular, it has meant that members of the IOR School have had little access to the resource of postgraduate research students with the ability and the time to carry out fundamental research on aspects of the strategic choice approach and its relationship with other related bodies of theory. More significantly, it has meant that there has been little opportunity for the kinds of sustained interaction between generations which become possible within the context of established academic programmes. The interactions which have led to the development of the ideas presented here have been primarily with experienced decision-makers. What the approach set out to do is to make more explicit some of the important types of judgement which practitioners normally learn to make on the basis of experience rather than taught skills.

So it is important to ask how far this kind of experience can be made more directly accessible to the successors of these decision-makers in future generations, through the educational process. As already mentioned, in Chapter 9, there has already been a substantial experience in the *training* of experienced decision-makers in the philosophy and methods of strategic choice. However, this has usually taken the form of quite brief events addressed to people whose time is at a premium; and for those of us involved in a training capacity, the event has had to be seen either as an adjunct to or a diversion from the various applied projects through which the main thrust of development has been sustained.

Meanwhile, the dearth of readily accessible published material, written with educational objectives in view, has until now made it difficult for lecturers in educational institutions to incorporate the ideas into their main teaching programmes. This is a gap which, it is hoped, *Planning under Pressure* will do something to fill.

But there are deeper challenges to be faced if the strategic choice approach is to play its part in the education of future generations of decision-makers. For, if its strength lies in the potential it offers to help people make more sense of their own experiences of making complex decisions under pressure, it has to be asked how far it can be realistically taught to young people, most of whose life's experience of the complex world of organisational decision-making is yet to come.

To arrive at pessimistic conclusions on this point would be not only defeatist but also irresponsible. Even in their adolescence, most people now encounter problems of considerable complexity and interconnectedness — about what skills to develop, where to live, how to travel, how to budget their expenditure, how to relate to others with conflicting views and aims. Often, too, negotiations on such matters are required. So there is no reason why such problems should not provide foundations of experience which can be built on in preparing them for the more weighty challenges of organisational and inter-organisational decision-making that many of them will face in their later lives.

The fear is that the rigidity of many educational systems, with their inherent bias towards well-structured and examinable forms of knowledge, will impede progress in directions such as these. But these systems in aggregate have vast human, financial and material resources on which to draw. If this book can play its part in indicating the shape of the challenge to be faced in preparing people for responsibilities in the world of complex decisions, then the hope must be that those people within the world of education can find imaginative ways of building on our experience — and their own — to overcome the constraints of their environments and design appropriate forms of learning experience for those who pass through their hands.

For the need to equip emergent generations to work effectively on complex problems is an urgent one. We who are involved in the continuing development of the strategic choice approach do not have the skills or the resources to devote the level of effort to this task that it requires. For innovation in planning and management methods is a never-ending task. Inevitably, progress raises expectations; and these expectations, in turn, generate dissatisfactions with the existing state of the art. If these dissatisfactions are not energetically addressed, the result will be a gradual ossification of methods and ideas, leading in time to disillusionment and to sacrifice of the progress already made.

Although we have sought to present the current state of the art in a readily accessible form, we do not ask that those in the world of education and training should accept it as it stands. Indeed, we are concerned that our ideas about planning as a process of strategic choice should be scrutinised critically from diverse scientific perspectives; should be tested against a range of experiences; and should be evaluated carefully by those who face the day-to-day pressures of student expectations and demands.

So the influence and inspiration of those who are immersed in the world of education will be essential if future decision-makers are to be helped to make use — selectively and adaptively — of the ideas presented here. For these ideas are built on interpretations of many peoples' experiences in planning under pressure — people whose working lives are finite, even though there can be no respite in the challenges facing the many organisations, large and small, which share responsibility for the future of the world.

A Guide to Further Reading

Introduction

A considerable amount has been written about the strategic choice approach and its applications prior to the publication of this book. However, people have told us that they find much of it inaccessible, in that it remains buried in conference proceedings, reports to government departments and other sponsors, and internal working papers.

The inaccessibility of much that has been written is an unfortunate, but perhaps inevitable, result of the pressures under which the strategic choice approach has developed, and found its way into planning and policy processes over the last two decades. These pressures have themselves been varied enough. They include the pressures on ourselves and our collaborators to complete major projects; to negotiate new contracts; to achieve a synthesis of approach within an inter-disciplinary and often inter-organisational team; to prepare a written paper as a contribution to the proceedings of a conference at which one has agreed to speak.

Amongst these pressures, the well-known incentive for the individual scientist to build up an impressive list of published journal articles has not figured as prominently as it might have done had we been seeking to develop scholarly careers from a stable university base. So too many pieces of writing which we would have wished to polish up for publication have had to remain unpublished, under the continuing pressure to maintain the momentum of applied work. Of the project reports that have so far been produced for particular clients, some have been confidential. However, even where no such restrictions apply, these reports were often written primarily for a particular client readership; so the findings sometimes refer to institutional and procedural contexts which the general reader might find unfamiliar.

For all these reasons, it seems appropriate to end this book not only with an alphabetical list of references, but also with a brief structured guide to further reading, including some comments on accessibility and on relevance to different reader interests.

Principal Published Sources on the Development of the Strategic Choice Approach

The book *Local Government and Strategic Choice* (Friend and Jessop, 1969/77) was first published in 1969 by Tavistock Publications of London — a division of Associated Book Publishers whose association with the Tavistock Institute of Human Relations has an important historical basis, even though for many years now there has been no formal organisational link. The book was first reprinted in 1971 as volume SSP84 in the Tavistock Publications Social Science Paperback Series. Publication rights were subsequently transferred to Pergamon Press, who published the second edition in 1977, as Volume 14 in the Pergamon Urban and Regional Planning Series.

Because of the death in 1969 of one of the book's co-authors — Neil Jessop, first Director of the Institute for Operational Research — the second edition made no changes to the main text of the book; but it included a new foreword and a postscript by John Friend, as surviving co-author, setting the book in context of developments over the intervening eight-year period. While the main text of the book describes in some depth the way in which the strategic choice approach emerged from the experience of the Coventry project in the mid-sixties, the foreword to the second edition re-appraises the content of each of its four main sections in the light of subsequent events. The purpose of the postscript to the second edition is to report the early experiences in application which followed during this same eight-year period.

Published Sources on the Development of the AIDA Design Method

The design method of Analysis of Interconnected Decision Areas (AIDA), which is one important element in the broader strategic choice approach, emerged from a Tavistock Institute project which was roughly concurrent with the Coventry project and was concerned with problems of communications in the building industry (Crichton, 1966). The report of a short pilot study which preceded this was also published (Higgin and Jessop, 1965). Following a well-established British scientific tradition, the invention of AIDA was first registered in a short article in the journal *Nature* (Harary, Jessop, Luckman and Stringer, 1965), while a fuller account was published in the operational research literature two years later (Luckman, 1967). A monograph was produced in 1971 following a research project on applications of AIDA to engineering design problems and copies of this are available through the Tavistock Institute (Morgan, 1971).

Published Applications of the Strategic Choice Approach

The first published applications of the strategic choice approach as such — including an account of the application in the north of England on which the South Side Story is loosely based — are to be found in the report of the

LOGIMP experiment (Friend, Wedgwood-Oppenheim et al, 1970). One of the applications of this period was described further by Bunker (1974) and there have been some published descriptions of the series of applications to County Council structure plans in England, focussing in particular on the development of a multi-level approach to the use of strategic choice in this context (Bather, Williams and Sutton, 1976: Hickling, 1978). An application to recreational planning has been published by Ferguson (1979) and a number of reports of applications in the Netherlands have been published in English (Dekker et al, 1978: Dekker and Mastop, 1979), including a brief report on an application at national policy level (Van de Graaf, 1985).

However, for reasons discussed in the introduction to this section, several of the most significant applications of strategic choice ideas have not been published, even though in some cases they have been written up for particular clients. It is hoped to go some way towards remedying this situation by producing an edited volume of case studies as a companion to the present book.

In concluding this section, mention should be made of one book and some published papers which describe the use of strategic choice ideas not so much directly as an aid to decision-making, but as a means of analysing the realities of complex decision processes, within the context of research studies sponsored by research councils and government departments. The book *Public Planning: the Inter-corporate Dimension* (Friend, Power and Yewlett, 1974) made extensive use of strategic choice methods in this way. Among the papers in journals which fall into this same category are Friend and Hunter (1970), Floyd (1978), Friend (1976), Friend (1977), Friend (1980) and Friend, Laffin and Norris (1981). Among authors who have made use of the UE/UV/UR framework in analysing planning processes and practices are Ormerod (1983) in a paper on corporate planning in Britain's National Coal Board, and Hall (1980) in his book on great planning disasters. Also, issues of evaluation method in strategic choice have been reviewed by Dello (1985).

Translations and Reprints

In 1973, a German translation of *Local Government and Strategic Choice* was published by Bertelsmann of Dusseldorf (Friend and Jessop, 1973). This was abridged though the omission of the first three and the last three chapters, because these were more specific to the British local government system of the time. A Danish translation of chapter 5 — describing the general view of planning as a process of strategic choice — appeared in the journal *Byplan* in 1971 (Friend and Jessop, 1971). An account of the strategic choice approach has also appeared in an Italian book on town planning methods (Balbo, 1975). An introductory booklet on the strategic choice approach which was first produced in 1974 (Hickling, 1974) has provided the basis for subsequent editions in Dutch (Hickling, Hartman and Meester, 1976), French (Hickling, Wilkin and Debreyne, 1980) and Portuguese (Hickling, 1981). These translations are far from identical, as they reflect progressive adaptations to the original text as well as contributions by the respective co-authors and translators. A revised English language version of the original was published in Canada (Hickling, 1976) and subsequently further adapted and extended as an internal Tavistock Institute document (Hickling, 1979). Particular chapters of the book *Local Government and Strategic Choice* have been reprinted in edited volumes on urban planning methodologies (Robinson,1972) and on systems behaviour (Open Systems Group, 1981).

LINKAGE

Between April 1977 and February 1983, seven issues were published by the Tavistock Institute of Human Relations of an occasional journal/ newsletter by the name of LINKAGE, concerned with issues of inter-organisational decision-making and planning with a primary emphasis on the provision of community services at local level. LINKAGE was seen as a means of reporting on developments within the Institute's planning processes programme in a more informal and speedy way than through more conventional channels, while also promoting interchange between practitioners concerned with inter-organisational issues. A total of sixty articles appear in the seven issues of LINKAGE, about half of them written or co-authored by members of Institute staff and reporting on new developments both in general theory and in various fields of application.

Among the contributions which may be of most direct interest to readers of this book are:

LINKAGE ONE — April 1977
Noad A and Friend JK. Linkage in the Provision of Local Services: The Search for New Ideas.
Noad A, Bailey L and Norris ME. Area Co-ordination: Problems behind the Solution.
LINKAGE TWO — November 1977
Friend JK. Community and Policy: Co-ordination from Above or Below?
Friend JK and Noad A. Inter-organisational Linkage: Towards a Useful Theory.
LINKAGE THREE — July 1978
Noad A and King L. Area Co-ordination: A Way Forward.
Friend JK and Spink P. Networks in Public Administration.
Power JM. Reticulist Activity and Institution Building.
Friend JK, Noad A and Norris M. Progress in Understanding Linkage.
LINKAGE FOUR — April 1980
Plowden W. Innovation and Public Policy.
Stringer J. Industrial Contexts for Inter-organisational Linkage.

LINKAGE FIVE — December 1980
Laffin MJ and Friend JK. Leave it to the Professionals?
Hickling A, Luckman J and Friend JK. Co-ordinating Development Programmes: Can Meetings Help?
LINKAGE SIX — December 1981
Schon DA. Organisational Learning as an Operational Idea.
Friend JK. Joint Working: A Cautionary Tale.
Jago L and Norris ME. Training in Inter-organisational Working: An Experimental Course.
LINKAGE SEVEN — February 1983
Friend JK. Planning: The Art of Responsible Scheming.
De Melo A. Coping with Turbulence: Articulated Incrementalism.
Norris M. Catalysts of Coppers? The Design of Intermediary Bodies.
Jago L et al. Strategies for Working between Organisations: A Training Experience Reviewed.

Complete sets of the seven issues can be obtained from the Tavistock Institute of Human Relations at the address given at the end of this section.*

Project Reports and Unpublished Papers

Summary reports on several of the studies of planning processes and inter-organisational arrangements which have been conducted by the authors, with various collaborators, will be found in the issues of LINKAGE referred to above. The following fuller reports to government departments may also be of interest to some readers:

1975 Carter K, Friend JK, Pollard J and Yewlett CJL. Organisational Influences in the Regional Strategy Process. Tavistock Institute Internal Document IOR846 (92pp).

1977 Floyd M, Friend JK, King L and Sutton A. Monitoring for Development Planning. DOE Research Report No 23. London: Department of the Environment (114pp).

1977 Carter K, Friend JK and Norris M. Regional Planning and Policy Change. London: Department of the Environment (115pp).

1978 Friend JK, Lind WG and McDonald S. Future Regional Reports: A Study of Form and Content. Edinburgh: Scottish Development Department (64pp).

1979 Hickling A, Friend JK and Luckman J. The Development Plan System and Investment Programmes. London: Department of the Environment (181pp).

1980 Sutton A, Friend JK and Hickling A. The Analysis of Policy Options in Structure Plan Preparation. London: Department of the Environment (407pp).

1980 Hart DA, Hickling A, Norris M and Skelcher CK. Regional

*It is hoped to hold a price of £11.00 including post and packing (UK) and £14.00 airmail (other countries) for approximately three years after the publication date of this book.

Planning Methodology. Tavistock Institute internal document 2T/436 (87pp).

1984 Friend JK. Strategic Choice in North East Brazil: A Report to the British Council. Tavistock Institute internal document 2T/496 (28pp).

Enquiries about reports published by government departments should be addressed to relevant departmental libraries. Enquiries about Tavistock Institute documents should be addressed to the Institute's Publications Secretary at the address given on page 315.

Training Aids

A 55-minute *video tape* on strategic choice, entitled 'Strategic Choice — Planning to Learn', was produced in Canada as a training aid, by Alan Sutton and Bert Painter. It covers a brief introduction to process and philosophy; some shots of groups in action; and some interviews with participants about their personal experiences. Copies of the video tape can be supplied on rent or purchase from Allen Hickling at the address given on page 315.

Enquiries

Authors

Readers are invited to get in touch with either author if they wish to make further enquiries about:

— availability of computer software for strategic choice;
— training services and materials;
— advice on applications;
— points of contact in particular countries or regions;
— arrangements for strategic choice workshops;
— any new publications on strategic choice and its applications.

On all these fronts, the position evolves from year to year, and the authors intend to produce periodic bulletins to keep the picture up to date. Their correspondence addresses are as follows:

John Friend
Barleyland,
Thornhill Lane,
Thornhill,
BAMFORD,
Near Sheffield,
S30 2BR
UK   Telephone 0433-51544

Allen Hickling
Allen Hickling and Associates,
2 The Old Bakery,
Church Road,
Long Itchington,
RUGBY, Warwickshire,
CV23 8PW   Telephone 092-681-7048
UK   Fax   0926-25542

Both AH + A and IOP (which stands for Inter-Organisational Planning) operate flexibly as network organisations; that is, their resources lie not only in the skills of their respective principals, but also in the extensive networks of working relationships they have built up with other individuals and organisations throughout the world. The names of many of those involved at the time of going to press will be found in the list of acknowledgements in the authors' preface. While the two networks differ in their membership and spread of interests, there are substantial overlaps — each author remaining close to the centre of the network of the other, so that enquiries can be handled in a flexible way.

Tavistock Institute Publications

Most of the internal Tavistock Institute documents referred to in the Guide to Further Reading and in the list of References that follows are stored on microfiche at the Institute. Copies can be obtained at a cost to cover reproduction, packing and postage from the following address:

The Publications Secretary,
Tavistock Institute of Human Relations,
Tavistock Centre,
120 Belsize Lane,
LONDON NW3 5BA
UK   Telephone 01-435-7111

References

ACKOFF RL (1970) A Concept of Corporate Planning. New York:Wiley
ACKOFF RL (1974) Redesigning the Future. New York:Wiley
ASHBY WR (1956) An Introduction to Cybernetics. London:Chapman and Hall
BALBO M (1975) La Pianificazione come Processo di Scelte Strategiche. In: P Ceccarelli (ed) Potere e Piani Urbanistica. Milano:Franco Angeli Editore
BATHER NJ, WILLIAMS CM and SUTTON A (1976) Strategic Choice in Practice: The West Berkshire Structure Plan Experience. Reading, UK:University of Reading, Geographical Paper No 50
BATTY SE (1977) Game-Theoretic Approaches to Urban Planning and Design. In: Environment and Planning B *4*, 211-39
BEER S (1966) Decision and Control. Chichester:Wiley
BENNETT PG (1985) On Linking Approaches to Decision Aiding: Issues and Prospects. In: Journal of the Operational Research Society *36*, 659-69
BENNETT PG and HUXHAM CS (1982) Hypergames and What They Do: A 'Soft OR' Approach. In: Journal of the Operational Research Society *33*, 41-50
BION WR (1961) Experiences in Groups. London:Tavistock Publications
BUNKER R (1974) Making Decisions in St Albans. In: Built Environment 1974, 316-8
CHECKLAND PB (1981) Systems Thinking, Systems Practice. Chichester:Wiley
CHILD J (1972) Organisational Structure, Environment and Performance: The Role of Strategic Choice. In: Sociology *6*, 2-22
CLARK AW (1976) Experimenting with Organisational Life: The Action Research Approach. New York:Plenum
CRICHTON (ed) (1966) Interdependence and Uncertainty: A Study of the Building Industry. London:Tavistock Publications

DALKEY NC (1969) The Delphi Method: An Experimental Study of Group Opinions. Memorandum RM-5888-PR. Santa Monica, Calif:Rand Corporation

DEKKER F and MASTOP P (1979) Strategic Choice: An Application in Dutch Planning Practice. In: Planning Outlook 22, 87-96

DEKKER F et al (1978) A Multi-Level Application of Strategic Choice at the Sub-Regional Level. In: Town Planning Review 49, 149-62

DELBECQ AL, VAN DE VEN AH and GUSTAFSON DH (1975) Group Techniques for Programme Planning. Glenview, Illinois:Scott Foresman and Company

DELLO P (1985) Strategic Choice and Evaluation: Some Methodological Considerations. In: Faludi A and Voogd H (eds) Evaluation of Complex Policy Problems. Delft: Delftsche Uitgevers Maatschappij

DOYLE M and STRAUS D (1976) How to Make Meetings Work: Jove

EDEN C and JONES S (1984) Using Repertory Grids for Problem Construction. In: Journal of the Operational Research Society 35, 779-90

EDEN C, JONES S and SIMS D (1983) Messing about in Problems. Oxford:Pergamon

EDEN C, JONES S, SIMS D and SMITHIN T (1981) The Intersubjectivity of Issues and Issues of Intersubjectivity. In: Journal of Management Studies 18, 34-47

EDEN C, WILLIAMS H and SMITHIN T (1986) Synthetic Wisdom: The Design of a Mixed Mode Modelling System for Organisational Decision Making. In: Journal of the Operational Research Society 37, 233-42

EMERY FE and TRIST EL (1972) Towards a Social Ecology: Contextual Appreciation of the Future in the Present. London:Plenium

ETZIONI A (1968) The Active Society: A Theory of Societal and Political Processes. New York:The Free Press

FALUDI A (1973) Planning Theory. Oxford:Pergamon

FALUDI A (1984) The Return of Rationality. In: Breheny MJ and Hooper AJ (eds) Rationality in Planning. London:Pion 1984

FALUDI A (1986) Critical Rationalism and Planning Methodology. London:Pion Press

FALUDI A (1987) A Decision Centred View of Environmental Planning. Oxford:Pergamon

FALUDI A and MASTOP JM (1982) The IOR School — The Development of a Planning Methodology. In: Environment and Planning B 9, 241-56

FERGUSON MJ (1979) A Strategic Choice Approach to Recreation Site Resource acquisition. In: Town Planning Review 50, 325-45

FISHER R and URY W (1982) Getting to Yes. London:Hutchinson

FLOYD M (1978) Structure Plan Monitoring: Looking to the Future. In: Town Planning Review 49, 476-85

FRIEND JK (1976) Planners, Policies and Organisational Boundaries: Some Recent Developments in Britain. In: Policy and Politics 5, 25-46

FRIEND JK (1977) The Dynamics of Policy Change. In: Long Range

Planning *10*, 40-7

FRIEND JK (1980) Planning in a Multi-Organisational Context. In: Town Planning Review *51*, 261-9

FRIEND JK and HUNTER JMH (1970) Multi-Organisational Decision Processes in the Planned Expansion of Towns. In: Environment and Planning *2*, 33-54

FRIEND JK and JESSOP WN (1977) Local Government and Strategic Choice: An Operational Research Approach to the Processes of Public Planning (Second Edition). Oxford:Pergamon. [First Edition (1969) — London:Tavistock Publications]

FRIEND JK and JESSOP WN (1971) Hvad er Planlaegning. In: BYPLAN *23*, 134-40

FRIEND JK and JESSOP WN (1973) Entscheidungsstrategie in Stadtplanung und Verwaltung. German translation by Zwirner WGO. Dusseldorf:Bertelsmann

FRIEND JK, LAFFIN MJ and NORRIS ME (1981) Competition in Public Policy: The Structure Plan as Arena. In: Public Administration *59*, 441-63

FRIEND JK, POWER JM and YEWLETT CJL (1974) Public Planning: The Inter-Corporate Dimension. London:Tavistock Publications

FRIEND JK, WEDGWOOD-OPPENHEIM F et al (1970) The LOGIMP Experiment: A Collaborative Exercise in the Application of a New Approach to Local Planning Problems. London:Centre for Environmental Studies (refer to Tavistock Institute of Human Relations)

GUPTA SK and ROSENHEAD J (1968) Robustness in Sequential Investment Decisions. In: Management Science *15*, 13-18

HALL P (1980) Great Planning Disasters. London:Weidenfeld & Nicholson

HARARY F, JESSOP WN, LUCKMAN J and STRINGER S (1965) Analysis of Interconnected Decision Areas: An Algorithm for Project Development. In: Nature *206*, 118

HART DA, HICKLING DA, NORRIS ME and SKELCHER CK (1980) Regional Planning Methodology. London:Tavistock Institute of Human Relations. Internal Paper 2T/436

HAWKINS L and HUDSON M (1986) Effective Negotiation. Melbourne:Information Australia

HICKLING A (1974) Managing Decisions: The Strategic Choice Approach. Rugby:Mantec (refer to Tavistock Institute of Human Relations, London)

HICKLING A (1976) Aids to Strategic Choice (Second Edition). Vancouver:University of British Colombia, Centre for Continuing Education

HICKLING A (1978) AIDA and the Levels of Choice in Structure Plans. In: Town Planning Review *49*, 459-75

HICKLING A (1979) Aids to Strategic Choice Revisited. London:Tavistock Institute of Human Relations. Internal Paper 2T/226

HICKLING A (1981) Abordagem da Escolha Estrategica. São Paulo:Fundacão do Desenvolvimento Administrativo

HICKLING A (1982) Beyond a Linear Iterative Process. In: Evans B, Powell J and Ralbot R (eds) Changing Design. Chichester:Wiley

HICKLING A (1985) Evaluation is a Five Finger Exercise. In: Faludi A and Voogd H (eds) Evaluation of Complex Policy Problems. Delft: Delftsche Uitgevers Maatschappij

HICKLING A, HARTMAN R and MEESTER JG (1976) Werken met Strategische Keuze. Alpen aan den Rijn:Samson Uitgeverij

HICKLING A, WILKIN L and DEBREYNE F (1980) Technologie de la Decision Complexe: Des Aides pour l'Elaboration des Choix Strategiques. Bruxelles:Universite Libre de Bruxelles, Centre E Bernheim pour l'Etude des Affaires

HIGGIN G and JESSOP WN (1965) Communications in the Building Industry: The Report of a Pilot Study. London:Tavistock Publications

HILL M (1968) A Goals-Achievement Matrix for Evaluating Alternative Plans. In: Journal of the American Institute of Planners *34*, 19-28

HILL M (1985) Decision-Making Contexts and Strategies for Evaluation. In: Faludi A and Voogd H (eds) Evaluation of Complex Policy Problems. Delft: Delftsche Uitgevers Maatschappij

HOWARD N (1971) Paradoxes of Rationality: The Theory of Metagames. London:MIT Press

JAGO L and NORRIS M (1981) Training in inter-Organisational Working: An Experimental Course. In: LINKAGE SIX. London:Tavistock Institute of Human Relations

JAGO L et al (1983) Strategies for Working between Organisations: A Training Experience Reviewed. In: LINKAGE SEVEN. London:Tavistock Institute of Human Relations

JONES S and EDEN C (1980) OR in the Community. In: Journal of the Operational Research Society *32*, 335-345

KELLY GA (1955) The Psychology of Personal Constructs. New York:Norton

KELLY GA (1972) A Theory of Personality. New York:Norton

LICHFIELD N (1966) Cost-Benefit Analysis in Town Planning. A Case Study — Swanley. In: Urban Studies *3*, 215-49

LICHFIELD N, KETTLE P and WHITBREAD M (1975) Evaluation in the Planning Process. Oxford:Pergamon

LICHFIELD N (1985) From Impact Assessment to Impact Evaluation. In: Evaluation of Complex Policy Problems. Delft:Delftsche Uitgevers Maatschappij

LINDBLOM CE (1965) The Intelligence of Democracy: Decision Making through Mutual Agreement. New York:Free Press, London:Collier-MacMillan

LUCKMAN J (1967) An Approach to the Management of Design. In:

Operational Research Quarterly *18*, 345-58

MACHOL R (1976) Principles of Operations Research: The Sutton Effect. In: Interfaces *7*, 106-7

MASON RD and MITROFF II (1981) Challenging Strategic Planning Assumptions. New York:Wiley

MILLER EJ and RICE AK (1967) Systems of Organization. London:Tavistock Publications.

MORGAN JR (1971) AIDA — A Technique for the Management of Design. IOR Monograph No 2. London:Tavistock Institute of Human Relations.

NORRIS ME (1985) Operational Research and the Social Sciences: Review of Local Government and Strategic Choice. In: Journal of the Operational Research Society *36*, 870-2

OPEN SYSTEMS GROUP (1981) Systems Behaviour (Third Edition). London:Harper & Row

OPENSHAW S and WHITEHEAD P (1986) The Decision Optimising Technique: History, development and progress towards a future machine based planning system. In: Willis KG (ed) Contemporary Issues in Town Planning. Aldershot:Gower

ORMEROD R (1983) Corporate Planning and its use of OR in the NCB: A Personal View. In: Journal of the Operational Research Society *34*, 461-7

PHILLIPS LD (1982) Requisite Decision Modelling. In: Journal of the Operational Research Society *33*, 303-12

RAIFFA H (1968) Decision Analysis. Reading,Mass:Addison-Wesley

RICE AK (1965) Learning for Leadership — Inter-Personal and Inter-Group Relations. London:Tavistock Publications

ROBINSON I (ed) (1972) Decision-Making in Urban Planning: An Introduction to New Methodologies. London:Sage

ROSENHEAD J (1978) An Education in Robustness. In: Journal of the Operational Research Society *29*, 105-11

ROSENHEAD J (1980) Planning under Uncertainty: II A Methodology for Robustness Analysis. In: Journal of the Operational Research Society *31*, 331-42

SAATY T (1980) The Analytical Hierarchy Process. New York:McGraw-Hill

SCHARPF FW (1972) Komplexitat als Schranke der Politischen Planung. Politische Innovation und Gesellschafliche Wandel: Politische Vierteljahresschrift

SCHNELLE E (1973) Metaplan: Op Zoek naar Doelstellingen Leerproces van Medewerkers Betrokken. Amersfoort:DHV

SCHON DA (1971) Beyond the Stable State: Public and Private Learning in a Changing Society. London:Temple Smith

STRINGER J (1967) Operational Research for Multi-Organisations. In: Operational Research Quarterly *18*, 105-20

SUSSKIND EL (1987) Breaking the Impasse: Consensual Approaches to Resolving Public Disputes. New York:Basic Books

SUTTON A and WILKIN L (eds) (1986) Related Socio-Technical Approaches to the Management of Uncertainty. Dordrecht:Martinus Nijhoff

THOMAS H and SAMPSON D (1986) Subjective Aspects of the Art of Decision Analysis. In: Journal of the Operational Research Society *37*, 249-65

TRIST EL, HIGGIN GW, MURRAY H and POLLOCK AB (1963) Organizational Choice. London:Tavistock

VAN DE GRAAF R (1985) Strategic Choice in LPG Policy. In: A Faludi and Voogd H (eds) Evaluation of Complex Policy Problems. Delft:Delftsche Uitgeres Maatschappij

VICKERS G (1965) The Art of Judgement. London:Chapman and Hall

WEDGWOOD-OPPENHEIM F (1972) Planning Under Uncertainty. In: Local Government Studies *2*, 53-65

Answers to Exercises

Chapter 2 — Exercises: Answers and Comments

1. There would be 13 additional decision links. Figure 12 shows 8 decision links, out of a maximum possible of 21. As was mentioned in passing in the chapter, the maximum can be worked out by calculating that each of the seven decision areas could be connected to each of the other six — making 42 links in all, which reduces to 21 when double-counting is allowed for. Alternatively, you could draw in the thirteen extra links on a copy of the decision graph; which could help you in appreciating how confusing and lacking in structural information a fully connected decision graph becomes.

2. There are various possibilities for rearranging the graph after you have added the two additional links. For example, try redrawing it with GAS SITE? and GRIFF SCHL? out to the right; WEST ST? swung around to the top; and DIST LIFE? shifted to the centre of the ROAD LINE?/SHOP LOC'N?/CENT'L SITE? triangle. You should then be able to avoid crossovers between decision links — though this would not necessarily remain possible if still more decision links were added. This example illustrates how a little skill and judgement in positioning can make structural relationships more clear.

3. In the modified decision graph of question 2, you will find that there are five fully interconnected triads. They are:

ROAD LINE?/WEST ST?/SHOP LOC'N?
ROAD LINE?/SHOP LOC'N?/CENT'L SITE?
ROAD LINE?/SHOP LOC'N?/DIST LIFE?
SHOP LOC'N?/CENT'L SITE?/DIST LIFE?
ROAD LINE?/CENT'L SITE?/DIST LIFE?

Note that ROAD LINE?/SHOP LOC'N?/DIST LIFE?/CENT'L SITE? also forms a fully connected cluster of four decision areas. You might decide to choose either this or any of the five triads listed above as a problem focus within which to explore what combinations of options were available: but you might wish to take other non-structural information into account in making this choice.

4. A quick glance at Figure 17 shows that schemes E, G and I are the only ones including the 40-year option in DIST LIFE?, so these three would be removed. This exercise illustrates how easy it can be to test the effect of removing specific options when decision schemes are presented in the form of a tree.

5. Schemes G and I in Figure 17 both involve the combination of 40YR in DIST LIFE? with OPEN in CENT'L SITE?, so would be eliminated. This again is not hard to see simply by inspecting the tree. Of course, you can do this kind of exercise very quickly with a computer — which can be useful if you have larger trees to handle and if you want to explore the effects of many different changes in assumptions.

6. These two extra option bars would eliminate schemes A, B, C, D and F, in addition to G, which was already ruled out by the option bar introduced in question 5. So, only schemes E and H would remain: in practice this would probably lead you to ask questions as to whether other option bars could be removed to open the range of choice up again.

7. Removal of the SOUTH — IND option bar in Figure 16 would allow two additional schemes to be introduced:

SOUTH — GAS — IND — 20YR
SOUTH — GAS — IND — 40YR

The information to allow you to work this out is contained in the option graph of Figure 16; but you may have found it useful to refer to the tree in Figure 17 as well, to find out the answer quickly.

8. Looking at the map in Figure 18, you might wonder why there was no link shown in Figure 12 between the WEST ST? and CENT'L SITE? decision areas, given that the two sites are adjacent. However, you would be wise then to refer back to the fuller descriptions of these two decision areas in Figure 10. It is important to bear in mind that locational connections are not the *only* possible grounds for introducing links between decision areas: there may be no *decision* links at all between choices on adjoining sites while, conversely, choices relating to non-adjacent sites may be linked for financial, functional or other reasons. The map could also cause you to wonder whether there might be a direct link between DIST LIFE? and GRIFF SCHL?, given that the school looks as if it could serve the neighbourhood. However, the map on its own gives you far less information than would be available in practice to anyone with a detailed knowledge of the area, its people and its services. So, the point of this exercise is that there is not *necessarily* any relationship between a decision graph and a physical map: adjacency is only one of many kinds of relatedness which may (or may not) be reflected in a decision graph.

9. The answer to this question is even more open than that to question 8, for similar reasons. You might wonder why Figure 16 shows an incompatibility between NORTH in ROAD LINE? and GAS in SHOP LOC'N?, given that the gasworks site seems to be so remote from the northern road line; or you might wonder why an option bar appears between SOUTH in ROAD LINE? and IND in CENT'L SITE?. And would not IND in CENT'L SITE? make it difficult to keep the shops in Main Street which runs alongside, suggesting a new option bar? But these again are questions rather than answers; questions that could be put to people with more specific knowledge of local circumstances, yet even then might not have clear cut answers. For option bars are essentially *working assumptions* about which combinations are possible and which are not.

Chapter 3 — Exercises: Answers and Comments

1. The CAPITAL: comparison area could, if desired, be split into two elements concerned with construction works and property aquisition; or the RESIDENTS: comparison area into separate elements concerned with confidence and quality of life — though these could prove much harder to separate in practice. Other distinctions could be made between different types of employment within JOBS:, and between different sources of INCOME:. This is not to suggest that it will usually be a good thing to divide comparison areas into smaller and smaller elements: the point of the exercise is simply that there are differing levels of abstraction that can be thought about in formulating an appropriate set of comparison areas for working purposes.

2. You will probably have found this a hard question to answer because of the way ranges are used to express uncertainty in Figure 20. A statistician would tell you that there is no sound way of deducing the assessments for H compared to B in terms of numerical ranges for CAPITAL:, INCOME: and JOBS: without making further assumptions about whether the sources of variation in the B versus A and H versus A comparisons can be considered as independent. Working on mid-points of ranges, you might say that H was likely to cost about 350k more than B; to generate about 50k per annum less income than A; and to generate about 25 more jobs — but it is only in the case of INCOME: that you could be fairly confident that H will yield less than B, because the ranges do not overlap. A reasonable inference to make from the two RESIDENTS: assessments is that B will probably generate much more confidence than H.

3. B would now yield more income and jobs than A for the expenditure of less capital: so it is likely that the only hesitation in expressing a preference for B would lie in the assessment that it would 'probably' generate more confidence among residents. This suggests a *possibility*, however remote, that it might leave them feeling less rather than more confidence. So could the conditions likely to lead to this outcome be at least briefly explored?

4. The changes proposed in question 3 would swing the INCOME: and JOBS: ranges over into corresponding positions on the right hand side of the advantage comparison chart. It now seems that any possible advantage to A in terms of the RESIDENTS: assessment could be at most marginal: this would be outweighed by the significant-to-considerable advantage to B in terms of CAPITAL:, even before taking the INCOME: and JOBS: advantage to B into account. This suggests there is no real risk in eliminating A as inferior to B — unless, of course, there could be advantages in other comparison areas not yet included in the list.

5. Comparing the 'best guess' points of the CAPITAL: and INCOME: ranges as presented in Figure 21, the balance of advantage is likely to be in favour of B because the CAPITAL: advantage to B appears as 'considerable' and the INCOME: advantage to A as only 'significant'. But the two ranges indicate that there is quite a lot of uncertainty in this judgement; there is at least a possibility that the net financial advantage could be to A if the capital advantage to B were on the low side of the range and the income advantage to B on the high side. Further examination of this could mean looking both into sources of uncertainty in the money amounts involved, and into any time discounting assumptions used to weigh income against capital.

6. The capital cost indices for schemes C, D, E, F and G would reduce by 200k each, becoming 1800k, 1900k, 1950k, 1750k and 1800k. The costs for H and I would reduce by 150k each, becoming 1900k and 1950k respectively. The new order of preference on capital cost would be B, F, (C, G), (D, H) and, lastly, (A, E, I), using brackets to indicate ties. The arguments for shortlisting B and E still apply as in Figure 22; but A is less attractive and might be replaced by D, C or G.

7. Figure 22 shows that there are two schemes — B and C — which differ *only* in the choice of location for the shopping centre. Because B is given a higher residents' confidence rating than C in Figure 22, it seems that residents' confidence will be higher if it is proposed to retain the MAIN shopping location rather than move it to KING.

8. The informal soundings in response to the ?VALJOB uncertainty area were assessed in Figure 24 as leading to a much greater gain in confidence in comparing A against B than the market survey aimed at the ?SITEJOBS uncertainty area; yet the delay is less and, instead of an estimated fee of 20k, the only resource demand is 'some demands' on the time of busy policy-makers. These demands would probably have to be very severe to outweigh the expenditure of 20,000 monetary units, so the second exploratory option appears to be very much more resource-effective than the first.

9. Rearranging the tree, there are three action schemes which leave open the choice of two alternative decision schemes in the longer term: these are 10YR-HOUS, 20YR-OPEN and 40YR-OPEN. The other three action

schemes leave open no flexibility for the future. Of those mentioned above, however, cross-reference to Figure 22 shows that only the 10YR-HOUS action scheme leaves open more than one decision scheme scoring RRR or above on the residents' confidence index. So on these grounds 10YR-HOUS is the most *robust* of the six possible action schemes.

10. In the SHOP LOCATION? row of Figure 26, MAIN STREET would disappear from the first cell — though you could replace it by '*NOT GASWORKS SITE*'. You would now enter in the deferred choices column something like 'in x months decide shop location [Main Street or King Square]'. There are all kinds of steps you could consider — for example, consulting the local traders; detailed costing or design exercises; or discussions with a supermarket company which might help finance the development on King Square.

11. The figures in Figure 27 give you a little more information about the numbers of 'stakeholders' in some of the decisions that are being faced over the future of South Side in relation to the wider metropolitan area. But of course, the size of their stakes will differ and these differences would probably have to be weighed up politically. Note however there is no financial or economic information in Figure 27 (apart from a hint about the economic condition of existing traders). Some kinds of financial information might be easily obtained from municipal sources, while other kinds could be more inaccessible. Given the pressures on the South Side Working Party, they would have to make some quick judgements in the *value* of any such information to the decisions they face before deciding whether to invest time and resources in obtaining and processing it — which helps to illustrate the more general points about exploratory options discussed in Chapter 3.

INDEX

accommodating uncertainty, 7, 8
accountability, 99, 108
   politics of, 269
accountable roles, 267, 269
accuracy, 108
Ackoff, Russell, xiv, xvi, 89, 296, 317
action, choice of, 117
   commitment to, 19
action research, 251
action scheme, 70, 71, 83, 182, 212, 225, 229
action set, 71
actions, as element in commitment package, 73, 231
adaptation to change, 182
adaptiveness, 107, 250, 254
advantage, balance of, 59, 65, 191, 207, 224
   judgement of, 57, 59
advantage comparison, 58, 59, 83, 260, 281
adversarial working, 247
agenda, 13, 18, 96, 100, 235
agenda building, 110
AIDA, 27, **39**, 47, 52, 143, 304
aims, 9
alcohol problems, 298
alternatives, 29, 57
Amsterdam, xv, 205
analysis, depth of, 132, 175
Analysis of Interconnected Decision Areas, *see* AIDA
applications of strategic choice, 250, 294
approach, *see* A-TOPP
appropriate technology for strategic choice, 25, 51, 91, 258
arbitration, 287
areas of concern, 64
arena, political, 211, 267, 289
armchair strategic choice, 92
Ashby, Ross, 182, 317
assessment
   method of, 185, 187
   relative, 55, 56, 83
assumptions, 64, 187, 212, 219, 228
assumptions behind option bars, 149
A-TOPP framework, 85, 106
Australia, soil conservation in, vii
authority, point of, 96
   to decide, 238
autonomy, loss of, 97
Avon County, 277

backroom work, 252, 271
Balbo, M., 317
Bath, University of, 300, 302
Bather, Nick, 295, 317
Batty, Susan, 287, 317
Beer, Stafford, 289, 317
Bennett, Peter, xvi, 294, 299, 317
Bion, W., 302, 317
Birmingham, University of, 85
black box, 17, 86
blackboards, 259
Blu-tack, 259
board of management, 18, 96
boardroom, 296
boundaries, drawing of, 6
Bowen, Ken, xvi
Bradford, University of, xiii
brainstorming, 111
branching point, 45, 159, 227
Brazil, 137, 207, 251
Breure, Bram, xvi
British Coal, 297, 311
British Council, 137
Bryant, Don, xv
Bryant Jim, xvi
budgets, 101, 103, 144, 243, 284
building industry, communications in, 39, 310
Bunker, Raymond, xii, xiii, 317

calibration of advantage scale, 193
calligraphy, 260
Canada, xii
capital expenditure, 53, 55, 185
cards, use of, 115, 205, 263
Carter, Ken, xv, 313
categories
   of decisions, 93, 113
   of impact, 178
   of uncertainty, 11, 69, 215
centralisation vs decentralisation, 297
certainty, 21
chains of decision areas, 123
chairing role, 18, 100
changeability of policy orientation, 183
Checkland, Peter, 89, 317
Child, John, 296, 317
choice
   levels of, 115, 161, 231
   personal vs collective, 2

329